New England Outpost

New England Outpost

War and Society in Colonial Deerfield

RICHARD I. MELVOIN

W · W · NORTON & COMPANY

NEW YORK · LONDON

FIRST EDITION

THE TEXT OF THIS BOOK *is composed in Caledonia, with display type set in Baskerville. Composition and manufacturing by The Maple-Vail Book Manufacturing Group. Book design by Marjorie J. Flock.*

Library of Congress Cataloging-in-Publication Data
Melvoin, Richard I.
    New England outpost.

    Bibliography: p.
    Includes index.
    1. Deerfield (Mass.)—History.   2. Massachusetts—
History—Colonial period, ca. 1600–1775.   3. Frontier
and pioneer life—Massachusetts—Deerfield.   I. Title.
F74.D4M4   1988   974.4′22   87-34749

ISBN 0-393-02600-0

W. W. Norton & Company, Inc., 500 Fifth Avenue, New York, N.Y. 10110
W. W. Norton & Company Ltd., 37 Great Russell Street, London WC1B 3NU

1 2 3 4 5 6 7 8 9 0

For My Family

Contents

Contents

• MAPS •

Preface

JUST OFF Interstate 91 in South Deerfield, Massachusetts, sits a large low-budget motel, which for years held a restaurant called The 1704. Half a mile away, in the middle of South Deerfield, the Bloody Brook Tavern serves a largely local clientele. There is a historic heritage in Deerfield, but it can be curious: The restaurant and the bar were named for famous local Indian attacks.

In Old Deerfield itself, some five miles to the north, the museum houses of Historic Deerfield, Inc. offer a more appealing vision of the town's past. Freshly painted and filled with fine antiques, these colonial homes sit peacefully on Deerfield's lovely, pristine "main street." The lofty trees, the lovely homes, the working farms of the town, and the beauty of the Deerfield Academy campus all make frontier violence seem ages away.

And in fact it has been ages since the Bloody Brook Massacre of 1675 and the more famous Deerfield Massacre of 1704 devastated the town. Still, those attacks have occupied the minds of townspeople—and some students of early American history—for the three centuries since they took place.

This project was started because of those two dramatic events. As I settled in to work, however, I quickly began to appreciate how rich Deerfield's past was. This soon made me feel that a larger history of the town deserved telling. Although townsman George Sheldon wrote a massive, majestic two-volume *History of Deerfield* in the late nineteenth century (with four hundred of his fourteen hundred pages devoted solely to genealogy!), his view of the incidents and the world that surrounded them was limited. Although Sheldon carefully chronicled the attacks on his town, he left many vital questions unanswered. Rather than just berating the enemy for its "savagery," why not consider how and why the Indians and French fought as they did? And why attack Deerfield? What importance, if any, did it hold? What was its place in the wider world? Beyond these questions of war, what was an early New England frontier town such as Deerfield like? Who would live in such a place, and what kind of town would develop? It was thus the famous incidents—yet also the questions behind the incidents—that carried me along.

Further study made me realize that these questions deserved exploration not just for Deerfield but for New England generally. Although much excellent history written in the last twenty years has looked at "the New England town," little has centered on frontier communities. Yet a look at any map of colonial New England, whether in 1650 or 1750, reveals that a great number of towns sat on "the frontier." In addition, relatively little recent work has focused on war, and still less on the effects of war on local settlement. Yet war was a fundamental part of life in early America. A man or woman who lived to adulthood in colonial times almost by definition lived through war. Deerfield's first sixty years were marked by four wars—almost thirty years of conflict. Those numbers are painful, but they are hardly unique.

In 1780, John Adams wrote to his wife, Abigail, "I must study politics and war that my sons may have liberty to study mathematics and philosophy . . . in order to give their children a right to study painting, poetry, music. . . ." Here, too, my goal is not to seek new heroes or any glory in war. Rather, it is to study the impact of war on society—in this case, on a frontier town over three generations. One cannot understand early New England—early America—without coming to grips with these two issues of the frontier and war. They are not sidelights. Rather, they did much to define New England's colonists and colonies.

A third theme that Deerfield's story invites is the intertwining of native American history with colonial history. Again, this town's past is unusually fertile. Deerfield's history cannot be complete without study of the Indians who first lived on the town site; of inter-Indian conflict that opened the land for English settlement; of Indian-English relations before, during, and after wars; of the roles of different Indian groups in the English-French struggles for North America; and of the nature of Indian warfare. These themes do not comprise merely parts of Deerfield's story, either. They also help make Indians subjects rather than objects in the study of the past: The Indians become active agents in history, not simply pawns or objects in European peoples' stories.

In sum, studying Deerfield over the past nine years was like getting on a tame horse for a quiet trail ride and then having the beast bolt for a gallop over the countryside. The ride was long, exhilarating, daunting at times, and not at all what I bargained for; I saw far more than I expected; and the journey, while no smooth path, proved infinitely more rewarding. I hope this book conveys at least some of what I saw.

Acknowledgments

I T IS A PLEASURE to get to thank people for their support over the past few years. The staff of Historic Deerfield, notably Don and Grace Friary, Ritchie Garrison, Kevin Sweeney, and particularly the library team of David Proper and Louise Perrin, gave enduring support to my work. My friends and colleagues at Deerfield Academy have encouraged my efforts, bucked me up when I needed it, and helped me keep this work in balance amidst the joys and demands of school life. I also thank the headmaster and the Academy's Summer Grant Committee for their financial support.

I was fortunate also in having excellent scholarly guidance. As a dissertation this project came under the direction of Kenneth Lockridge, my chairman, and John Shy—two fine scholars, and good and kind men, whose complementary ways of exploring material and ideas gave me even more than they may realize. In the evolution of thesis to book came further substantial help. Thanks are due to Gary Nash, Alden Vaughan, John Demos, Bill McFeely, Skip Mattoon, David Dunbar, Antonia Woods, Philip Morgan, Dan Richter, and Pat Tracy. Thanks also to Jim Mairs at Norton, who showed encouraging confidence and provided long-lasting support. All these people improved the book; the remaining problems I cheerfully claim as my own.

Finally, great thanks go to my family. No one could be more fortunate in having a large and wonderfully supportive extended family (buddies included) to keep one going. Closer to home, though, special thanks go to my wife, Barbara Glass Melvoin, and my daughters, Sarah and Rebecca. The latter two have cheered on their father's "Indian book" with admirable patience. Meanwhile, their mother supported the project in

her own, right way. At times that meant reading over the manuscript, some chapters more times than she would wish to remember. At other, more important points, it meant telling me
when to stop working and come home. Most important, all
three helped me keep this project in perspective and have
continually reminded me about what is really important in life.

R. I. M.

September 1988
Deerfield, Massachusetts

Introduction

THREE DRAMATIC BATTLES leap out of the celebrated past of an isolated little colonial village in western Massachusetts.

Late in the summer of 1664, the Pocumtuck Indians are nervous—and rightfully so. In June the Mohawks, easternmost of the five Iroquois nations, sent a peace party to the Pocumtuck village on the Connecticut River, some fifty miles east of the Mohawk settlements in New York. For much of the seventeenth century, the Mohawks have wreaked havoc on the Algonkian Indians of the northeast. Although recently hurt by losses from war and disease, they remain as powerful as any military force, Indian or European, in the region. For most of the last half century, the Pocumtucks have lived at peace with the Mohawks; they have even been allies. In fact, in May of 1664 the Pocumtucks had hosted peace negotiations which included the Mohawks, Dutch, English, and Sokokis, the Pocumtucks' neighbors to the north.

Perhaps the Mohawks insulted the Pocumtucks at that May meeting. Perhaps the Pocumtucks had long chafed under Mohawk domination, and recent Mohawk losses encouraged them to break this pattern of domination. Perhaps the thirty Sokokis, living with the Pocumtucks since the Mohawks had attacked and destroyed their village the previous December, goaded them into action. Whatever the reason, when the Mohawk peace party arrived at Pocumtuck in late June the Pocumtucks murdered them all, including the Mohawk prince Saheda.

The Pocumtucks thus have good reason to be anxious. And their fears are soon justified. With European forces staying out of this inter-Indian conflict, late in 1664 the Mohawks send a large war party to the Pocumtuck village and fort. No record of the battle remains. Local legend has it that the Pocumtucks first turned the Mohawks back, but when they followed the retreating force they fell into a deadly ambush. No matter what the details really are, the results were immediately clear. The Pocumtucks, before this the largest Indian force in the middle Connecticut valley, are destroyed. The village and fort are no more. The survivors scatter, joining other bands of Indians to the south, east, and north. As 1664 draws to a close, the fertile valley of the Pocumtucks lies open.

Eleven years later, again late in the summer, a village at Pocumtuck again lives in fear of the consequences of the events of June. In 1675, though, the people of Pocumtuck are not Indian, but English.

Since 1670, when English men and women first settled at Pocumtuck, the village has grown quickly. By 1675 it holds a little over two hundred people. But they are threatened by war. In June, fighting broke out between Indians and English in southeastern Massachusetts, a hundred miles away. That distant conflict, now called King Philip's War, has widened and spread—to other Indians and to the west. In fact, the center of hostile Indian activity has been moving toward Pocumtuck. In early August the hamlet of Brookfield, some forty miles southeast of Pocumtuck, is destroyed after repeated attacks. After a similar series of strikes, the same fate befalls Northfield, Pocumtuck's only English neighbor to the north—and less than fifteen miles away.

On September 1, 1675, the Indians strike at Pocumtuck. They kill one soldier, drive the fleeing settlers into the town's two fortified houses, and burn seventeen outlying houses and barns. Soon after, Pocumtuck's women and children are sent away to stay with friends and relatives in safer towns farther down the Connecticut valley. Some fifty men, townsmen plus garrison soldiers, try to hold the town.

They cannot. An attack on September 12 results in more death and destruction. Still Pocumtuck clings to life. It is not only the valley's northern sentinel now, but in its fields the village also holds a vast quantity of grain, grain that valley settlers may need to survive the winter. Realizing that, regional authorities order the garrison at Pocumtuck to bring the grain south to greater safety. With Captain Thomas Lathrop's troops as reinforcements, on Saturday morning, September 18, 1675, some fifty soldiers plus fifteen Pocumtuck "teamsters"—village men recruited to help—load the grain onto carts and head south.

About five miles south of town the convoy slows to cross a streamlet called Muddy Brook. At that moment, Muddy Brook is transformed into Bloody Brook, as hundreds of Indians attack the English party. The surprise is complete and the victory total. When the ambush is finished, over sixty Englishmen lie dead; of Pocumtuck's fifteen men, only one survives. One-third of the town's men have been killed.

Within a few days valley authorities decide it is futile to try to hold Pocumtuck any longer. The garrison is abandoned, and the Indians soon burn the remaining buildings. Once again, Pocumtuck lies destroyed.

Almost three decades have passed and "Pocumtuck" is no more. But a new village has arisen on the old site. Shunning the former Indian name, the English settlers now call the place Deerfield. By 1704 the town has grown to 260 people. The size of the town suggests stability. Yet like its predecessors Deerfield lies alone and exposed on the frontier. There are still no English settlements west of Deerfield for fifty miles, until one reaches the Hudson River and New York. Nor are there English towns north of Deerfield at all. To the east, too, lie forty miles of wilderness.

As in 1664 and 1675, the late summer of 1703 has been a time of great anxiety. Activities of late spring have once again brought forth these fears. In May, early in the conflict known as Queen Anne's War, New York governor Lord Cornbury sent word that French soldiers and allied Indians from Canada were heading for Deerfield and the Connecticut valley. As of September a stressful summer has passed peacefully. Then in October, a small Indian force strikes, capturing two Deerfield men. Tensions heighten; the town strengthens its fortifications; the Massachusetts General Court sends soldiers to help protect the town. As of December, though, all is quiet. The cold and snow of winter now promise further respite, for in 1704 wars are not fought in the depths of winter.

But now the quiet of late winter is about to be shattered. Two hours before dawn on the fateful leap-year morning of February 29, 1704, Deerfield's inhabitants lie asleep inside the town's palisade. Because the Indian threat remains, all the town's residents, including the twenty Massachusetts soldiers just arrived from Boston, sleep in the dozen houses inside the fort. The other thirty or so houses outside the palisade lie empty. A watchman is assigned to patrol the town through the night. In the pre-dawn hours, however, he proves unfaithful to his duty. That breach of faith soon proves fatal.

Two miles north of town, just across the Deerfield River, lies a military force of two hundred to three hundred French and Indians. These men have traveled close to three hundred miles to reach this spot. Now they are ready to attack. Silently they cross the river and traverse two miles of open farmland toward the sleeping town. They are able to move quietly, for deep snow dampens all sound. Winter aids them in another way as well. Heavy drifts have piled snow against the walls of the fort, drifts so high that the attackers can easily scale the walls. Without a night watch to contend with, the warriors quickly move inside. The signal comes—a cry rings out—and the attack begins.

Although the townspeople fight back bravely, the French and Indian force is too strong and their advantage too great. Even the reinforcements who charge up from Hadley and Hatfield cannot turn the tide. At battle's end, the survivors grimly assess the town's losses. Fifty-six English men, women, and children lie dead; another 109 have been captured. In all, three-fifths of the town's people are gone. Almost half the houses have been burned.

Unlike the villages of 1664 and 1675, Deerfield is not abandoned this time around, but only because the region's military commander will not allow it. As it is, the town barely clings to life. It is years before survival is assured.

These three events have given Deerfield much fame over the years. The town gained immediate notoriety throughout New England after the events of both 1675 and 1704. That fame grew after 1707 when Deerfield's minister, the Reverend John Williams, published his view of the events of 1704 in *The Redeemed Captive Returning to Zion*. One part jeremiad and one part gripping captivity narrative, the book proved to be an eighteenth century "best-seller," going through six editions before 1800. The story of 1704 received still wider attention late in the nineteenth century when Francis Parkman made "The Sack of Deerfield" a chapter in his volume *Half Century of Conflict*.

The significance of these events has proven less clear than their fame. There was nothing vitally strategic about Pocumtuck or Deerfield in 1664, 1675, or 1704. Deerfield never proved particularly important after all the attacks ended, either. By 1750 it was simply an increasingly prosperous little farm town. By the 1800s it had become a sleepy rural village that the industrial revolution passed by.

Yet the stories that spin out of this place form a rich tapestry of early New England life. There are stories about the Indians who lived there, the lives they led and the problems they faced; about English settlers striving to build a town; about the inexorable destruction of the Indian natives of New England; about the decades English settlers lived under the almost constant threat of war; about the difficulties of frontier existence; about the complex relationships among different European and Indian forces, in trade and politics as well as in war; about violence and death. Deerfield was not "typical"—its drama and violence hardly make it representative of "the New England town." But the events and actions and people that make it special can tell us much of what early New England was all about. The tapestry that emerges has a unique pattern; yet the strands that form it could be found in many different places throughout early America.

PART ONE

Pocumtuck

Native Peoples, Native Lands

I N THE CENTER of the little village of Deerfield, Massachusetts, just off the town common, stands a huge buttonball
tree. A remarkable eighteen feet in girth, it offers shelter
from rain or sun to the students of Deerfield Academy who
scurry beneath it on their way to classes. From the base of the
tree, the view in any direction is calming and pastoral. The tree
has stood there for over four hundred years. The view has not
always been so peaceful.

The struggle to take and hold this place, and the lives of the
people—Indian and English—who came and left and came here
again, comprise the essence of this story. It is a story of wars, of
violence that engulfed this frontier town for half a century. Yet
it also must be a story of the ways of life of the peoples who lived
here. To understand early America's wars, it is important to
grasp how both native and European peoples coped with the
conflicts and their effects. Who were the natives who first lived
here? When did they leave, and why? What Europeans would
then come to live in such a place, and how would they live?
Knowing simply who survived this century of struggle in America is not enough. The details, the richness of this story offer far
more in coming to understand life in early America.

Anyone who has ever been to Deerfield regards it as a special
place. That has been the case for a long time. In the mid-
nineteenth century, a chronicler of history, trying to imagine
how the English settlers must have first viewed the land, put it
in words they might have used:

We at length arrived at the place we sought after. We called it Petumtuck, because there dwell the Petumtuck Indians. Having ascended a
little hill, apparently surrounded by rich meadow land, from that spot
we beheld broad meadows, extending far north, west, and south of us.
In these meadows we could trace the course of a fine river, which
comes out from the mountains on the north west, and running north-
erly, through many miles of meadow, seemed to us to run in among
the hills again, at the north east. The tall trees of button wood and elm
exposed to us its course. That meadow is not soft and covered with
coarse water grass, like that around us here [in Dedham], but is hard
land. It is the best land we have seen in this colony; we dug holes in
the meadow, with the intent to find the depth of the soil, but could
not find the bottom. At the foot of the little hill we stood on, it is a plat
of ground sufficiently high to be out of the reach of the spring floods.
Providence led us to that place? It is indeed far away from our plantations, and the Canaanites and Amalekites dwell in that valley, and if
they have any attachment to any spot of earth, must delight to live
there. But that land must be ours. Our people have resolute and pious
hearts, and strong hands to overcome all difficulties. Let us go and
possess the land, and in a few years you will hear more boast of it in
this colony, as a land good for flocks and herds, than could ever be
justly said of the land of Goshen, or any part of the land of Canaan.[1]

To begin the story of Deerfield, then, one needs a sense of
how special the site is. For before there were English, before
there were Indians, there was the land.

"It is the best land we have seen . . ."

The Connecticut River is a big, strong piece of water as it
cuts south through western Massachusetts. From its headwa-
ters high in Vermont, it swallows up tributaries as it drives
down through Massachusetts and Connecticut to the Atlantic.
While it drains the gentle mountains to both east and west, it
also shares its waters with the rich bottomlands in the valley.
In the seventeenth century it was a river loaded with salmon
and shad, its basin rich in potential farmland, its nearby forests
filled with game.[2]

Less than a mile below what both the English and Indians
would call the "Great Falls" of the Connecticut (now Turner's
Falls, Massachusetts), the Deerfield River meets the wide and

powerful Connecticut. The confluence of waters is unusual. Because the Deerfield flows into the Connecticut against the current, often in spring the Connecticut pushes the Deerfield's waters back upriver a couple of miles. That water spills silt and nutrients out the Deerfield's banks, onto rich bottomland of Deerfield. For this reason, Deerfield has always had a good quantity of extraordinarily fertile land.

The land is not only rich but protected. From the plateau on which the town now stands, miles of open, level fields extend up and down a tight little valley. To both east and west quickly rise the kind of worn mountains that typify the Berkshires. At Deerfield they "lock in" and protect the town site. To the east a five-hundred-foot rise looms over the town, falling off quickly on the opposite side where it drops down to the Connecticut River. The western mountains rise more gradually, yet also serve to close in the town. In the winter the hills serve to keep out some of the snow that neighbors to the east and west receive. In the summer they wall in the heat and moisture so that there are days when the sun does not burn through the heavy mist until midday. The corn can be head high by early July, and even tobacco flourishes in this unusual pocket of land.

Deerfield is also distinguished by a plateau, about a mile long and perhaps half a mile wide, that rises in the middle of this narrow valley. It is difficult to imagine a more ideal site for settlement: On three sides, north, west, and south, the land drops cleanly away to the open farmland. In the middle of the plateau the land stands a bit higher still, forming what the early colonists called "Meetinghouse Hill," an appropriately raised spot for the spiritual center of a Puritan town. A high spot on a plateau, surrounded by rich farmlands, drained and nourished by a river skirting this central place, all locked into a tight, buffered valley . It is no wonder that Indians and English alike coveted the area.

"There dwell the Petumtuck Indians. . ."

For much of the seventeenth century, and likely at least a century before that, no one questioned who controlled this land. It was Indian land: used, maintained, improved, and shared—if not outright owned in an English sense—by the Pocumtucks, one of the Algonkian Indian tribes of New England.[3] In 1630 great numbers of Algonkians, probably many thousands, lived in the Connecticut River valley. A half century later, practically none remained. As late as 1638 the Pocumtucks themselves were healthy, strong, and amiable enough to sell five hundred bushels of corn to weak and hungry Englishmen beseeching them from infant valley settlements below.[4] Fewer than thirty years later the tribe was decimated, with only scattered fragments remaining. Yet the destruction of the Pocumtucks took place in 1664, eleven years before King Philip's War, the apocalyptic Indian-English struggle for New England. What happened?

Here Deerfield's legacy offers a great challenge—and opportunity. The challenge lies in seeing that some of the vital clashes in early American history took place *between Indians*. Europeans may have sometimes played a role, but inter-Indian conflict could be fundamental. The opportunity thus comes in exposing this complex layer of history. In so doing, a new appreciation emerges of the native actors on America's stage, even if they do not appear in later acts.[5] In this way, the Pocumtucks help illuminate an important larger part of America's past.

Who were the Pocumtucks? First, they were Algonkian Indians. As members of that great body of tribes in the northeast of what is today the United States, they shared the same basic linguistic family and practiced similar life-styles. Experts disagree on the nature of the Pocumtuck dialect, and hence tie its people with different tribes, from the Wappinger to the Nipmuck to other Indians down the Connecticut River.[6] Still, the sense is clear that the Pocumtuck Indians spoke and lived much like their neighbors.

And the Pocumtucks had many neighbors. Centering the compass on the Pocumtucks, one might have looked first to the east, where lived the Nipmucks, or Nipnets; farther east, in the cradle of Massachusetts Bay, dwelled the Massachusetts tribes. Farther off, the southeast held the Wampanoags and the Narragansetts, New England's largest tribe, while directly below, in central and southern Connecticut, lived the Mohegans and also the Pequots, "the terror of the surrounding tribes." To the west, some fifty miles across the Berkshire Mountains, the valleys below Albany embraced the Mahicans, neighbors of the Wappingers.[7] North of the Pocumtuck site lived various Western Abenaki bands; the closest of those was the Sokoki. Farther off, in present-day Maine, dwelled the Eastern Abenaki.[8] As of 1600, the Indians of New England totaled somewhere around 100,000 people.[9]

The size and strength of the Pocumtucks are not entirely clear. Some earlier historians called them a tribe; others considered them a "confederacy," claiming a population as grand as 5,000 in villages stretching fifty miles up and down the Connecticut valley.[10] Most likely, though, the Pocumtucks fit among the many "segmentary tribes" in the valley: a few hundred people, local, autonomous, and without extensive internal organizational structure.[11]

At the same time, the Pocumtucks appear to have been a larger and more influential group than many of their neighbors. The various records that place them north near present-day Vernon, Vermont, and south as far as the Farmington River in Connecticut suggests a larger population. As early as the 1630s, the Dutch accorded them respect as a " 'great' or numerous tribe."[12] By the 1640s "a very large & a strong fort" stood at Pocumtuck.[13] According to a longtime student of New England Indians, the Pocumtucks were "said to have kept the Ware River Valley, twenty miles from home, so clear that from a Brookfield hill a deer could be spotted four miles distant," a feat implying influence over far-reaching lands. Another historian has termed the Pocumtucks "that most influential of Connecticut valley bands."[14] From all this it seems possible that the Pocumtucks numbered at least 500 to 750 people, and perhaps as many as 1,200, as of 1600.[15]

From all indications, these Pocumtucks lived simply, comfortably, and quite well. Like other Indians of southern New England, they farmed, hunted, fished, and gathered "their daily bread."[16] While they cultivated a range of plants, including "kidney beans, squash, Jerusalem artichoke, and tobacco,"[17] their great staple was maize—corn. According to William Morrell, an Episcopal clergyman who observed and waxed poetic about New England in the early 1600s, corn was "[t]heir strength of life," "the staff of all their lives."[18] Growing corn was "perennial and systematic,"[19] and whether boiled, roasted, baked, ground, or dried, it was used in dozens of recipes. In general, grain "made up perhaps one-half to two-thirds" of the Indians' diet.[20]

The Pocumtucks and their neighbors did not limit their diet to corn, or their methods of food gathering to cultivation. The changing seasons brought a regular rhythm of different foods to Indian meals. Morrell lauded the diverse opportunities for bringing in food in his poem when he wrote of New England:

> O happie planter, if you knew the height
> Of planter's honours where ther's such delight;
> There nature's bounties, though not planted are,
> Great store and sorts of berries great and faire.

In early autumn, not just berries but such fruits of the forest as acorns and chestnuts supplemented the Pocumtucks' diet.

Autumn also brought the season for hunting, which provided both food and clothing. Morrell writes of "deare, and beares, . . . foxes both gray and black . . . with muscats, lynces, otter, bever / With many other which I here omit / Fit for to warm us, and to feede us fit." Deer served as the major animal food source, providing up to 90 percent of mammal meat.[21] More than simply accepting what they found, the Indians devised methods to encourage deer and other game to come to certain fields. In *New England's Prospect*, one of the first reports about the region sent back to London in the 1600s, William Wood explained that when "the INDIANS burn the woods in November, when the grass is withered, and leaves dried, it consumes all the under-wood and rubbish."[22] This would keep a "deer pasture" "open, and its herbage . . . succulent."[23] During the winter the Indians supplemented their supplies of stored food with the benefits of further hunting and ice fishing. When in spring the ice broke up and spawning runs began, they would harvest the shad, alewife, and salmon near some of the Connecticut's major falls. By mid-spring, while fishing and hunting likely continued, fields were sown and the seasonal cycle turned once again.[24]

These means of food gathering, and especially the centrality of corn in the natives' lives, helped dictate other important elements of New England Indian life. First, they helped define the roles of Pocumtuck men and women. The men became the hunters and fishermen, often working away from the home. They were also the warriors. In addition, they would train the young boys in all these skills. By contrast, the women did most of the work required to keep a family fed and warm. Morrell's poem embellishes this stark contrast of roles: "Thus all worke-women doe, whilst men in play / In hunting, armes, and plea-sures, end the day." Plymouth governor Josiah Winslow's Eurocentric 1624 account of the New England natives noted, "The women live a most slavish life; they carry all their burdens; set and dress their corn, gather it in, and seek out for much of their food; beat and make ready the corn to eat, and have all household care lying upon them."[25]

How the Indians stored their corn tells a great deal more about their way of life. The Pocumtucks and their neighbors kept corn, and sometimes nuts as well, in underground storehouses or trenches. Valuable during times of war or emergency, this also gives evidence of a planned agrarian economy. With the Indians thus prepared, they display "the very opposite of improvidence."[26]

A third significant element of Pocumtuck life dictated by corn was the very places these Indians lived. Because they depended so much on corn and planted it intensively, the Indians settled into regular, "semi-permanent village locations," rather than maintaining the loose, nomadic, even chaotic life-style of legend. While they would make a "major shift of residence from summer to winter," this constituted "routine and customary movement centering in summer around the cornfields, in winter around the wood and warmer (less wind swept) bottom lands."[27] This, too, Morrell noted: ". . .Distrest / With winter's cruel blasts, a hotter clime / They quickly march to. . . ."

Whether in winter or summer, most Algonkians lived in simple villages, little more than clusters of huts. These huts were made by bending flexible poles to make domelike frames, circular or oval at the base, which were then covered with mats or bark. While the village served as the "basic face-to-face unit of population,"[28] the nuclear family was "the basic unit of Algonquian life,"[29] a point emphasized by the separate dwellings that held each family.

The village also served as the "basic sociopolitical unit."[30] Each village had chiefs, called sachems or sagamores, and larger tribes were marked by a level of sub-chiefs as well. This leadership role was usually inherited, and it appears that the lines of descent in at least some tribes were matrilinear.[31] Both men and women served as sachems, and thus in at least some tribes Indian women held political power. One Pocumtuck squaw, Mashalisk, apparently held enough power to sell land to Englishmen, which she did at Pocumtuck in 1672.[32]

While most New England Indians lived in small villages, some dwelled in more substantial settlements—in forts. These forts, described in numerous colonists' contemporary accounts, might be fifty to one hundred feet in diameter, shaped square, round, or oblong. Often they would have "a ditch and breast-high embankment," the latter made with stakes as a palisade.[33] While the Pocumtucks lived in many villages down the Connecticut valley, their main fort stood just northeast of present-day Deerfield, on a rise still known today as Fort Hill.[34]

As William Morrell looked on this "new England," its natives, and their way of life, he concluded that this was, "In briefe, a briefe of what may make man blest." It is difficult to disagree. Rich and fertile land, abundant game, an economy that went beyond subsistence, stable social, political, and territorial structures—all marked this existence as indeed "blest."

"The Canaanites and Amalekites dwell in that valley. . . . But that land must be ours."

Actually, the English colonists who came into the Connecticut valley and saw Pocumtuck as early as 1637 were not nearly so zealous as this romantic 1819 vision suggests. The early English men in the valley acted carefully, often courteously, and sometimes deferentially in dealing with the Pocumtucks and their Indian neighbors. Still, no matter how lawful, careful, or deferential they were, in fifty years the Indians were gone, and the Connecticut valley held a strand of growing English settlements.

From the very first, European-Indian contact in the valley proved ill-fated. Between 1633 and 1635, even before any English towns were established, European pioneers brought a paroxysm of death to the Indians, in the form of a virulent epidemic. The disease, probably smallpox though possibly measles, swept through the defenseless natives. A report from Dutch traders who spent the winter with a thousand Indians somewhere "up the Connecticut River" claimed that all but fifty of those died.[35] Discussing a similarly devastating epidemic near Plymouth, contemporary Nathaniel Morton held that so many Indians died of the "great mortality . . . so as the twentieth person was scarce left alive.[36] It is also possible that the earlier, 1617–1619 epidemic that decimated the Indians of the Massachusetts Bay region reduced the inland population as well, even before the 1633–1635 outbreak. Some English saw this as an "opening up" of "virgin land"—a striking internal contradiction that speaks volumes about the English attitude toward the land and its natives. Some saw the change as providential. Morton certainly did: "God hath very evidently made way for the English, by sweeping away the natives by some great mortalities . . . at Connecticut, very full of Indians a little before English went into those parts."[37] Even without such Eurocentric, expansionist, or theological claims, the facts—like the deaths—remained. Before much contact, then, the Pocumtucks and their brethren lost vast numbers to an unseen, unknown, unimagined English menace.

That the source of the menace remained unknown to the Indians is clear. This comes most poignantly in looking at a striking act of Indian friendship, an act of the Pocumtucks. It is an inland tale of Squanto, a Connecticut valley story of Thanksgiving.

In late winter of 1638, the General Court ordered William Pynchon, founder of Springfield, to go upriver and obtain five hundred bushels of corn from the Indians to aid the struggling settlers of the valley. Unsuccessful as he worked up through different villages, Pynchon finally found help when he came to the Pocumtuck fort. There the natives loaded his canoes with food, at the nominal cost of five shillings per bushel. The valley below was fed, perhaps even saved.[38] The Pocumtucks received money for this, to be sure. Yet beyond that, the event proved rich with signs of the valley's future. It showed a prosperous and friendly Indian village, free from fear and well provisioned. It also presaged the rise of Indian-English trade and the growth of English settlement in the region. Finally, it hinted at the central role that the Pynchon family would play in the region's development.

The Pynchons dominated life in the upper Connecticut valley from the establishment of Springfield in 1636 through the end of the century. William Pynchon came to Massachusetts Bay from Essex, England, in 1629/1630 and served as the colony's first treasurer. Within a few years he migrated to the Connecticut valley and established a great fur and beaver trade with the Indians, while working the other end of the trade with merchants of both Boston and London. In time, he also came to trade on behalf of the colony, and he aided in Indian affairs "out west." This work was expanded by his son John—"the Worshipful Major Pynchon"—"magistrate, mediator, businessman" and the financier for most of the settlements in the Connecticut valley—largely because he was the only valley resident with significant credit resources.[39] Under John Pynchon's control and drive Springfield flourished. The promise of similar success, coupled with the expansion of Springfield itself, pushed English settlers up and down the valley over the next thirty-five years—to Northampton, Hadley, Hatfield, Brookfield, Enfield, Suffield, and Deerfield. While this expansion did not have to force removal of the native population, it meant that the Pocumtucks and their allies would at least be sharing the region's resources.

In some respects, the Indians were partners in all this activity. While they likely did not understand at first the implications of land sales, they did sign deeds throughout the seventeenth century. And if they did not understand a deed's significance in 1636, they almost surely would have by 1675.[40] More compelling, though, among the growing Indian-English ties were the economic bonds. The whole fur trade, the initial basis of the Pynchons' wealth, depended on the Indians' supply of furs and beavers. Early on at least, the Indians liked the trade, for it brought them "a new prosperity," as one historian has put it. Trinkets and clothes soon gave way to tools, metals, and weapons, as the Indians were launched into a new economic orbit where trade supplanted self-sufficiency. Yet trade could be a trap:

The Indians were quite willing to neglect their own individual arts and substitute the English products. Indeed, it would have been a people excessively bound to a ritual of accustomed life and materials that would have refused goods as preferable to their own as those of the Europeans. They could not have been expected to understand the danger of building up a reliance on a trade sure to be transitory.[41]

Transitory it was. The fur trade in the valley peaked in the 1650s and had largely ended by 1675. Yet new patterns, new needs and desires had been implanted. Beyond that, the fur trade brought with it rivalry among Indians for furs, which led both to more warring and to a greater sense of territoriality among Indians. Tribal middle men arose, and tribal trading posts as well, all of which led to still more conflict.[42] A wheel had begun to spin, and most Indians did not even know they were on it, much less how to get off.

Meanwhile, as Indian and colonist interacted in matters of land and trade, the colonists imposed on the natives their English laws and government, at least to some degree. As early as 1637 the Pocumtucks learned that they were under the "protection" of Connecticut when that colony sent three men to Agawam to "treate with Indians . . . concerning the tribute towards the charges of our warres." The English asked the "Pacumtucketts" to contribute one and a quarter fathoms of wampum for each man in the tribe to gain Connecticut's protection. While there is no record that the natives paid this "tribute," the request alone is telling.[43]

It was generally in more desultory matters that the Pocumtucks and other aboriginal neighbors made their mark in colonial law and governance. Indian cases do not abound in the early Hampshire County court records, but they do regularly appear. The Puritans held the Indians liable for the same sorts of offenses that they did their fellow English men and women: drunkenness, breach of Sabbath, fornication, theft. There are also cases where Indians received restitution for the wrongs of their English neighbors. For instance, in a 1667 case where some Northampton youths destroyed an Indian's canoe, the court ordered payments to the native for his losses. Still, the essential point here is that the Indians were being put under English law, whether they liked it or not.[44]

While the colonists apparently wanted—or at least assumed—some legal control over Indians, some distance between the peoples remained. In 1657, for example, Connecticut authorities asked the Pocumtucks to turn over an Indian named Mashupanan, whom they were allegedly hiding, because they claimed he was responsible for a "horrible bloody act" down at Farmington.[45] The merits and results of the case notwithstanding, this Connecticut request is illuminating. It demonstrates that settlers would request, not demand, an Indian from a tribe; that they recognized tribal differences; that they respected Indian sovereignty. Thus, it can be said that while valley Indians were under English law, they were not wholly of it.

When it came to actual conflict between different tribes, the English had still less control. Although the Indians and the English of New England did not fight for almost forty years, from the Pequot War of 1637 to King Philip's War in 1675, the English were constantly concerned about conflicts among Indians. And conflicts were many. While the English were sometimes "players in the game" and tried to influence events, they monitored conflict more often than determined it. They were as yet one force among many.[46]

Intertribal warfare exposes a vital dimension of seventeenth-century Indian life. In maneuvering through complex struggles for power and control among Indians from Long Island to Maine, as well as among the Europeans—English, French, and Dutch,— the natives displayed great dynamism. In this respect, they proved hardly the helpless victims of European growth, but rather were active agents in their fate. In particular, the Connecticut valley Indians fought amongst themselves as well as with outside tribes, and their wars predated contact with the English.[47] Different tribes also displayed diverse degrees of political organization and military prowess. One student of Indian politics has gone so far as to write, "The forms of an Indian society were always in flux, and the balance of forces within society were [sic] always shifting. When the white man intruded upon the situation, he simply became another issue to be dealt with in the context of a continuing internal struggle."[48] While this view is too simplistic, especially given English military strength by 1675 and the Europeans' effects on the Indians' economy, English records regarding the Pocumtucks and their neighbors generally support this view.

For their part, the Pocumtucks made their marks throughout the English records of this period as a prominent Indian force. Most notably, they engaged in wars or skirmishes with a number of different tribes of southern New England off and on from at least 1640 into the early 1660s. A United Colonies (New England Confederation) commissioners' petition of 1659 hints at the Pocumtucks' power, for it focuses on the Pocumtucks "and their Confederates," and appeals to "the Pocumtuck Sachems."[49]

One important conflict affecting the valley's Indians in the seventeenth century was a protracted struggle between the Mohegans and the Narragansetts, a struggle in which the Pocumtucks allied with the Narragansetts against the Mohegans and their hated leader Uncas. This fight began in the 1640s, largely as a struggle for control of the lower valley and of local Indian survivors of the Pequot War of 1637. It built also as a clash between two Mohegan leaders, Uncas and Sequasson. Members of the Pocumtuck confederacy sheltered Sequasson when Uncas managed to drive him north, but in 1646 Uncas successfully raided the Pocumtucks and captured his rival. From that point on until 1660, the Pocumtucks joined different alliances against Uncas and the Mohegans. In 1648 they met with a fighting force of Narragansetts, Niantics, and Mohawks at their fort at Pocumtuck which numbered as many as a thousand.[50] Although the alliance did not lead to action at that time, a "Narragansetts-Pocumtuck-Mohawk axis" held firm for the next decade.[51] In the mid-1650s the Pocumtucks also joined with the Podunk and Tunkiss tribes against the Mohegans. Only as 1659 came to a close did this conflict wane.

While the English stayed clear of actual fighting, they apparently tried to effect a balance of power in the region by aiding one side: the Mohegans. Through those years Uncas benefited greatly from that pairing, while earning the enmity of many Indians for it. The English appear to have had little actual control over the conflicts and still less over Uncas. Instead, it seems that Uncas proved the dynamic one, using the English to his best advantage, gaining aid and protection when he needed it, then waging war as he saw fit. He becomes, in this light, a master of seventeenth-century New England *realpolitik*.[52]

On the other side of this conflict, the tone of the English exchanges with the Pocumtucks suggests care, even forbearance at times. While the English sought to curtail Pocumtuck strikes against Uncas, they also respected the confederacy enough to request action, not demand it. In this vein, in 1657 the English authorities asked Pocumtuck sachems why they fought Uncas, a query that bespeaks more a learning session than an effort to control the natives.[53] In 1659 they wrote to the Pocumtucks of their continuing concern that the Indians, "in theire warrs and quarrells amongst themselves . . . presse soe neare . . . and sometimes into the houses of the English."[54] The Pocumtucks responded in kind. Reassuringly their message read, "The old league of ffriendship betwixt the English and our selves; we are resolved to keep. . . . And as for any wrong done to any of the English it is not done with a sett purpose to breake with the English." Yet in the same message, the Pocumtucks laid out some less reassuring goals and expectations:

We desire the English Sachems not to perswade us to a peace with Uncas although he promeseth much he will perform nothinge; wee have experience of his falcenes; alsoe wee desire that if any Messengers bee sent to us from the English they may bee such as are not lyares and tale carryers but sober men; and such as we can understand. . . .[55]

At the very least this is a message between equals.

All of this does not mean that the English held no power or influence over the Pocumtucks and their neighbors. From the 1630s on, the trade that William Pynchon had established with the Indians had altered their economy and culture. By 1660 valley Indians had traded with the English for a generation. They had traded off land as well, and they had seen English imposition of laws. The very fact of English communication with Indians had to affect Indian politics, and "the Puritan predilection for meddling . . . led them frequently to interfere with such tribes in the name of justice and peace."[56] Then, too, English efforts to control Indians could spur challenges to a sachem's powers—by the English if their efforts were rebuffed, and by the Indians themselves if the English succeeded.

Still, while the English involved themselves in Indian conflict, they did not dominate it. In fact, the 1650's brought repeated evidence of their "inability . . . to resolve any major disagreements among Indian groups."[57] As late as 1660 they were still just one force among many. For their part, the Pocumtucks proved themselves one of the more important Indian groups in the region, fighting or allying with Indians not only of the valley but as far south as Long Island and west as the Mohawk territory. Through the middle years of the century, the Pocumtucks strove to keep an even keel among the different forces of the region, Indian and European. For a generation, amidst a backdrop of native and European interdependence, they succeeded.[58]

What finally allowed the English access to the Pocumtucks' land at Deerfield had little to do with any Europeans. What transpired between 1660 and 1665 was neither greater English agitation, nor disease, nor trouble with other Algonkians. What happened to the Pocumtuck Indians was war with the Mohawks—and when the warring had ended, the Pocumtucks had been shattered forever.

From the very first European chronicling of Indian life, the Mohawks stand apart. The easternmost of the five tribes comprising the Iroquois nation in the seventeenth century, the Mohawks made life difficult for the Dutch, French, English, and other Indians alike. While New England's prospect was bright in William Wood's eyes in 1634, he greatly feared this "cruel bloody people" who fought other Indians with "brutish savageness, spoiling their corn, burning their houses, slaying men, ravishing women." This stood in stark contrast to the frequent yet far less destructive wars of New England Indians which depended on stealth and strategy, cost tribes few lives, and were often ritualistic.[59] The Mohawks were "more desperate in wars than the other Indians," and further practiced "inhuman cruelties."[60] In 1648 Roger Williams termed the Mohawks "more terrible and powerful than the English."[61] A French observer in 1659 similarly related, "Insolent in disposition and truly warlike, they have had to fight with all their neighbors."[62] Even Daniel Gookin's generally sympathetic 1674 study of New England Indians was no kinder. He claimed their "manner was to rob, kill, and spoil, their neighbor Indians far and near," that they were "given to rapine and spoil," to "cruel and murtherous practices," and were "much addicted to bloodshed and cruelty."[63] In the Connecticut valley, William Pynchon called them "the terror of all Indians."[64]

Mohawk influence extended "far and near" during the seventeenth century. A long-running war with the Hurons north and west of the Mohawk valley resulted in the decimation of those Indians by 1660. Similar strife with Algonkian tribes of New France yielded a similar fate. Even the French winced from Mohawk blows. These two forces battled for well over half the century, with only occasional interludes of peace. Some of this conflict involved only small-scale raids. Other periods, however, like the mid-1660s, brought out armies composed of hundreds of warriors.[65]

Why the Mohawks fought so frequently and so fiercely with other tribes has long been a vexing question. One sociological study of the Iroquois suggested that "blood vengeance or feud" lay at the heart of this trait; as with any feuds, wars would continue "long after the causes were lost in oblivion." Important recent research indicates that the Iroquois practiced "mourning-war," where fighting was undertaken in order to take captives to replenish forces depleted by war or disease.[66] One critical factor as the seventeenth century progressed was the role the Mohawks played in the fur trade. Mohawks served at times as vital middlemen for Dutch, French, and English traders. At other times they proved predators on that trade. Strategically situated in upper New York, with control of the Hudson and Mohawk rivers plus access to the St. Lawrence valley, Mohawks sought to solidify their potent position, and as rivalries grew, so did their ferocity.[67]

Mohawk activity was hardly confined to the lands north and west of their valley. Almost all of New England felt the Mohawks' influence during the 1600s. At least as early as the 1620s, the Mohawks were invading New England, in particular to war with the Mahicans in the south.[68] While large-scale fighting took place only in the late 1620s, Mohawks and Mahicans were apparently "hereditary enemies," and warring between them continued on and off for another forty years.[69] Meanwhile, by 1628 the Mohawks had already established a "domain of power" over the Indians of the middle Connecticut valley.[70]

While long-term struggles may have been unusual for the Mohawks, other raids were not, to the dismay of the Algonkian tribes. By about 1640, "Mohawks had been running small war parties into the valleys of the Connecticut and the Merrimac, killing the people and burning the villages of the indigenous tribes." Mohawk tentacles extended to bands as far south as Long Island, as well as to Eastern Abenaki down the coast of Maine. With such reach they brought "complete terror" to the northeast and made that terror "one of the basic facts of Algonkian life during the entire seventeenth century."[71] In fact, endemic Mohawk terror can even be considered a cause of significant population decline among New England's Indians through this period.[72]

Sometimes these eastern Iroquois made alliances within New England and embroiled themselves in others' battles. For instance, in the Pequot War the Mohawks aided the English and cut off the Narragansetts. While this can be seen as evidence of the peace that the English and Mohawk shared for much of this period, it also shows how the Mohawks grabbed an opportunity to cripple New England's strongest tribe when it could.[73] In 1648, as aforementioned, Mohawks allied with those same Narragansetts, as well as the Pocumtucks. By then their concerns centered on the Mohegans and their leader Uncas, who may have been becoming too firm an English friend.[74]

The 1650s saw relative stability in Mohawk-Algonkian relations. Although the 1648 pact between the Mohawks, Narragansetts, and Pocumtucks had not led to any fighting, the alliance served to restrain new conflict. Not that there were no pressures. From 1649 through 1651, the French Jesuit Father Gabriel Druillette labored to build a "French-sponsored, anti-Iroquois alliance.[75] By 1650 he had enlisted a number of Algonkian tribes, including the Sokokis, Pennacooks, Mahicans, and Pocumtucks to join his previous converts, the Abenaki and Montagni. When he tried to get the English to join in 1651, however, Druillette failed, and this likely led the Pocumtucks and their neighbors to resume ties with the Iroquois.[76]

Other pressures arose as well, with economics playing a key role. Although the English failed to recognize it, Indian conflict in the Connecticut valley often stemmed from efforts "to control or benefit from the wampum trade.[77] This trade proved an enduring concern for Indians trading with the Dutch as well as with the English—in other words, the Mohawks as well as New England's Algonkians. In fact, since at least the 1640s Mohawk activity in the Connecticut valley had turned on the issue of "access to a major source of wampum in the Narragansett and Niantic villages.[78] Pressures on land, arising from spreading English settlement, were growing as well. The Pocumtucks and their neighbors thus found themselves in a perilous position. To the west loomed the Mohawks; to the south, the Narragansetts and Mohegans. English pressures on land and trade continued to build. Through the 1650s the Pocumtucks had to perform a "diplomatic juggling act," appeasing the Mohawks, asserting their independence from the English.[79]

For over a decade they succeeded. But the fragile balance of power in the Connecticut valley soon broke apart under the weight of so many pressures. As the region's fur trade declined, the Indians fought for control of the trade that would bring them the European goods on which they now depended. A concurrent decline in demand for wampum made economic pressures still greater. Steady English settlement growth up the valley threatened the region's ever tighter natural resources.

Meanwhile the Mohawks faced other pressures. Devastated by population losses from war and disease through the 1650s, they returned to war as one way of replenishing their numbers, via the taking of captives. Through this same period, Mohawk fears also intensified that the French were succeeding in encircling them with a chain of hostile, allied Indian bands.[80]

The result of these pressures was war. The warfare was both new and old. On the one hand, new and growing pressures precipitated the outbreak. On the other, a historic "ethnic-linguistic divide between Algonkian and Iroquois, which had been overshadowed for a generation in New England and New Netherland, returned to the surface in native politics."[81]

Mohawk activity against New England tribes quickly intensified. In 1659, they reportedly set off against "the Abnaquiois" (Abenakis) to the east.[82] A report the next year indicated that they were now fighting against different Indian forces—Western Abenaki, Mahicans, and the "people of the east," likely Kennebecs and Penobscots.[83] Even after a 1661 treaty was signed with the eastern Indians, reports of war continued into 1662.[84] A Dutch memorandum from the summer of 1662 further implies that the Mohawks and "Kinnebeck Indians" had not yet made their peace.[85] At this same time another two hundred Mohawks were off fighting the Ottawas, an Upper Algonkian force.[86] And to the south, Mohawks and Mahicans soon resumed fighting.[87]

Conflict soon closed in on the Pocumtucks. When the Iroquois raided an Abenaki village in 1660, the Abenaki received help from the Sokoki, the Pocumtucks' neighbors just to the north. In 1662 the Sokoki attacked a Mohawk village, and in 1663 some Mohawks were killed, probably by Sokoki, near Pocumtuck.[88]

The Indians of the middle Connecticut valley quickly showed that they wanted no trouble with those Iroquois. With John Pynchon of Springfield drafting the letter, the Indians of Agawam, Pajassuck, Norwootuc, Wissetinnewag, and Pocumtuck wrote to the Mohawks to plead their innocence in the matter. Indeed, they wrote, they "deplore it exceedingly, repudiate the deed . . . [and] are resolved to keep up their intercourse and friendship with the Mohawks as before."[89] While apparently accepting this explanation, the Mohawk response noted that "if the sawages would send hither some of their people with presents, then the friendship and peace would be much firmer."[90] Meanwhile, they did not let the purportedly guilty Sokokis rest easy. In December 1663 they struck the Sokokis at their southernmost village of "Asquakeeke"—Squakeag, less than twenty miles above Pocumtuck—"breaking open their stores of corn and spilling it on the ground."[91] Within a few months Squakeag lay abandoned.

By spring of 1664, a vortex of forces, both Indian and European, whirled around Pocumtuck. The Iroquois, fearing French intervention in these conflicts, sent a peace delegation to Quebec—but Algonkians, likely including Pocumtucks, ambushed and smashed it. The Dutch, their beaver trade with the Iroquois hurt by recent strife, urged the Iroquois to make peace with the New England Indians. The English in the Connecticut valley, disturbed by the recent fighting in their region, tried to pressure the Pocumtucks into making peace with the Mohawks.

With all these forces spinning, in late May of 1664 an entourage of two Dutch, two Mahican, and three Mohawk negotiators arrived at Pocumtuck, where they were soon joined by five Englishmen from Northampton. Although affairs were not wholly resolved, the Pocumtuck attitude appeared to promise peace. Reviewing their relations with the Mohawks, the Pocumtucks recalled that they "had no war for thirty-six years and have not troubled ourselves about our neighbors [the Sokokis] . . . at war with them last year." Mirroring the Mohawks' request of the previous year, the Pocumtucks added, "Let them send us a present, then we will release their prisoners and bring a present to their country, thus to renew our old friendship."[92] The Mohawks acceded. Leading the delegation was a Mohawk "prince," Saheda, a leader "much beloved by . . . the Indians on account of his knowledge."[93] Bearing gifts, Saheda and his entourage of perhaps fifteen men left Fort Orange on June 21 and entered the Pocumtuck fort a few days later. They never stepped out again.

Perhaps the Pocumtucks resented Mohawk efforts to dictate the peace. Perhaps Saheda angered them. With the Iroquois besieged on so many fronts, perhaps the Pocumtucks now felt that the Iroquois no longer posed a threat. It is also possible that the Sokokis talked the Pocumtucks into this act, for in the aftermath of the Mohawk attack on the village at Squakeag and its subsequent abandonment, some thirty or forty Sokoki had come to live in the Pocumtuck fort.[94] The Dutch, at war with the English and ever straining to strengthen their Mohawk alliance, claimed that Englishmen in the fort put the Pocumtucks up to the act. Whatever the reason, the bald facts remain: The Pocumtucks killed Saheda and his entire entourage. They had thrown a brazen challenge at the Mohawks.

The Pocumtucks had sown the wind; they would soon reap the whirlwind. By July Dutch reports of the event had been filed at Fort Orange and Mohawk outrage duly noted, though no action yet took place.[95] Late summer brought a major change in the imperial history of the colonial northeast: The English moved into New Netherland, quickly forced a Dutch surrender, and consolidated control up the Hudson River, including Fort Orange, near the center of Mohawk power. Yet however important this might ultimately prove, it did not change Iroquois-European relations. In fact, like the Dutch, the English of New York already had strong ties with the Indians and tended to support them during inter-Indian clashes.[96] Thus, in late September they had no qualms about, first, promising to provide the same "wares and commodities" to the Mohawks that the Dutch had and, second, on September 25 agreeing "[t]hat the English do not assist the . . . Pacamtekookes, who murdered one of the Princes of Maques, when he brought ransoms & presents to them upon a treaty of peace."[97]

Understandably, the English wanted firm, lasting bonds with the northeast's most powerful Indian tribe. In that light, the first act makes perfect sense. The second action, however, made them minor players in a larger, deadlier Indian game. While this agreement may have seemed inconsequential to the English, in effect they had signed the Pocumtucks' death warrant.

Soon after securing English support, the Mohawks launched a war party across the Hudson, down the fifty miles of the "Mohawk Trail" into the Upper Connecticut valley. Precisely how and when they attacked the Pocumtuck fort, what strategy they used, and what losses they suffered lie unknown. Local legend has it that the Mohawks first attacked the fort straight on, suffering significant losses. Then, when they pulled back, the Pocumtucks followed and fell into a fatal ambush. However, the battle actually went, when it was over the Pocumtuck tribe had been destroyed. The fort and village were laid waste, the people slain or scattered.

The destruction of the Pocumtucks did not mark the end of Mohawk incursions into New England. Though hostilities abated slightly in 1665–1666 due to renewed French efforts against these Iroquois, occasional forays continued. Some were of broad scale and highly organized, such as a 1666 strike at Podunk, near Windsor.[98] Others were isolated strikes by small Mohawk bands, such as a 1669 attack on Northampton and two other locales by "Indians called Maguaws [who] made spoyle among the Cattell."[99] In 1669 a whole host of New England tribes banded together to send a force of six hundred or seven hundred men against these hated "Maguaws." While some marched as far as two hundred miles to attack the Mohawk fort, they were repulsed and driven back into New England with heavy losses.[100] It may well be that some Pocumtuck Indians joined in this pan-Algonkian effort against the Mohawks. As a cohesive force, though, the Pocumtucks had ceased to exist. Although Algonkians no longer left New England to attack the Mohawks, the opposite did not hold. The Mohawks proved to be a critical force affecting New England's Indians during King Philip's War and even into the early 1700s. Their reach, too, remained great. Due in part to these Iroquois, by the 1670s Eastern Abenaki Indians in Maine had become so battered that significant numbers of those Indians left their homelands for the greater security that the French offered in Canada.[101] When Mohawks moving through Connecticut in 1678 killed or captured twenty-four "ffreind Indians . . . near o^r English houses," the Connecticut Indians complained to the colonial authorities, and Connecticut complained to New York—but no one could do much to or about the Mohawks.[102]

Indians were not the only victims of Mohawks. Well into the 1690s, colonial authorities received "almost constant complaint" that the Mohawks were continuing "the old Iroquois habit of attacking settlers' property on their way to and from Albany." While the "chief targets were corn and livestock," vandalism was common, and killings occasional.[103]

Thus, the Mohawks proved a dominant—perhaps the dominant—force in western New England in the seventeenth century. That they destroyed the Pocumtucks may seem gruesome, but it was not unique. Indians held significant power in colonial New England longer than many settlers wanted to think, and at least some Indians stood not only above English law but also beyond English power. Such were the Mohawks.

As for the Pocumtucks, it is clear that English exploration and settlement had made an impact on the tribe well before 1664. By 1660 their economic system, their land, and their law all bore signs of the growing English presence. Yet ultimately it was other Indians who destroyed them. The impact of the Europeans on the Indians' economy, life-style, and culture surely affected and in some cases induced these wars, but for Pocumtuck the point remains: Indians warred, and Indians destroyed Indians. The story of seventeenth-century New England, of Indians and Europeans, of contact and trade and settlement and destruction, does not run in linear fashion. Rather, it spins out a whirl of forces, some English yet many Indian.

"Let us go and possess the land . . ."

In 1665, English explorers from Dedham completed a one-hundred-mile journey. Forty miles north of Springfield, they forded the Connecticut River and climbed up the east side of the five-hundred foot rise looming before them. Their reward was to gaze down on the beauty and tranquility of the Pocumtuck valley. The timing of these Dedham men in finding this "open" valley was exquisite. Appointed by their townspeople to find a place in which to lay out an eight-thousand-acre grant from the General Court, they looked down upon the open plateau, the rich meadows, the river, and the protecting mountains to the west and apparently saw no residents. And so, understandably, they took the land.

Here, then, was another story of the Bay repeated on the River. It was a story this time not of Thanksgiving but of discovery. When the Puritans landed in Massachusetts Bay in 1629 to begin their holy experiment, they praised God for blessing them with such good, open, virgin land. Of course the land was not virginal.[104] For decades, if not centuries, Indians had lived there. But the Indians of Massachusetts Bay had been decimated between 1615 and 1620 by a plague brought, albeit unknowingly, by earlier European explorers. To the English, though, the land appeared open and thus blessed.

As disease had decimated the Indians of Massachusetts Bay by 1620, so had Mohawks blotted out the Indians of Pocumtuck by 1665. Soon after, English settlers came to Pocumtuck, saw it as open, and quickly secured it. In fact, the land was no virgin, but the suitor did not care.

The Pocumtuck valley would, in time, bear many English children, but not before it suffered greatly in pain and loss of blood. The Pocumtuck Indians never came back in force to the valley, but over the next half century there would be other, jealous native suitors.

TWO

"Some Controversey," and New Proprietors

THE POCUMTUCK VALLEY did not lie open for long. Within a year of the Mohawks' devastating attack of 1664, English explorers had viewed the land and secured the rights to it from the Massachusetts General Court. Within six years, English settlers were farming there. Within ten years, the little village of Pocumtuck had been granted official town status.

Understanding how the colonists settled Pocumtuck brings into focus a number of larger themes of early New England history. Pocumtuck's story helps show how Massachusetts expanded; how the English dealt with the Indians they were dispossessing; the reasons and ways new towns grew; how they were organized; and the roles religion, politics, and economics played in expansion. Pocumtuck's story also proves special for Massachusetts because it links east and west in the years after 1665. The people who held title to Pocumtuck and legally organized its settlement came from Dedham, near Boston. Yet the pioneers who built and actually settled in the new town came from one hundred miles west—from settlements south of Pocumtuck in the Connecticut valley. Out of these two distinct groups—proprietor and resident, owner and settler, east and west—came the new town.

"Some controversey . . ."

Dedham's land grant at Pocumtuck was born in controversy. Its very conception came about because of the work of one of the prominent characters of seventeenth-century New England, the Reverend John Eliot. Born in Essex County, England, in 1604 and trained at Cambridge, Eliot apparently possessed no exceptional background, education, or intellect for working with the native Americans. One way in which he did excel, however, was dedication. Starting in about 1645, Eliot devoted the rest of his life to converting the Indians of Massachusetts to Christianity. He struggled to learn the Algonkian language, he lectured to the Indians, he raised funds in America and especially in his native England to support his holy work, and he helped establish the Society for the Propagation of the Gospel in New England. For all of this labor, though, Eliot realized that he needed a way to engage the Indians more fully in a Christian way of life. To do this, he set out to establish "praying towns," Christian Indian villages built on an English scale and pattern.[1]

After a "difficult search for available land" for his first praying town, Eliot relates, finally in 1651 "the Lord did by his speciall providence, and answer of prayers, pitch us upon the place . . . at Natick."[2] Within a year a town was thriving at this fine site on the Charles River, some eighteen miles southwest of Boston. Within another quarter century, Eliot's and others' labors had produced fourteen towns and had engaged as many as twenty-five hundred Indians.[3]

Eliot's work upset the townspeople of Dedham almost from the start. Their concern stemmed not from the minister's work but from its locale, for Eliot's first and foremost praying town at Natick stood in part on Dedham land. The Indian presence did not come as a complete shock to the Dedhamites: In 1650 the General Court had authorized Eliot to settle his praying Indians there. Still, from the very start Dedham considered this "a matter of great Concerne^mt in many respects" and formed a committee of town leaders "to take a carefull & speciall veiw of the Land."[4]

Their worries soon proved justified. For the next dozen years, Dedham fought, argued, and pleaded with the colony's legislature and courts, raising claims, promises, and fears, and always based on the same theme: the town's loss of land. No fewer than six times in the years from 1651 to 1660 did the General Court acknowledge a challenge to the Indians' version of Natick's boundaries. Yet the town received no satisfaction.[5]

Finally, in May of 1662 the united proprietors of Dedham, some forty-seven strong,[6] sent a lengthy petition to the governor, lieutenant governor, assistants, and deputies at the General Court.[7] In response, the General Court pushed for "a final issue of the controversy." Its order shows studied balance. While affirming Dedham's "legal right to compensation for lands lost," the Court also acknowledged its own "incouragement of the Indians in their improovements" of lands which the Court had granted them. Therefore, the Court ordered "that the Indians be not dispossessed of such lands as they at present are possessed of," and that a committee be established to assess Dedham's "damages" and to establish fair compensation.[8]

Some six months later the committee made its report. It turned out that Dedham's protests were justified. Contrary to the original grant, Eliot's Indians now lived on both sides of the river at Natick. What's more, the Indian settlement on Dedham did now "Containe Fowre Thousand Acres, or thereabouts": Their original two thousand acres had *doubled*. Weighing this, the General Court provided generous compensation. In the "final issue of the Case," the order of May 27, 1663, read, the Court "judgeth it meet to grant Dedham EIGHT THOUSAND ACRES OF LAND in any Convenient place, or places not Exceeding two, where it can bee found free from former Grants."[9]

"Any convenient place . . ."

It took Dedham well over a year to find an open and desirable site. In late fall of 1664, however, just weeks after the Mohawks had destroyed the Pocumtucks and their fort, the selectmen "heard of a considerable Tract of good Land . . . about 12 or 14 miles from Hadley." At its next meeting, in January, the town voted to proceed to lay out the land there. On May 22, four townsmen sent to survey the land returned from their journey

west. They reported that they had successfully laid out the
eight thousand acres. The name of the place, they reported,
was "Pecumptick."[10]

At its autumn session, the General Court confirmed Dedham's acquisition when townsman Joshua Fisher brought forth
a map of the land along with a written summary of its borders.
The plat embraced the heart of what Fisher as well as the
Indians called Pocumtuck. Now Dedham was to "make a toune
of it, to majntejne the ordinances of Christ there once wthin
five yeares."[11]

Dedham's timing in all this was fortuitous. The town laid
claim to Pocumtuck a scant six to eight months after the Mohawks had destroyed the Pocumtuck Indians' fort and village.
That depredation must have been massive, even total, for the
Dedham and General Court records betray not one word of
Indian lands, dwellings, or peoples. Yet Dedham's citizens were
neither naive nor stupid. On May 22, 1665, the same day they
welcomed their explorers home, they raised this "Indian issue." Acknowledging that it would "appeere that some Indians
are like to clayme a Title" on the land, which needs to "be
cleered," the selectmen announced that Ensign Daniel Fisher
and Eleazer Lusher should go and "treat with . . . Capt Pinchion, and empower him to contract wth those said Indians for
the buyeing out of all thier Right or clayme in the prmises."[12]
Captain Pynchon—not William Pynchon, Springfield founder
and Connecticut valley pioneer, but rather John Pynchon, his

ON THE OPPOSITE PAGE: This is a copy of the one surviving piece of a map
prepared in Pocumtuck in about 1671. It shows the layout of lands for the
northern half of town. This includes home lots, in the map's lower right
quarter; first-division farmlands, in the meadows to the north of the home
lots; and second-division farmlands, on the west side of the Deerfield River.
At the very top of the map are also noted four "farms" (1 through 4), given by
Dedham to the four men who went out and surveyed Pocumtuck in the 1660s.

The numbers on the map represent the holdings of the different proprietors of Pocumtuck and were drawn by lot, in Dedham, as planned by the
town. The differences in lot sizes were based on the number of "cow commons," or proprietary shares, that each proprietor held. (For further explanation see Chapters 2 and 3.)

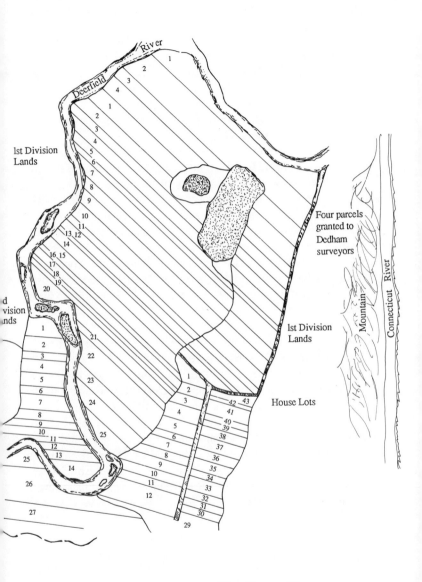

The Town Plan
of Early Deerfield:
Pocumtuck, ca. 1671

son—now dominated the valley, as the Dedham selectmen
clearly knew. By this act, the people of Dedham showed they
were not ignorant that "other people" had lived on their newly
claimed lands. The way they resolved this matter illuminates
the hearts and minds of these Puritan pioneers.

It is to the Puritans' credit that they recognized that Indians
might well "clayme a Title" to the land. And yet, that town
meeting of May 22, 1665, was the only time the Dedham citizens paid attention to the actual rights of the Indians of Pocumtuck. Five weeks after the town sent Fisher and Lusher off to
engage John Pynchon, the town turned the whole affair of the
eight thousand acres back over to the selectmen.[13]

From then on, the "worᵖfull Capt Pincheon" did most of the
work.[14] Over the next three years he executed no fewer than
four different deeds with surviving Indians of the Pocumtuck
valley (a fifth was signed in 1672).[15] Since the deeds all used
Indian and not English place names, it is impossible to know
precisely what Pynchon and Dedham actually secured. In this
case, however, such precision does not seem critical. For a total
cost to Dedham of £96.10—Pynchon's "bill" to the town—Pocumtuck was now theirs, apparently free and clear.[16]

While the land—and the Dedham proprietors' con-
sciences—may have been free and clear, the purchase of Pocumtuck raises many issues about the Indian-English relations
of this period. In exploring what one historian has labeled "the
deed game,"[17] it appears that in this era most New Englanders
tried to follow the law when obtaining land from the natives.
The sticking point, however, is that the law was English law.
This English ethnocentrism is evident in the English view of
what they called "virgin land"—land which of course was already occupied, by the Indians. The English believed that land
that was not being used—that is, settled, farmed, and enclosed—was open land, *vacuum domicilium*,[18] and was free for
the taking. John Winthrop, the first governor of Massachusetts
Bay, gave credence to this view. In response to the query,
"What warrant have we to take the land?" he wrote:

That which is common to all is proper to none. This savage people
ruleth over many lands without title or property; for they enclose no

ground, neither have they cattle to maintain it, but remove their dwellings as they have occasion, or as they can prevail against their neighbors.[19]

Not only seventeenth-century New England Puritans held this view, either. No less a utopian philosopher than Thomas More struggled when confronting the potential problem of "uncooperative" peoples in his ideal world. Although he tried to work through the problem, ultimately More called for occupation and conquest if native tribes could not peaceably be convinced.[20]

Part of an explanation for what seems to be such English arrogance comes from the special sense of mission that buoyed New England's Puritans. In "God's Promise to His Plantation," John Cotton, one of the great early Puritan preachers, hearkened back to the Old Testament when he declared that God "had given them their land for a possession": "this placing of people in this or that company, is from God's sovereignty over all the earth, and the inhabitants thereof." When considering how "God makes room for a people," he proclaimed that one way was "when He makes a country though not altogether void of inhabitants, yet void in that place where they [will] reside."[21] The Pocumtuck proprietors could appreciate that. What Cotton was generally declaring was a seventeenth-century version of manifest destiny.

Puritan visions of land rights and legal jurisdiction further affected relations with Indians. When English colonists took over Indian land, they took over both property *and* sovereignty, land *and* law.[22] In looking at the Pocumtucks' situation, the English imposed their laws even before they owned the Indians' land. Well before deeds had been signed, the English were bringing natives into English courts for various violations of English law—drunkenness, breach of the Sabbath, and the like.[23] As long as the Indians wanted to continue to live in the region, they apparently had little choice.

This Puritan ethnocentricity becomes still clearer through analysis of the sales of Pocumtuck land which took place in the 1660s. The first and most glaring piece of evidence about Dedham's attitude toward Indian rights is that the town did not even raise the issue of gaining title to the Indians' lands at Pocumtuck until after the tract had been laid out. Joshua Fisher brought back his map of the land in early May of 1665; only on the 22nd of that month did Dedham raise the issue of right title. In other words, the land had been surveyed and studied before the issue of ownership even came up. Mirroring this attitude, the General Court approved the specific tract in October 1665— a good six months before Pynchon secured any title to it.

Like most other English of this period, the Dedham proprietors also ignored the difference between English and Indian concepts of land ownership. Algonkian Indian claims to land were based on "collective *sovereignty*," not "individual *ownership*." Within villages, Indians maintained a fluid view of land. What mattered was not actual personal ownership of the land, but rather what was on it. In other words, "use" was the critical issue.[24] Looking at villages as whole entities, village sachems, whether male or female, held general authority over the land. Not only did these sachems hold rights "like . . . eminent domain" over all land, but apparently to make a sale of land "legitimate in Indian eyes it had to be approved by the grand sachem."[25] This last position does imply, nonetheless, at least a theoretical awareness of the possibility of selling territory.

The surviving deeds show how Pocumtuck fit into this tangled web of questions about land. The five extant deeds were each signed by different Indians. In fact, no fewer than eight Indians ceded Pocumtuck land to the English in these five documents. Only one of them, Chauk, claimed he was "the sachem of Pocumtuck," and there is no evidence to support the assumption that he was the grand sachem—if there was one— or even one of the tribe's sub-chiefs, who were also titled "sachems." In fact, Pynchon and the Dedham proprietors may have bought the lands from any Indians who would sell it.

Selling land implies Indian acceptance of the English concept of land ownership, which cannot be confirmed. It also implies compensation, a selling price. Here it appears Pynchon took full advantage of the Indians. Of the available deeds, the first one with Chauk lists only "good and valuable Considerations" in the terms of the deed. The next two, of 1667, list nothing. Only in a 1672 deed securing more land south and east of the village did Pynchon itemize his terms. And that payment was nominal at best.[26] For a five-mile-long tract of rich bottomland along the Connecticut River, an "old woman" named Mashalisk received retirement of a debt of "ten large beavers" plus some other debts of her sons, "sixty fada of wampum . . . cotes . . . some cotton & Severall other small things."[27]

Questions about proper authority to sell lands also emerge. The surviving deeds are filled with Indian place names rather than English surveying and descriptive terms, so it should be conceded that the English were working with unfamiliar language. Still, a review of these Indian deeds reveals that Pynchon and Dedham bought at least two tracts of land twice![28] Admittedly, Pynchon may have been acting diligently in following Massachusetts law, which required extinguishing all Indian claims. Still, since different Indians sold the land each time, it appears that not only did the English bargain with whomever they could to secure lands, but that neither they nor the Indians themselves had a clear sense of who owned what. That no single sachem guided the Pocumtucks in the 1660s now appears obvious.[29]

Lest this seem wholly one-sided, it should be noted that in at least two of the five deeds, the Indians maintained some rights to their land. In the first deed Pynchon secured, in 1666, the Indians retained "Liberty of fishing . . . in ye Rivers or waters & free Liberty to hunt deere or other wild creatures, & to gather walnuts chestnuts & other nuts thing & c on ye Commons."[30] Still, it is hard to measure how realistic this was for either party. While the Indians staved off eviction through such clauses in their deeds, they may have gained little real advantage from them as English settlement pressed in.

By 1669 the proprietors from Dedham had secured their eight thousand acres and legalized their claim. They did it largely on their own terms, but then again, by 1669 in the Pocumtuck valley, those were the only terms that mattered. The Mohawks had guaranteed that. To their credit, the men of Dedham had by legitimate means sought land due to them for a legitimate grievance; received compensation for it from the General Court; followed Massachusetts law in finding and securing their new land; surveyed it properly; sought and received the colony's blessing for their efforts; negotiated with Indians for rights to the land; signed carefully drawn deeds with both English and Indian witnesses; and made their actions public. In some respects, the Pocumtuck Indians appear to have negotiated well. A decimated, scattered tribe was able to sell its land, not merely lose it (and indeed, sold some of it twice); kept some hunting, fishing, and gathering rights; and by acquiring English neighbors gained some possible protection from future Mohawk attacks.

Yet the picture is not all bright. These self-assured Puritans claimed Indian lands before ever meeting with the Indians. They also failed to consider—or at least acknowledge—any possible differences with the Indians in concepts of land ownership or proper Indian authority to sell such land. They also secured real bargains with the less powerful and possibly uncomprehending Indians. Finally, and most enduring, they imposed their laws, standards, and beliefs on the surviving natives.

Little more than twenty years from the time John Eliot had begun his holy work at Natick, Dedham had received land in compensation and those new lands were now open and titles clear. The people from Dedham were free to settle a new plantation at the place called Pocumtuck.

"A new plantation"

Even with the land free and clear, Pocumtuck's new owners had a number of questions to consider. Who within Dedham actually owned the land? How much of it did different towns-people own? Who had the authority to divide up the land and how could it be done fairly? Who would move to the new plantation? Who should govern the new lands and by what rules? When might an independent town emerge?

Taken together, town records from Dedham and Pocumtuck provide a good picture of how one early New England town was spawned from its parent. In the control and distribution of land, the layout of the town, and the system of town governance, Pocumtuck followed generally common regional practices. In other ways, however, Pocumtuck proved to be quite unusual. A number of Dedhamites speculated with Pocumtuck lands, an activity usually not associated with seventeenth-century New England towns. In addition, the town's birth arose from the efforts of two wholly separate groups that show vastly different strains of the early New England frontier. The Dedham proprietors of eastern Massachusetts were formal, careful, and legalistic in drawing up a plan for a Puritan town. Yet almost all the actual residents of Pocumtuck came from the west. They proved to be a different cut of men and women. Both proved essential in establishing the town.

The group that oversaw early Pocumtuck's affairs after 1665 was "the Dedham proprietors." But who were they? To answer this requires a return to Dedham's past.

When Dedham had been a small, covenanted community in the years after its founding in 1636, virtually all townsmen had participated in the full life of the town. That meant not only voting at town meetings and attending church but also sharing control of the town's abundant lands. If Dedham's men at the town meeting decided they wanted to parcel out new shares of land for each of them, they were free to do so. By the early 1650s, however, as new settlers kept moving into Dedham, it became clear to the original inhabitants that they were giving up more and more land—but more important, rights to future lands—to virtually all new townsmen. For this reason, in 1656 the town separated its proprietors—the legal owners, regulators, and distributors of the town's undivided lands—from its mere "inhabitants." All seventy-nine men who held lands in town as of 1656 were made proprietors. But that 1656 division bound the townspeople and "their heyres and assignes for ever."[31] New settlers could purchase already divided and privately held land, but would gain no proprietary rights unless they specifically purchased them from a townsman or were specially granted them by the proprietors.[32]

The Dedham townsmen (no women were included in the original distribution of proprietors' shares) never intended to parcel out those shares equally. That kind of "democratical" step would have been anathema to them.[33] Rather, they worked out a marvelously convoluted system for distribution of shares based on current wealth. First, they established that the total number of shares would approximate the total number of acres in the town's cow commons: 532 acres. Then, the total value of the estates of all proprietors was divided by this number to establish the amount of estate a man must have to own one proprietary share. By this method, they granted one proprietary share for every £18 worth of estate, real and personal. These proprietary rights they called, appropriately enough, "cow commons," and indeed, they carried with them equivalent grazing rights on the actual cow commons in the center of Dedham. What is crucial here, however, is that these rights also entailed a proportionate share of any future divisions of Dedham's undivided lands. To handle fractions of shares, they further declared that one cow common would equal five sheep, or goat, commons. Thus, John Kingsbury, with an estate worth £183.10, received the rights to ten cow commons and one sheep commons (10 times £18 plus 3.5 / 18—about 1 / 5 cow, or one sheep commons). And Kingsbury and his heirs would retain these rights as long as Dedham still had lands to divide.[34]

After three years of ironing out problems, in February of 1659 the townspeople of Dedham approved their proprietary system, with a total of 522 cow commons and 2 sheep commons—remarkably close to their target of 532 shares. Ten years later, these rights proved the basis for rights to the new lands at Pocumtuck.

As the 1660s drew to a close, interest in the new lands at Pocumtuck heightened. Dedham's proprietors did not face any great pressure to leave their town, yet the new lands were starting to cost them time and money. The town had underwritten a number of trips by townsmen to visit and survey the lands and in 1665 had voted to tax each proprietor two shillings for each cow common he owned in order to support "the mayntenance of an orthodoxe ministry" at Pocumtuck. In October of 1667 they were required to pay another rate, of four shillings per cow common, to cover John Pynchon's purchase of all Indian rights to the land. Later in 1667, Lieutenant Cooke reminded the town "that the time prfixt by the Generall Court for the planting [of] a Towne at Pocompticke doe shorten."[35] Beyond that, at least some proprietors were getting interested in making use of the tract.

A few months later came the event which galvanized the Pocumtuck proprietors into action. At Dedham's town meeting on May 18, 1669, one "Samuell Hinsdell of Hadley in the Countie of Hampshire" came forward. "[H]aveing purchased some ppriety [proprietary rights] in Pocumtucke in the Land Granted and layed out to the Inhabitants of Dedham, and made empremt [improvement] by ploughing Lande there," Hinsdale "demaunded the layeing out of the Rights he had so purchased . . . that he might settle himselfe upon it and pceed in empvemt thereof." Since the Dedham leaders could "see no cause to forbid him seing himself . . . to beare the venture of the place"— in other words, to venture in and settle there—they decided "to move the ppriators to pmote the layeing out each Inhabitants Right there."[36]

The next step came in November of 1669 when the town meeting suggested that the proprietors ought to "drawe Lotts in the first optunitie, that it might be better knowen wher each mans ppriety will lye." From the first Massachusetts Bay settlements in 1630, proprietors had divided up town land by choosing lots randomly so as to make the actual distribution of land as fair as possible. This does not mean that each man received the same amount of land. All men were not equal, in age, status, wealth, or family size. But if they did not receive equal shares of land, they still could have equal chances of getting the best lands and locations. For this reason, proprietors divided a township's land into different types—plowlands, meadows, swamp, woodlands—and divided these into lots for each proprietor. That way no one would gain undue advantage over another by having a large, single lot of particularly good land in one spot. Although the Massachusetts General Court did not formalize rules for proprietors to follow until the early eighteenth century, strong traditions led town proprietors to follow these elaborate procedures.[37] Here the Dedham proprietors' work with Pocumtuck typifies seventeenth-century New England practices.

The proprietors settled down to business at Lieutenant Fisher's house in Dedham on May 22, 1670. Attendance was impressively high. Not only did a majority of the Dedham proprietors appear, but at least some of those who could not made sure they had proxies there. Samuel Hinsdale came all the way from the Connecticut valley, as did "Joh: Pincheon Esqr"— John Pynchon, who had purchased some commons rights to Pocumtuck. The proprietors first decided to hire an "Artiste," upon "moderat tearmes," to go to Pocumtuck and determine where the different divisions of land should be—house lots, first and second division (or quality) plowing land, meadows, woodlots—and to lay out the first set of lots. Then the artist / surveyor, along with a town committee, was to figure out where to put the meetinghouse, "high wayes," and church lots.

The proprietors tried to be scrupulously fair. They were careful to check not just the proportion of land set off for each proprietor, but all the "quallitie thereof; so that "equitie may be attended to each" proprietor in "every sort of land." They also decided that to make sure no one got an unusually good or bad tract of land, "no man shall laye out more than 20. Cowe Comon rights together in one place."[38] Anyone with over twenty cow commons rights would have to get land via two (or more) separate drawings for lots in a given division. The group further made sure that all plowlands would "runne easterly and westerly," apparently to give everyone equal sun as well as access to the river. Finally, after all rules were established, the proprietors drew lots for the first division of farmlands.

While a major step toward establishing a town, the dividing of farmlands did not include the choosing of house lots. This required further work by Dedham's "artist," followed by another drawing of lots to determine where each proprietor's home site lay. His report came a year later, on May 16, 1671. Forty-three house lots were laid out on both sides of a six-rod-wide "common street" that ran north and south on a one-mile-long elevated "banke or ridge of land"—the central plateau. While the location of each man's homesite among the forty-three laid out was drawn by lot, size was once again based on the number of cow commons each proprietor held.[39] In other words, the proprietors had first determined the location of each proprietor's house lot based on a random drawing and then worked out each lot's size based on the number of cow commons each proprietor held.[40]

The general plan for Pocumtuck reveals a good deal about the goals as well as experiences of the Dedham proprietors. The very fact of a town plan, with house lots and various sorts of farming lands laid out precisely before settlement even began, speaks volumes about them. These settlers certainly were pioneers, but hardly the isolated, fiercely independent individuals of American legend. Instead, they designed a town with the houses all grouped together and with the farmlands, woodlands, and fields stretching out from around the center.[41] With houses placed close up along the main street, their front doorways facing one another, the proprietors directed Pocumtuck's people inward, away from the wilderness and toward one another. Part of this scheme doubtless came from their fears of the frontier; another part reflected a Puritan concern for watchfulness; another suggested the manorial system of England that so many Dedhamites had left behind.[42] In other words, Pocumtuck's plan was both old and new, English and Dedham-based, dependent on religious concerns and designed for frontier exigencies—and probably both conscious and unconscious.

In planning Pocumtuck, the Dedham proprietors appear to have acted like the founders of most other New England towns of this period. From that perspective, the next step would be for Dedhamites to settle their new town. But Dedham's proprietors did not move to Pocumtuck. In fact, many promptly sold their rights, often to far-off Connecticut valley people. Within three years Pocumtuck became a town—yet without the people of Dedham who had designed it.

An isolated frontier village perched on the edge of English settlement, Pocumtuck strained patterns of seventeenth-century New England town building. Distance encouraged speculation and absenteeism, two developments foreign to the Puritans of early New England. Because of these developments, Pocumtuck's story cuts against the grain of early New England history. The Dedham proprietors may not have even considered the possibility of speculation and absenteeism when they first gained Pocumtuck's lands in 1665—yet by 1675 these forces had played a major part in the young town's development.

When Dedham had borne two offspring towns in mid-century, Medfield in 1649 and Wrentham in 1662, it had done so for specific reasons. First, the town had begun to face population pressures. Also compelling was Dedham's "urge to create buffer settlements" to the south and west. Since these new towns were nearby, migration to them was easy and since Dedham was actually sponsoring the new settlements, townspeople readily moved to them.[43]

In the Connecticut River valley, town foundings reflected other problems and goals. Northampton began in 1654 because economic pressures drove settlers up the valley from the towns below. Hadley got its start in 1659 when religious controversy at Hartford and Wethersfield drove a group of zealots to plant a new church upriver.[44]

In these cases and others like them, distinct groups of townspeople had grievances and the aggrieved groups moved out. Whether the problems were economic, political, or religious, specific issues led these pioneers to found new towns. And these new towns, like Medfield and Wrentham, were invariably near their mother towns. But Pocumtuck was different. Dedham's offshoot was both exposed and far distant. In addition, there was no aggrieved party in Dedham in the 1660s: No clear group or issue or problem led to the founding of Pocumtuck. Certainly Dedham had been upset when John Eliot received his lands at Natick in the 1650s, but that issue lay between Dedham and the General Court, not among people within Dedham. Besides, Dedham was hardly desperate for land, and surely not such distant land. After all, all those with proprietary rights to Pocumtuck were by definition Dedham proprietors, and that meant that they already held lands and rights to future divisions in Dedham itself. By contrast, Pocumtuck lay in isolated, dangerous wilderness one hundred miles away. Indeed, on at least three occasions, Dedham explorers to Pocumtuck in the mid-1660s were rewarded for their service with new parcels of land—in Dedham.[45]

Pocumtuck was different: more like a gift, a bonus, unexpected compensation, even more a bit of "spare cash" than a necessary new division. While this claim may sound strained, a look at records both within Dedham and without reveals that even as some Dedhamites were carefully laying out Pocumtuck, others were already trading shares and speculating heavily in the new venture.[46]

When Dedham had made the "final settlement" of its proprietors in 1659, the list included seventy-nine names. When the Pocumtuck proprietors got together in autumn of 1669 to establish a rate of "payment to Capt Pincheon for the purchase of the Indians rights there," the list of those to be taxed stood at eighty.[47] In other words, at that point virtually all the Dedham proprietors still held their rights to Pocumtuck. In the next eight months, however, a wild scramble went on in Dedham for those rights. By the time the lots were drawn in May 1670, only thirty proprietors held rights. Further, of those thirty, nine were men who had not even appeared on the previous year's list. Among these were Samuel Hinsdale, the Hadley resident who had already been "ploughing land" at Pocumtuck, thereby pushing the proprietors into action in 1669; Hinsdale's father, Robert; and none other than John Pynchon, who showed up in Dedham for the drawing of lots suddenly in command of a huge share of fifty-four cow and four sheep commons.[48] Also among the nine was a Hatfield resident named Samson Frary. He was much more than a mere proprietor. In fact, when Pocumtuck's "artist" laid out the town house lots in 1670–1671, he measured the street beginning at the "falling ridge of land at Samson Frary's celer." In other words, Frary must have already been there, and was, along with Hinsdale, among the first residents of Pocumtuck.[49] In summary, by early 1670 control of Pocumtuck's lands was rapidly changing. Almost sixty out of eighty of the Dedham proprietors had already given up their rights to Pocumtuck, while at least two pioneers from the west had pushed onto the land even before they had gained rights to it.

Interestingly, some trading or selling of rights and lands had been going on well before 1670, even if the proprietors had not formally approved it. By 1667 John Pynchon had already bargained for cow common rights with Joshua Fisher and John Allin, Dedham selectman and pastor, respectively. Pynchon also made a major purchase in late October of 1667 from another Pocumtuck speculator: Massachusetts governor John Leverett! For £6 plus "Severall Barrells of Tarr," Pynchon received from Leverett Anthony Fisher's 150-acre "farm," plus cow common rights which had come from at least two other Dedham men.[50]

That all this activity was "obviously speculative" on the part of at least some of the proprietors is clear.[51] Out of seventy-nine men on Dedham's 1659 proprietors' list, Ensign Chickering had the largest single holding of proprietary rights, with seventeen cow and four sheep commons, and only four men held more than twelve cow commons. The 1669 tax rate on Pocumtuck proprietors shows a similarly broad distribution of rights.[52] By 1670, however, the holdings of Pocumtuck rights looked radically different. Of the only thirty "present ppriators," over half held twelve or more cow common rights, and seven held more than Ensign Chickering's former high of seventeen cow and four sheep commons. Perhaps even more telling was that four "giants" had emerged among the proprietors, each holding between forty-six and sixty cow commons. Ensign Phillips and Peter Woodward, Jr. were Dedham natives, yet Samuel Hinsdale and John Pynchon were certainly not—and of the four, only Hinsdale ever ended up living in Pocumtuck. In fact, of the sixteen individuals holding the largest proprietary shares for Pocumtuck in 1670, only four ever settled in Pocumtuck and not one resided there after 1680. Indeed, of the entire group of thirty proprietors in 1670, only six ever went to live at their new plantation, and only one of these was a Dedham townsman. With so few men controlling such a large percentage of Pocumtuck's proprietary rights, Dedham's new plantation appeared to be a speculative venture in the west controlled by distant easterners—the very antithesis of the mainstream of seventeenth-century town development in Massachusetts.[53]

The outburst of speculation did not begin immediately with Dedham's acquisition of Pocumtuck in 1665. In fact, as of 1667 few proprietors had done anything with their Pocumtuck rights. They had served simply as "money in the bank." Even when the first taxes were levied on the Pocumtuck proprietors, shares did not turn over much, perhaps due to the fact that no one paid the tax.[54] However, between Samuel Hinsdale's pushing the proprietors into laying out the town in May 1669 and the levying of the next tax rate in September of that year, it became clear to the Dedham proprietors that a new plantation was to be built. This time they would have to pay their taxes, and for many, that distant land at Pocumtuck was just not worth it. Selling their rights might recoup their investment and a little more. On the other hand, for those men willing to put up some money, take a risk, and buy up the proprietary rights to Pocumtuck, speculation in Pocumtuck rights appeared promising. The grant was sizable, it held some rich, open farmlands, and it might produce a nice profit. Certainly speculation held risks, but settlers were steadily moving up the Connecticut valley through the 1660s and relations with valley Indians seemed stable. In sum, the place looked promising and the risks worth taking.

In all this, Pocumtuck's development seems out of kilter with the flow of seventeenth-century New England history—if for understandable reasons. With its skewed circumstances, though, the new settlement appeared less a city upon a hill than just a village in the valley. Its origins suggest that within fifty years of the founding of Massachusetts, speculation and economic gain may have already been supplanting the utopian vision of the colony's first generation.

For three years after 1670 the proprietors of Dedham managed to keep at least a tenuous hold on their distant town. The Dedham town book shows that at least some of the continuing sales of land and proprietary shares were recorded.[55] Further, knowing that Dedham still legally controlled governance of Pocumtuck, the new village dutifully sent back representatives to Dedham to discuss town affairs.

Yet during this same three years Dedham's hold over Pocumtuck kept slipping. Although some Dedham proprietors maintained their interest in Pocumtuck's affairs, still more sold out. Some failed even in the "cleereing of accounts with Major Pinchion" that had begun five years before. The town meeting in Dedham in April 1672 revealed that the Pocumtuck proprietors still owed close to £10 of the original £96.10 due to the Springfield entrepreneur.[56]

Dedham also failed, or refused, to provide even the basic political leadership through a Dedham town committee that the new Pocumtuck settlers were seeking. In early February of 1673 Samuel Hinsdale, representing "the inhabitanc at pocomtick," requested of the Dedham town meeting that a committee be chosen, "invested with all such poure [power] nesesary," to handle the settlement's "afires."[57] That spring Hinsdale returned to implore the town to "consider" the Pocumtuck settlers' case and "the dificaltyes that are upon them by reasone of thier remoatness." This time Dedham responded. It empowered a five-man committee of Dedham and Pocumtuck residents, including Hinsdale, to oversee the bringing of "sutable inhabitance"; to "order their herding . . . cattel and regolating . . . swine"; to "make orders about fence"; and to "have liberty to procure . . . an orthodox Minester to dispenc the word of god amogst them."[58]

This step gave a clear signal that Dedham's power was being transferred to the inhabitants of Pocumtuck. But for those inhabitants, even this was not enough. Back to Pocumtuck went Hinsdale to meet with his fellow residents, and back east he came again. This time, though, he journeyed not to Dedham but to Boston, to the General Court, where he offered up a "peticon of the inhabitants of Paucomptucke." Rather than accepting control of Pocumtuck by a five-man committee which included Dedham proprietors, the infant town sought complete freedom from Dedham. And they got it. Exactly two months after Hinsdale had pleaded with Dedham for help, the

General Court answered the plea, granting Pocumtuck's petitioners "the liberty of a touneship." Not only that, the court
dramatically increased Pocumtuck's land holdings, from eight
thousand acres to a tract "seven miles square," provided only
that the town get an "able & orthodox minister" settled there
within three years. Further, the Court established a new committee made up solely of local settlers to oversee the admitting
of inhabitants, granting of lands, and ordering of all the town's
"prudential affairs."[59]

Dedham did not protest. Perhaps they knew that this infant
settlement had little chance of surviving on New England's
frontier without such independence. Besides, most of the Dedham proprietors had already pulled out of the venture. In any
event, less than two years after Dedham had laid out its satellite
town of Pocumtuck, the town had broken out of Dedham's
orbit. A combination of unusual circumstances had made
Pocumtuck a curious proprietary venture in the first place; now
the actual settlers—the residents—would manage the affairs of
the new town. Pocumtuck had its freedom. It quickly busied
itself with the daily life of a tiny new frontier community.

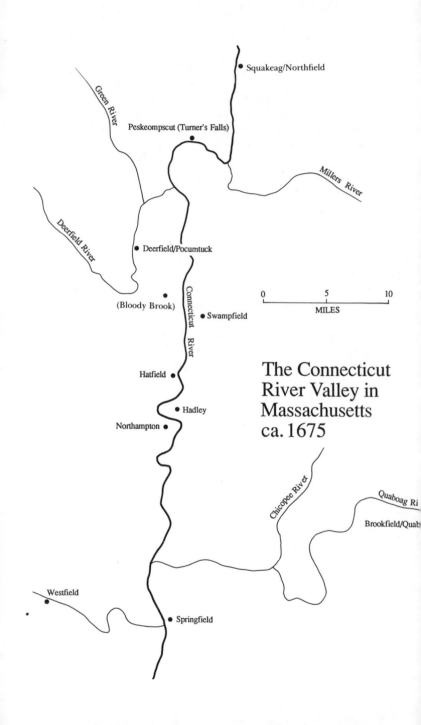

Green River

Squakeag/Northfield

Peskeompscut (Turner's Falls)

Millers River

Deerfield River

Deerfield/Pocumtuck

Connecticut River

(Bloody Brook)

Swampfield

0   5   10
MILES

Hatfield

Hadley

Northampton

The Connecticut
River Valley in
Massachusetts
ca. 1675

Chicopee River

Quaboag Ri

Brookfield/Quab

Westfield

Springfield

THREE

"Make a Toune of It"

TELLING THE STORY of Pocumtuck's life in the first years after 1673 is no easy task. Evidence is scanty—mostly the scattered shards of a town record book, early county records, and genealogies. Even so, there is much to tell about what kind of people Pocumtuck's pioneers were and what kind of seventeenth-century frontier town New Englanders would build.

If active local government is one classic sign of a healthy town, then Pocumtuck was born in good health. Pocumtuck's settlers had been holding town meetings even before they gained their independence from Dedham in May of 1673, and they continued this all-inclusive participatory process. In November of that year, twenty-four men placed their "Marcks" on the minutes of the first formal meeting of Pocumtuck's "Inhabitants, and proprietors."[1] The issues discussed were typical of any new town: rights to woodlands, support for the ministry, and questions about property lines. Subsequent meetings also focused on land issues: who should handle boundary disputes, how one might acquire more land, how newcomers might gain land. Pocumtuck also started to choose town officers such as constables to handle local matters.[2]

As the town book shows, land—its quality, quantity, distribution, and use—was an area of paramount concern to Pocumtuck's new residents. In terms of quality, the settlers of Pocumtuck knew they had placed themselves on fertile ground. For one thing, the native Indians of the region had farmed there. For another, the very fact that the settlers had planted themselves at the narrow northern end of their seven-mile-long grant—far from their only neighbors, at Hatfield to the south—implies that they knew where good earth was and were willing to accept isolation for it. As for quantity, Pocumtuck had plenty. By 1672 the town had already weathered a boundary dispute with Hatfield. Although the General Court ruled that Pocumtuck had encroached over one and a half miles south into Hatfield lands, it compensated Pocumtuck with land to the north of the eight-thousand-acre grant.[3] When the General Court expanded Pocumtuck's size the next year from eight thousand acres to seven miles square, Pocumtuck's abundance was assured.

Distribution of Pocumtuck's land proved equally smooth. By 1674 the town was settling boundary disputes among townspeople; more important, it was promoting settlement by granting house lots, acreage, and commons rights to newcomers. The town supported growth in another intriguing way. In November of 1673, the town meeting decided that all proprietors would "laye downe all their wood lands now in proprietye to Comon"— in other words, make their nearby woodlands open and available to anyone.[4]

Finally, on the issue of land use, Pocumtuck quickly established a smoothly functioning system that balanced communal desires and needs with those of the individual. The town followed a pattern seen in parts of both old England and New England of what was loosely called a "common-field" system. Townspeople owned their own farmlands individually, as laid out in long strips. Actual farming, however, was a group enterprise. Townsmen worked the lands together, relying on shared labor; town regulation of such matters as fencing and grazing seasons further supported this communal venture. In addition, grazing land and woodlands were held in common and regulated by the town. To plow their rich fields, Pocumtuck townsmen also shared the oxen, yokes, and chains that some in town owned or that they bought together.[5] By 1675 Pocumtuck's settlers were producing wheat, malt, hops, peas, barley, rye, and hay, while Indian corn—maize—quickly proved to be Pocumtuck's staple, as it was for the entire region. Cattle and a few pigs roamed the pastures. Most men had one horse, and many held two or more. Pocumtuck's pioneers had quickly moved to produce at least "moderately comfortable lives" from the soil.[6]

One land problem nagged at settlers of the new town: the issue of absentee proprietors. Many distributed parcels of Pocumtuck land lay untouched during the town's early years. A few Dedham men apparently just let their land and rights slip away, never claiming or selling their cow commons. Other Dedhamites sold out, though not always to Pocumtuck settlers. Edward Richards had received one hundred fifty acres for helping explore Pocumtuck in 1665, but by 1673 he determined it was of little use, or perhaps could bring a profit, and sold it off. Thomas and Hannah Fuller likewise "cashed in," selling their twenty cow commons and house lot in 1674.[7] Still other proprietors, who paid their taxes or leased their lands, legally maintained footholds in Pocumtuck, though they received no additional distributions of land from the town. In general, Pocumtuck now controlled its lands, though open spaces among the house lots and fields dotted the village.

Prominent among the men to whom Pocumtuck did give land in 1674 was a Mr. Samuel Mather. Mather received a large sixteen-cow-common allotment of lands and rights from the town meeting, but that was understandable: He was the town's new minister. Following the General Court's dictum that Pocumtuck establish a ministry within three years, the townspeople accomplished a task often difficult for new frontier settlements. Mather's background fit Pocumtuck's needs well. A recent graduate of Harvard College, he had received proper training; only twenty-three years old, he had the youth and energy the new outpost needed; as the nephew of the famous Boston clergyman Increase Mather, his pedigree was impressive. The town tried to make Mather feel welcome. It established what was, in the context of a new outpost, a good starting salary of between £40 and £50 annually. In addition, the town soon started to build a meetinghouse, and soon after that a home, for the young minister.[8] In return, prepared in the orthodoxy of seventeenth-century Harvard, Mather gave his flock clear, orderly, logical sermons in the "plain style," as he taught them to seek piety with rationality.[9]

Living conditions in the new settlement proved spartan but adequate. While their farmlands were rich, villagers lived in sparsely furnished houses. Permanent furniture other than a bed was apparently rare, as were most luxury items.[10] Still, settlers busied themselves putting up good fencing around their homes, and new settlers found the town desirable enough to give up former estates. Moses and Rebecca Crafts felt confident enough to sell off family lands in Boston, while Barnabas and Sarah Hinsdale from Hatfield even gave up their "Mansion house" there to come.[11] Another sign of maturity came in 1674 when the county court granted Crafts allowance "to keepe [an] ordinary there and sell wine and strong liquor." Hampshire County's judges fretted at the time about "too much idle expence of Precious time and estate in Drinking Strong Liquors," especially by "many of our youth." Accordingly, they ordered barkeeps to sell only to citizens that were "Governors of Families of Sober Carriage." Pocumtuck must have had enough qualified "Governers," since Crafts did get his license.[12] The town even gained new neighbors who eased Pocumtuck's isolation. Both Northfield to the north and Swampfield to the south were established between 1672 and 1674, as a new generation of valley towns continued to grow. In sum, life at Pocumtuck seems to have been quite promising.

Yet for all these signs of successful settlement, there were also hints of problems. Pocumtuck had grown quickly after 1671, fed by a rising stream of newcomers. Generally Puritan towns carefully screened newcomers. Yet with Pocumtuck's settlers virtually all "new," there seemed no control. Similarly, when New Englanders founded a town in the seventeenth century, they usually drew up a covenant, both civil and ecclesiastical, to reflect the communal commitment of the assembled group. Yet Pocumtuck's people bound themselves together in no such covenant. In terms of land holding and distribution, Pocumtuck's citizens had taken a big step toward ordering their plantation when they gained the "liberty of a township" in 1673. A great deal of speculation had already taken place, however, and absentee owners like John Pynchon of Springfield and Henry Woodward, Jr., of Dedham held large tracts of land, numerous house lots, and great numbers of commons rights. Perhaps they were helping Pocumtuck by promoting settlement and growth through their ventures, yet they could wreak havoc on the young town. Beyond all this, Pocumtuck's settlers had few possessions other than their new land. That land might in time bring them prosperity, yet for now these pioneers were only subsisting.

Thus the bright picture of Pocumtuck, the thriving young town, has darker hues, hints of problems. A proper and full view requires a push past study of the town's institutions and daily life to the people themselves. Who were they? Where were they from? What were they like? Put simply, who would come to live in such a place?

What Manner of Men—and Women?

For a frontier outpost, Pocumtuck had grown quickly. By 1675, within six years of its first English settlers and just two years after the town had gained independent status, the population stood at about two hundred. Sixty-eight were adults: thirty-nine men and twenty-nine women. The men ranged in age from eighteen to sixty-six; the women varied similarly. Large extended families and solitary male settlers were found among the population, explorers from afar and farmers from neighboring villages just below. Wealthy, established men helped secure Pocumtuck, as did poor young stragglers. There was even a group of pioneers who had helped found other towns and who now moved to do the same at Pocumtuck.[13]

Basically, it was a young man's town. In fact, over three-quarters of the men in town in 1675 were between the ages of twenty-one and forty. As of 1675 the whole group of men averaged a little over thirty-five years of age. The evidence for the women suggests similar youthfulness: an average age of thirty-one.[14] This appears consistent with other young towns in early New England.[15]

A span of some six years separates the averages at which the men and women of Pocumtuck first married. Men tended to hold off getting married until their mid-twenties, with an average age of just under twenty-five. In fact, only three men were found to have married before the age of twenty-two; on the other end, only three men did *not* marry before the age of thirty. By contrast, the women of Pocumtuck entered marriage significantly earlier. Pocumtuck's women first married when they were about nineteen years old. In fact, Anna Hawks Hastings proved to be the "old maid" of the group, having married in 1672 at the ripe old age of twenty-three.

These numbers suggest that marriage for men and particularly women of Pocumtuck came earlier than in many other New England towns. For the men, the difference with other towns was small, just one or two years. For the women, the gap is closer to three years.[16] These figures for Pocumtuck suggest that the people who would come to such a place might often have been "young marrieds" who sought the open land that a new town could provide.[17] Perhaps also some of these people married at Pocumtuck relatively early in life due to the town's youth, size, or the lack of traditional barriers like family or local custom. That the frontier brought people together more rapidly than safer, more settled areas is another possibility.

Pocumtuck also held a number of men and women who had already married more than once in their lifetimes. The surviving records show that as of 1675 at least eight of Pocumtuck's twenty-nine known husbands had married after their first wives died. By the same token, no fewer than seven of the women who came to Pocumtuck did so with second husbands. Death often knocked at the doors of seventeenth-century New Englanders, as Pocumtuck saw in the 1674 death of Zechariah Field, only thirty years old. His wife, Mary, had to go on and take care of their two young surviving sons (another had died early). She did so, at least in part, by marrying Robert Price, a valley resident who would later resettle the family at Pocumtuck.

This degree of remarriage is not surprising. Second marriages in early New England were quite common and also came quickly, for they were at times matters of necessity. Thus, the fact that roughly one-quarter of Pocumtuck's men and women had remarried by 1675 makes it similar to such varied places as Plymouth, Andover, and nearby Northampton.[18]

In the families of this frontier town, as in the rest of early New England, children abounded. As of 1675, Pocumtuck's

families had brought 131 children into the world, 69 boys and
62 girls. Put another way, these generally young families had
borne an average of about five children,[19] roughly the same
number as families in other towns.[20] It is true that couples like
the Hastings and Stockwells had only one or two children at
this time, but they had been married for just two or three years.
More common would be the Frarys, who lived on a small lot
near the center of town. Samson and his wife, Mary, had been
married for fifteen years—two years more than the town's average—and had had five children, three daughters followed by
two sons. The Frarys had faced their share of sorrow, for they
lost their third daughter, Susanna, and first son, John, early in
life. A few doors south of the Frarys lived John and Mary (Bullard) Farrington. They had one of the largest clans, having
raised eleven children since their marriage in 1649. They were
known to have lost only one of their eleven, Judith, at an early
age, and Mary bore their last child—their sixth son, Thomas—
at Pocumtuck more than twenty years after their first child had
been born.

One particularly telling point about life in Pocumtuck comes
in looking at the numerous ties between families in town. From
this comes a sense of tight interweaving among the little village's two hundred souls. John and Jane Plympton, formerly of
Dedham and Medfield, came to Pocumtuck after they bought
proprietary rights from their old Dedham neighbor, John Bacon.
They may well have moved to be near their daughter Hannah,
who had married Pocumtuck settler Nathaniel Sutlieffe. Within
three years another daughter would be the wife of another
Pocumtuck resident. Samson Frary's wife, Mary, was probably
happy to see Samuel Daniels move from Dedham to Pocumtuck during this same period, for Daniels was Mary's brother.
Richard Weller doubtless felt pride in helping establish Pocumtuck along with two of his four sons, his eldest, John, and his
youngest, Thomas.

In many early New England communities, a handful of families cast unusually long shadows.[21] In Pocumtuck it was the
Hinsdales and the Hawkses. The Hinsdales dominated Pocumtuck's citizenry as did no other family. The clan was well known

both in the valley and back east. Samuel was Pocumtuck's first
known English settler, coming north from Hadley in 1669 at
age twenty-six. He obviously believed in the future of the plantation, for by 1670 he had amassed forty-six cow and three and
one-half sheep commons. His father, Robert, had been among
the first settlers of Dedham and among the founders of Medfield. By 1670 he, too, had gotten onto the list of Pocumtuck
proprietors, although he held a more modest eight cow commons.

And Robert and Samuel proved to be only the start of the
Hinsdales' Pocumtuck legacy. By 1675, four of Robert's other
sons were living in the town: Thirty-six-year-old Barnabas, his
wife, Sarah, and four children; Experience and Mary and their
two daughters; John and his family; and single, youngest son
Ephraim had all settled in the community. Even their sister
Mary was in Pocumtuck, married to Daniel Weld. In short,
over a fifth of Pocumtuck's couples included a Hinsdale. Perhaps this helps explain why Samuel was chosen to represent
the town in its dealings with Dedham and the General Court in
1672–1673: He was representing the family!

Family patriarch Robert Hinsdale provided the link with the
other large clan in Pocumtuck: the Hawks family. In 1671, a
few years after the death of John Hawks of Hadley, widower
Robert Hinsdale married Hawks's widow, Elizabeth. Happily
for her, Elizabeth did not lose touch with her six children when
she and her new husband moved to Pocumtuck. Her eldest
daughter, Elizabeth, was married to Joseph Gillett of Pocumtuck; daughter Anna and her husband, Thomas Hastings, moved
into town soon after their marriage in 1672; eldest son John and
his family moved in before 1675; and in a second-generation
match mirroring the surviving parents, Elizabeth's daughter
Mary married Robert Hinsdale's son Experience. Through all
this activity, Hawks children found themselves in six of Pocumtuck's homes.

While it is impossible to measure the impact of all these ties
on the town, they probably served to make the frontier community still closer. It certainly seems that such extensive family
networks would help keep a community spirit among the vil-

lagers. As Pocumtuck's isolation might drive people together, so, too, its small size and its extensive family ties likely made Pocumtuck a close-knit town.

The places Pocumtuck's settlers came from tell still more about what the new town was like. These men and women came from all over Massachusetts, from no fewer than thirteen different towns, from both the Bay to the east and the Connecticut River valley below. Many Pocumtuck people had moved many times in their lives. Further, not only did Pocumtuck hold a number of transient New Englanders, but it also held at least a handful of first-generation English emigrants.[22] At the same time, within this broad range of origins and experiences lay well-defined patterns of movement. Two-thirds of both the men and the women of Pocumtuck came up from the three valley settlements immediately below: Northampton, Hadley, and Hatfield. Of the remaining third of the residents, half the men and four-fifths of the women came from Dedham and its "offspring" Medfield. Only a handful of settlers trickled in from other towns.

Interestingly, the Dedhamites who came were not from among the original Pocumtuck proprietors. In fact, John and Mary Farrington proved to be the only original Dedham proprietors to settle at Pocumtuck.[23] More typical were Samson and Mary Frary. They had lived for a time in Dedham and Medfield, yet they were Hadley residents when they purchased proprietary rights to Pocumtuck sometime before 1670. By contrast, Quinton Stockwell had lived in Dedham for a few years, though he did not hold any proprietary rights (probably because he was not a Dedham resident when rights were assigned in 1656). Apparently a poor and struggling fellow, he took his new wife, the former Abigail Bullard, out to Pocumtuck without having secured any particular rights or land.[24]

Looking back, it appears that Dedham and Medfield residents, or former residents, learned about Pocumtuck from present or former neighbors and that a handful decided to try their luck out west. That these men and women knew of Pocumtuck's rich and abundant soil is understandable. All Dedham's efforts to establish Pocumtuck between 1664 and

1671 surely brought home news of the new land. Residents or former residents also would have had the best chances to secure land and rights from old friends and neighbors, perhaps at good prices.

By far the greater percentage of Pocumtuck's settlers, however, came from nearby Northampton, Hadley, and Hatfield. Many forces impelled them to move north. In fact, each of the three towns showed signs of unrest in the 1660s that may have pushed people out.

In 1659 settlers from Hartford had established Hadley in the aftermath of a religious dispute. In building their new village, as with their former town of Hartford, Hadley's settlers had settled on both sides of the town's river. But troubles arose quickly, for that river was the broad and mighty Connecticut. Within eight years, complaining of "extreme and intolerable . . . difficulties and dangers," ninety of Hadley's "west-siders" petitioned the General Court for a declaration of independence from their townsmen on the east bank. Often unable to attend church, since the journey across the river was difficult, they sought their own minister and the "liberty to be a society of ourselves."[25] After three years of sometimes acrid negotiations, Hatfield broke free and became incorporated on May 31, 1670. However, the damage done to both the old town and the new may well have shorn the spiritual and civil bonds which had held Hadley's first settlers together. Within five years, eleven men and seven women from Hadley and Hatfield moved to the new village of Pocumtuck.

The vicissitudes of life in Northampton, too, suggest strong reasons for leaving. This valley town was founded in 1653 by twenty-four male petitioners. A 1661 church covenant shows seventy-five men and women in town, a sign of modest growth. By 1674, however, Northampton held 108 men and the total town population stood at close to 500. That rapid population growth may well have driven settlers to new and open lands— to Pocumtuck.[26]

Exacerbating the strains of growth in Northampton were signs between 1665 and 1671 of restrictions on the rights of some of its citizens. In 1665, a number of people in town issued a petition seeking "ancient rights libertyes and previledges." The petition was not asking for provincial political rights, since a number of signers had already been made freemen. Apparently Northampton's citizens, or some of them, were not getting local rights they felt they deserved—and the list of signers included no fewer than seven future settlers of Pocumtuck.[27] Perhaps even more serious, amidst a summary of "orders" about Northampton's settling appears this cryptic note of February 12, 1671/1672: "The vote that the Comons should not be divided made." Northampton was not dividing up its common lands for settlers—and in fact did not do so for twenty-one years, from 1663 to 1684. Moreover, new settlers after 1660 were usually required to buy their house lots.[28] In sum, these Northampton affairs suggest obvious reasons for people to leave town.

Beyond these local issues in Hadley, Hatfield, and Northampton was another factor that drove people to Pocumtuck. Many were "outlaws" from other communities. Among the men and women who came up the valley were a number of lawbreakers. Their stories show that Pocumtuck's pioneers were not all proper, God-fearing Puritans.[29]

In the early 1660s John Allen and John Earle of Northampton were accused of "irregular voting for select men" in town. A decade later Earle's wife, Mary, was convicted of lying "in bed together" with Northampton's Thomas Root, "at wch time alsoe they had Rhum to Drinke." By 1675 the Earles and the Allens were Pocumtuck residents. In March of 1674 Martin Smith of Northampton was accused of "offering some abuse to Jedediah Strong's wife . . . laying hold on her to Kiss" her, and making her "somewhat affrighted." Although Smith came to court "condemning himself and seeming sorrowful," the judges showed grave concern for such "lasciviousness." Smith soon brought this spotted record to Pocumtuck.

In 1672 Hatfield's Philip Barsham stole eight bushels of wheat and meal from fellow townsmen Samuel Dickinson and Eleazar Frary. Fined forty shillings, plus fifteen lashes, plus damages to Dickinson and triple damages to Frary, his future in Hatfield could hardly have been bright. He, too, soon moved to Pocumtuck.

Hadley's Robert Hinsdale faced a very different problem
when he was brought to court in 1674. Hinsdale's first wife had
died around 1668, and his second marriage, to Elizabeth Hawks,
was not working out. In fact, the two partners had come to "live
asunder": Hinsdale, "in a raged manner as is sayd rejecting
her," had moved out as a sign of "conviction of her disorder
towardes him." This the court found "utterly unjustifyable" in
both civil and "divine law." In addition, all this had apparently
led to further troubles, notably "wanton & Lascivious Carriage
soe Gross & odious" that the court ordered Hinsdale to bear
"10 stripes"—lashes—or else pay a £5 fine. After this public
marital tumult the Hinsdales quickly left Hadley, and Pocumtuck was a close, easy alternative.

By 1675 Pocumtuck also held two residents with even longer
records. In 1667 John Stebbins, Jr., had been sentenced to ten
lashes or a forty-shilling fine (his father paid the fine) in Northampton for complicity in a burglary/runaway attempt by three
local youths. In 1674 he was embroiled in another case, as five
people accused him of "lascivious carriage." In 1670 Zebediah
Williams, also of Northampton, was convicted of "misbehaving
himself in time of ye public Ordinances of ye Sabbath many
tymes" and was sentenced to fifteen lashes. Only because of his
mother's plea in court and his "promise of amendmt" were the
lashes dropped and a fine of £5 substituted. A year later he was
again accused of "disorderly carriage," and in 1672 he was fined
for "laughing in meeting." After May of 1673 and yet another
fine, this for "mispence of tyme" at another's house, he headed
north for Pocumtuck.

All of this does not mean that Pocumtuck harbored all the
region's reprobates, the dregs of valley society. After all, these
cases pertain to barely a quarter of Pocumtuck's families. Still,
troubles with the law seem to have been one force which impelled people to leave their old towns to try fresh starts elsewhere. Then, too, more established valley towns may not have
wanted such citizens, and Pocumtuck provided an easy option.
After all, given its locale, youth, and size, Pocumtuck could
hardly afford to be too picky about who settled there.

Beyond all this, one other force[30] linked many of Pocumtuck's first settlers. They lived connected to a chain of debts, a chain of dependence. At the other end of the chain was the dominant figure of the Connecticut valley in the seventeenth century: the "worshipful Major Pynchon."

Explorer, merchant, magistrate, mediator, speculator, and financier, John Pynchon dominated western Massachusetts for almost the entire second half of the seventeenth century. As landholder, his seigneury extended from his home in Springfield, where he held a staggering 2,000 acres—one-fifth of the town's land—to his 510 acres at Suffield, his 200 acres at Brookfield to the east, and his 54 cow commons' worth of land and rights at Pocumtuck, more than one-tenth of the total in the entire town.[31] As a military man he served as the highest-ranking officer in the valley. As public official he sat on both the General Court and the Governor's Council; locally, he held power as justice of the Hampshire County Court. An established mediator with the Indians, he served his region through forty years of negotiations. This work with Indians, begun through his dominance of the region's fur trading, led him to become the foremost explorer and settler of titles for new towns in the valley. Pynchon helped oversee the establishment of no fewer than five valley plantations: Northampton in 1653, Hadley in 1660, Hatfield in 1672, Swampfield (later Sunderland) in 1673, and of course Pocumtuck between 1665 and 1671.[32]

Part of Pynchon's success as a town founder lay in the fact that he also served as a town financier, the one man with enough capital to buy Indian rights. At least part of his pay probably came in the form of land rights in the new towns. He also speculated, buying up land in these new towns. This certainly was true at Pocumtuck. Between 1665 and 1670, before Dedham had even divided up its new lands, Pynchon went from holding no interest in the new plantation to becoming its second-largest shareholder.

All of these activities served the Springfield magnate well in yet another sphere, for Pynchon was also the dominant merchant and trader in the valley. Beginning with his father's fur trade, John expanded that local exchange into a whirl of food, livestock, cloth and pins, gunpowder and knives, lace, hats, buttons, and blankets.[33]

It is in the areas of land and trade that Pynchon came to affect Pocumtuck's life so greatly. Almost one-third of Pocumtuck's first townsmen appear in Pynchon's account ledgers of the 1660s and 1670s. This suggests that Pynchon was Pocumtuck's key trader in its first years, providing the young, isolated frontier post with vital goods and supplies. Not incidentally, this service helped increase Pynchon's fortune—and also put many Pocumtuck men into debt.

Most of the debtors in town came from among Pocumtuck's young, struggling farmer families.[34] In fact, almost half of the town's married men can be found in Pynchon's books between 1660 and 1675. The types of exchanges ranged broadly. Some settlers dealt with Pynchon for land: Two bought house lots and land from him, one leased commonage, and another received credit in Pynchon's general store by plowing and clearing his Pocumtuck land for him. Others worked to pay off their debts to Pynchon by building fences on his land, "helping daub ye chimney," mowing, "shingling," or most commonly exchanging goods. As for supplies, Pocumtuck's young settlers bought just about anything from Pynchon: cotton, "knitted," pins, barrel pork, books, horses, cotton ribbon, "hide leather," sugar, shoes, even an "inkhouse."

The size of the debts varied greatly. Some settlers accumulated small debts for various items over two or three years, totaling perhaps £5, cleared the ledger, and then built up new sets of debts. In such cases Pynchon provided vital supplies—and service—for this simple agrarian economy.[35] Yet there was also Pynchon the entrepreneur, the lender, the speculator, the man playing for higher stakes. Pocumtuck's Joshua Carter had a string of debts between 1662 and 1675 which went as high as £25. In 1670 alone, John Earle borrowed almost £50 for a horse-trading scheme. He was paying off that loan amidst other deals with Pynchon for the next five years.

While the size, type, and duration of debts varied widely, John Pynchon clearly played a vital role in the lives of many

Pocumtuck men. Dealing with the poorer, younger families the most, he helped these people even as he helped himself. Coupled with the huge impact he had on Pocumtuck's very founding and the vast amounts of land he had secured in town, Pynchon proved to be an important, if absent, figure in the new plantation.

Bringing together all the information about settlers' ages, families, wealth, previous activities, and mobility yields new and richer ideas about what Pocumtuck was really like. One strong impression is that Pocumtuck held distinctly different types of settlers. While such categories are never perfect, the four offered below suggest a way to get a fuller sense of the town's first generation.

One group of settlers who came to Pocumtuck can be called *perpetual pioneers*. These men and women were generally older and wealthier than most other settlers. All or almost all their children were grown. They had helped establish other settlements, had been active in civic affairs in their previous residences, and were often local if not regional leaders. The group also stayed largely clear of John Pynchon's chain of dependence, for its people were well established and independent of such needs. Roughly one-fifth of Pocumtuck's townspeople belonged in this group.

One such perpetual pioneer was Francis Barnard. Born in England in 1617, he spent his early adulthood in Hartford, where he became a maltster. In 1659 he helped found the town of Hadley. He achieved both financial and political success there, notably in the latter category for three sessions as juror of the Hampshire County Court and two elected terms as Hadley constable. Yet in November of 1673, at age fifty-six, there was Barnard at the Pocumtuck town meeting, helping direct local affairs.

Barnard serves as a good model of these well-established pioneers. He did not need to leave his home; indeed, he had achieved a great deal there. It was Pocumtuck's good fortune that he and others like him brought their skills and experience to the new town.

About half the town's adult population comprised Pocum-

tuck's second group of settlers: the *frontier farmers*. With both
husband and wife under forty years of age and a number of
children at home, these families had typically moved up the
valley to Pocumtuck from Northampton, Hadley, and Hatfield.
Essentially, they were subsistence farmers. They did not have
much property, either real or personal, and they were the people most commonly in debt to John Pynchon, but by settling in
Pocumtuck they had gained the chance to make a good living
by farming Pocumtuck's fertile fields. John Hawks, Jr., came
from Hadley to Pocumtuck in 1673 along with Martha, his wife
of six years, and their two young children (a third had died
young). As of 1675, the thirty-year-old Hawks owned a house
lot and sixteen cow commons of land. Joshua and Mary Carter
had moved up to Pocumtuck by 1673 as well. Married twelve
years as of 1675, Carter and his wife had four children. When
he died later that year at the age of thirty-seven, he left a
personal estate of only £15.10.

Pocumtuck also held a small group of men who did not fit the
farming mold. Perhaps one-tenth of the town's men had *special
skills* or practiced occupations that separated them from their
brethren. These included the minister, the tavernkeeper, the
doctor, the carpenter, and the millwright. Like the bulk of
Pocumtuck's adults, they tended to be young, married and with
children, though often not natives of the valley region. Many of
these people farmed as well, but their special skills make them
noteworthy. This is a group typified by single, twenty-four-
year-old Reverend Samuel Mather, just four years out of Harvard,
and William Bartholomew, a thirty-four-year-old carpenter from
Roxbury.

Finally, Pocumtuck had a group of independent single men,
in their late teens or twenties, who comprised roughly one-fifth
of the adult men. A motley crew, they included drifters, independent youths sowing wild oats, even young men cast out of
their homes or towns. Yet they aided Pocumtuck greatly as
hired hands. Typically men "without houses or farms of their
own and with little or no property," their work—in the fields,
building houses, running mills, or clearing land—provided a
boon for the young town.[36] A number eventually settled into

marriage and family at Pocumtuck. Others were killed fighting in the Indian wars. Some simply dropped out of sight. For the bulk of these men, these years at Pocumtuck may have been only a stage in life, but it was a stage visible at—and important to—the young outpost.

Early Pocumtuck in Perspective: A Frontier Town

Pocumtuck's early years were not spectacular or dramatic, but they were rich in the events and activities that would bring a town to life. In comparison with other towns of seventeenth-century New England, the town appears both typical and special. In many respects Pocumtuck seems a classic young New England village. Its system of distributing land followed a well-established pattern of granting proprietary rights. Like other New England towns, Pocumtuck's layout mixed practices of old England and New England. While the town never looked exactly like Sudbury or Newbury, Hingham or Dedham, it combined traditional elements with those that fit the site and the people's needs, as other pioneers had done at other plantations.[37]

Town government, too, acted in classic early New England fashion. As a new town, Pocumtuck depended on the town meeting. "The town" or "the inhabitants" decided the minister's salary and granted house lots; selectmen held important, yet limited, power. Moreover, meeting records invariably note that decisions were made not by "the majority" but by "the town." Like other early New England towns, Pocumtuck was ruled not by "mere" democracy, with its inherent divisions of majority and minority, but by consensus.[38] Pocumtuck also drew no distinction between "the town" and "the proprietors," a blending of control over government and land often seen in early New England towns. This community was also Christian. Within a year of its 1673 General Court directive, Pocumtuck had found a minister and was building both house and meeting-house for him.

At the same time, though, there are signs that Pocumtuck did not fit so well the classic image of "a New England town."

It certainly was unusual in the way it was claimed amidst the
Dedham-Natick controversy of the 1650s and 1660s. Pocumtuck's situation in the years around 1670, with easterners controlling the land and westerners moving in and settling it, was
also unusual. Further, while a Christian community, Pocumtuck was not closed. Instead of a small group of pioneers band-
ing together to forge a covenant before settling the town,
Pocumtuck's inhabitants first had encroached upon, then trickled
onto, and finally rushed to the new site. New settlers arrived
constantly, apparently without first purchasing land or gaining
the approval of other settlers. In this regard, then, the town
was neither closed nor corporate. Nor, apparently, was it utopian. Early government by consensus shows signs of amity, but
no record exists of any covenant, actions, or events binding the
townspeople together.

Two other ideas help characterize Pocumtuck better. First,
it was basically a "second-generation" town. Established largely
by the children of the founders of Massachusetts and Connecticut, by 1675 many of those children had lost their parents'
fervor for the "mission to New England." Pocumtuck's men
and women took their religion seriously, and their meeting
record shows that they worked together. But the utopian dream
was fading.[39] Pocumtuck was not the covenanted community
that first-generation New Englanders had tried to plant. And
that is not surprising, since most of the town's citizens did not
belong to that first generation, either.

Pocumtuck's second critical characteristic is "the frontier,"
for Pocumtuck was surely a frontier town. In the study of seventeenth-century New England that word has specific meaning. Recent scholarship claims that frontier towns were young,
struggling, largely egalitarian with a limited wealthy class; often
settled by family groups but with some independent young
men; without political influence in the county or colony; with
the town deciding issues by vote of all the inhabitants; and with
"rapid change" as a constant. All this fits Pocumtuck.[40]

Yet there is more. The number of Pocumtuck residents who
had previously been in trouble with the law suggests that frontier towns attracted—or accepted—settlers who were escaping

from bad records back home, thrown out, or seeking a new start. Also telling is the web of influence that John Pynchon wove around and through Pocumtuck. His control over land and trade, the great number of ties he had with Pocumtuck's poorer, young frontier farmers, and the strings of debts so many residents had suggest that the frontier brought with it considerable indebtedness and dependence as well.[41]

Interestingly, Pocumtuck's position on the frontier apparently did not bring any particular frontier mentality. At least, if "frontier" should imply "defense," it failed to do so at Pocumtuck. There is no record of any military preparations at Pocumtuck before 1675. There was no fort, no call for militia, no special contact with Springfield or Boston about Pocumtuck's defenses. Perhaps the establishment of so many other new valley towns during this period—Hatfield in 1670, Northfield in 1672, and Swampfield and Brookfield in 1673—made Pocumtuck feel safe.[42] In any event, no signs of insecurity emerge, save perhaps that so few Dedhamites came.

Given Pocumtuck's locale, such a sense of security seems surprising. While a map of Massachusetts in 1675 shows an increasingly intricate network of settlements in the east, in the west it shows only a narrow knife of towns piercing up the Connecticut valley into the wilderness. Pocumtuck stood on the knife's edge, not quite at the very tip that was Northfield, but far up the blade. To the west stood fifty miles of forest, with no fellow colonists east of the Hudson River. To the north, past the hamlet of Northfield fifteen miles above, lay over two hundred miles of wilderness. Eastward, across the Connecticut River, no Englishmen lived within forty miles. Even Hatfield, the closest established southern neighbor, lay a good twelve miles distant.

Pocumtuck's isolation was heightened by other forces. Since the General Court had granted the town its liberty the legislature had simply left it alone, and no Pocumtuck resident sat in its chambers keeping lines of communication and aid open. Even the Connecticut valley itself, for all its ties to Pocumtuck, held fewer than three thousand colonists. In many ways the town stood alone.

And yet Pocumtuck also serves as an excellent model for understanding the interconnectedness of early New England because it demonstrates that, for all its complexity, seventeenth-century New England was essentially a small area with a small number of people whose events were intertwined. The region was a tightly spun web. Indeed, Pocumtuck's life up to 1675 shows a startling degree of the entire region's history tied into a single town. The town's origins bind it, first, to New England's Indians, to colonial Indian policy, and to the Reverend John Eliot's missionary efforts. Negotiations over the Natick land tie Pocumtuck to the Bay, to Dedham, and to the General Court. Pocumtuck's land came open due only to inter-Indian strife—an important, if little understood, element of seventeenth-century life. Negotiations for the land tie Pocumtuck to Puritan land policies, to English-Indian relations, and to John Pynchon, the Connecticut valley's most influential seventeenth-century figure. Speculating for Pocumtuck land made even Massachusetts governor John Leverett part of Pocumtuck's past. And Pocumtuck's settlers connected the new plantation to many of New England's older towns while showing migration patterns of both Massachusetts Bay and the Connecticut River valley. In all these ways, Pocumtuck helps tell the story of early New England because it played parts in so many scenes.

Thus it remains difficult to assess Pocumtuck as a frontier town. It was small, new, western, exposed, rapidly changing, and economically dependent. Yet it also grew quickly; showed signs of tradition and order in land use, government, and religion; had neighbors fairly close by; was bound in many ways to the rest of New England; and betrayed no feelings that it was in any danger.

It is possible that all of the above contradictions do fit together. Perhaps this is what New England's frontier was like in the seventeenth century; small, rough, changing, yet held together by a strong, inherited, English, Puritan, agrarian sense of order. New England frontiersmen and women would not differ radically from their more established brothers and sisters; the lines of order, mission, and tradition ran too strong and too deep. So perhaps Pocumtuck *was* the New England frontier. It was just not the western frontier of modern American lore.

Isolated and intertwined, part of the old and yet something new, the young frontier town of Pocumtuck headed into the century's last quarter. But this town would not live to see 1700, at least not in the same form or by the same name. If the people of Pocumtuck could have seen the year's horizon, what the dawn of 1675 would bring from the east, they might have abandoned their settlement and even their region. The Indians of southeastern New England came out of the sun, blazing to reclaim their lands, and Pocumtuck would prove unable to withstand the fire of King Philip's War. In the town's next scene, then, Pocumtuck would play another—and this time more violent—part in New England's drama.

FOUR

The Wheel Turns: Pocumtuck and King Philip's War

NATIVE AMERICANS had been part of the English colonists' lives ever since explorers had settled in the Connecticut valley. Though decimated by diseases that the English had carried with them, the "River Indians" had treated and traded with the English since the 1630s, especially during the region's mid-century fur-trading boom. While southern New England had experienced violent conflict in the Pequot War of 1637, after that the peoples of the upper Connecticut valley, from all English accounts at least, coexisted amicably.[1]

For many years before 1675, a pair of Indian forts stood close by the English settlements of the valley, one just outside Springfield and a second midway between Northampton and Hatfield on the western shore of the Connecticut River. In addition, the region's Indians maintained what were probably seasonal villages at, at least, three other locales: up the valley near Northfield at the place the Indians called Squakeag, east of Pocumtuck near the Connecticut "Great Falls" at Peskeompscut, and forty miles southeast of Pocumtuck near the new village of Brookfield—Quaboag to the Indians.[2] Also, Indians who had sold lands to the English often retained hunting, fishing, and gathering rights, as some of the Pocumtucks had in negotiating with John Pynchon.

Another index of peaceful coexistence lies in the court records of Hampshire County. From the beginning of those records in 1660 through the next fifteen years, Indians appeared in a range of ordinary local legal affairs. In one intriguing case in Northampton in 1667, the court gave restitution to a native whose "broken Cannow" had been "taken forth and used and abused by diverse young persons." Each of the fifteen youths involved was required to "pay the said Indian 4d. a peece" to help repair or replace the vessel.[3] The fact that an Indian would paddle into town and leave his canoe—and that he could get restitution from an English court for abuse of his property—suggests respectful interchange between colonists and natives.[4]

At the same time, that court record exposes tension between the two cultures. Almost half of the cases involving Indians concerned liquor, a destructive combination which English traders apparently fostered. Thefts by Indians constitute most of the other cases. These cases suggest the strained relations which prevailed elsewhere in New England. Since their first contact with Europeans, the native population of New England had suffered dramatically. From 1600 to 1675 Indian numbers had declined from roughly 100,000 to between 10,000 and 20,000.[5] English settlers continued to buy or take over new lands. Indian economic dependency set up by traders altered traditional native patterns of living. Missionaries thrust themselves into Indian settlements, often gaining more resentment than converts.[6]

The natives also suffered repeated indignities as their role evolved from that of the colonists' benefactors and even saviors in the first years to becoming squatters in an English colony. In 1671 one young Indian chief betrayed his deep-seated anger when he spoke of his father, the great Indian chief and English friend Massasoit:

When the English first came, [my] father was as a great man and the English as a litell Child, he constraened other indians from ranging the English and gave them coren and shewed them how to plant and was free to do them ani good and had let them have a hundred times more land, than now the King had for his own people.[7]

The speaker was Metacom, soon to be known far better by his English-given name: King Philip.

The story of the causes, conduct, and results of King Philip's War of 1675–1676 is well known. Forty years of Indian degre-

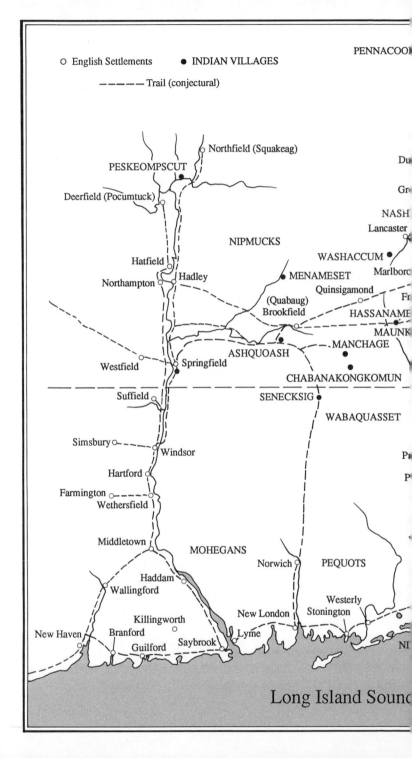

O English Settlements ● INDIAN VILLAGES

----- Trail (conjectural)

PENNACOO[...]

Northfield (Squakeag)

PESKEOMPSCUT

Deerfield (Pocumtuck)

Du[...]

Gr[...]

NASH[...]

Lancaster

NIPMUCKS

WASHACCUM ●

Hatfield

Northampton ○ Hadley ● MENAMESET Marlbor[...]

Quinsigamond

(Quabaug) Fr[...]

Brookfield HASSANAME[...]

MAUNK[...]

── MANCHAGE

ASHQUOASH ●

Westfield ○ Springfield ● CHABANAKONGKOMUN

Suffield SENECKSIG ●

WABAQUASSET

Simsbury ○ Windsor

Hartford ○ Pr[...]

Farmington ○ P[...]

Wethersfield

Middletown MOHEGANS

Haddam Norwich ○ PEQUOTS

Wallingford

Killingworth New London Westerly

New Haven Branford Stonington

Guilford Saybrook Lyme NI[...]

Long Island Sound

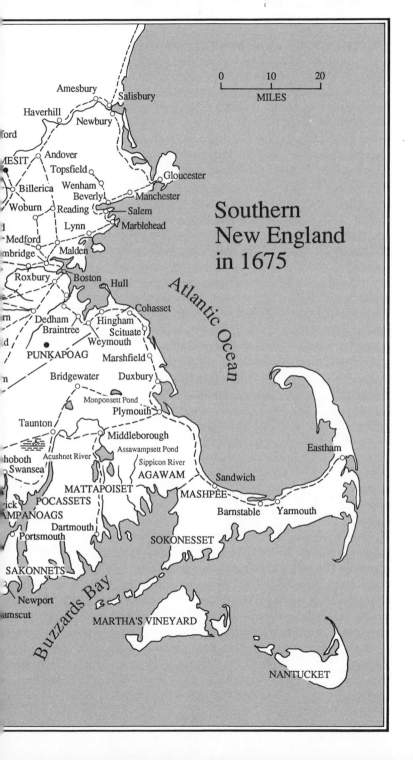

Southern
New England
in 1675

Atlantic Ocean

Buzzards Bay

0 10 20
MILES

Amesbury
Salisbury
Haverhill
Newbury
ford
Andover
MESIT
Topsfield
Billerica
Wenham
Woburn
Beverly
Reading
Medford
Lynn
mbridge
Malden
Roxbury
Boston
Hull
Dedham
Hingham
Braintree
Scituate
Weymouth
PUNKAPOAG
Marshfield
Bridgewater
Duxbury
Monponsett Pond
Plymouth
Taunton
Middleborough
Assawampsett Pond
hoboth
Acushnet River
Sippican River
Swansea
AGAWAM
Sandwich
MATTAPOISET
MASHPEE
ick
POCASSETS
Barnstable
Yarmouth
MPANOAGS
Dartmouth
Portsmouth
SOKONESSET
SAKONNETS
Newport
amscut
MARTHA'S VINEYARD
NANTUCKET
Gloucester
Manchester
Salem
Marblehead
Cohasset

Eastham

dation mixed with a series of immediate incidents led to fifteen months of horror for both natives and colonists.[8] By the time the war was over, New England's Indians were nearly eradicated—by death and destruction, by flight to other regions, and by sale into slavery. The English victors suffered grievous losses as well: Twenty-three of Massachusetts' towns were attacked and one-tenth of its men were either killed, wounded, or captured. In fact, in terms of the proportion of casualties suffered in a population, King Philip's War remains to this day the most destructive war in American history.[9]

This fierce battle for New England, the region's last and greatest Indian challenge to English colonization, had its own particular violence. In fact, if contemporary accounts can be believed, the savagery practiced by both sides fulfills the most lurid fantasies of chroniclers of frontier life. One contemporary colonist claimed that Indians used "exquisite Torments and most inhumane barbarities": "cutting off the Head, ripping open the belly, or sculping the Head of Skin and Hair . . . wearing Men's fingers as bracelets about their necks." Reports from Indian ambushes at Northfield and Whately in late summer of 1675 included soldiers' heads cut off and put on poles, burnings at the stake, and at least one victim "found with a chain hooked into his under jaw, and so hung up on a bough of a tree."[10]

For their part, the English soldiers also took scalps—and sometimes were paid bounties for them. They indiscriminately killed old men, women, and children in at least two major military encounters, the "Great Swamp Fight" against the Narragansetts in December of 1675 and at Turner's Falls in May 1676. They, too, put their enemies' heads atop pikes. Captain Samuel Mosely revealed yet another English horror when he reported the interrogation of a captured Indian in the fall of 1675. Only after he completed his report did he add the chilling postscript: "This aforesaid Indian was ordered to be *torn to peeces by Doggs* and *she* was soe dealt with all [emphasis added]."[11] The Puritans also sold some of their captured enemies into slavery, at least 184 in August and September of 1676 alone. Even more disturbing, the English visited the sins of the father upon the son, a clear break with English law, in sending

Philip's nine-year-old son into slavery. The General Court evidently felt this verdict was merciful, since the alternative they considered was death. [12]

What follows here is not an attempt to explain or excuse this war and its terror. Neither does it represent an attempt to condemn either the Indians who attacked or the English who, by dint of a half century of settlement and growth, had already become the Indians' conquerors. Instead, this chapter focuses on the effects of the war on a single town and the role that the town and its region played in that much wider war. Pocumtuck was not the most important site of fighting during King Philip's War. But it did turn out to be directly in the path of the whirlwind. Thus, Pocumtuck's story becomes a study in miniature of a region at war.

"Ashes to ashes, dust to dust"

In January of 1675 John Sassamon, a Christian Indian and secretary to the Wampanoag sachem Metacom, went to the English authorities at Plymouth with the news that his tribe was plotting a general Indian uprising against the English. Sassamon paid for this act with his life. When three Wampanoags were tried and convicted in early June for his murder, English settlers read the verdict as proof that Philip was plotting against them. The Wampanoags believed their three brothers' claims of innocence, however, and with their executions Indian anger flared. Colonists living near the tribe sighted bands of armed natives, some of whom were painted for war; there was a report that the Indians had sent their women and children away from their village below Swansea on the Mount Hope Peninsula in southeastern Massachusetts. On June 20, 1675, Indian warriors plundered and burned English houses close to their settlement. The first blood was shed three days later, and on June 24 war broke into the open at Swansea, with at least nine English killed and two wounded. King Philip's War had begun. [13]

Even before armed conflict had started, the Massachusetts Bay Colony had mobilized troops. Now these troops joined a small, defensively oriented band from Plymouth to try to contain Philip and his forces. Though the Indians soon slipped away from Mt. Hope, the three hundred colonial troops had reason to hope they could contain the natives near Pocasset on a peninsula to the east. However, the drive stalled while the Massachusetts forces attempted to make sure of the support of the Narragansetts.

Meanwhile, the Wampanoags attacked Rehoboth, Swansea, Dartmouth, and Providence. The English retook the field in mid-July and, realizing they needed to trap the natives to defeat them, moved down into the Pocasset swamp country. But they were fighting on unfamiliar soil using unfamiliar tactics—as a contemporary noted, like "fighting a wild Beast in his own Den."[14] Between the difficult fighting, short supplies, and particularly poor tactics and overall strategy, the English effort to contain the uprising failed miserably. On July 30, a report filtered out that Philip and his followers had slipped past the area's troops and were moving northwest into central New England.[15] The war had exploded, and the concussive waves soon rocked the Connecticut valley.

It took only three days for the west to feel the first blow. On August 2 Indians ambushed the Massachusetts militia company of Captain Edward Hutchinson three miles outside the tiny new village of Quaboag, or Brookfield, some forty miles southeast of Pocumtuck and twenty miles east of Springfield. Hutchinson's survivors raced to the town to warn the locals. The village's eighty men, women, and children were soon under siege. It was forty-eight hours before other Massachusetts troops were able to rescue them. Although most of the townspeople survived, the town did not. Most buildings were burned by Indian torches, and from then on Brookfield served only as a garrison. Even in that limited form the town survived only a few weeks. By the fall it lay abandoned.

As the settlers of Pocumtuck and the Connecticut valley heard this news, they must have realized that a distant, local uprising had suddenly become a real and immediate war. A new plantation close by had been lost, blood spilled—and by whom? Philip's Wampanoags had not struck Brookfield. The local Indians, the Nipmucks of central Massachusetts, had done the deed. The war was spreading, not just onto local land but to local natives as well.

The valley lay quiet through the middle of August, save only an incident up at Northfield where Indians drove off some sheep. Tension continued to mount, however. As Hartford and Boston both armed the valley for war, Major John Pynchon, the valley's military commander, reported on August 22 that his soldiers headquartered in Hadley "expect nothing but ye enemy to insult & fall upon ye remote Townes . . . they are in great feares." Although a twenty-man garrison stood guard at North-field, the soldiers were worried that the number was too small. Ten soldiers had also been sent to Pocumtuck, yet there was talk of "calling off" the garrison entirely, which must have frightened the village. [16]

Part of the terror sweeping the valley lay simply in not know-ing who the enemies were. If solely the Wampanoags had been fighting, the valley could have breathed more easily. But the war had already spread to the Nipmucks. Fearing that the River Indians—the surviving Pocumtucks, the Norwootucks, and the smaller, local tribes—might turn next, on August 24 the Con-necticut valley authorities called in representatives of the re-gion's tribes and demanded that they turn in their weapons. The natives stalled, then fled under cover of darkness. Hotly pursued by militia from Hadley under Captains Richard Beers and Thomas Lathrop, the Indians turned and surprised the English soldiers at Hopewell Swamp, near the infant settle-ment of Swampfield, killing nine soldiers during the three-hour encounter. [17]

English intervention had come too late. With armed conflict and bloodshed along the Connecticut, and a pitched battle less than ten miles from their homes, Pocumtuck's citizens knew they were in grave danger. More generally, the entire region's settlers realized that the war had now embroiled local, formerly friendly tribes. This flew in the face not only of years of stable relations but even of a specific peace pact which area settlers and Indians had signed just two months before. But there was nothing the English could do about that now. [18]

Obviously the Indian view of these events differed sharply.

Either Philip himself, his emissaries, or perhaps simply the appeal of his cause was leading other New England Indians to join him. The colonists' own records show that Indian tribes throughout southern New England quickly learned about Philip's campaign, and while not all tribes joined him, a great number soon came over. Through the entire war in the west in 1675, the Wampanoags never fought a battle alone. Local forces were always engaged, at times exclusively.[19]

By September, with Philip free and at the head of hundreds of allied Indians, the war came down upon the valley in full fury. Pocumtuck took the first blow. On September 1 about sixty Indians struck, first killing one of the town's garrison soldiers out "looking after his horse," and then directly attacking the town. Although the settlers all safely fled into the town's two fortified houses, they did not have enough armed men to challenge the attackers. Thus they had to remain inside while the Indians burned seventeen of the outlying houses and barns.[20] The next day Indians struck fifteen miles above at Northfield, attacking "several men that were gone out of the fort," and killing eight. Unaware of this latest disaster, on September 3 Captain Beers took "about thirty-six" men up from Hadley to the fort at Northfield to "fetch off the garrison." He never arrived. On the morning of September 4, Indians attacked his troop three miles south of Northfield, killing Beers and close to twenty of his men. The rest fled back, in haphazard fashion, to Hadley. The next day Major Robert Treat, Connecticut's commanding officer in the valley, led upwards of one hundred men to Northfield. This troop, too, was fired upon, but they reached their destination safely. Looking over the situation, Treat quickly decided to "bring off the garrison." In his view the situation must have been desperate, for the troops left that same night, leaving cattle there and even soldiers' corpses unburied.[21]

With Northfield abandoned and soon burned by the Indians, Pocumtuck now stood, exposed and alone, as the region's extreme frontier outpost. Brookfield to the east, Northfield above, even tiny Swampfield six miles below—small, young plantations all—had disappeared in the course of a few short weeks.

And yet Pocumtuck was neither deserted nor defenseless.

Since the war had moved west, both Massachusetts and Connecticut had sent reinforcements into the upper Connecticut valley. Doubtless these soldiers helped Pocumtuck's townsmen strengthen the village's two garrison houses—fortifications which Massachusetts demanded of its frontier towns.[22] Pocumtuck drew further strength from its own militia, the able-bodied men of the town who took on military service as a regular duty of town life. Even so, while the authorities ordered the men of Pocumtuck to remain at the outpost, the women and children probably did not stay. With Northfield's villagers resettled in valley towns below, Pocumtuck likely sent its dependents and women to safety there as well. The townsmen and the troops, perhaps fifty in all, tried to hold on.

Their grasp slipped. On Sunday afternoon, September 12, twenty-two men trying to go from one garrison to the other for a town meeting were surprised by the Indians. Although only one soldier was killed, the attacking force drove the others into the garrison they were heading for. Then, with the troops enclosed, the Indians proceeded to burn the other garrison house and one other home, kill a number of horses, and cart away "horse-loads of beef and pork" to their rendezvous on Pine Hill one mile north of town. While the soldiers fumed with the enemy so close, the colonial force was too small to risk an attack. Rain that night made counterattack still less feasible. By the time Captain Lathrop brought enough soldiers up from Hadley to challenge the Indians, they had fled.[23]

Pocumtuck's situation became still more desperate. By now there seemed little doubt that, as Northampton minister Solomon Stoddard noted, "most of the Indians in the country" had turned against the colonists. John Pynchon plaintively echoed the region's mood: "We are endeavoring to discover the enemy, and daily send out scouts, but little is effected. Our English are somewhat awkward and fearful in scouting and spying, though we do the best we can. We have no Indian friends here to help us."[24]

Yet still Pocumtuck clung to life. One reason, beyond the obvious desire to keep any town alive, stood out. In stacks in the Pocumtuck meadows stood over three thousand bushels of corn. With a besieged valley to feed, the food's value was obvious. With a share of the grain belonging to none other than Pocumtuck entrepreneur, valley merchant, and military commander John Pynchon, desire to salvage the grain may have gained official sanction. Perhaps most important, reports were trickling in that, in this summer of war, food supplies were dwindling. As the corn stood in Pocumtuck's fields, the General Court was less than a month from declaring the "great danger of a famine."[25]

With all these forces and fears bearing down on the valley, the military decided to bring Pocumtuck's corn down to Hadley and greater safety. Captain Thomas Lathrop took his company up to the town and, aided by the remaining townsmen, loaded the grain onto carts. On Saturday morning, September 18, while Captain Mosely and his Pocumtuck garrison sent out scouts, Lathrop and about fifty soldiers, plus fifteen "teamsters"—Pocumtuck men recruited to help drive the caravan—headed south.

As Deerfield's chronicler George Sheldon tells the story, "Southward along the narrow Pocumtuck path, through the primeval woods, moved Lathrop and his men—brave, fearless, foolish. Confident in their numbers, scorning danger, not even a van-guard or a flanker was thrown out."[26] Lathrop, a contemporary later recorded, had "taken up a wrong notion" that the Indians would never assault such a large group, and thus moved slowly, without protection. That error soon proved fatal.[27] About five miles south of town, the convoy slowed to cross a small, muddy brook. Increase Mather later claimed that the soldiers were so unafraid that they even left their arms on the carts and started to pick grapes by the stream.

At that moment the Indians struck. Hundreds of warriors—Wampanoags, Nipmucks, Pocumtucks—charged Lathrop's bewildered and outnumbered forces as the muddy brook became, forevermore, Bloody Brook. Although Mosely's militia soon reached the site, they could do little more than drive off the Indians from their scalping. The slaughter was already complete. Over sixty men lay dead on what one contemporary called "that most fatal day, the saddest that ever befel New-England."[28] It was, indeed, a disaster—as bad a defeat as any the English suffered in the entire war.[29] Among the slain lay fourteen Pocumtuck men; only one escaped.

That night Mosely led his troops back to the Pocumtuck garrison. When he awoke that next Sabbath morning, he rode his forces back to the site of the disaster so that they could bury the dead—only to find Indians there "stripping the slain."[30] Driving away the enemy, Mosely's men carried out their gruesome task, laying the bodies in a common grave at the site.

Returning to Pocumtuck, Mosely's soldiers faced another sickening scene. A detachment of the victorious Indians appeared across the river from the town, insolently "hanging up the garments of the English" slain at Bloody Brook. Even more insulting for the soldiers, some of the Indians taunted the survivors in good English. They were from among John Eliot's former "praying Indians," his English-speaking Christian converts. Still other Indians then passed close by the remaining garrison house in town. With only twenty-seven soldiers left, though, Mosely dared not attack.[31]

Pocumtuck was defeated and now even humiliated. Within two days the Connecticut authorities notified John Pynchon of their "sense about quitting the Pocumtuck garrison."[32] Pynchon quickly agreed. Within a few days the colonists abandoned Pocumtuck, and the Indians soon burned the remaining buildings. As Hadley minister John Russell wrote of the valley's woes, "The light of another day hath turned our yesterdays fears into certainties and bitter lamentations for the distresses and calamities of our brethren and friends."[33] From the ashes of the Pocumtuck Indians' fort in September of 1664 to the ashes of the English Pocumtuck settlement in September of 1675, the wheel had turned full circle. An Indian village had lived and died there; now, so too had an English settlement.

As Pocumtuck's survivors assessed their losses, they seemed huge. Their entire town was gone—about thirty houses, plus barns and outbuildings, all their lands, and much if not all of their harvest. The buildings were of course gone forever; the land, though still held legally, had no value. The settlers also lost much personal property. They managed to save some horses and cattle, as well as various tools and cooking utensils. They also salvaged a handful of books—likely account books and Bibles—and a few beds. However, no other furniture survived, and only a few dishes did, some wooden, mostly pewter. All of this suggests that Pocumtuck's settlers left quickly and carried but few possessions with them.[34]

More daunting than the loss of property was the loss of life. Over one-third of Pocumtuck's men—fourteen in all—had been killed at Bloody Brook. That slaughter had made widows of nine women, almost one-third of the wives in town. Each was left with children, as few as two, as many as eight. In all, in a town of two hundred people, forty children lost their fathers that September 18.

The dead ranged in age from under twenty to fifty-eight. Key leaders were lost. Most notable was Samuel Hinsdale, Pocumtuck's first settler, 1673 constable, and representative in negotiations with Dedham and the General Court. While the war struck a number of families hard, the Hinsdales suffered the most. Not only were Samuel and his father, Robert, killed at Bloody Brook, but so were two of Samuel's brothers, Barnabas and John, and their brother-in-law Joseph Gillett.[35]

In the face of these losses, most of Pocumtuck's survivors drew down to safety in the valley towns below. The vast majority headed for Hatfield, Hadley, or Northampton. Three families pushed even farther south, and three headed east toward the Bay. No matter where they settled, however, the lives of Pocumtuck's survivors, particularly those families with children, remained difficult. Forced to dwell in other people's homes, living with the terror of a war that had already taken friends and family, retaining only a handful of salvaged possessions, unsure whether their lands would ever be restored, many without fathers or husbands—Pocumtuck's lot was sad indeed. Its English settlers had, at least for now, followed the Pocumtuck Indians into shattered exile.

At the same time, Pocumtuck did not die quietly. Bloody Brook's earthquake had sent tremors of war through the entire Connecticut valley. And contemporary chroniclers throughout New England told of it, often in blazing language. Back in

Boston, Reverend Increase Mather wrote about the ambush, and Samuel Sewall commented on "that lamentable fight" in his diary.[36]

In fact, it is in accounts like Mather's that Bloody Brook took on larger significance. The defeat was so terrible, so "aweful," that it became a symbol for New England. When Mather wrote of that "black and fatal day," that destruction "all in one little Plantation, and in one day," he strove to understand its meaning. Why had "the Lord himself seemeth to be against us, to cast us off, to put us to shame"? The answer lay in "the sinful *Degenerate Estate* of the *present Generation in New-England.*"[37] In another of his works of this time, Mather claimed that God had used the horrors of this war "as an heavy Judgement which should come to punish that sin of mens unfaithfulness. . . . Is it nothing that so many have been cut off by a bloody and barbarous Sword? Is it nothing that Widows and fatherless have been multiplied among us? . . . Alas that New-England should be brought so low."[38]

The General Court obviously agreed. It made October 7, 1675, a "day of Humiliation," of solemn prayer and contemplation. In passing "Lawes and Ordinances of warr" six days later, it moved to include proper religious practices as part of its military code.[39] On November 3 the Court detailed the region's failings, declaring that the colonists had "neither heard the word nor rod as wee ought . . . hence . . . the righteous God hath heightened our calamity." The sins of the people included "neglect of discipline in the churches," especially regarding the children, and "manifest pride openly appearing amongst us in that long haire, like weomens haire, is worn by some men . . . either their owne or . . . perewiggs." Men and women alike were accused of "excesse . . . the evil of pride in apparrell . . . vajne, new strainge fashions, both in poore and rich, with naked breasts and armes." "Comon swearing and cursing," "the shameful and scandelous sin of excessive drinking, tipling, & company keeping in tavernes," and "private unlicensed houss of enterteinment" threatened the colony, as did the "sin of idleness." Shopkeepers and merchants were setting "excessive prizes on their goods," while men and women were riding from

town to town "merely to drinke & revell."[40] It was all these sins
that had caused God to pass his dreadful judgment.

Though this legislative jeremiad took the colony far beyond
consideration of Pocumtuck alone, the connection between the
two remains. God did not visit such horror upon his people
without cause. As much as any incident in the war's first year,
Bloody Brook forced the colonists of New England to consider
well the paths of their lives. In this way Pocumtuck's destruction served the Lord and provided meaning for all of New
England.

Through the autumn of 1675 King Philip's War continued its
sweep down the Connecticut valley. With four young outpost
towns already destroyed, the natives now attacked the older,
more established towns. Within the next six weeks Northampton, Springfield, Hatfield, and Westfield all bore the scars of
Indian attacks. Springfield's losses were especially high, for on
October 4 Philip's forces destroyed thirty houses and twenty-
five barns. Hatfield absorbed a major blow on October 19 when
a huge Indian force assaulted the town, destroying numerous
houses and leaving seven settlers dead and ten wounded. Not
until the cold of mid-November did the fighting ease.

In the meantime the extent of crisis showed itself in other
ways. The Hampshire County Court could not open for its fall
session, since it was "obstructed by ye wars." The General
Court levied two new taxes on the colony within fourteen weeks,
both specific responses to "the great & dayly growing charge of
the present warr." And the threat of serious food shortages
continued to grow. In fact, on November 3, the General Court
decided that "grajne inned in the barnes of . . . inhabitants"
allowed "the enemy" too great a chance for destruction or theft.
Therefore, farmers lost control of their own produce: Militia
and selectmen were empowered to secure the grain within local
garrisons. Although the actual fighting eased with the coming
of winter, official actions in the last months of 1675 showed that
this had become all-out war, a struggle even for survival.[41]

The English were not entirely defenseless against this Indian
campaign in the west. They reported that the Indians suffered

significant casualties in a number of their attacks: as many as eighty killed or wounded at Brookfield in early August, twenty-six killed in the Hopewell Swamp ambush of August 24, as many as one hundred casualties at Bloody Brook.[42] Further, Connecticut and Massachusetts rapidly mobilized and deployed troops throughout the valley. At times the colonial armies even tried to take the offensive in the war in the west. Notable was a colonial mission led by Captain Joseph Sill in mid-November which journeyed into "Nipmuck country" and destroyed a great deal of corn which the Indians had stored for the winter.[43] Still, in 1675 this attack proved the exception, not the rule. For the most part, the colonists fought defensively, fortifying their towns and trying only to hold on to what they had.

It was a grim Christmas for the English of the Connecticut valley. Losses were staggering. Four of their towns had been destroyed, the remaining five attacked. Even the surviving towns had each lost houses, barns, and livestock. Miraculously, no children and only one woman had been slain. However, 145 men had been killed in the fighting, one-third of whom were not Massachusetts soldiers but local settlers.[44] Many others had been wounded, and a handful captured. Pocumtuck's survivors spent the winter in the remaining valley towns, holding on to what few possessions they had been able to cart away, living in cramped quarters with friends or relations on the reduced frontier, coping with reports that Indians had already settled at Pocumtuck,[45] contemplating their lost homes and fallen brethren. The winter solstice marked a cold and dark time indeed for the survivors of Pocumtuck.

The Fall of Pocumtuck: Another View

As the English had suffered in this first year of war, the Indians had enjoyed great triumphs. From the natives' perspective, their 1675 campaign in the Connecticut valley proved a huge success. More than merely scattering attacks around a region, King Philip's cause had mobilized increasing numbers of Indians who consistently executed effective plans of attack. Both coherent strategy and successful tactics marked their campaign.

Claiming a clear Indian strategy requires some caution, for there exist, of course, no "Memoirs of King Philip" or captured native war records to support such claims. Yet the English record can illustrate the Indians' ways. Enough information about the various Indian attacks and battles of King Philip's War survives to reveal Indian methods that the colonists—and often historians as well—saw only as madness.[46]

A careful study of the incidences of war in the Connecticut valley in 1675 reveals a clear and cogent Indian plan. Between August 2 and 4, two major assaults forced the abandonment of Brookfield. From August 15 through about September 6, Northfield faced four separate attacks. When that town was abandoned after the fourth raid, the Indians quickly moved in and leveled it. Similarly, after four attacks on Pocumtuck between September 1 and September 19, townspeople left their village and the Indians promptly burned it. Infant Swampfield, just a few miles south of Pocumtuck, also disappeared amidst this tumult.

Adding up these depredations yields a picture of a rational and effective Indian strategy. While the natives threatened settlers throughout the valley, they keyed on one town at a time. Brookfield, the most isolated village and the one in the middle of Nipmuck country, took the first series of attacks in early August. When it was gone, so, too, was the easternmost link of the valley settlements to Boston and the Bay. Moving northwest, the Indians then systematically reduced the two northernmost outposts along the valley's frontier line during September: first Northfield and then Pocumtuck. In doing this, they actually pushed the frontier back down some twenty-five miles.

The next major attack, however, took place not at Hatfield, the town next southward, as would be expected, but well below at Springfield, on October 5. But this strike actually reinforces belief in the Indians' savvy and strategy. Three key points support this. First, after the reduction of Northfield and Pocumtuck, survivors had fled to the nearest towns below and the military authorities had bolstered the garrisons there, placing soldiers at Hatfield, Hadley, and Northampton. Inhabitants of these towns doubtless prepared for the next expected blow. For this reason Indians might have anticipated only limited success had they attacked there. Second, by this time the Indians probably realized that the colonial military force trying to protect the west was too small to be divided up among all the various towns. Instead, it stayed largely in whole, mobile companies, moving through the valley as needed. By mid-September much of that force had moved up to protect the northernmost settlements. In fact, on October 4—the day before the Indian attack—Springfield's own militia had headed north.[47] Finally, just below Springfield sat an Indian fort, an outpost of the River Indians with whom the settlers had lived peacefully for the past forty years. Philip's forces used it well. The post provided sanctuary for "several hundred of the enemy Indians" as they slipped past the now-guarded towns to the north and prepared to launch their attack on a suddenly defenseless Springfield. By thus modifying their general plan, the Indian attack on October 5 sent Springfield up in flames. Two weeks later, the last major attack of the fall took place back up the valley at Hatfield, the site of the previously expected blow—and after the dazed colonists had moved to distribute their limited number of soldiers among *all* the valley towns.

Through 1675, then, the Indians waged a coherent campaign which effectively reduced the frontier and successfully drove back English settlement. The colonists were not blind to such successes. In the aftermath of Bloody Brook one observed that "now those wretched [caitiffs] begin to talk of great matters, hoping that by degrees they might destroy all the towns hereabouts, as they had already begun."[48]

The tactics the Indians used suggest further intelligent decision-making. Most of the twenty-four attacks on the nine valley towns in 1675 involved small numbers of Indians, from a handful up to perhaps seventy-five men. They were virtually all surprise attacks, whether upon a town, individuals, or small groups in the woods or fields. The September 12 blow at Pocumtuck came on a Sunday as the men headed for meeting and prayer. Indians once swept down on Hatfield while the colonists were in the midst of putting up the frame of a new house. One Pocumtuck man was attacked by a party of Indians who leapt out at him from under the bridge he was crossing. All these attacks allowed for quick action, good chances for success, and minimal losses. Even the six larger assaults by more than seventy-five men used the same basic stratagem of surprise. By doing this the Indians avoided the risk of high losses that open, frontal assaults would bring. The Indians had no desire and no need to square off with the colonial forces. And the proof of the success of their tactics was obvious.

The colonists were well aware of the Indians' tactics. Throughout 1675, however, they only complained about them rather than adapted to them. Typical of the English reaction is the aggrieved tone taken by the Massachusetts Council in Boston on August 30, 1675:

[I]t is the Manner of the Heathen that are now in Hostility with us, contrary to the Practice of all Civil Nations, to Execute their bloody Insolencies by Stealth and Sculking in small Parties, declining all open Decision of their Controversie, either by Treaty or by the Sword.[49]

William Hubbard placed such Indian tactics on a lower moral plane: "[T]hey durst not look an Englishman in the face in open field; nor ever yet were known to kill any man with their guns unless when they could lie in wait for him in an Ambush, or behind some shelter, taking aim undiscovered."[50] As a soldier and not a writer, John Pynchon betrayed a more frustrated and less patronizing view when he grimly wrote: "And when we go out after the Indians they doe soe sculk in swamps we cannot find y^m & yet do waylay our people to there destruction."[51] Not until February of 1676 did the General Court order that its soldiers "be improoved in scouting & warding, to prevent the sculking & lirking of the ennemy about the . . . townes, & to give tymely notice of approaching dainger."[52]

The Indians had good reasons for focusing their 1675 offensive on the upper Connecticut valley. Indian settlements which lay up near Pocumtuck and Northfield had been increasingly

threatened by rapid English expansion, with Hatfield, Pocumtuck, Northfield, and Swampfield all established between 1670
and 1673. Attempts to bring the Indians under English jurisdiction and political authority, an additional offshoot of English
colonization, may have soured relations further. By 1675 Indian
farming, fishing, and hunting were all adversely affected by this
rapid growth. As the English moved into Pocumtuck and
Northfield, the Indians lost some of the richest farmland in the
entire valley. By late November of 1675, when their caches of
corn were destroyed by colonial militia, the Indians faced the
threat of starvation. In responding to their loss of food, the next
spring the Indians followed the plan of Canonchet, a beloved
and respected Narragansett chief, and planted a reported three
hundred acres of corn in their old fields at Pocumtuck and
possibly similar acreage at Northfield.[53] In other words, driving
the colonists south may have been done at least in part to regain
those lands for farming. Similarly, valley Indians had always
depended on the abundant fish of the Connecticut River, and a
prime locale for great catches of salmon and shad was the Great
Falls—located squarely between the new settlements of Pocumtuck and Northfield. That the Indians coveted this spot
becomes still more evident in noting that some five hundred
Indians encamped there in the spring of 1676. Finally, Indian
hunting in the area was undoubtedly hurt by the burgeoning
English presence. Certainly if furs sold indicate availability of
game, then the region had already been shorn by around 1660,
as diminishing trade in Springfield showed.[54]

To sum up this Indian viewpoint, then, the warring native
forces launched a well-engineered campaign in 1675. They had
goals in the west—military, economic, and geopolitical—and
they used intelligent means to achieve them. As of late 1675,
the Indians were successfully fighting an effective seventeenth-
century guerrilla war.

1676: The War Slows

As winter's respite from war ebbed, the massed native forces
in the west made plans for not only the Connecticut valley but

all of southern New England. In late March two colonial captives were treated to a full display of massed Indian might. The Indians then promptly sent them scurrying back to New England's officials, where they reported that as many as three thousand Indians were banded together. These two captives also reported the basic Indian plan: "first, to destroy Connecticut in the spring, then Boston in the Harvest."[55]

With this scheme in mind, the Indians soon resumed their attacks. Between March 1 and June 12, 1676, they launched fifteen assaults on the surviving towns of the Connecticut valley. The types of attack remained the same—surprise raids, large and small, at any place, at any time. Within this general trend, the larger attacks suggest a continuation of the 1675 plan to push back the colonial frontier. Of the five large assaults in 1676, one took place at Hadley and two each at Hatfield and Northampton, the three northernmost settlements.

In attacking these three upper valley towns, the Indians apparently believed that the waves of English settlement could be broken and pushed back even farther. Perhaps the sea of settlers could not be stopped entirely, but the natives would no longer merely watch the erosion of their lands. The number of larger Indians attacks in the spring of 1676 suggests this growing confidence. With less probing of colonial defenses needed in this second year of the war, the Indians now hit harder more often, using smaller raids more for distraction and terror.[56]

By mid-spring of 1676 the Indians seemed on the verge of great success in the Connecticut valley. Good strategy, proven techniques, and a large, mobile force all suggested successful policy. In addition, there was no colonial force anywhere near the area large enough to destroy the Indians, especially if they stayed close to their recently added lands in the upper valley.

Yet western Massachusetts did not become Indian territory. In fact, by July scarcely a native could be seen in the entire valley. By September Philip was dead, his troops slain, scattered, or enslaved, and the war over. What happened?

In essence, four major developments demoralized Philip's forces. First of all, the five major attacks by his forces on valley settlements all failed. A great force of more than three hundred

Indians assaulted Northampton early on the morning of March 14. Northampton suffered five men killed and another six wounded, plus a handful of houses and barns burned—but the Indian force was repulsed. These Indians turned on Hatfield later that same day, but had even less success. Two days later at 2 A.M. they struck Northampton again, but an alert sentry sounded the alarm. Losing their surprise, the Indians drew back, taking only some horses and sheep. More than two months later they launched a major attack on Hatfield, but the settlers once again were armed, alert, and effective in their defense. On June 12, this time at Hadley, the same story was repeated. Clearly the colonists had learned from the misery of the previous year, and while small attacks could not be stopped, big ones could be blunted.

The second major development of 1676 was that while Indian strategy had remained consistent, colonial tactics had changed. Massachusetts had strengthened its militia laws, improving training, urging better use of watches and scouts, and making residents more responsible for the fate of their towns. Then, too, the General Court had gotten tougher on its citizens, not only haranguing them for their sins but also forbidding militiamen from leaving their towns.[57] And 1675 had made the soldiers themselves wiser and tougher. The first year of King Philip's War had been a learning experience for the English. Frustrated for eight months, by 1676 they had adopted both Indian fighting techniques and more effective defenses.[58] Thus, by May of 1676 one finds Thomas Savage, commander at Hadley, steering the colonial authorities away from the previous "way of following the enemy up and down in the woods . . . in which they . . . can take advantage of us," and instead urging attacks on the Indian settlements where they "plant and fish on . . . the river."[59]

Savage proved remarkably prophetic. Just three days after he posted his letter, the English provided the Indians with the third demoralizing blow. Given the course of the war the previous year, the Indians never expected much colonial offensive action, and surely not from large forces. For this reason, the "Falls Fight" of May 19, 1676, at Turner's Falls (what the Indi-

ans called Peskeompscut, or the "Great Falls"), five miles
northeast of Pocumtuck, shocked Philip's forces. In his careful
1896 study *Soldiers in King Philip's War,* George Madison Bodge
provided a thoughtful, balanced account of the events leading
up to this battle:

After the withdrawal of the army under Major Savage, the Indians
seemed to have relaxed much of their vigilance, watching mainly for
opportunities for plunder wherever the English became careless and
exposed themselves or cattle to the chance of capture. In the mean
time the situation of the Indians was becoming desperate. The Narra-
gansets with their allies and many of the Wampanoags had been forced
in an almost destitute condition upon the Nipmuck and Pocumtuck
tribes for support. These unwanted numbers soon exhausted the never
abundant resources of the local tribes, and when Philip's promises of
a speedy victory over all the river towns with plunder of their goods
were not realized, when the great chieftain Canonchet was taken and
slain, and having met the repulses at Northampton and Hatfield, they
were reduced almost to starvation. . . . [Now] the Indians gathered to
the fishing places upon the river in large numbers, hoping here to
supply their wants and secure a stock of provisions till they could
accomplish the destruction of the towns and secure the corn and cattle
of the English. Knowing that the garrisons were small, and feeling
secure from attack both by numbers and distance, they grew careless
in sending scouts or placing guards. Hearing . . . that the English had
turned some of their cattle out into Hatfield meadows, a detachment
was sent out upon May 12th, and succeeded in "stampeding" about
seventy head of these cattle, and driving them safely into the woods.
This fresh outrage was carried out with impunity, and so enraged the
English that they urged to be led out against their enemies at once,
and when [an escaped captive named Thomas] Reed . . . came in on
May 15th, and disclosed the carelessness of the Indians, it was resolved to wait no longer.[60]

As Bodge indicates, the Indians were not faring as well as the
English might have thought. Still, they remained "secure and
scornful, boasting of the great things" they had done and would
do. In addition, Peskeompscut, their site on the Connecticut
River, was providing needed food in the form of the abundant
shad and salmon. And just five miles away, Thomas Reed had
seen Indian corn planted again at Pocumtuck.[61]

Between May 15 and 18, Captain William Turner gathered together an English troop at Hatfield. Unlike most colonial forces, this one consisted mainly of valley settlers, plus volunteers from the regular soldiers. On the night of May 18, Turner's group of over one hundred fifty men headed north, past the ruins of Pocumtuck and across the river north of town, and looped up above the Indians at the falls. Then, with no Indian guards posted, just before daybreak the soldiers crept into the sleeping camp. As Increase Mather reported it, "our Souldiers came and put their Guns into their Wigwams . . . and made a great and notable slaughter amongst them."[62]

If Bloody Brook was a massacre, so, too, was the battle at what became known as Turner's Falls. Many Indians were killed in the first seconds of the attack as they lay asleep in their tents. Others died before they could offer resistance. Still others ran to the river, leaping into canoes or headlong into the waters, but a vast number of these died as they hurtled over the massive falls. More "were chased to the shelving rocks along the banks and there shot down."[63] In all, the colonists killed outright some one hundred Indians; roughly one hundred forty more died trying to escape via the river. Perhaps even more brutal is the fact that this assault was perpetrated considerably against "old men and women," for Reed's report of May 15 had indicated only "60 or 70 fighting-men" at Peskeompscut.[64]

More than a surprise, more than a galling defeat, the slaughter at Turner's Falls demoralized the Indians. Although nearby natives rushed to the falls and routed and scattered Turner's forces, killing the captain and thirty-seven others, the Indian losses were horrifying. Compounded by their own offensive failures of the spring, this foray cut deeply into Indian hopes.

By late May, then, Philip's forces had been badly shaken. The failure of their major assaults all spring must have been discouraging, to say nothing of their shock and dismay after the attack at the Great Falls. Yet there was still more. By now, "many of them were destroyed by fevers and fluxes, with other Distempers falling amongst them."[65] There were also reports of "some Quarrel amongst themselves," of warriors "now strangely divided and separated the one from the other."[66] In April the

Colonial War Council in Hartford had sent a party of friendly Indians to Philip's allied forces to negotiate a prisoner exchange as well as offer peace to any sachem desiring it. Though the Narragansetts rejected them, the Pocumtucks and Nipmucks were receptive to these plans. Even though nothing ultimately came of the exchange, this division suggests serious problems. Still another report indicates that the Indians were "disappointed of their fishing and put by their planting, [and] began to fall at variance amongst themselves" with some local tribes now "quarrelling with *Philip* for fetching all this Mischief about."[67]

For all this, though, the English still had not come close to actually defeating the Indians. It took another force to drive Philip out of the west, where he remained reasonably secure, to the east and his destruction. This fourth and decisive development of the war had little to do with the English. Instead, other Indians—the Mohawks—played the pivotal role.

In the first six months of 1676, a series of Mohawk attacks crushed Philip's forces, both physically and spiritually. In February, reportedly three hundred of these eastern Iroquois assaulted some five hundred of Philip's men forty miles east of Albany near the Hoosick River, where they were encamped for the winter, and routed them.[68] In March they cut off a party of Pocumtucks and Nipmucks heading "to Canada, with captives taken at Lancaster, to be exchanged for powder," killing two Pocumtucks.[69] Then on June 12, "while the *Indian* men were thus fighting against *Hadley, the . . . Mohawks* came upon their Head-Quarters, and smote their women and Children with a great Slaughter, and then returned with much plunder." At least fifty of Philip's Indians were reportedly killed, perhaps as many as one hundred forty.[70]

Contemporary English reports reinforce the importance of the Mohawks' role. In one 1676 account, a Pequot sachem affirmed "that the said *Mohucks* were the only persons likely to put an end to the war, by hindering the enemy [Philip's forces] from planting and forcing them down [east] upon us."[71] William Hubbard also reported that "some of the *Mohawks* (a sort of fierce and salvage *Indians* yet mortal Enemies of these . . .)

had fallen upon some of *Philip's* Party and destroyed many of them."[72]

Although the Mohawk attacks mark the turning point of the war, until recently their influence has been overlooked. That is not surprising, since historians have traditionally reflected the colonists' view of a singular "Indian enemy."[73] However, a closer look at the dynamic between Indians and Indians reveals how crucial the Mohawks were. As of 1675 factionalism divided the Indians of New England—and in fact had done so for decades.[74] More important, though, it was Indians from outside New England—the Mohawks—who had dominated the region's inter-Indian wars through the seventeenth century. In the sixty years before King Philip's War, Mohawks had clashed with Indians in New England from Long Island to the coast of Maine—with Mahicans, Western and Eastern Abenaki, Penobscots, Kennebecs, Sokokis, and of course dramatically in 1664 with the Pocumtucks. As of 1675, the Mohawks stood powerful and distant, the strongest single Indian force in the northeast, and a power with which all men, English and Indian, had to reckon.

While the English authorities in Boston were certainly aware of Mohawk power, they did not betray much understanding of intertribal relations or the independent strength of these powerful Iroquois. Settlers out west apparently knew more than Boston did about what was transpiring between Philip and the Mohawks. On April 29, 1676, eight of them wrote to the General Court, "All intelligence give us cause to hope that the Mohawks do still retain their friendship for us and enmity against our enemies. Some proofe of it they have of late in those they slew higher up this river"—Philip's intercepted party to Canada. "And further proof it is thought they would soon give," the message concluded.[75]

The Massachusetts leadership did not seem to understand these complexities. Apparently they felt that New York authorities, notably Governor Edmund Andros, could simply order Mohawk attacks but had chosen not to do so. Both during the war and after, Bostonians complained bitterly about how the Mohawks had fought against the colonists in the war and how

New York had betrayed them by supplying the enemy Indians
with arms and ammunition. Andros fired back in kind. Reporting on this acerbic exchange, Edward Randolph reported to the
Council of Trade in 1676 that Andros

hath proved very friendly and serviceable to the Massachusetts in this
warr . . . he offered and would have engaged the Mohawks and Ma-
quot Indians to have fallen upon the Sachem Philip and his confederates; but his friendship advice and offers were slighted. Nevertheless
Collonel Andros out of his duty to His Majesty kept the aforesaid
Indians from taking any part with the Sachem Philip.[76]

Randolph's report was dead wrong—but it is most instruc-
tive, for it exposes the extraordinary clash of forces brought
about by this war.[77] In January of 1676 Andros did strongly
"Incourage" the Mohawks to attack Philip's forces near Hoosick, and in early February they drove Philip off. In fact, Andros
later took credit for supplying and supporting the Mohawks in
that attack.[78] Randolph's report also conflicts with Andros's own
claim of July 5, 1676, that the Indians fought quite well against
Philip: "Our Indians, the Maques, &C . . . have done very
great execution on your Indian enemy."[79] Finally, Randolph
implies that Andros *would* have sent the Mohawks out to fight,
had New England's leaders desired it, but that they never
asked—a position that makes no sense, given Massachusetts'
later complaints.

In truth, Connecticut and Massachusetts had asked for help—
but Andros's terms, which included Mohawk pursuit into western New England, were unacceptable. The reasons run deep.
On one level, Andros and his ally Randolph were fighting for
the crown's favor in a continuing struggle with Massachusetts
for royal support from home. Part of that depended on how
successful Andros was—or appeared to be—in controlling the
Indians, especially the Iroquois.[80] On another level, since he
had become governor of New York Andros had been trying to
take over all of Connecticut's lands west of the Connecticut
River, a move which New Englanders obviously opposed.[81]
Thus, influence over the Mohawks—given their sway over Indians throughout New England, their ability to control terri-

tory, their potential for aiding or crippling New England in its war against Philip, and their impact on Massachusetts-New York-English relations—was critical.

In the face of these factors, Boston's angry claims that Mohawks fought on Philip's side gain greater significance—and some credence. At least two contemporary reports argue that some Mohawks did. In the winter of 1675–1676 Philip assembled a force variously estimated at nine hundred, fifteen hundred, and twenty-one hundred warriors, and some three thousand Indians in all. Included were not only Algonkians of New England but also Mahicans, Scaticookes, and even "5 or 600 French Indyans" from Canada—French Mohawks.[82] By 1676 the Jesuits in Canada had drawn several hundred Mohawks away from the Iroquois and under French control at Caughnawaga, near Montreal. It appears that some of them were prepared to fight along with Philip against the English enemy—and thus possibly against their Iroquois allies.

Amidst these complexities, understanding the Mohawks' actions is difficult. Yet perhaps the best path to understanding is also the most logical. Rather than questioning whether and how Andros controlled the Mohawks, a better solution lies in the possibility that Andros simply did *not* "control" them. He apparently was on good terms with them, for the arrangement was mutually beneficial.[83] But in 1676 that hardly means that he controlled them.

In light of these ideas, the Mohawks' role in King Philip's War becomes clearer and more understandable. In the winter of 1675–1676, as is well documented, Philip went to the Mohawks to enlist their aid. While some may have joined him—for Indians were not wholly unified by tribes or completely controlled by their sachems—most Mohawks did not. In fact, soon after Philip was rebuffed they once again went to war with New England Indians.[84] After all, although anti-colonial Indian action during 1675 and 1676 dominated the English settlers' lives, "intertribal warfare did not cease."[85] In this case, the Mohawk attacks of 1676 were simply the latest in a long series, albeit influenced by the English and their conflict.

What happened to Philip's forces from January to June, then, is that they had to fight two wars at once. The only one that most colonists knew or cared about was the one that dominated their lives—the assaults on their homes and villages. However, Philip's Indians were fighting their way south and east while keeping an eye to the north and west. In this context, the three Mohawk attacks make sense. The February rout of Philip's forces from the Hoosick River area drove Philip away from safety, back toward the English; the interception of the party heading to Canada for ammunition cut supply lines to Philip's deteriorating forces; and the June 12 raid on the Indian camp while the warriors were attacking Hadley destroyed people, property, and certainly security.

Other evidence strengthens this view of inter-Indian war still more. When Turner's men launched their dawn raid on the sleeping Indians at the Great Falls on May 18, many of the Indians reportedly ran from their tents crying "Mohawks! Mohawks!"[86] Why else would they make this cry except that they lived in fear of those enemy Indians? A letter that same day sent news from Hadley that "the Maques have fallen upon the enemie & slayne 79 of them." Even though this dispatch was inaccurate, it suggests the influence of the Mohawks. Of similar importance is another report detailing new Mohawk attacks in northern New England.[87]

Finally and most critical, the whole end of the war rests on the Mohawks' attacks. Why else would Philip's forces have left western Massachusetts after June 12 if not for the Mohawks? The Indians had already seen great success in the Connecticut valley, destroying five English towns and pushing settlement south a good twenty-five miles while also recovering at least two old village sites and valuable farming, fishing, and hunting territory. Indian corn was already in the ground, at least at Pocumtuck.[88] Beyond all this, one must consider Philip's alternatives. Moving east toward Boston was no bargain, for that is precisely where greater colonial military strength lay. Yet move east he did. Going south was of course impossible, but why not west or north? Or why not simply stay? Apparently all those routes were eliminated by the Mohawks.

In summary, King Philip's Indians in western Massachusetts were not defeated by the English. The strategies and methods the Indians had employed in the war against the colonists in the Connecticut valley had proven successful, and even the surprising resistance in 1676 resulted more in stalemate than setback. The Indians did not leave the valley because of discouragement, disease, or even the one shocking colonial assault. They left, ultimately, because they were driven out by other Indians. The Mohawks continued to dominate Algonkian tribes in 1676 much as they had throughout the century. This time, though, with the Algonkians already embroiled in an all-out war with the English, the stakes proved higher. Philip's forces succumbed to this dual-front war, and the result was decimation and disintegration.

After the double disaster of June 12—the Indians' setback at Hadley while the Mohawks were attacking their camp—Philip's valley forces broke apart. The surviving Nipmucks and Pocumtucks headed west and north to seek refuge with the Mahicans, Scaticookes, Abenaki, and Caughnawagas; most Wampanoag and Narragansett survivors fled to Canada and Maine; and Philip and his remaining forces headed back south and east where they met their end two months later.[89] Over the course of the war, Philip's army had held some 2,900 warriors, from a total allied Indian population of roughly 11,000. Approximately 2,430 of these Indians were killed or captured in this war.[90]

William Hubbard wrote in 1677, "The *Indians* being thus dispersed in several Ways, were strangely confounded, and destroyed one Parcel after another, until there was none left."[91] As for the Mohawks, they continued to display their strength, their independence, and even their insolence as they made occasional raids into western New England for four more years, taking cattle, attacking settlers, and also killing and capturing a handful of the colonists' surviving "ffriend Indians."[92] Only in 1680, after years of trying, were New England agents able to get the Mohawks to end this strife.[93] To do so, they had to travel to Albany, where the English and Iroquois were forging their

Covenant Chain. New York now held virtually all English influence over the Mohawks—although influence did not mean control.[94]

King Philip's War had already turned into an Indian hunt when Philip himself was shot and killed back home, near his base at Mt. Hope, on August 12, 1676. From that point on, the colonists of southern New England faced virtually no more organized resistance from the Indians. From the Connecticut valley came one isolated report of stolen cattle in August, but basically all was quiet. In general, "central and western Massachusetts appear to have been almost completely denuded of their aboriginal inhabitants."[95] Moreover, from this point on "most Indian-white relations in the interior of southern New England were conducted on an individual rather than a tribal basis."[96] The war had made a decisive mark on the history of Indian-English relations in the region.

Back in the west the settlers of the Connecticut valley began to put the pieces of their lives back together. Yet the pieces did not all fit, for it was a different valley. Death and destruction had taken their toll on the region's three thousand settlers, and where there had been nine towns, there now stood five.

In some senses Pocumtuck had not died. Although its settlers had left their village, many maintained their claims to it. When Nathaniel Sutlieff and John Mun enrolled as two of Captain Turner's 1676 soldiers, they were listed "of Deerfield"—Pocumtuck's alias.[97] Experience Hinsdale's 1676 probate inventory listed his nine cow commons of land "at derefd"—although it was accorded no value at the time.[98] Thus, the idea of this town, and perhaps its resettlement, remained alive. Then, too, some of Pocumtuck's men continued to help fight the war.[99] Pocumtuck's survivors also attained unusual status in the war's last months. Though required to stay in the towns to which they had migrated, the General Court exempted them from having to pay taxes in those towns.[100] In other words, the Court recognized that they had not forsworn their plantation and may well have expected them to return and rebuild.

From the Indian perspective as well, Pocumtuck lived, and for them had even come back to life, at least for nine months.

With the English settlers driven from the village after September 1675, Pocumtuck and other Indians had returned to the site. As they had before the Mohawk assault in 1664, they planted their corn and fished the Great River nearby. Two summers of war all around the site had not altered its role. Through 1675 the English had farmed it and taken its food—although that food was intercepted by the Indians at Bloody Brook. In spring of 1676 the Indians had sown the fields; by autumn the colonists reaped the harvest.

Thus did wheels of life and death and war turn around Pocumtuck in 1675 and 1676. The great wheel of King Philip's War had sprung Indian campaigns from southeastern New England out to the west and to Pocumtuck, and in its revolution it had rolled over and destroyed the young village. Yet even as that great wheel turned there spun a wheel within a wheel. Indians fought other Indians in the west during 1676, and when that wheel had whirled full cycle, Philip and his forces had been turned back toward the east. The great wheel finally dropped Philip back at Mt. Hope and ceased its destructive turn.

Inside the great wheel of colonial-Indian war, tucked inside even the smaller wheel of inter-Indian strife, lay Pocumtuck. It lived and died as both a native American place and a colonial place during these years of war. Famous for a time and important for others, at the end of 1676 it lay empty. The place called Pocumtuck held no one at all.

Pocumtuck Epilogue: "A Dwelling for Owls..."

GENEALOGIES OF early New England commonly include, after children's names and birthdates, the note "d. young." It means that the child died young, often in infancy, a fate which befell perhaps one-quarter of the region's offspring.[1] It is also a fate which a handful of New England's towns suffered, especially as victims of warfare. Pocumtuck was one of those towns.

Yet Pocumtuck's colonial parents were to try again. Although no English ventured back to the place during King Philip's War, by the time the war was over in late summer of 1676 the Connecticut valley held almost no Indians.[2] By the summer of 1677 a handful of Pocumtuck's pioneers had returned.

Only a few men went back to rebuild Pocumtuck. The women and children stayed in the towns below—for the dangers were still great—while fifty-seven-year-old Sergeant John Plympton and a handful of younger men began to rebuild their homes.

Just before dark on September 19, 1677, two years and a day after the slaughter at Bloody Brook, and one year after King Philip had been killed and "his" war ended, a band of Indians struck again. Surprising Pocumtuck's few outnumbered settlers, they killed John Root and captured three men and a boy: Sgt. Plympton, Quinton Stockwell, Benoni Stebbins, and eight-year-old Samuel Russell. Quickly the Indians bound the colonists and led them off. About a mile north of town, the Pocumtuck captives met up with seventeen prisoners from Hatfield—men, women, and children. They had been taken earlier that same day, suffering also the burning of four houses, four barns, and some stacks of corn, and the deaths of twelve townspeople.[3]

With no state of war with any Indians in 1677, valley authorities were not sure where to turn. Immediately they suspected the Mohawks, who had been raiding the area not only before and during but even after King Philip's War. A band of Mohawks had been sighted outside Hatfield on September 18, just one day before the fatal raid.[4] The Connecticut Council wrote as much to New York governor Andros, asking him to see if he could control those natives—and got an immediate, scathing reply. Andros sympathized with the Council and the "wofull disaster & murthers," but he pointed out that the enemy was "from whence unknown" and that accusing him or the Mohawks was "slander."[5]

The Connecticut Council was both right and wrong. It was correct in that the Mohawks did continue raiding into the Connecticut valley until at least 1680. But the Mohawks usually attacked other Indians, not English settlers. More fundamentally, the Council was wrong in this case, for the Indian attackers this time were not Mohawks, as Pocumtuck captive Benoni Stebbins learned during his march and captivity. The twenty-six Indians in the band, eighteen of whom were fighting men, were "Norwooluck" Indians plus one Narragansett, all natives of southern New England, led by the chief Ashpelon.[6] This suggests that native survivors of King Philip's War had attacked as an act of revenge, an ominous sign for the colonists of the valley. Also ominous was the fate of the prisoners. The Indians killed three, and Pocumtuck's Sgt. Plympton died horribly, burned at the stake. Most significantly, though, the others were marched to Canada—to the French. In fact, Stebbins reported that these Indians had fled north and lived with the French in the aftermath of King Philip's War, and that the French had "Incouradged them" to take captives, paying £8 apiece. Furthermore, if this first foray went well, "the French Indians did intend to come wth them the next time."[7]

This assault and captivity of 1677 thereby mark a turning point in the wars that engulfed Pocumtuck for half a century. In this case the Indians who struck came from New England, but the inspiration for their attack did not. It was the last time Pocumtuck suffered at the hands of local Indians, and yet it was only the beginning of decades of French-supported attacks.[8]

After a long and circuitous march north, the band of Indians and captives arrived at the French frontier town of Chambly in early January of 1678. Following the band trekked two heroic Hatfield settlers, Benjamin Waite and Stephen Jennings. Each bereft of his wife and children, the pair carried messages and ransom money north with them. Their courage was rewarded—and the £345 raised in the Massachusetts towns and General Court doubtless helped—as they redeemed the survivors late that winter. By late May the prisoners were back in Albany, where Pocumtuck survivor Quinton Stockwell wrote to his wife that "though wee met with greate afflictions and trouble since I see thee last, yet now here is opportunity of joy and thanksgiving to God."[9]

The mood back in the valley hardly matched Stockwell's joy. The 1670s appeared for many to be "a time of calamitie,"[10] a reflection of the way many New Englanders saw King Philip's War: God's way of striking down a sinful people. In the aftermath of that war, many now considered the valley reduced to a "Wilderness state," a region teetering on the edge of destruction.[11]

Pocumtuck's survivors, scattered among the valley towns, were demoralized. Sergeant Plympton, one of the town's pioneers, was dead. A handful of intrepid young settlers had been driven anew from the plantation site. Still more women had been widowed and children rendered fatherless.[12]

This is not to say that Pocumtuck received no support at this time. To redeem the Hatfield and Pocumtuck captives, in October of 1677 the General Court had sent out directives to help raise money "in recovering of those of our people who are now in captivity with the barbarous heathen."[13] Late that month the Court had directly addressed the exposed towns of Hampshire County, ordering "that each towne then doe endeavor the new modelling the scittuation of their houses, so as to be more compact & live neerer together, for theire better deffence against the Indians." "And as a further provission for the security of those towns," the Court continued, "it is ordered, that a garrison be stated at Deerefeild, and . . . that the inhabitants of the place doe repajre thither this winter . . . and provide for the setling thereof in the spring." The plan also directed a garrison of twenty soldiers to Pocumtuck "to preserve & secure the place," supported in part by "our brethren at Connecticot."[14]

But all this was not enough to assuage the surviving settlers' despair. After a winter without activity, on April 30, 1678, they plaintively responded to the General Court's energetic call: "We the small Remnant that are left of Dearfield's poor inhabitants (that desolate place) . . . prostrate ourselves at yor Worship's feett in this our sorrowful complaints & fervent desires."

Basically, the settlers said, there was little hope for the town: "our estates are wasted . . . we find it hard work to Live in this Iron age . . . our houses have been Rifled & then burnt, our flocks and heards Consumed, the ablest of our Inhabitants killed." In fact, their former settlement had become "a wilderness, a dwelling for owls and a pasture for flocks." In addition, the war had scattered the townspeople throughout the valley, and the minister, Samuel Mather, was languishing and now considering offers from other towns.

In spite of all this, "the Remaining Inhabitants . . . desire [to] returne and plant that place again." It remained "as rich a tract of land as any upon the river," and could be "a bulwark to the other towns," and "disheartening to the enemie." A major problem, however, lay with the town's absentee proprietors, "eight or nine" who "are never like to come to a settlement amongst us" yet who controlled almost half the town's lots and land. Thus, the townspeople "humbly beg . . . that some expedient way might be found out to Remove that impediment."[15] Could the General Court help?

The answer was no. In October 1678, six months after the settlers sent their plea, the General Court answered the petition by quietly asserting that the Court "judgeth it meet to refere the peticoners to the properietors for the attayning of their interest."[16] In other words, if Pocumtuck's settlers wanted to take over the land that absentees held, they were going to have to deal directly with them. The colony was not about to start taking away people's lands, even those of absentee proprietors.

The decision was apparently too much for Pocumtuck's pioneers to overcome. While some individuals or even families may have gone back to the place after 1677,[17] "the town" effectively ceased to exist.

On October 2, 1678, a proclamation was issued from the General Court in Boston. Endorsing a recommendation from "the Commissioners of the United Colonies . . . to prostrate themselves joyntly before God" as a plea for humility and as pardon for transgression, the Court declared Thursday, November 21, "a day of Fasting and Prayer." The Court hoped to call "forth strong and unanimous cries unto God for the obteining of his Grace and favour."[18]

Even the most hopeful and upright people of Pocumtuck must have felt the irony of such a day. Their town had been destroyed, its people scattered. Efforts at resettlement had brought still more death and discouragement. Any former settler of Pocumtuck would have to be a strong Christian indeed not to taste New England's fruits as bitter on this Thanksgiving day of 1678, in the year of the end of Pocumtuck.

PART TWO

Deerfield

FIVE

"Plant that Place Again": Deerfield, 1680-1688

SOMEWHERE in the 1670s a curious thing happened to Pocumtuck. The town's name changed: "Pocumtuck" became "Deerfield." This change evolved slowly and unevenly. As of 1673 all records, whether from Dedham, Hampshire County, or the town itself, called the place Pocumtuck. Yet in 1674 the town book referred to local land "within the township of Deerfield." In the Hampshire County Court session of March 29, 1676, the justices referred to John Allin "of Deerfield alias Pacomtuck." They then proceeded in other cases to use the former name three times—and the latter twice more. In 1679 the Registry of Deeds mirrored the confusion in a reference to land at "Pacumptook alias Deerfield."[1]

No clear reason emerges for this change. Perhaps the deer in the valley and on the hills nearby inspired the colonists; perhaps after King Philip's War townspeople grew weary or resentful of an Indian name for English land; perhaps they just wanted to be in step with their neighboring new "fields"—Southfield (Suffield), Northfield, Swampfield, Brookfield. In any event, the change of name aptly fit the place's fate, for by 1678 Pocumtuck no longer existed.

By 1680, though, settlers both old and new began to build a town at the old site up the Connecticut River valley. Like a phoenix, Deerfield grew out of the ashes and aspirations of Pocumtuck. Within a decade, Deerfield was a growing, independent frontier town.

The New Generation, 1680–1688

Apparently Deerfield had no trouble attracting people for its resettlement. By 1688 Deerfield held about 235 people, a number already greater than Pocumtuck's 200 in 1675, and one which suggests health and vigor in such a new frontier settlement. No fewer than fifty-four men, old and new alike, had settled in town.[2] Many had families: Of those fifty-four, at least forty-one were married.[3] And these couples had produced about 140 living children who now dwelled in town.[4]

Like the group that had built Pocumtuck in the 1670s, Deerfield's 1680s settlers were young. As of 1688, the men averaged about thirty-five years of age, and almost three-quarters were under forty. The women also reflected the new town's youth, averaging about twenty-nine years of age. Deerfield's youthful population is understandable. As a rule, "settlers of new towns were generally young people because the opportunities for gaining wealth and prestige were greater there than in the more established communities." Besides, town building required energy and resourcefulness.[5]

Marriage age further shows the youthfulness of Deerfield's adults. Like Pocumtuck, on average men first married before they reached twenty-five years of age.[6] In fact, nearly three-quarters had married by age twenty-five and more than nine-tenths by age thirty. The women's data are even more striking: an average age at first marriage of nineteen. In this respect, Deerfielders both did and did not match the patterns of other towns in the region. Generally, Deerfield men were like others in New England. They often waited until they had a home and enough land and independence to settle down and raise a family, marrying in their mid-twenties. On the other hand, Deerfield's frontier women married markedly earlier than women in other locales. Deerfield's average of nineteen is the same as Pocumtuck's was, and is one to four years younger than a range of other, less isolated places in New England.[7]

Deerfield's earlier marriages for women apparently came about because it was a frontier town. In this light, it is telling that virtually all adult women in Deerfield were married. Women were a "precious commodity" at such a distant place, fewer in number than the men and obviously needed.[8] At the same time, especially if they migrated to a frontier town like Deerfield with their parents, young women remained at least some burden until they got married and moved out. Thus, women may well have married earlier in frontier outposts such as Deerfield.

People at Deerfield not only married early; when a spouse died, the survivor often married again. This practice did not reflect any lack of love for the departed spouse, but rather was a product of custom and even "sheer functional necessity."[9] A look at Deerfield's forty-one married men shows that at least eighteen married more than once and at least four of those eighteen married three times. As for the women, no fewer than twenty-two of forty-five, also almost half, married more than once. Given these numbers, it is not surprising that widows often married widowers: Deerfield shows at least five such cases during this period.

Compared with other towns in early New England, Deerfield had quite a high rate of remarriage, a sign that death may have been more common on the frontier than elsewhere. Given the relative youth of Deerfield's adult population in 1688, the remarriage rate seems still more grim.[10] As a young frontier outpost with open lands and opportunities, Deerfield may have attracted young adults who had recently lost spouses and were seeking a "fresh start." On the other hand, the difficulties of frontier life may have caused a higher death—and therefore remarriage—rate. Certainly the fourteen women of Pocumtuck who were widowed in 1675 could attest to that.

Given Deerfield's patterns of early marriage and frequent remarriage, it is not surprising that the town held a large number of children. As of 1688, 36 Deerfield couples had produced 174 children, 89 boys and 85 girls. Nine children were reported to have died young, though the number was doubtless higher.[11] While couples had as many as seventeen children, as of 1688 Deerfield families had borne an average of just under five children each. This makes Deerfield families one to two children larger than in other New England towns, a difference attributable perhaps to the earlier marriage age for women.[12]

Since Deerfield in the 1680s was being built over the ruins of 1670s Pocumtuck, the town faced the possibility of two distinct groups settling the place: returnees and new pioneers. Overwhelmingly, however, the latter dominated the settlement. As of 1688 the Pocumtuck survivors comprised only one-fifth of Deerfield's fifty-four townsmen.

A breakdown of the ages of Deerfield's men further illustrates the gap between old and new. Deerfield, like Pocumtuck had been, was a "young person's" town, something quite understandable and even necessary for the success of a young frontier outpost. In keeping with this, the men who came anew to Deerfield in the 1680s were much younger than the returnees from Pocumtuck. They averaged thirty-two years of age, while the Pocumtuck returnees averaged forty-eight—the older survivors of an earlier, different town.

And Pocumtuck's hold on the place kept slipping away. By 1704 six of the eighteen Pocumtuck returnees were dead. In addition, the two big clans which had been such a large part of Pocumtuck's generation of 1675 barely survived. Of the Hawks family, John Hawks returned, but neither his mother nor his three sisters did, all of whom had lived there with their husbands and families before 1675. The Hinsdales' status had changed even more dramatically. With five family men killed during King Philip's War, it was not until Samuel Hinsdale's son Mehuman, Pocumtuck's firstborn English child, reached maturity that Deerfield had another Hinsdale man in town.

While Pocumtuck survived in Deerfield in limited fashion, Dedham's links disappeared entirely. In the decade after 1680, most Dedham proprietors still holding land and cow commons in Deerfield sold them off to the town's new residents. While a few claims lingered into the 1700s,[13] by 1688 not a single Dedham proprietor lived in Deerfield nor did any even appear on the town's division of lands. Less than twenty years after the Dedham proprietors had drawn lots for Pocumtuck's lands, the people who had received the eight-thousand-acre grant were gone from Deerfield's life. The town belonged overwhelmingly to its residents.

Deerfield did maintain one of Pocumtuck's patterns. Its new men and women, too, came most often from close by, moving upriver from the valley below.[14] Three-fifths of Deerfield's new men came from the closest three valley towns of Northampton, Hadley, and Hatfield. Another quarter came from valley towns farther downriver: Springfield, Suffield, Hartford, and New Haven. The remaining handful came from the Bay—from Boston, Roxbury, and Watertown.

The women's story reads similarly. Over three-quarters of Deerfield's women were local, coming from Northampton, Hadley, and Hatfield—or from within Deerfield itself, where these settlers' daughters often married resident men. Virtually all others came from scattered towns farther down the valley: Brookfield, Farmington, Windsor, Wethersfield, Pomfret, New Haven. Not one woman of this generation, however, came directly from the Bay.

In sum, Deerfield's new men and women were overwhelmingly valley people who moved short distances to get to Deerfield. Throughout Hampshire County in the late seventeenth and early eighteenth centuries, the constant threats of Indians and the frontier forced more consolidation than expansion.[15] Thus, unlike the geographic or speculative leaps of the Dedham grantees, moving to Deerfield during this period reflected an incremental, not radical, step for its pioneers. The townpeople knew the locale, or at least knew much about it, and certainly knew the region. Deerfield still stood as a frontier outpost, but the post was manned by pioneers who inched—not swept—the frontier ahead.

While this new group of pioneers settled Deerfield, a small number of absentee landowners retained rights in town. Interestingly, three of the valley's ministers held cow commons in Deerfield in 1688. And so, still, did John Pynchon. Always an owner, never a resident, Pynchon retained considerable land and rights in Deerfield through the 1680s.[16]

Pynchon's connections with Deerfield and the surrounding area extended well beyond his ownership of land in town. In

1685 he convinced the Massachusetts General Court to grant
him one thousand acres "nere to Millers River, above Dearefeild, & nere ye great river," so that he could start a mining
venture—"to finde out metall."[17] More important, he maintained many ties to Deerfield through his role as the region's
dominant trader.[18] As of 1688, at least one-fifth of Deerfield's
men were actively involved in trade, rental, or other form of
exchange with Pynchon.

Like Pocumtuck's earlier generation, many of the debts
Deerfielders owed to Pynchon were small and the ledger of
items short. In 1678 Joseph Barnard owed 3s. 4d. for two quarts
of rum; in the early 1680s he went £2 into debt for a list of
"severalls"—cloth, buttons, knives. Cordwainer Godfrey Nims
paid off over £4 worth of debts accumulated in the 1670s for
items like cotton ribbon, sewing materials, and hide leather by
giving over to Pynchon several pairs of shoes he had made.
Sometimes the debts proved more weighty. Simon Beaman's
father had run up debts of £47.4.4 by 1675, and the family
added to those in the next five years. To pay them off, the whole
family went to work for Pynchon in 1680, and even that effort
was not enough to retire the debt.[19] With general stores in
Northampton and Hatfield, the Springfield trader kept his lines
of credit to Deerfield open and flowing.[20]

Also important for many Deerfielders was Pynchon's use of
his lands in town. In 1677 he engaged Philip Mattoon in an
eleven-year lease of one large holding. Mattoon put himself in
a deep hole with Pynchon from the very beginning, for he
signed the lease just months before Pocumtuck was attacked by
Indians and abandoned. Not only did Mattoon thus have to pay
rent on empty land during the years before resettlement, but
the contract required that he pay an escalating annual rent,
starting at thirty shillings the first year and ending up at eighty
shillings the eleventh. It further required the young lessor to
build Pynchon "a good dwelling house . . . well built & com-
pleately furnished," thirty by twenty feet with ten-foot ceilings,
plus a barn forty-eight by twenty-four feet with fourteen-foot
ceilings. For his part, Pynchon supplied "Two good . . . Cows."[21]
Mattoon further compounded his indebtedness by running up

a string of debts for "severals" between 1686 and 1693. And Mattoon was hardly Pynchon's only local real estate client: Several other Deerfield men either leased or bought land from the Springfield merchant.[22]

In sum, Pynchon kept extensive lines of exchange open with Deerfield through the 1680s. Whether through small purchases at his general stores or large investments in land, he maintained a tightly spun web of credit and debt.

Yet another striking characteristic of Deerfield in the 1680s is the number of townspeople who had gone to court for breaking the law. No fewer than thirteen of the town's fifty-four men—and four of its women—had faced county court actions in the years before 1688.

The cases that went to the Hampshire County Court showed a broad range of offenses. Five future Deerfield men and three women were fined during the 1670s "for wearing of Silk . . . in a fflaunting manner [or] for Long Haire and other Extravegences." At first glance this action seems unimportant. However, the court record shows that the justices were deadly serious, for apparently a youthful rebellion had broken out in western Massachusetts. When the judges inveighed against such acts as "Contrary to honest & sober order" and "not Becomeing a Wilderness State," they did not merely cry idly in the wilderness. Instead, they admonished and fined twenty-four young people in Northampton, eighteen in Springfield, four in Westfield, and twenty-three in Hadley and Hatfield. Coupled with a vague yet disquieting court report of a February 1676 riot in Hadley—what one historian has termed "a general attack on all authority"—involving at least one future Deerfielder, the era of King Philip's War appears to have been a time of great turmoil for the valley.[23]

Other criminal activities involving future Deerfield settlers in the fifteen years before 1688 show a range of misdeeds. Carnal temptation certainly took its toll. In 1674 Martin Smith was fined twenty shillings "for trying to kiss Jedediah Strong's wife on the street." Three years before that, nineteen-year-old Thomas Wells was taken to court "for miscreant acting wth ye Negro wench servant to Mr. Russel." The partners had different versions of what transpired, "shee sayeth he threw her down, he denyes it . . . sayeth she set by him & pulled up her clothes & lay bare before him." In any case, Wells confessed to his "sinful dalliance" and was to be "well whipted on his naked body by his father in presence of the constable"—or pay a twenty-shilling fine.[24] Also serious, if common, was the 1678 case of John and Mary Evans, in court for "ffornication . . . a matter heinouse & Shameful." The problem lay not in the Evanses' marriage, but rather in the fact that their first child arrived well before their ninth month of marriage. For this crime John Evans bore twenty lashes, and Mary ten.[25]

The Stebbins family had its own ledger of troubles. As discussed above, John Stebbins, Jr., had been found guilty of being an accessory to a 1667 crime in Northampton involving break-ins and robberies while townspeople were in church. That caper also included a plan among three "lads" to run away to Canada, all of this abetted by a local Indian. In the years after 1680, John, a former Pocumtuck resident, returned to Deerfield, while the other two participants in that escapade, John's brother Benoni Stebbins and Godfrey Nims, also settled in town.

Each of these three Deerfield settlers also lengthened his own criminal record after the 1667 incident. In 1674 John was "complained of" for "lascivious carriage." In 1685 Godfrey was convicted and fined "for defaming or slaundering" Mr. Joseph Hawley of Northampton over the fair sale of a house. Benoni compiled the longest record. The string included a 1676 fine for wearing silk; a 1678 fine upon his wife for wearing silk, which Benoni refused to pay, thereby "openly affronting the Court" and drawing his own fine; a 1680 case of "non payment of a debt" to John Pynchon; another nonpayment of debt, in 1682, to Joseph Parsons of Springfield; and a 1684 case involving Benoni's failure to care properly for his apprentice.[26]

Still more Deerfield men were involved in still other cases. Jonathan Wells was fined ten shillings for failing to attend to his duties as a juror for the county court. Joseph Barnard, who along with his wife and Wells had been fined in the 1676 "silk" case, was convicted in 1681 of selling liquor to the Indians, as was his partner, future Deerfielder Joseph Seldon. Seldon compounded his problems, and got fined forty shillings two years later, by "buying furres of the Indians" while again bartering with liquor.[27] Philip Mattoon's crimes were more violent. In 1678 he was convicted of card playing "at an unseasonable tyme of the Night," striking and threatening one man, abusing another's cellar and goods, and "breach of the King's peace."[28]

Last, James Brown perpetrated a particularly long "train of abuses" before coming to Deerfield. In September of 1674 Brown went to court for his "gross miscarriages in Breaking up ye House & seller of Thomas Meakins, Sr." and stealing nine gallons of "strong liquors & doing other damages." For this crime Brown had to pay triple damages, plus £3 in court costs, and, gravest of all, he and his partner were "Branded on their fforheads for their Burglary with ye letter B." Yet even this failed to settle Brown down. At the very next court session, in March of 1675, he was "complained of" by Hatfield's John Graves "for breach of ye Peace . . . beating him about ye head & face" while Graves was that winter in the meadow loading his sled with wood. At that same court session he was further accused of "Prophaning ye Sabath Laughing & Sporting in ye time of Publique Ordinance," for which he spent four hours in the Northampton stocks. In light of all this, a 1684 debt action against him seems minor, almost an "improvement."[29] By 1688 Brown had settled in Deerfield.

While these actions yield no clear conclusion, the fact that nearly one-quarter of the town's men were convicted of some crime in the county court is significant. Between inappropriate dress and sins of the flesh there emerges a picture of a young town, a frontier outpost, that was a refuge for valley people who had previously gotten in trouble with the law. Perhaps these were people who felt that Puritan rules of propriety were too rigid. It is also possible that, as the valley's rudest and most exposed town, Deerfield was the region's "escape valve," the place to which people in trouble could flee. Deerfield's demographics—its small and youthful population, preponderance of men, and lack of established families—also suggest greater likelihood of trouble than in more established towns.[30]

Although it is difficult to know whether Deerfield's citizenry
was unusual, there are some clues. On the one hand, the frontier town of Kent, Connecticut, endured no apparent problems
other than a general pattern of debts, most of which were settled without recourse to the courts.[31] On the other hand, seventeenth-century Springfield was "a contentious, disruptive
and factious" town which saw a great deal of crime. John Pynchon's court record from 1660 to 1690 was filled with records of
Springfield residents much like those of Deerfielders, although
Springfield seems to have been far more riddled with ongoing
private or family feuds.[32]

Less diverse, stratified, and strife-torn than Springfield, while
at the same time far more isolated and alone, Deerfield appears
to have been more a haven for former troublemakers than a site
of continuing criminality. In other words, it appears to have
been a place for people to make a fresh start. Still, that men
with such records of abuses could settle in town makes it appear
that Deerfield, like Pocumtuck, was not a utopian, covenanted
community of entirely upright citizens. No enclave of families
pledged to build and protect it; no clear goals or vision marked
its founding; no spirit of community mission dominated its early
years. Deerfield was a frontier town—not the mythical lawless,
hell-raising town of the American West, but not a 1630s closed
utopian commune, either. It was a new settlement on a still
fragile frontier that evidently was willing to take in just about
anyone who wanted to move there.[33]

A general profile of Deerfield's settlers in the 1680s looks
much like that of Pocumtuck's pioneers of the 1670s. Each held
a small group of older, established, financially secure men who
provided leadership and stability. The majority of men in each
town were "frontier farmers"—young, with small families,
without much money or property, often in debt, and occasionally leaving behind previous troubles in other towns. For them,
Deerfield provided a classic "fresh start": land and a share in a
new town's growth, governance and opportunity, all tempered
by the risks of life in a raw, rude, exposed new settlement. Men
with special skills—a cordwainer, a weaver, carpenters, a minister—again comprised a small part of the town's population.

Most also farmed: Deerfield could not yet afford pure specialization in occupation. Young, single, independent "hired hands"
also continued to play a role, especially by providing the town
with vital labor.

If there was a group which made Deerfield different from
Pocumtuck, it was the "settlers' sons." Obviously, Deerfield
and towns like it continually had young men growing into maturity and independence from their families, but this group
seems particularly noteworthy in Deerfield, where so many did
not move up and out but stayed. In this respect, Deerfield
mirrors the experience of Andover, Massachusetts, where over
80 percent of the first generation's sons stayed in town. In
Andover that degree of persistence has been attributed to "pro-
longed paternal authority and influence over sons."[34] In Deerfield, however, circumstances were sharply different. As a
frontier settlement anxious to build up its population, Deerfield *gave* new lands to settlers' sons.

The women of Deerfield are less visible in the historical
record but were no less important to the life of the town. Deerfield's women played, on a daily basis, a multiplicity of roles
that were essential to the town's very survival. Housewife and
mother, consort and mistress, neighbor and Christian—they
were all of these.[35] In addition, they often helped their husbands with their work: In a new town like Deerfield, struggling
to get on its feet, men and women did whatever was needed.
Given Deerfield's youth and poverty, no wife could afford to do
otherwise. And virtually all of Deerfield's women were indeed
married. Throughout this range of roles, then, women were
instrumental in building the town. Indeed, Deerfield's women
merit recognition, even in the routine life to which most of
them were confined, for they were as vital in their ways to the
town's survival as the men.

1680–1688: Reconstruction

The town these men and women built in the 1680s grew
steadily. After the General Court had turned aside the Pocumtuck survivors' request for aid for resettlement in 1678, those

townspeople had abandoned all efforts for two years. By 1680, though, a group of Pocumtuck's survivors tried again. When "some of the Proprs of the Town or place comonly called Deerfeild" showed "themselves desirous" that the county court "appoint some meet persons. . . . In order to the setling of Plantations new beginning," the Hampshire County Court responded. On March 30, 1680, the court named a committee of five prominent county men to oversee resettlement. For the next eight years these five men—all justices of the peace in the county during this period—took on the "complicated and time-consuming duties" of organizing and overseeing settlement of the fledgling town.[36]

Within a year their work bore fruit. On December 12, 1680, the committee brought together "a meeting of ye Comittee & proprietors of Deerfield att Northampton." The meeting, though brief, was not without its achievements. The main efforts involved granting lands and proprietary shares, tasks that would fill the town's ledger for the next decade. Although only three men were granted any cow commons at that gathering, it is noteworthy that all three were new proprietors. Deerfield was enlisting new pioneers for its venture.[37]

Over the next year, the town followed the Massachusetts laws for those "people who are intended to resettle the Villages deserted in the late war." They made application to the governor and council for resettlement; their appointed committee for resettlement went to "view and consider the place"; and they petitioned the General Court so that the committee could receive full power for "the better regulation of ye prudential affaires there."[38] All was in order and so the General Court granted the petition on May 27, 1681.

It is quite possible that the first of Deerfield's new inhabitants moved up the valley that summer, for by the next two meetings of the committee and proprietors in March of 1682, the group was listed simply "of Deerfield" and no longer additionally "att Northampton." At these meetings, the committee and proprietors addressed a problem which had plagued Pocumtuck: absentee proprietors. As Pocumtuck's survivors had found in the late 1670s, speculators and absentee owners could clog up town settlement and expansion by letting their lands and home lots lie vacant. In fact, the March 30, 1682, meeting granted land to four new settlers—but all "on the North [far] side of the Deerfield river at the mouth of the green river," some three miles north of town.[39] Since so much of the land in and around the town center was locked in older proprietary holdings, new settlers could get land only away from the town center. In light of this problem, the proprietors and committee decided that in the future settlers would gain title to newly granted lands only when they did "come and settle in Deerfield and Inhabit there three years."[40]

The issue of absenteeism clearly nagged at Deerfield's builders, so much so that the citizens even petitioned the General Court again, as they had in 1678, for release of all lands and proprietary rights of those owners not actively involved with resettlement. Here the Court proved "not . . . satisfied" with such a Draconian measure, though it did suggest that if each proprietor gave up one-tenth of his acreage, the town could garner enough land to provide "a very probable way to gaine more usefull inhabitants for planting & settling." Taking land from "orphants," however, as the townspeople had actually suggested, was unacceptable.[41]

Even with the continuing problem of absenteeism, Deerfield was alive and growing. By late spring of 1682, the General Court acknowledged that the town had not merely proprietors but "inhabitants." Still, town institutions were fragile. For one thing, there was no minister. Reverend Samuel Mather never rejoined his flock at Deerfield. As the inhabitants' woeful 1678 petition had hinted, after Bloody Brook Mather had removed down to Hatfield. There, as he despaired of waiting out his calling to an abandoned settlement, he began to weigh other offers. A bequest of land at Westfield from his father, Timothy, in 1677 may have tempted him further. By 1680 he had endured long enough and headed for Branford, Connecticut. Two years later he took his place at the pulpit at Windsor, where he would spend the next forty-six years.[42] Not until 1686 would Deerfield have another minister.

Nor did Deerfield have its own independent local govern-

ment. Until 1688 Deerfield continued to live under the control
of the town's outside "prudential committee." There were no
slates of town officers elected, no regular town meetings. Settlers dealt with only one local issue—land—and even there the
outside committee oversaw all transactions. Perhaps symbolic
of this restive time is the fact that of the four men who had
pleaded Deerfield's case for resettlement in 1678, two never
even returned. [43]

At least townspeople actively participated in the town government's most important single activity, the distribution of
land. The drive for Deerfield's rich farmland took different
forms. Some men leased land in town. [44] More significantly,
some of the previous landowners at Pocumtuck began to sell
out. Virtually no one had sold land between 1675 and 1682, for
after the war the land in the abandoned town had been practically worthless. With resettlement, though, the land had value
again. William Bartholomew had given up on the Deerfield
venture soon after the failed 1678 petition and moved his family
from their temporary home in Hatfield down to Branford, Connecticut. In 1685, he got rid of his Deerfield holdings, selling
half his twenty cow commons and two-thirds of his house lot to
former Hatfield neighbor Daniel Belding. Similarly, William
Clark, Jr., showed no interest in maintaining his father's stake
upriver of his home in Northampton. In 1685 he sold his holdings to Hadley's Henry White. [45]

Deerfield's new settlers had to be pleased with another pattern of sales: A number of Deerfield absentee landowners with
holdings dating back to the 1670s sold them off during the
1680s. In 1683 Eleazer Farrington of Boston sold off land and
rights that his father, John, of Dedham, had held since 1671.
They went to Northampton's Isaac Sheldon, Sr., the patriarch
of a Deerfield family that within a decade would produce a pair
of vital town officers. In 1686 Charlestown's Peter Turffs, Sr.,
helped another Deerfield family settle when he sold off two
discrete divisions of land and two corresponding house lots to
Jonathan Wells. A year later Turffs sold off yet a third original
Dedham holding to Deerfield's Simon Beaman. Like Farrington, Turffs had held all his lands and rights, intact and un-

touched, since the first Dedham proprietors' division in 1671.[46] And these were precisely the kind of unused holdings which had so demoralized Pocumtuck's resettlers. But now the spaces on the town plat were being filled by owner-settlers. By 1688 nearly one-sixth of *all* Deerfield's proprietary lands and house lots—lands that had lain empty—were filled.[47]

Inheritance of Pocumtuck lands proved to be another key issue in Deerfield's resettlement. When fourteen Pocumtuck men died at Bloody Brook, they left a thicket of legal problems of land ownership through which their descendants had to hack. Some cases were simple, as wives and children survived to share inheritances. But when wives legally entitled to maintain land for their young children remarried and moved, who could use the land? It took some time for Deerfield newcomer John Evans, the new husband of Mary Hinsdale, Experience's widow, to get court approval for use of his stepchildren's lands.[48]

For all of this, however, the single most important way that Deerfield attracted people to settle was simply by offering them land and, in some cases, proprietary rights. From December 1680 until April 1687, the "Inhabitants of the town" made fifty-two grants of land, either to prospective newcomers or to residents seeking additional lands. These fifty-two grants went to forty-one different men, only four of whom had been settlers at Pocumtuck before 1675.[49]

For the most part Deerfield parceled out land grants in a clear and coherent way. During this period, twenty-six of the forty-one men who received grants got house lots, almost always of four acres. Deerfield was seeking settlers, not just inviting local interest or speculation. Of the remaining fifteen grantees, almost all were settlers who had house lots from previous grants or purchases and who now received additional holdings. These ranged from odd lots of woodland and house-lot extensions to the exchange of parcels and even one grant of "an Island" in the Deerfield River.

The geographical pattern of the granted house lots shows still more of the townspeople's desire to make Deerfield work in the face of absentee owners. Of the house lots granted, only five were for sites on the town's main street. This is understandable since the town's original forty-three house lots had been divided and granted back in 1671, and only proprietors who had failed to pay their taxes had lost their lands to the town. Thus, as of the 1680s the old main street was largely blocked to new settlement. Instead, all the remaining grants of home lots came in two newly created hamlets, each roughly two miles from Meetinghouse Hill.

The town planners first looked south, to a little plateau which they called Plumtree Plain, or Wapping. Here they marked out a new street and placed eight house lots along its north-south axis. The second new hamlet, called Green River, lay in the opposite direction, two miles north of town and across the Deerfield River at the place where the Green River joined the Deerfield. Here Deerfield's planners laid out twenty house lots, ten on each side of an east-west street. By 1688 they had parceled out fifteen of those lots. To make the Green River settlement viable, the town also gave nine of the new "northern" pioneers twenty acres of farmland up in the same area across the river. In this way the settlers would not have to make daily river crossings to farm their land.

In this expansion to two new village sites, Deerfield was following a seventeenth-century New England town pattern: When a town got too crowded, it planted new settlements nearby. Much as the people of Dedham had done in establishing Medfield and Wrentham, Deerfield had sown new seeds at Wapping and Green River. However, Deerfield had no intention of granting these hamlets their independence, nor did their citizens desire it. All were Deerfield residents, full-fledged voters at town meeting, often leaders of the community, expected as much as "main streeters" to attend church. The town center might not be able to hold any more new settlers, yet the town continued to grow.[50]

Even as Deerfield was granting new lands to settlers during the 1680s, it also gave out a flurry of what were called "wanting lands." These were lands which townspeople found "wanting," or lacking, when they measured their lands and compared their findings to the legal, recorded size of their grants. Inhabitants grew concerned about such shortages as early as 1684. In response, the committee for resettlement appointed a three-man commission "to Messure mens allotments . . . and to bring an account of what Land is wanting in every mans allotment." Aided by two other residents, the group was then empowered "to lay out to such as want land as neer as they can to each mans want." Since the land shortages often involved prime, well-located first-division acreage, the commission had to consider both quantity and "what it wants on quality."[51]

From late 1684 to spring of 1688 Deerfield made thirty-three grants of wanting land to twenty-nine different settlers, both old and new. Land shortages most often appeared in the first-division farmlands, and since this best and best-situated land could not really be replaced with equal acreage of equal value, the town usually compensated for quality with quantity. Although occasionally wanting land was matched "acre for acre" with other town lands, or at a ratio of 1.5:1 or 2:1, most Deer-fielders received three acres of new land for every acre found wanting, and in two cases the compensation reached a level of four to one. The acreage was often significant, too. Although a few decisions involved only an acre or two, the average grant for wanting land was almost eighteen acres. Five petitioners received over thirty acres of compensation, and one was granted sixty-four acres for sixteen lost acres of meadowland.[52]

While one might expect to find some explicit *quid pro quo* behind all this granting of land, there really was none. All persons in town with home lands or meadowlands abutting the meadow's boundaries had to "maintain the meddow fence lying against their so granted lands,"[53] but that was standard for any New England town which employed a common-field system. Rather, Deerfield was just anxious to get settled and stable, and the best way to do that was to give settlers land. Eighty-five separate grants of land in fewer than eight years, only one-seventh of which went to returning settlers or their heirs, sounds like a vast giveaway. In fact, it was considerable, totaling well over eleven hundred acres.[54] Yet it was not unreasonable. For one thing, Deerfield had abundant acreage—a township seven miles square—so there was plenty of land available, even after all this. For another, an isolated, once destroyed frontier outpost like Deerfield needed to attract settlers. While memories of Bloody Brook and the destruction of Pocumtuck had receded, those events were only a decade past. Thus, if Deerfield's cost for getting new settlers was land, then the cost was not high. After all, in the late medieval, subsistence-farming world of seventeenth-century New England, land was the most important thing a person could own. It meant home, shelter, food, security, independence. In this light, Deerfield did not pay a bad price at all to secure a growing population.

While the town's resettlement committee and inhabitants encouraged new settlers with grants of land, the town proprietors—the group legally impowered to distribute town land— were also at work. In 1688 they dramatically narrowed the difference between proprietors and "mere inhabitants" when they decided to parcel out wood lots along "Long Hill," a long ridge south and east of town. These lots were apportioned, as were all such divisions in Deerfield, based on the number of shares each proprietor held.[55] Here Deerfield followed the standard pattern of land distribution for early New England towns. What made this division so noteworthy, though, is that of the fifty-one men listed to receive wood lots—and therefore holding proprietary shares—thirty-three were new to Deerfield; only eighteen were from among the 1670s settlers of Pocumtuck. In other words, in addition to receiving grants of land, almost all the newly established settlers in Deerfield had now also received proprietary rights. This meant not only more land for each in 1688, but also a voice in proprietors' meetings and a share in any future divisions of town lands. Pocumtuck's "old order" had changed indeed.

For all this upheaval, the wood-lot list also shows that the town's settlers perpetuated the great care that their Dedham ancestors had shown in establishing clear title for all lands. The 1688 list of cow commons totals 557 shares. Subtracting from this the 33 new shares granted in 1680–1682, there remains a total of 524 commons—only one from the total that the Dedham proprietors had determined back in 1659. It is an impressive sign of consistency and care amidst the rapid turnover and uncertainty of the early frontier. It also serves as a reminder of how much land mattered in this 1600s agrarian world.

Although land issues dominated Deerfield's official records through the 1680s, the town displayed other signs of growing maturity and independence. A most heartening sign that the new plantation was taking hold came in 1686, when townspeople shifted their attention from the soil to the soul. At the January 5 meeting that year the town voted "to Incourage Mr. John Williams to settle amongst them to dispense the blessed word of truth unto them." To entice the twenty-one-year-old minister, just three years out of Harvard, the citizens made him a generous offer: to build him a house "42 foot long 20 foot wide with a lentoo"—a lean-to—"on the back side," plus fence his four-acre home lot on Meetinghouse Hill, build him a barn within two years, "break up his plowing land," and give him a starting salary of £60, with the promise to increase that to £80 within four or five years.[56] Whether for the salary and benefits, the proximity to his classmate and cousin William Williams just settling as a minister at Hatfield, the chance to leave teaching in Dorchester, or perhaps just the appeal of Deerfield's ministerial post, Williams accepted the position.

From all indications it was a fine match. Williams took the pulpit by the summer of 1686.[57] A year later he strengthened his bond with the valley when he married Eunice Mather, daughter of the late Northampton minister Eleazer Mather. The townspeople of Deerfield soon showed their approval of the young pastor by granting him "a certain piece" of meadowland in December of his first year in town, twenty acres more up on the Green River the next winter, and by 1688 eight cow commons' worth of land and rights.[58] The ultimate confirmation of this match came on October 17, 1688, when, in the presence of his townspeople and fellow clergymen, John Williams was ordained a minister at Deerfield. The town's flock had found a faithful shepherd, one who would guide them for the next forty-one years.[59]

The other major sign that Deerfield had reached maturity came in the realm of Deerfield government. Progress here was not as dramatic as an ordination could show. Instead, starting from the county-appointed absentee committee in Northampton in 1680, there gradually evolved in Deerfield an independent town government. For the first few years after resettlement efforts began, the "prudential committee" directly ran or oversaw town governance. The committee could decide almost any local matters, from whom to allow into town to the rules for land distribution; in the absence of a minister, it could even choose the songs and sermons for appointed readers on Sundays.[60] As late as 1686 the inhabitants were still acting "with the Consent of the Comitte," "allowed by the Comitte," "by consent of the proprietors with the Committe," even in granting small parcels of land.[61] But after 1686 these overseers began to pull back. In late winter of 1686/1687, although still under committee direction, Deerfield elected its first slate of local officials. The town voted six men, including one Pocumtuck veteran, to be "select men Towns men or overseers" and to "Continue in office until othr be Chosen and they discharged."[62] To assist the selectmen the town also chose a tax commissioner, a town clerk, three "serveighers," and three haywards. The open-ended terms of office are curious, but perhaps telling. Evidently this group would take over town governance but would stay under the committee's supervision until the committee approved the normal annual elections that were standard for independent Massachusetts towns. Thus, although the town directed its selectmen to act "prudentialy," the committee remained cautious. The December 20, 1687, town meeting record shows this, noting that clerk Joseph Barnard dutifully "attested" to the meeting notes "before ye Comitte," which then "allowed these notes & grants."[63]

Independence finally came in 1688. That year, which saw the end of the floodtide of land grants, and likely saw a flood of emotion with John Williams's ordination, also marked Deerfield's emergence to full-fledged status as a Massachusetts town. The meeting notes for that year now referred only to "the Inhabitants of Deerfield." No note of "the Committee" occurred in any form. A year later the records began: "30th May 1689:

Att a Leagal town meeting in Deerfield. . . ." The town was truly on its own.[64]

The year 1688 proved important for all of Massachusetts for another reason. That year marked the end of the short-lived Dominion of New England under its hated English governor Edmund Andros. In that context it is possible that Deerfield seized its "leagal" status to fend off possible problems of rightful control in the face of Andros's threats to Puritan land titles. However, the town had not depended directly on the General Court, nor had the Court been heard from, for many years. The Court-appointed "Committee" had directed Deerfield's affairs for over eight years. By 1689, with abundant lands distributed to a new generation of settlers, an independent ministry, and a working town government, Deerfield was ready to live on its own. Andros's threat may have sharpened Deerfield's desire to show its freedom in May 1689, but essentially the town had already eased from committee control to independence.

As 1689 dawned, Deerfield's hundred men and women could feel pleased about what they had wrought. From the ashes of Pocumtuck had arisen a new town with a largely new population. It was not a covenanted, closed New England community, and it had its share of less than upright citizens. In fact, it appears to be no accident that the young frontier town of Deerfield—the most isolated and exposed town in all of western Massachusetts—held a large number of newcomers who were young, had debts, or had been in previous trouble with the law. Yet, however young, however fragile or tenuous, Deerfield was alive. It had taken almost a decade for the town to regain people, political order, a minister, and independence. Now it could hope to enjoy a steadier, more settled existence.

SIX

A Communal Frontier Town

DEERFIELD MATURED in the years between 1689 and 1704. No longer a little village consumed by rebuilding and controlled by outsiders, it achieved a steady rhythm of life that the struggling outposts of 1670s Pocumtuck and 1680s Deerfield never had. By 1704 Deerfield displayed a largely closed, closely knit population; almost universal male participation in town governance; an interdependent, subsistence agrarian economy; and a high level of church membership. Deerfield hardly met the popular modern concept of the frontier as a haven of democracy, opportunity, and individualism. Rather, it was a small, poor, inbred communal outpost.

One sign of the increasingly closed nature of the town is that, essentially, Deerfield did not grow. The town that held about 240 people in 1688 held roughly 260 in 1704.[1]

Not that there were not internal changes. Of the fifty-four men who had resettled the town in the 1680s, little over half remained fifteen years later. Fifteen had died by 1704—a sobering mortality rate of almost 30 percent. While some of those men's families stayed and their widows remarried, the town was struck hard by these losses. In addition, eleven other men, including at least seven with families, had left by 1704.

Yet Deerfield maintained its size—largely through the emergence of a new generation. Between 1689 and 1704 thirty-nine new men and twenty-six new women became Deerfield citizens. Of these, twenty-two of the men and seventeen of the women were "Deerfield children"—the sons and daughters of settlers.[2] This provides a mixed message about the town's health and growth. On the one hand, Deerfield had survived long enough to produce its own next generation. In fact, at least eight of Deerfield's "sons" married Deerfield "daughters."[3] On the other hand, only seventeen "outside" men and nine "outside" women settled in Deerfield during these fifteen years. Apparently the attractions of New England's northwest frontier had ebbed.[4]

With Deerfield's population so inbred, it is not surprising that many of the townspeople were bound in a web of family ties. Although no one or two families dominated the town as the Hinsdales and Hawkses had before Bloody Brook, Deerfield was certainly a "family town." The Smeads provide a good example of this. William and Elizabeth Smead had helped settle both Pocumtuck in the 1670s and Deerfield in the 1680s. Seven of their children settled in Deerfield with spouses who were also residents. The Smeads thus tied together eight different Deerfield families. And the ties had further twists: Sisters Judith and Thankful Smead married brothers Eleazer and John Hawks, and Mehitable Smead married Jeremiah Hull and, after his death, Godfrey Nims—all men from Deerfield.

Yet late-seventeenth-century Deerfield was not entirely English, local, and inbred. A handful of Indians, blacks, and Frenchmen lived in and around the village in the years before 1704.

Although the Connecticut valley's Indians had been decimated by King Philip's War, a few scattered natives remained in the region. Hampshire County's deeds of 1686 reveal that an Indian living below Springfield was upheld as "the true & lawfull heyre" of some Westfield lands that were previously his grandfather's. In 1694 an Indian was brought to trial for the theft of a horse and some other items; here the county court was at least allowing Indians due process. Most intriguing, Deerfield knew of the continuing presence of Indians because in 1703 the town witnessed the marriage of resident Robert Price's twenty-year-old daughter, Elizabeth, to "Andrew Stephens, an Indian."[5]

Blacks, too, were part of the Connecticut valley scene—though virtually all as slaves or "servants." In 1692 a black couple was brought before the county court on a charge of fornication. The court record a decade later reveals a "Betty Negro" being sentenced to ten lashes for her "Base Toung," a charge corroborated by "Tom Negro." A 1694 Hatfield assessor's list gives evidence that the town's minister, Reverend William Williams, as well as a number of other inhabitants owned "negro" slaves. In Deerfield itself, a list of townspeople in 1704 includes the names Parthena and Frank, two "Negroes" who were servants of the Reverend John Williams; a second list includes a possibly free black man listed only as "primus, Negro." At his death in 1733 former Deerfielder John Sheldon (by then of Hartford) owned a black couple, their child, three other "boys," and a girl.[6]

A handful of Frenchmen also lived in and around Deerfield. In September 1692 John Butcher, "A Frenchman," went to court in Springfield for breach of Sabbath, while within four months "Captain John German the French man" was charged with "violently throwing the worshipful Coll Pynchon over a barrel of rossin"![7] Once again, Deerfield also held such outsiders within. In early February of 1704 the town welcomed newlyweds seventeen-year-old Abigail Stebbins and Frenchman Jacques Denieur (anglicized in some records to Denyon). By some accounts, 1704 Deerfield held two other Frenchmen as well.

That these people lived in or near Deerfield certainly modifies impressions of the early New England frontier. The existence of blacks in the Connecticut valley, much less their lot as slaves to at least two Puritan ministers, is itself a powerful statement about early New England society. The presence of French and Indians suggests that the "frontier line" should not be drawn too firmly. While perhaps a clear line of division during wars, this edge of English settlement was apparently a zone of exchange, coexistence, and even intermarriage for at least some people of different colors, cultures, and nationalities.

The frontier also stretched women's roles. Although women sat separately from the men at church and could not hold office or participate in town government, they played other notable roles beyond their traditional tasks. Deerfield's first known schoolteacher was a woman, Hannah Beaman, who began her service by the early 1690s.[8] More frequently, women's actions became visible via involvement in county court actions. Sometimes they ended up in court facing criminal charges (see Chapter 5); more frequently they figured in land transactions and settlements of estates. When husbands died, widows, termed relicts, were often appointed administrators of their husbands' estates. By a 1647 Massachusetts law, when a husband died without a will, the relict received one-third of his personal property, at least for her lifetime. When young children were involved in such cases, the court would often entrust the entire estate to the widow, with the proviso that she apportion the estate appropriately when the children married or came of age.[9]

Land sales also brought women into legal matters. A common pattern was for husband and wife to cosign a deed: "John Severans with Mary his wife have Sealed & Subscribed & acknowledged. . . their act & deed"; "Symon Beamon & Hannah his wife came personally & acknowledged their hands & seales thereto." Sometimes this took place because the family was selling off lands that had come down to a woman through her family. Thus, when Benjamin and Elizabeth Hastings sold a house lot to Godfrey Nims in 1694, "Elizabeth did freely & voluntaryly Relinquish her Right of Dowry in ye premises." Husband and wife often worked together in this way, as when James Brown of Deerfield sold land in 1697 "off his own ffree Will & alsoe with ye Consent approbation & good likeing of Remembrance Brown his Well beloved Wife." Finally, in 1692 two Connecticut valley women, both widows, independently consummated a deal for land—a striking example of women's rights in court.[10]

As Deerfield's population stabilized in the years from 1689 to 1704, the town began to build in other ways. In the aftermath of autonomy in 1689 came a series of municipal projects. First was the construction of a mill. In 1689 Deerfield's inhabitants ordered the selectmen to hire Hatfield millwright Captain John

Allis. When he died amidst "preparations" in 1690, the town quickly brought in Joseph Parsons, Sr., of Northampton to take over construction.

Deerfield's generous contract with Parsons suggests how important this mill was to the town.[11] Assuming he could get "a good suficient and substantial corn mill . . . set up and fit to grind" within six months, Parsons would "take for his tole for Grinding" one-eighteenth of all barley malt, one-fourteenth of all wheat, and one-twelfth of all other grain ground there. As long as he wanted to maintain the mill these benefits would be his. On the other hand, if at any time after completion Parsons wanted to quit the site, he had "free liberty . . . to desert and leave [the mill] into ye towns hands."

That was not the only enticement. Just to come to Deerfield, the town offered Parsons two tracts of land totaling over fifty acres. Further, during construction Parsons was given "ye help of 6 Catle and Two men" to get the millstones in place. Parsons paid no taxes on his mill. If the mill burned down, he had the right of first refusal on reconstruction. The Northamptonite was even "granted . . . the Stream" on which he built as long as he maintained the mill. About the only constraint the town put on Parsons was that if the new mill did "not answere ye end and expectation of ye owners and town"—that is, if the mill simply did not do its job—then the town could find another place to build. Even in this case, though, Parsons would get "first offer" of the new mill contract. Deerfield obviously coveted the facility. Not surprisingly, Parsons liked the deal. By summer of 1693 Deerfield had its mill.[12]

The town launched a second project in 1694. Pocumtuck's meetinghouse had been consumed by the flames of King Philip's War, and it is likely that its 1680s successor—if a separate building existed at all—was only a small, crude edifice.[13] With the town better established by the mid-1690s, and with Reverend John Williams's tenure extending toward a full decade, Deerfield's inhabitants determined that "a meeting house. . .the bignes of Hatfield meeting house"—some thirty feet square—should be built.[14]

While construction progressed smoothly over the next two

years, the town soon had to grapple with another complexity of
building a new church. At the same time that pineboard pews
were going into the new building, the town charged a five-
member committee with the sensitive job of establishing a seating plan for the new church. Here was a task sure to make any
committee squeamish. The charge itself sounded simple: Develop a seating plan based on the "age [e]state and dignity of
the townspeople."[15] But there was no set formula by which the
committee was to weigh the three criteria and arrive at a single
ranking. And the committee knew that seating was a touchy
local issue, since it provided the town with what one historian
has termed "a new edition of the social register."[16]

After three years of handling such matters of internal and
external construction, in 1697 Deerfield saw John Williams
ascend to his new pulpit. Meanwhile, work on the meetinghouse continued. Within three years the town decided that the
"galleryes" upstairs could now be "compleatly finished." Then
in December of 1701 the whole seating process began anew.[17]
Deerfield had a new meetinghouse, and another sign of a ma-
turing town as well: a clear and now changing pecking order.

The third major new facility the town added during this decade was a school. Education was a vital part of New England
Puritan life, and the high percentage of Deerfield men that
owned books suggests a high degree of literacy, something true
throughout the region.[18] Even without a formal school, townspeople had gained reading skills through lessons at church:
Education meant more than just a schoolhouse.[19] At the same
time, however, Massachusetts law required towns of forty or
more families to provide formal education. Thus, in 1698, after
years of irregular schooling at various sites in town, Deerfield
decided "that a School House be built upon ye Town Charge,"
measuring twenty-one by eighteen feet.

The way Deerfield taxed its citizens for school expenses is
revealing. Although all townspeople were taxed to pay for the
new school and schoolmaster, families with children between
the ages of six and ten, "whether male or female," had to pay
an additional tax, "whether y^a [they] send such children to
School or not." Apparently the town expected parents to send

those six- to ten-year-olds to school. Yet four years of schooling was enough. Children under six or over ten who wished to attend school had to pay an additional rate.[20]

Once established, the school was set into the larger pattern of local governmental affairs. Each year after 1698 the town chose a school committee to "hire a meet person or persons to teach ye towns children to read and write," to "repair ye towns school house . . . at ye towns charge," and to provide "firewood to ye scholars." Inhabitants were particularly pleased in 1703 when they successfully "bargained" to get new resident Mr. John Richards to teach. His pay suggests that they cared a great deal about school. Richards got £25 for this seasonal work—at a time when the town was unable to pay John Williams his salary of £70.[21]

While more mundane, construction of new roads provided yet another sign of Deerfield's maturity and expansion. Although roads already ran through Deerfield's meadows, in 1694 the town meeting voted that "a highway" be built across the Deerfield River "to the land on the west side" called Carter's land. A year later a committee was empowered to make sure that "ye town street" was maintained at its full and proper "breadth of six rods," and even "laid out wider" by Meeting-house Hill. In 1701 a town-appointed committee planned two new highways, one to meander through the fields west of town across the Deerfield River, the other to run to the "uper end" of the "Green River lands" over two miles north of town. Two years later the town set out yet another new road, this one going directly west from town across the Deerfield River into the foothills beyond New Fort Meadow. Deerfield was shooting out roads like vines, irregular in paths yet bearing fruit along the way.[22]

Amidst all this construction, late-seventeenth-century Deerfield displayed other patterns of stability and order. As the town grew, it developed a regular rhythm of existence, a pulse, a clear, steady, yearly cycle of life. This order and rhythm emerge most clearly through a study of the record of Deerfield's town meetings.

The meeting record provides abundant signs of greater regularity. In the 1680s when Deerfield was run by its outside "prudential committee," the town met infrequently, with perhaps a meeting or two between January and April, but then little else until late in the year. Some years there is record of only a single meeting. Further, when the outside committee ran Deerfield, the town only once elected a slate of officers and only occasionally chose committees to handle specific issues or grievances.[23]

Town governance changed dramatically with the town's independence in 1689. Within five years a new pattern was clear. Regular meetings now took place three times a year, in March, September, and December. While special circumstances occasionally dictated special meetings, in general the three meetings sufficed—and gave the town a regular pattern of governance.

Each of these seasonal meetings had its own regular agenda. March was the time to elect town officers for the year.[24] These included the selectmen, tax commissioner, surveyors and haywards, fence viewers, tithingmen, the "sealer" or clerk of market, the "packer" of pork or beef, the town clerk, the constable, and often appointees to measure out new lands or highways during the next year. In all, roughly twenty men took office each March.

As farmers prepared for spring planting, March also became the time to handle local land issues. In addition to distributing new and "wanting" lands, this gathering also set the year's rules and regulations for land use. For instance, with a common-field system for its meadows, all Deerfielders had a stake in the proper maintenance of the common fence. Almost all residents owned land in those meadows, and to keep animals out each landowner was required to maintain the fence at the edge of his own acreage. In this light, it is not surprising that at the March 1692 meeting the selectmen, having "taken great care . . . y^t [that] all defects in ye common fence may be repayered," ordered fines of one shilling per rod of fence per day for any defective fence still standing—or, more properly, not standing. To make identification of land and fence clearer, in March of 1698 the town set up rules for carving into the stake at the north end of each man's common fence "ye first two letters of his name," with stiff penalties for noncompliance.[25] Planning major town projects like the new mill or new fortifications also came in March, as did planning for the year's schooling. The new year was beginning, and Deerfield began it by choosing its leaders, distributing and regulating soon-to-be-planted lands, and planning new projects. The townspeople, the earth, and the town all gained new life in the spring.

September's meeting was quite different. Usually there was only one major item of business. At this harvest-time gathering, the town would determine "ye Time for opening ye meadows or corn field." 1697's decision is typical: "on Monday at night being ye fourth of October." Why a full town meeting for such a decision? Again, Deerfield's common-field system speaks volumes, for "opening the fields" meant that the town's livestock could now graze where crops had stood. This had to be a town edict because individuals needed to know how much time they had to harvest their crops. Even the detail "at night," common in Deerfield's records, suggests the importance of this decision. September's meeting might also bring discussion of other items—a dispute over an exchange of land, reminders to maintain common fence, standards issued about proper branding of animals to be let free in the fields—but essentially the substance of the meeting matched the affairs of that time of year. Autumn brought an end to the harvest, and the meeting echoed the rhythm of the season.[26]

The cycle of town and farm life carried through the December meeting. As ever, land issues would crop up, such as a forfeiture declared on unused land. Unusual incidents of the year now ending might arise, too. The December 1696 meeting included a pair of these. Joseph Brooks was allowed to keep his three new cattle and one horse tax-free for the year, since he had bought them to replace animals "killed by ye Enemie" earlier that year, and Eleazer Hawks was granted twelve shillings to compensate for losses in a house fire the year before.[27]

The bulk of each December meeting, though, was devoted to setting "rates," or taxes: to raising the money needed to maintain the town and its services for another year. Each December the town would first decide how it would "apprize" each man's "ratable estate." This first step was needed before the town could establish its tax base. How should an acre of meadow be valued? How much for an ox, a cow, a horse? Then came the tougher questions. How does one adjust appraisals of land with "respect to distance of lands from home" or "for goodness" of lands? What adjustment should be made for an animal's "Age and goodnes"? The town would set the standards; the elected "apprizers" would work from there.[28]

After values were set, rates were determined: How much should each person pay for each pound's worth of estate? Then, beyond that, how would townsmen pay? Here one can see the common crops that Deerfielders grew as well as their relative values. Indian corn was worth two shillings of tax per bushel, rye and barley three each. "Fated [fatted] pork" was another common medium of exchange, used almost as frequently as Indian corn, and valued at 2½ pence worth of taxes per pound.

The taxes raised paid for town improvements, such as the new meetinghouse, or more commonly for annual expenses like the maintenance of the school. Sending a representative to the Massachusetts General Court was a great expense for a small town, one Deerfield incurred only infrequently during the 1690s. The town's largest single annual expense went for the other chief focus of the December meeting: the ministry. December not only brought the collection of taxes but also the settlement of the minister's salary and perquisites. How much should the town pay young John Williams in 1689? The December meeting agreed on £70. Should he be allowed to use the empty town lot next to his own, as he requested? The 1692 December meeting said yes.

Thus was December a time to look back on the year now ebbing, to handle the normal residue of problems that any town would have, but mostly a time to end the year by settling local taxes and expenses. Given that early winter was also the time when settlers would have close to their maximum in grain and produce still stored away, it seems a wise time to take the town's share in taxes. And then, after the cold and snow of the next two months, the whole cycle would begin anew. Deerfield lived by the words of Ecclesiastes: To everything there is a season, and a time to every purpose under heaven.

As the wheel of life turned steadily in Deerfield through the 1690s, other rhythms emerged. By 1704 Deerfield displayed distinct patterns of government, economy, religion, and social order. While each of these bespoke separate elements of frontier life, together they represent something that neither Pocumtuck nor the Deerfield of the 1680s had: a stable, clearly defined frontier existence. The single word that best captures that existence is *communal*.

Town government became inward-focused in the years after 1689. Frontier Deerfield maintained a striking degree of autonomy and isolation—from a political as well as geographical viewpoint. While the town maintained some ties with Boston, overall the provincial government had little hold on the distant town. In the 1680s the General Court had approved Deerfield's outside committee, but then it left Deerfield alone. The Governor's Council occasionally issued general orders for Massachusetts towns, such as setting rules for local establishment of schools. In practice, though, Deerfield had great freedom in following such laws. In truth, the town regulated itself.[29]

In addition to being some distance from provincial control, Deerfield apparently either did not care or could not afford to send regular representatives to sessions of the General Court. Massachusetts law declared that every town in the province holding "forty freeholders and other inhabitants qualified by charter to elect" was required to send one representative to the Court. Towns with between thirty and forty such men were "at liberty to send one, or not," and those with fewer than thirty could send one or "join with the next town in the choice of their representatives, they paying a proportionate amount of the charge."[30] By 1689 Deerfield had roughly forty freeholders, which makes its status unclear. What is clear, however, is that in the fourteen sessions between 1689 and 1704 it sent representatives only three times. Further, although neighboring Hatfield sent a representative every year, there is no evidence that Deerfield ever approved or financially supported its neighbor's choice.

Deerfield may have sent representatives so rarely because it was so expensive. Maintaining a representative at the General Court cost about £10 per year. Towns without much money or with different priorities, such as constructing a meetinghouse or building a road, might well spend their money "at home." Still, such circumstances made Deerfield all the more isolated.[31]

While Deerfield steered clear of Boston, the provincial government did not pay great attention to Deerfield and the west, either. In the years after Governor Andros's expulsion in 1689, the Governor's Council was dominated by a disproportionate number of men from Boston and the east. Hampshire County seemed far removed—by distance, by wilderness, by frontier problems.[32] Even more isolating for Deerfield, Massachusetts governors failed to select a single justice of the peace—the most prestigious local office—from Deerfield in the years before 1704. While it is true that many frontier towns did not have justices, the absence of such a leader in Deerfield enhances the sense of the town's isolation and even impotence in the larger political world.[33]

Closer to home Deerfield had closer political ties. At least occasionally the Hampshire County Court reviewed Deerfield's governmental setup and leadership. In 1693 the court was presented with Deerfield's list of local officials plus "Orders made by the select men" which the Court then "allowed . . . confirming the same." The next year both Deerfield orders and "by lawes" passed through the court's hands, as well as a list of the town's slate of officers.[34] Deerfield also stayed tied to the courts by its steady contribution of jurors to sessions in Northampton and Springfield. No fewer than six Deerfield men served between 1689 and 1695.

Even here, though, there is evidence that the townspeople, and the town, kept their distance. In 1694 Jonathan Wells of Deerfield was fined ten shillings for failing "to attend the Dutyes of ye Jurors."[35] More compelling is the sharp decline of cases involving Deerfielders in the court record during this period. While it is possible that the town's citizens all refrained from unlawful activity, more likely is that the town took care of problems on its own. For one thing, the town constable could handle many cases. For another, taking alleged criminals and witnesses to county court was a time-consuming and expensive proposition, one Deerfielders likely wished to avoid.[36]

Overall, then, at the county level, too, Deerfield's ties were limited. This isolation is perhaps best symbolized by a Hampshire County Court action of 1691 where the justices decided to improve the county's highway from Springfield north—but stopped well below Deerfield, at Northampton.[37]

Deerfield pulled away still more from the valley as its ties with John Pynchon lessened. Although Pynchon still dominated the region's courts and was the General Court's chief link to the valley, his role in Deerfield diminished sharply in the years after 1689. Not only did Deerfielders trade less with him, but he sold off a good deal of his Deerfield land during this period. In fact, the only sign of new activity at all in the 1690s came in a four-year land lease that Pynchon set up with John Hawks in 1699.[38] The Springfield magnate's contact with Deerfield continued via official judicial, military, and Indian matters, but affairs of land and debt and credit had come to an end.[39]

While Deerfielders had limited involvement with provincial and county affairs during this period, local matters provided an entirely different story. Virtually all Deerfield townsmen served in town government. This widespread sharing of officeholding was a vital part of what made Deerfield communal.[40]

Each March the town would vote into office roughly five selectmen; four to six fence viewers; two or three surveyors, haywards, and tithingmen; a varied number of tax assessors; a town clerk; a constable; a clerk of market; and a packer of meat. Townsmen also chose a moderator for each meeting. In sum, in a normal year approximately twenty men would serve—in a town of perhaps sixty adult males. Over time, the results were dramatic: Almost every town resident participated in town government. In fact, not one man who lived in Deerfield from 1689 through 1704 was not "chosen."[41] Equally dramatic, each man served an average of almost five years in one office or another.

In some respects, Deerfield's local government patterns were like those of other New England towns. While twenty offices represents a considerable number for a town so small, the number is not unusual. Nor was the degree of participation in Deerfield's government unique. An average of five years of service in this period also appears common. Small, young outposts required an egalitarian approach to town governance, where many people would rotate officeholding.[42]

Where Deerfield was unusual is in the way the town so quickly grabbed newcomers and younger settlers and integrated them into its government. Whether the town carefully examined prospective settlers before admitting them, as the General Court ordered in 1676, is not known. However, almost as soon as people settled in town they were thrust into office. There was no "trial period" for newcomers where they stood on the periphery of town government, no delays of long years while the town decided whether to accept them as full-fledged residents. The frontier brought its own needs, its own drives and demands, and one was participation—help—in administering the affairs of the town. For this reason, within a year of his arrival in Deerfield in 1698, William Arms was serving the town as a fence viewer. Soon he was made a town constable, and tithingman the year after that.

Deerfield's "sons" also quickly moved into office, often before the age of thirty. Nathaniel Sutlieff, Jr., son of one of the Pocumtuck pioneers who fell at Bloody Brook, became a fence viewer in 1700 at age twenty-seven. John Smead, son of Pocumtuck veteran William, took on the same office in the same year at the same age. In other towns in Massachusetts, most men did not move into even minor political offices before their thirties.[43] Yet in Deerfield, public service was common, a sign of citizenry, even a sort of rite of passage for newcomers and young men.

Not all jobs were equal. Most Deerfield men, whether recent arrivals or established residents, began their public service as surveyors, haywards, or, most commonly, fence viewers. These tasks involved focused, seasonal work, some menial and some supervisory. The town had some protection from possible incompetence since they were limited in scope and involved groups of men. At the same time, these kinds of jobs could provide an "apprenticeship of public service": The town could get a low-risk look at its men and their abilities.[44] Turnover was rapid: Townsmen usually served only one or two years in these tasks. Many then moved on to higher office. In the fifteen years between 1689 and 1704, twenty different Deerfield men served as surveyors, twenty-one as haywards, and a remarkable forty-five as fence viewers.

Other offices rotated rapidly as well, but for different reasons. Of Deerfield's seventeen tithingmen between 1689 and 1704, only four served more than one term, and only one of these as many as three years. Tithingmen held particularly sensitive positions: They were "required faithfullie to act in inspecting y^{ir} [their] neighbors . . . to take care y^t ye Sabbath be not Prophaned by persons . . . exposed to many temptations and divertions."[45] As Puritanism filled its people with religious zeal, it also made them watchful of one another, both informally and officially. For citizens to gain such power over one another for long periods of time might skew a local sense of equality under God; it also could lead to friction in a small town. Thus, the job changed hands often.

If maintaining proper religious attitudes was a sensitive issue, doubtless so, too, was taxation. Given that estates were rated each year for tax purposes, it is no wonder that tax commissioners and assessors rotated almost every year. Evidently Deerfield residents did not want any citizens to hold this kind of power over others in town for long.

The one job in Deerfield which turned over absolutely every year between 1689 and 1704—and which never saw anyone return to the office later—was the constable. In this case townsmen were choosing someone from within to enforce the law, to provide the town's discipline—and its punishments as well—when necessary. It is hardly surprising that the town wanted to pass around such a task, since rotating it would mitigate against possibilities of systematic injustice. For their part, constables in many New England towns had no desire to serve any more than one year. Although the job's duties were vital to a town— "the collection of taxes, the warnings of town meetings, and the maintenance of order"—those duties were time-consuming and often stressful. Elected constables in some Massachusetts towns actually refused to serve, preferring to face stiff fines. Although no such refusal appears in Deerfield's early records, it seems that the price the town paid for service was that no man would have to stay in the office for more than a single term.[46]

While many jobs turned over regularly, others stayed markedly stable. Deerfield had only two clerks throughout this period. Joseph Barnard began service back in 1686, even before the town had become independent, and was elected annually until his death at the hands of Indians in late summer of 1695. In a special election that September, the town chose Thomas French, who then served without interruption through 1703. Apparently the town wanted consistency in the marketplace as well, for during these fifteen years only three men served Deerfield as clerk of market and three served as packer of pork or beef. One man, Eleazer Hawks, served as both sealer and packer for 1702 and 1703, and held either one office or the other through over half of this period.

Yet it was rotation rather than continuity which characterized the most important office in Deerfield: selectman. The town annually chose anywhere from two to seven of these "select men Towns-men or overseers." Selectmen held extensive powers in New England towns, and the job's prestige and duties were seen as sharply different from the "lesser offices" like hayward and fence viewer. Basically, these "select men" dealt with town affairs that arose between meetings, were not handled by town meetings, or were assigned to them at such meetings.

In many New England communities the selectmen formed the town elite, a group of established leaders. In Deerfield the case is more complex. Twenty-four different men served as selectmen in Deerfield between 1689 and 1704—more than in any other office except fence viewer. It is a striking claim of widespread sharing of leadership. At the same time, out of the twenty-four men who served, there emerged a core of political leaders. Just six men served four or more terms as selectman, and five of those six also served in the prestigious position of moderator (the sixth was Thomas French, Deerfield's second long-term clerk). Given that only seven men in town ever served as moderator before 1704, these five selectmen obviously dominate that group. Thus, Deerfield had a "pool" of "eminent members of the community."[47]

In general, though, the selectman list provides an index of impressively wide participation at the highest level of local government. Deerfield's townsmen shared the powers of selectman as or more broadly than other New England towns. A higher percentage of men in Deerfield served; they generally each served for fewer years, a further sign of shared leadership; and they also commonly moved back and forth between the "high office" of selectman and the town's many minor offices.[48]

Economic hardship likely pushed Deerfield toward such widespread participation. Officeholding, and particularly the job of selectman, was a financial burden for the men who served. The time put into local service and lost from one's occupation made it difficult for the less wealthy to serve for many years. In fact, in 1674 this problem had led Deerfield's neighbor Northampton to restrict men to serving no more often than every other year, "it being too great a burthen for the same men to be so often employ'd." This also helps explain the common ties between wealth and political leadership in any era: People have to be able to afford to serve in public office.[49]

In general, though, Deerfield depended on all its men to serve the town, to take on its daily and yearly tasks. Given the level of participation, it is not surprising that the town had a sizable group of men almost perpetually in one office or another. Five men served in four different offices during this period, often for more than one year; five men served in five jobs; and five served in six different jobs—and all this within fifteen years.

Not only did everyone serve, but everyone attended meetings as well. At the March 2, 1696, town meeting, the inhabitants "agreed and voted" that "a penalty of one shilling shall be laid upon every legall voter not attending town meeting."[50] All men probably voted as well. Province law required adult townsmen to own £20 of property before they could vote, but since almost all Deerfield settlers held town office, it would be unusual to deny any his vote. Besides, a small, isolated outpost like Deerfield could ill afford to be exclusionary.

Deerfield's ongoing concern for local affairs can further be seen in the fact that the town elected a new slate of officials every year. Men who served in almost any job, from selectman to tithingman to constable, did so for only one year at a time; if they served many terms in the same office, they were only rarely consecutive terms. Again, the burdens of office may have encouraged such turnover, yet the fact of that broad turnover remains.

Even the town's terse meeting records reinforce the sense of extremely broad-based polity. There is no mention in any of Deerfield's early records of separate selectman meetings. While such meetings undoubtedly took place, it appears that in early Deerfield "the town," and not the selectmen, decided major local matters. This is further seen in the number of town meetings Deerfield held and the wide range of matters which they addressed. By contrast, the selectmen of many other New England towns dominated their governments.[51] Finally, and significantly, at no time in these fifteen years is there any sign in the town records of close or even divided votes, whether over issues or election of officers. "The town," "the meeting," or "the inhabitants" always "agreed" or "approved" or "voted" on decisions.

It is difficult to describe this kind of government. "Democracy" does not fully characterize it. Granted, Deerfield was democratic in its most basic sense, that is, as a government "of and by the people." However, the term fails to convey any sense of the almost universal participation of townsmen, as voters at meetings but especially as officeholders. "Consensus" is another term that is helpful but limited. It conveys the point that the town decided matters in these years more by agreement of the whole than by votes of individuals. In that respect, Deerfield's government was "more" than democratic. This

characteristic was common in seventeenth- and eighteenth-
century Massachusetts towns. If they showed signs of being
"democratic," they were "democracies without democrats,"
"democracies in spite of themselves."[52] Their goal went beyond
democracy with its potential for division and contentiousness.

Deerfield was still more. It was democratic and consensual;
it was also all-inclusive, with all men attending town meetings
and serving in local office, often for many years. Not everyone
served the same number of years or in the same offices, and
some offices carried more weight than others, but virtually
everyone served. Although the town was not the carefully
planned utopian commune of early Massachusetts,[53] Deerfield
had achieved an extraordinary degree of popular involvement
in local government. Far from Boston, on the edge of the wilderness, Deerfielders had constructed a communal political
order.

In a number of important ways Deerfield's late-seventeenth-
century economy matched its politics. At the heart of the town's
economy was its land, and in the distribution and use of land
the town provided regulation and rough equity. Both enhance
the emerging vision of a communal frontier village.

First of all, Deerfield carefully controlled the distribution of
land to both old and new settlers. As in other early New England towns, Deerfield proprietors could and did receive additional lands from time to time, but when the town made a new
division of lands, all proprietors received their fair share. The
amount of land received depended upon the number of cow
commons, or proprietary shares, one held, so this system did
not produce equality of holdings. Still, the only surviving record of cow commons in Deerfield from this era, a 1688 wood-
lot division, reveals a generally even distribution. Lieutenant
Thomas Wells held the highest number of shares at this time
with thirty, and Benoni Stebbins had twenty-six, but the days
of a few men owning forty, fifty, and even sixty shares were
over. In fact, Wells and Stebbins were the only two men with
more than twenty cow commons. At the other end of the spec-
trum, newcomer Robert Price held a single share, but he was

unusual: Only seven men held fewer than five shares. The majority of Deerfield's men held between ten and twenty commons, and the entire group of proprietors owned an average of about twelve shares each.[54]

While Deerfield's proprietors continued to receive distributions of land, new settlers could also get land from the town without difficulty. Deerfield granted almost all newcomers the same amount of land, classically a four-acre home lot at Wapping or Green River and twenty acres of farmland. Newcomers would not own their land, though, until they had resided on it for three years. Deerfield wanted settlers, not speculators or itinerants.[55]

A final sign that Deerfield had firm control of its lands lay in the fact that by 1689 the original owners of Deerfield's lands, the Dedham proprietors, had all but disappeared from the record. Only three Deerfield cases involving Dedham proprietors arose between 1689 and 1704.[56] Other than that, Deerfield was autonomous when it came to land distribution, independent of the problems that had beset the town in the 1670s and early 1680s.

In addition to controlling distribution of new lands, Deerfield also carefully regulated land use. As in the 1670s, although individuals in town owned their own meadowlands, they farmed in common. This common-field system required that farmers live by common regulations, which were set at town meeting. Proper care for fences, when to "open the fields," grazing policies, rules for branding animals, penalties for "leaving creatures in the meadow"[57]—all were decided by the town. A man could not farm as he pleased or let his animals forage anywhere: He was part of a community-run operation. This communal orientation was reinforced by the fact that many townsmen shared bulls and oxen. These "common" animals met both practical and philosophical needs, the former because they reduced individual costs, the latter because they supported the vision of farming as a community enterprise.

The town determined still other elements of daily economic life that in another time or place might be private matters or handled by a committee. As discussed above, the town hired a millwright, oversaw the mill's construction, and regulated its profits and ownership. When the town raised taxes, it established the exchange rates of the various goods which people used to pay those taxes. When the minister was to be paid, the town—not the church members—decided on salary and method of payment.

Through all this, it is evident that the town directed many elements of its settlers' economic life. Beyond this local control, however, lay a whole economic system that reinforced settlers' interdependence. Deerfield's daily economic world was largely shared, closed—communal.

Essentially, Deerfield had an agrarian subsistence economy in the years before 1704. It was a town made up primarily of unusually poor farmers who each owned a house lot and some land—and little else.[58] The village did not exist at so primitive a level that each settler had to fend entirely for himself. In fact, the town saw growing specialization in the 1690s, as a number of men with particular skills moved into Deerfield. In addition to the minister, the millwright, and the teacher, Deerfield also housed a weaver, a tailor, and a maltster and cooper. Two men worked as "cordwainers"—shoemakers—and at least three considered themselves carpenters, while three others owned a number of carpentry tools. One man studied medicine. While most of these men also farmed, it is noteworthy that their trades and skills found their way to Deerfield during this period.[59]

There were other hints of commerce as well. Six men received the town's permission to use local pine trees to make resin and turpentine. A few men, not just outsiders like John Pynchon but locals, rented out extra lands. Townsmen also sold individual parcels of land or house lots without giving up commons rights.

Yet in essence Deerfield was a town of subsistence farmers.[60] Most owned various farming implements: horse chains, a cart and wheels, axes, a sickle, hoe, hayknife, sled, rope, scythe, fork, harrow. Along with farm tools would be farm animals. Almost all local settlers had one or two cows, an obviously vital source of milk and, in time, food and leather. Horses were common and essential, not just for mobility but as an alternative to much more expensive oxen for use in farming.[61] In the Deerfield of 1700, more than four out of every five men owned a horse, and many owned two or three. Sheep and swine were also common. Inside each man's barn would lie whatever craft tools he might employ.

In Deerfield's houses the belongings were sparse. As farm tools were essential outdoors, so were cooking implements indoors. Every home had its pots and pans, tongs, fire tools, trammels, and hooks. Plates and utensils were generally wooden, earthenware, or pewter. Furnishings were spartan. Everyone had a bed, but that was about the only sure piece of furniture. Chests and boxes were not uncommon, and many homes had chairs, but tables were rare.[62] Yards of fabric, the raw material for clothing, were frequently found. Deerfielders also, of course, kept a store of food. Most basic here was Indian corn, then wheat. Pork was the only meat commonly stored in Deerfield, and it was not all that common; and only one inventory from this period includes beef. A final common necessity was a gun and ammunition.[63]

Some Deerfielders had some nonessential items. Over one-third of Deerfielders owned at least one book during this period, most likely a Bible. Finery in the home might include some brass, pillows, or warming pans. John and Abigail Stebbins's daughter Hannah received some treasures upon her grandmother Ann Bartlett's death: a "mohaire Pettecoate, . . . a feather bolster, a dozen napkins . . . two feather pillows, curtains," yards of different cloths, fine linens, and a hat and case.[64] Such luxuries were rare, however.

Deerfield farmers, of course, did not all own equal amounts of land. Acreage varied along with the number of cow commons each man held. The gap between rich and poor in town, however, was not large. The top 10 percent of shareholders owned 21 percent of all proprietary rights; the bottom 10 percent held over 2 percent of those rights. In other words, no small group of individuals dominated landholding in Deerfield.

Landholding in Deerfield was not only roughly equal but staggeringly low compared with other New England towns at this time. In the years around 1700, Deerfield men owned an average of about sixty acres.[65] By comparison, settlers in early Dedham could expect to be granted roughly 150 acres in their lifetimes, and Andover residents 200 acres. Even though resident farmers would not initially use more than fifty to one hundred acres, the proprietors of the new frontier town of Kent quickly parceled out over one thousand acres to each shareholder. Only in Springfield, a town dominated by land tenancy and wracked by an actual shortage of land, did average acreage get anywhere as low as in Deerfield: just under seventy acres.[66]

Deerfield estate values mirror this pattern in landholding in both equity and poverty. Most Deerfielders held estates of roughly the same size, averaging roughly £87 (including both real and personal estate). Only three estates settled at this time were worth more than £100, and just one of these more than £200. On the other end, only four Deerfield men died with estates worth less than £50. Age was not a significant factor in the different sizes of estates.[67]

While total estate values give some sense of wealth and property in Deerfield, they need to be examined still more closely, for men often left considerable debts when they died—and they could turn an estate's value topsy-turvy. Joseph Barnard died with over £49 of debts, though his estate's final value was cushioned by its initial value of £230. John Allyn left £47 in debts, and with a total estate worth just £86, his estate's status changed far more dramatically. When David Alexander died in 1704, he left a personal estate (no lands valued) of £38—and debts of almost £44. In fact, of the Deerfield men of this period whose records survived, almost two-thirds left long strings of debts, strings which *averaged* over £28.

Owing to this mass of indebtedness, the values of the actual "free estates"—the final measure of estates after paying off debts—take on great significance, for these show by what margin a man's estate actually emerged "free and clear." The surviving records make Deerfield's men both more equal and even poorer. Free estates averaged less than £61, almost one-third less than the total estate values. Only two men held free estates worth more than £75, while three were worth less than £30.

The depth of Deerfield's poverty becomes clear when these

figures are compared with those of other New England towns. Even using Deerfield's initial average estate value of £87 and not the free estate average of £61, the differences are dramatic. In early Dedham, for example, personal estates alone (no land included) averaged £150, and total estates averaged £294.[68] Even in Hampshire County, much closer to Deerfield, people were far better off. In Springfield, residents who died between 1650 and 1702 left estates which averaged £209 in value.[69] Moving closer still to Deerfield, Northampton's first generation produced a record of impressive prosperity. Townsmen who died between 1661 and 1719 left estates with an average value of £395. Only five estates were worth less than £100, and only two of those less than £50.[70]

Deerfield's economic picture appears even starker when looking at what items cost at this time. This was a world where a house lot in town would cost £15 and meadowland could cost £1 to £4 per acre; a horse might cost £2 to £4, a cow the same; a pair of oxen £12; a gun and ammunition from 10 to 40 shillings. And in this world Deerfielders had free estates worth only £60.[71] The General Court even acknowledged Deerfield's lack of resources when in both 1696 and 1703 it offered financial support toward maintaining Deerfield's ministry, first £10 and later £20. By the second grant, the Court was writing about the town's "Extraordinary Impoverishing Circumstances," a clear signal that Deerfield was living close to the line.[72]

In light of all these circumstances—shared poverty, a general sameness of condition, limited resources, isolation, like occupations and life-style—it is not surprising that Deerfielders would become interdependent and community oriented. They needed one another to survive. One other facet of Deerfield's economic life brings this out still more dramatically. It is those strings of debts.

The debts that Deerfielders accumulated hold a key to still deeper understanding of the life of the town. For one thing, most townsmen had them: Credit and debit were apparently a way of life in the late-seventeenth-century Deerfield. Still more telling, however, is the fact that the strands were long and wove together a huge number of the people of the town. When Joseph Barnard died in 1695, he left debts of over £53 among thirty-six different people, twenty-eight of whom were men and women (especially widows) of Deerfield. Thomas Broughton's estate paid out over £48 of debts to thirty-eight people, twenty-five of whom were Deerfielders. Some debt totals did not run so high. Daniel Weld's added up to only £5.19. Yet the pattern remains: Weld's administrators paid out money to eleven people, nine of whom were fellow townsmen. Benjamin Barrett owed money to perhaps as many people as any: £50 spread around to fifty people, thirty-one of whom were of Deerfield. And the pattern continues, man after man. All told, townmen owed an average of £28 in debts to an average of thirty people, two-thirds of whom were fellow residents of Deerfield.[73]

That Deerfield men had debts does not make the town unique. Nearby Springfield faced "chronic indebtedness" during the late seventeenth century, while frontier Kent held "an astonishing amount of debt," with a similar pattern of numerous creditors. However, the explanations for these cases do not serve Deerfield well. In Springfield much of the indebtedness arose from the town's extraordinary dependency on one man: John Pynchon. Kent's situation is less clear, for there emerges no clear pattern of creditors, no sense of "class struggle," and no sense that indebtedness hurt economic opportunity in town.[74]

Deerfield's circumstances suggest more. With such a large number of debts owed to so many different people, it appears that if Deerfield was a subsistence farming community, it was a highly interdependent one. This was no town of independent yeoman farmers fighting to survive on their own. Instead, men and women freely, actively, willingly, and incessantly traded goods, services, food, resources, tools—perhaps just about anything. Actually, one item townspeople rarely used in trade was money. Indeed, the rare specific references to money suggest that Deerfield had more of a barter economy, with a complex network of constant exchanges.[75] This lack of specie is further seen in the fact that, as discussed earlier, townspeople paid their taxes with crops, not cash. Deerfield was evidently a cash-poor community and thus relied on a barter system. This system was not formally administered by the town, so it was not "state" run in any modern sense. Town government stayed apart, only regulating matters like rates of exchange and the measuring, packing, and sealing of goods. Yet the system depended on extensive community interaction. Most exchanges took place within the village, and those not made with Deerfielders took place with neighbors from nearby Hatfield or Hadley. People traded often, yet not in any pattern: No one or two or three men emerge as chief creditors or moneylenders.

It was, in sum, a vitally communitarian venture. The inhabitants depended upon, constantly traded with, and constantly indebted themselves to fellow citizens. Given Deerfield's rough, low standards of living, the town might not have survived otherwise. As with Deerfield's almost universal participation in town governance, as with the extensive regulatory policies of the town government, so in its web of credits and debts, Deerfield was living by—and even depending upon—its own special level of community cooperation. In daily economy as in governance, the frontier had turned people in on one another for help, support, and indeed survival.

No study of late-seventeenth-century Deerfield would be complete without a look at the role of the church in town life. Although only fragmentary evidence has survived, it yields the strong impression that church polity, too, buttressed the ideal of a closed, interdependent community.

Two main points dominate a view of the church's role in 1690s Deerfield. The first is that church and state were tightly knit together. In Deerfield, as in virtually all Puritan New England towns, town government held great power over church affairs. "The town" chose the minister, established his salary, and set the rates to pay him. The town was also responsible for constructing the meetinghouse, the local center of both civil and religious affairs. And payments for all these were based on town residence and property holding, not church membership. If one was absent from church, or misbehaved when there, the tithingman—a town-elected official—handled matters; if the case were serious enough, the town constable did. The public laws of the colony also ruled local churches. Civil statutes from the 1630s required that everyone in town must attend Sunday services and that towns must have their own "orthodox and learned ministers."[76] Deerfield complied in all this. The town brought John Williams to town in 1686 and supported his ministry throughout this period, supplementing his salary with occasional pieces of land and firewood. In 1695 the town built a meetinghouse, and throughout the decade it regularly elected tithingmen and constables to make sure residents got to it on the Sabbath as required. All of this makes Deerfield like the other Puritan towns of Massachusetts.

The second point about Deerfield and its church is less typical but no less important. It appears that Deerfield's church, like most in the Connecticut valley in the late 1600s, was following "Mr. Stoddard's Way"—and that "way" reinforced the communal spirit seen in other elements of town life. "Mr. Stoddard" was Solomon Stoddard, minister of Northampton from 1672 until his death in 1729 and one of the most influential clergymen in New England in this era. His "way" marked a new direction for the churches of New England.

In 1662, in response to declining church membership, Massachusetts ministers had convened a synod which brought forth what became known as the "half-way covenant." The synod declared that instead of the previous rigorous restrictions, the children of baptized persons could now themselves be baptized if they formally promised to live by scripture and be bound by church discipline. Although full church membership required "visible qualifications," this halfway measure could at least make the church more accessible to New England's younger generation. Northampton went further. In 1668, over the protest of their minister, Eleazer Mather, the church members passed their own "innovation": Any persons, young or old, need only be "not Scandelous in life" to receive baptism. "Honest life and good intentions" would be enough to qualify anyone for partial membership.[77]

As far as the Massachusetts ministers had gone, Stoddard went further still. Although he followed his new church's "revision" for a few years after his arrival in Northampton in 1672, he became distressed by how few halfway members confessed to an "experience of saving grace"—the only way persons could qualify for full communion and hence full church membership. In 1677 Stoddard took a huge step: He offered baptism to any adult or child who "accepted the creed," plus he offered full communion to any who "became satisfactory to him in their understanding of the 'principles of Christianity' and in their behavior." This opened the portals wide. During Stoddard's ministry "almost every adult in Northampton" became a church member.[78]

The significance for Deerfield of this radically new openness and inclusiveness depends, of course, on the extent to which Northampton influenced its neighbor to the north. Indications are that the impact was considerable. By 1690 Stoddard's views had come to dominate the region. By the force of both his intellect and his rhetoric, the Northampton minister spread his views. Soon, with the exception only of Westfield, "church after church in the Connecticut valley succumbed to 'Stoddardeanism.' "[79]

In a frontier outpost, especially one as young and exposed as Deerfield, Stoddard's ideas would be both appealing and practical. Full church membership offered spiritual solace, the transcendence that could help people look past their "distressed state." It could ease their isolation, their poverty. It could also offer villagers a "fresh start" in religion that paralleled the economic and social opportunities gained by moving to the frontier. Deerfielders thus would not seek church membership "because they lacked other forms of association."[80] Instead, the church was yet one more Deerfield institution that openly supported communal values. Open membership, encouragement of children to join the church, the requirement only to live a proper, God-fearing life—all would reinforce a communitarian way of life.

When placed together, all these views of Deerfield—political, social, economic, and religious—offer a panorama of daily life. Most people lived up and down the unbending mile of "the street"; a handful of families lived in a compact settlement at Wapping two miles below, with another few together at Green River two miles above. A fort consisting of stakes ten or twelve feet high surrounded the high ground in the center of town, enclosing the town common, the meetinghouse, and perhaps fifteen homes. Houses were situated, whether inside the fort or out, up along the street, on the front edges of the four- to five-acre home lots, facing in—for comfort, for protection, and for Puritan-inspired watchfulness as well.

There was not a great deal that was private in the little village. Townspeople saw and worked with one another constantly. The large number of town officers engaged in daily affairs, from fence viewers to haywards, kept people working together; universal church attendance further supported this inward bent; the common-field system relied on farmers' daily shared labor; and the closed, interdependent barter economy still further reinforced constant contact and cooperation. Once the town even voted to read in public "Bills of town debts"![81]

As the seventeenth century gave way to the eighteenth, people in Deerfield lived simply. Their lives centered on their lands and their work. While they had enough of necessities to get by—house and land, farm tools and household essentials—most had little more. The only "riches" Deerfielders had were their lands. And those lands were indeed unusually fertile. While they did not sell for more than in other places in New England, that is only because the richness of the soil had to be measured against the isolation of the town.[82]

An important question in any town's life is whether it is dominated by a few, by an elite. In Deerfield's case, the answer appears to be no. Local governance was marked by almost universal participation in town government. While seven office-holders emerged as a core of leadership, they did not dominate the town. Too many others served too often in too many positions of responsibility.[83]

Any claim of a political core based on socioeconomic class seems strained as well. Deerfield simply did not have wealthy men in the years before 1704. Granted, Joseph Barnard, one of the seven established leaders, had probably as large an estate as any man in town, but others in that political core had only slightly above average wealth, even when measured by Deerfield's extremely low standards.[84] These men may have been better off than many fellow townsmen, yet compared with

Hampshire County or virtually anywhere else in Massachusetts, they were far from wealthy. Deerfield followed New England's pattern of getting political leadership from those who could most afford to give it. As in other small, young, less developed towns, this proved to be a widespread group of only relatively better-off men.[85]

So lived Deerfield's men, women, and children in the years before 1704. They did not starve while living at this frontier outpost, but they surely did not live in luxury, either. Whether their task was killing their share of blackbirds—the quota in town was twelve apiece in 1699, with penalties for failure and half-penny bonuses for "extras"—or collecting "free" firewood—that which had "laid faln 3 months"—their lives involved work: work for themselves and for their community.[86] As Deerfield had moved out of its rebuilding period of the early 1680s and stabilized in the 1690s, there emerged a steady pattern of existence, a regular cycle of life. Deerfield did not "grow and prosper" in the classic sense. It did, however, establish a stable, active local government in which all townsmen served.

Deerfield's agrarian subsistence economy matched the community-wide interdependence of its politics. This town of poor farmers, aided by local craftsmen, was held together by a barter economy nourished by an extensive network of small debts, where townspeople owed each other all the time for endless goods and services. Local religious practices reinforced this communal way of life, for Deerfield's church apparently subscribed to the practice of open communion—and thus broad membership—that Solomon Stoddard had brought to the valley. Deerfield's 1690s shift in the makeup of its population, from newcomers moving in from the outside over to greater dependence on natural growth from within, makes this communitarian vision still clearer. Finally, complementing this was the interweaving of families. Thus, in its egalitarian political order, its barter economy, its open church, its closed society, its absence of an elite, and indeed in its poverty, the focus, the very nature of, town government, economy, and religion—of town life—was communal.

SEVEN

Living with Death: Deerfield, the New England Frontier, and War, 1680-1703

A S THE SEVENTEENTH CENTURY gave way to the eighteenth, Deerfield's local government, economic system, and religious practices suggest that the town was a "peaceable kingdom."[1] Yet this lovely phrase grants too much. There was no covenant in town, no public statement by the settlers of their goals, their dreams. Deerfield also readily took in outsiders—when they came. In fact, given the number of former lawbreakers who came to town, Deerfield seemed to take in anyone. And the town never threw anyone out, either: There is not one recorded case of anyone being "warned out" of Deerfield in the years before 1704. Likely the town did not want—could not afford—to make anyone leave the small settlement, for residents were too precious.[2]

Casting the town in this less idyllic light forces thinking about why townspeople lived as they did. Granted, their communal existence was consistent with the spirit and dictates of Congregationalism. Still, New England's Puritans lived a life of "practical orthodoxy,"[3] and while the "orthodoxy" in Deerfield was clear, the "practical" side deserves more attention.

Deerfield was an isolated little outpost in the late 1600s, and the isolation brought one set of responses. But Deerfield also stood in a region going through difficult times. Recently devastated by war with Indians, the Connecticut valley lived with the threat of further attacks. The region also showed signs of serious internal unrest. Coupled with the daily rigors of frontier life, these made Deerfield's lot that much tougher. The full story of how the town lived is not complete without a look at a darker, grimmer side of town life. Deerfield did not become the way it did solely because of lofty visions of Puritan communal utopias. Necessity, wars, and death all played roles in this drama.

Valley residents paid a heavy price for being pioneers on the edge of a "howling wilderness." Settlers had to clear and farm virgin lands, build their homes and villages, and construct their own local economy as well. These pioneers may have had ideas about how to do all these tasks, but the doing was not easy. Nature's forces made life difficult. Not only might the soil prove unyielding, but varmints plagued the region as well. The Massachusetts government paid £1 for every wolf killed in frontier towns. In 1695 alone Deerfielders earned £11.[4]

There were deeper problems as well. A kind of corrosion, an eating away from within, plagued the Connecticut valley. The problem was not just that crimes were taking place—though there was certainly that. Rather, an unease permeated the region. There was a sense that New England's mission was foundering in the valley far from the Bay—a distance measured spiritually as well as physically. When in 1675 the county court decided a case of a Deerfield couple that had been "living asunder," the justices decried the couple's actions in an extraordinary way. It was, they wrote, a "greate Cause to Lament & bewail ye fore hand of God agst us in suffering such vile enormityes to Breake out amongst us wch *as a flood doe threaten to overwhelm us* [emphasis added]."[5] This same tone, almost of a jeremiad, persisted through King Philip's War. In the 1676 case where a number of future Deerfielders were fined for their "flaunting manner" of "wearing silk, long hair and other extravagences," the court named a total of sixty-nine valley people, a startling number in a region of three thousand. Significant again was the way the judges phrased their verdict. They termed

such behavior "not Becomeing a Wilderness State" and foreign
to "ye Proffession of Christianity & Religion." In other words,
they worried that the valley was going to hell.[6]

Such worries continued after the war. When future Deerfielders John and Mary Evans were brought to court in 1678 for
fornication, the court called it "a matter Heinouse & Shameful . . . Especiallie at such a day of Calamatie as this."[7] But
there was no particular calamity at this time, and the war had
been over for two years.

Other fears gripped the region. In 1682 the Hampshire County
Court called in the selectmen of all the towns in the area to
force them to reinforce the laws about wearing "excesses" in
their clothing "beyound what the Law allowes."[8] More ominous, in 1675, 1683, and 1691 there arose valley cases of witchcraft, signs both of individual deviant behavior and of severe
community pressures.[9] Amidst all this Deerfield did not harbor
any particular evil, but even if the town itself was not corroded
by trouble, trouble was always nearby.

Part of what plagued the valley was the severity and even the
apparent arbitrariness of God's judgments. This emerged particularly in the valley's frequent confrontations with death. It
was all well and good that a settler might calmly "Resign" his
"Soule & Body unto ye hand of almightie God . . . my Com-
forter" upon one's death, yet "ye Afflicting hand of ye lord" had
not made life easy.[10] Death could come at any time and in any
way, as Deerfield well knew. Between 1680 and 1704, in a
village of just sixty men, sixteen died. Some had lived full lives,
like seventy-year-old Richard Weller and seventy-eight-year-
old William Brooks. Yet the list also includes twenty-four-year-
old Robert Alexander, killed on a 1690 Indian expedition to
Schenectady; civic leader Joseph Barnard, age forty-four, killed
by Indians in 1695 on his way to the local mill; and thirty-two-
year-old Thomas Broughton, killed by Indians in town in 1693.
Broughton's case widens the circle of death, for slain with him
were his wife and three children and also a neighbor's two
children.[11]

Not all Deerfielders died at the hands of Indians. In 1689 the
town lost twenty-three-year-old Anna Hinsdale Kellogg in

childbirth, the same fate that befel Joseph Petty's wife, Elizabeth, in 1702. Benoni Stebbins's wife, Mary, clung to life for
two months after she bore twins, but she succumbed on April
2, 1689. In the winter of 1694 fire consumed not merely Godfrey Nims's house but his young stepson, Jeremiah Hull, as
well.[12] Other county records from this period show how perilous life could be for youngsters. When a six-year-old Northampton girl died in 1684, an inquiry showed that "the cause
of her death was by a piece of turnep" caught in her windpipe.[13]
An even younger boy died one December when he "went out
to a sled without the dors and Indeavoring to get up upon the
sled halfe loaden with wood, a log Rowled down on the child."[14]

Life in and around Deerfield was not all grim. That townspeople worked together so extensively suggests a group of pioneers with shared goals. The town also had its ordinary measures
of life and growth. The average family had five or six children,
as many as in other places in early New England. Still, the
hardships of life frequently and often tragically reminded Deerfielders of their place in the world.

"Garrison and town . . .": 1688–1698

While everyday life on the frontier brought its own difficulties and dangers, the most tangible and immediate threat Deerfielders faced was war. Between 1688 and 1698 war again swept
into the Connecticut valley, driving back the frontier and taking
lives and property. Again the valley was caught in a crossfire
between rival Indian forces amidst a wider war. Once again
Deerfield bore a large share of the death and destruction.

Although warfare was not new to the Connecticut valley, the
enemies were. King William's War was the first of four so-called
"French and Indian" wars, as France and England struggled
from 1689 to 1763 for European control of North America. At
the same time, these wars were far more complicated than their
simple, Eurocentric titles imply, for Indians played critical,
active roles on both sides. King William's War embroiled a
number of different Indian forces, including most prominently
those of the Iroquois nation. When the war ended, the balance

of power between the French, English, and Iroquois had shifted significantly.

To understand the war from Deerfield's perspective—to understand the effects of war on a single place—requires a study of different wars. For this was not simply a European conflict carried over to America and fought by colonists. It was that—but it was far more. It also marked the escalation of an ongoing, shifting struggle by the Iroquois to maintain their strength and stature in North America. Strategically situated, these pivotal natives found themselves pressured not only between the English and the French but also by other Indian forces. For the people of Deerfield and the Connecticut valley, the conflict had still other consequences as well. At the start of King William's War, the valley frontier was a region of interaction between Europeans and natives; the colonists still distinguished between different groups of Indians; and "the frontier" was a fluid buffer zone of interchange. By 1698, that was no longer true: The war had hardened lines. All of these conflicts comprise this next chapter of Deerfield's story.

Europe had given a sigh of relief—and exhaustion—when in 1648 the Peace of Westphalia also brought with it a crucial balance of power on the continent. As the seventeenth century moved into its second fifty years, however, the France of Louis XIV came to dominate Europe. During this period, Louis made a series of attempts to enlarge France's power, which led him into war. One of these campaigns was the War of the League of Augsburg, or Nine Years War, of 1688–1697. The war pitted France against the combined forces of Rome, Spain, Sweden, the Dutch, and the smaller states of Bavaria, the Palatinate, and Saxony. These forces were directed by the Dutch leader William of Orange. When England's Glorious Revolution deposed James II, an ally of Louis, in 1688 and Parliament brought William and (James's sister) Mary in to rule, William brought England against France as well. The war proved indecisive, with much "toing and froing"; as early as 1693 "both sides had realized the impossibility of final victory."[15] The Treaty of Ryswick, which ended hostilities in 1697, reflected the inconclusiveness of the struggle.

As there was war in Europe, so was there war in America. What makes this ultimately important to Deerfield, so distant in time, place, and scale, is that war between England and France brought New England and New France—Canada—to war as well. In America the conflict became known as King William's War.

Within North America itself Europeans had other reasons for conflict. One is that the rivalry for the fur trade continued to intensify. As England and France pushed for more furs, they and their Indian partners advanced into new territories and closer to one another. The buffer between Europeans was shrinking. National pride also played a role. After all, the settlers of New England in 1688 saw themselves as English, not American, and those of New France were French, not Canadian.

Still, from a European perspective it was a curious conflict in America. No incident or particular new clash between French and English in America triggered it. Besides, each nation had reason to fear new fighting. In the late 1680s, New England was still recovering from the devastation of King Philip's War, while New France was reeling from Iroquois attacks earlier in the decade.

The English and French ministries' attitudes toward the war in America also made the conflict curious.[16] Although there were major differences between the English and French colonies in size, economy, population, aims, and administration, the two nations maintained essentially the same foreign policies. In time of war in Europe the colonies were expected to fight. Yet they were expected to provide for their own defenses. Further, while aid was low, expectations were high. While both France and England wanted their colonies to do battle, and even to conquer what they could, neither power would commit much in the way of men or matériel to the effort. On their own, then, the colonies took on the bulk of the fighting, but neither side was strong enough to defeat the other.

When word first came from Europe in summer of 1689 that England and France were at war, both colonial sides had visions of early major victories. The French under their new governor, the Comte de Frontenac, dreamed of capturing New York with coordinated expeditions by land and sea.[17] The scheme never got launched. Instead, by late 1689 the French were desperately trying to hold off Iroquois raids which were being reinforced by English aid from Albany. On August 4, 1689, fifteen hundred Iroquois struck at Lachine, near Montreal. Although the blow was not decisive in any long-term sense, its horror and scale terrorized the entire region.[18] Through the summer and fall, smaller raids kept New France edgy.

To turn the tide of these attacks, in early 1690 the French forces—mostly *coureurs de bois* plus allied Indians—struck back, destroying Schenectady, New York, and then Salmon Falls, New Hampshire, and Fort Loyal (Casco Bay) in Maine. The purpose of these thrusts was to put the English on the defensive.[19] Instead, they backfired. Spread as they were across the northern New England frontier, the attacks galvanized the colonies into collective action. Thus, for his trouble Frontenac now faced united and alerted English colonies. Under Sir William Phips, the English schemed to take Canada by capturing its heart and launched an expedition toward Quebec.

Although Phips's forces got closer to Quebec than Frontenac's had to New York, they were barely more successful. Phips did in fact reach Quebec, in October of 1690, but he had taken so much time getting there that he was repulsed merely by bad weather. Besides, Quebec's defenses were almost impregnable,[20] and so after a few days of jabbing and feinting, Phips weighed anchor and limped home. With that, the "major battles" of King William's War were about over.

To his credit, Phips had managed to take Port Royal in Acadia back in the fall of 1689, but beyond that, little else of consequence changed hands through the end of the war. Instead, it settled into *la petite guerre:* fearful watchfulness in towns and outposts punctuated by raids and counterraids.[21] While these attacks "spread terror among the isolated inhabitants of the frontier," they "contributed little toward a meaningful victory for either side."[22]

While ineffectual in broad terms, King William's War certainly made its mark on the Connecticut valley. Since the last

direct Indian attacks on the valley, on Hatfield and Deerfield
in September of 1677, the region had enjoyed over a decade of
peace. In the 1680s Brookfield and Northfield had joined Deerfield in rebuilding. But eleven years without war were all the
settlers would get.

In the summer of 1688 the Canadian governor, the Marquis
de Denonville (Frontenac's appointment was a year away), sent
a war party of allied Indians against the Connecticut valley
frontier. On July 27 the Indians struck at Spectacle Pond near
Springfield, killing five friendly Indians. On August 16 they
killed five or six colonists at Northfield, an assault which contributed to Northfield's abandonment once again, in 1690. That
these attacks took place in 1688, a year *before* England and
France went to war, is no accident. Rather, it bespeaks a "second war" that was being waged at this time, a war in which the
Iroquois played the central role.

While New England's immediate concerns about conflicts
with Indians had lessened after King Philip's War, patterns
of power and allegiance in the northeast continued to shift.
Indian-French, Indian-English, and inter-Indian relations all
changed—and the Iroquois invariably ended up at the heart of
the changes. Conflict did not arise solely over issues of territory
or military superiority. The fur trade, economic dependency,
alliances, political sovereignty, and population losses all played
key roles. The most important single development of this era
came in 1677, when the Iroquois and English forged the "Covenant Chain," a bond of friendship, alliance, mutual support,
and cooperation.[23] Although the chain binding these two powers would be stretched and strained over time, its existence
redefined the balance of power in eastern North America.

The Covenant Chain's significance emerged quickly after 1677.
Once in place, it helped the English get the Susquehannocks
to stop fighting with the Iroquois—a major Iroquois success in
the face of what had been a difficult and destructive war.[24] With
that flank secured, the Iroquois were free to turn their attention
to enemy Indians in the west. Yet the Iroquois were not all-
powerful in the 1680s. The previous decade had been one of
almost continuous warfare, especially against the Mahicans and

the Susquehannocks, and the costs had been high. Epidemics had also hurt the Iroquois off and on for decades. A new outbreak in 1679 forced them to go to war again to replace warriors lost to disease, via their practice of "mourning-war."

This concatenation of inter-Indian conflict and the emerging English-French battle for North America led the Iroquois into a "disastrous spiral of warfare."[25] Soon they were fighting out west, against tribes like the Illinois. Here the Iroquois were not challenging solely other Indians, however, for these western Indians were French allies. The English, led after 1683 by New York governor Thomas Dongan, encouraged the Iroquois, promising them the protection of English forces and reminding them of the Covenant Chain. As the French responded to the Iroquois challenge, then, the Iroquois found themselves ever more deeply embroiled in the English-French conflict.

The French attitude toward the Iroquois bespoke their acknowledgment that the Iroquois were the key force in the region's struggle. Through the 1680s the French alternately employed three policies toward the Iroquois: They tried to convert them to their side, they tried to split them up, and they fought with them. The first policy largely failed, for overall the Iroquois kept their chain with the English intact. The second had more success. As early as 1670 it was clear that the Iroquois, battered by war and disease, had been weakened. Although the 1677 Covenant Chain with the English reassured many Iroquois, both before and after that date others were lured by the promises and protection that the Jesuits, the French missionaries, offered. By the mid-1670s the Jesuits had "literally split Iroquois communities in two" as hundreds of natives, especially Mohawks, made their way to La Prairie and Caughnawaga, near Montreal.[26]

The third French policy—direct fighting against the Iroquois—gained strength through the 1680s as the vortex of war spun faster and faster. The Iroquois attacked western, French-allied Indians; those Indians and the French fought back. The English, led by Dongan, "fed . . . armed . . . rallied . . . [and] harangued" the Iroquois. In response, and buoyed by English promises of protection, the Iroquois "harassed New France from one end to the other."[27] Thus it is no surprise that French-allied Indians struck the Connecticut valley in 1688. Although King William's War had not yet come to America, war between the French and English and their Indian allies had.

Although the war that struck the valley in 1688 differed from King Philip's War in scope, duration, overall aims, and combatants, this did not mean that the patterns of war would be different. In fact, much of King William's War proved eerily familiar to the still-scarred survivors in the region.

Western Massachusetts waged much the same kind of war that it had in facing the Indians of southern New England in 1675–1676. Settlers were protective, trying only to maintain what they had built.[28] The Connecticut valley covered up like an outclassed boxer, hoping only to defend itself and not get knocked out.

The enemy thrusts came much as they had before. Virtually all were surprise attacks and ambushes. Although there was less destruction of property, and casualties were fewer than in King Philip's War, the settlers' losses were still great. In thirteen Indian raids between 1688 and 1698 the valley suffered at least thirty-seven dead, six wounded, and ten captured. At least one person was killed or mortally wounded in all but two of the assaults. As in the 1670s, raiding remained seasonal: Twelve of the thirteen attacks took place between June 6 and October 5. Though the raids were infrequent, the fact that they could come at any time and place forced the settlers once again into a state of constant preparedness and watchfulness. It turned out that the raids were smaller in scale than in the previous conflict, with no attacking party larger than forty or fifty Indians. That did not—could not—change the defensive posture of the valley's colonists, however.

In one respect the war showed a shift of enemy strategy. During King Philip's War settlers had to contend with strikes anywhere in the valley. In King William's War, the attackers from the north consistently hit northern settlements the hardest. Because of the 1688 attack, Northfield was already abandoned by the time of the next strike. Between 1693 and 1698, Hatfield took two blows, Hadley and Brookfield one each—and the northernmost outpost of Deerfield took six. Significantly, Springfield, Westfield, and Northampton to the south all escaped without a scratch.

The enemy itself, of course, had changed. In this war a range of Indian forces joined the French in attacking the valley. These Indians included groups variously termed Eastern, Abenaki, North, Canada, or simply "French" Indians. Most came from northern New England, especially from Maine, and included remnants of some tribes vanquished in King Philip's War. Likely they also included some Caughnawagas, or "French Mohawks." Thus the enemy was as expected. However, three of the raiding parties also included Scaticookes from across the Hudson—Nipmuck and Pocumtuck survivors who fled there from the valley after 1676. Their presence suggests that Indian survivors of King Philip's War had not forgotten their conquerors.

The pattern of attacks demonstrates continued intelligent and successful Indian strategy and method. By the absence of major forces in the area, it is apparent that the Indians were making no great attempt to defeat the English per se; indeed, they were not. Rather, the French and Indians were content to harass and frighten the settlers, to keep them on the defensive. In this regard, the continuation of surprise attacks served its purpose. By this strategy the Indians did not have to pay great attention to the region or maintain large forces nearby. Occasional forays, even with as much as a year or two between them, made settlers afraid to do more than keep constant watch and send out scouts.

By hitting northern valley settlements the hardest, the Indians may have hoped to push the frontier south, as the Indians in King Philip's War had done so successfully in 1675. If this is true, then the 1688 raid on Northfield served its purpose impressively. More likely, however, the Indians hit more up north because those were the first settlements they came to, because the villages there were smaller, and because those sites afforded the easiest routes of retreat. In this respect, one has to almost "redraw the map" of New England to understand attacks on the region. From the vantage point of settlers in Deerfield and the valley, the French-allied Indians were traveling great distances to attack them. These Indians' villages often lay over two hundred miles away, as did the protective forces of New France. If one looks solely at settlements, however, Deerfield was Canada's "neighbor," as near to Montreal as any town in New England.

Still, the Connecticut valley held no key to grand plans of the English, French, or Indians. Overall, western Massachusetts was a minor front in this war. The Indian attacks clearly hurt local settlers and settlements, but the overall impact of these assaults on the valley was less than in 1675–1676. Although the nature of war in western Massachusetts had not changed very much, the enemy, era, and full scope of the war had.

These different pictures, of a European war carried over to America and of a North American war that struck the upper Connecticut valley, help put Deerfield in perspective. In the first view, the town is but a tiny dot in a global picture; in the second, it becomes a larger, though still not dominant, part of a colonial conflict. A wide-angle lens focused on Deerfield brings the town's people and life into full view.

When war struck the Connecticut valley in summer of 1688, Deerfield was well along in rebuilding. It was not alone in this. Three years earlier the General Court had granted the chance to resettle to the former inhabitants of "Squakeage," or Northfield, some twelve or fifteen miles upriver.[29] Deerfield's neighbors at Hatfield, ten miles below, had also rebuilt and fortified their town after 1677. The successful Indian raid on Northfield in August of 1688 tore at Deerfield's sense of security, however. When Northfield's settlers abandoned their plantation less than two years later, Deerfields' once again lay exposed as the valley's northernmost post. It would remain that way for the next quarter century.

Even before Northfield was abandoned, Deerfielders realized they needed to fortify their town. Lieutenant Thomas Wells could tell them how fortunate they had been in not being attacked along with Northfield and Springfield in 1688. Just a few days before the July 27 attack at Springfield, eleven Indians who "lived amongst ye ffrench" had come to Deerfield and stayed with Wells, leaving the next day for Hatfield. Soon after, other Indians came to town and told Wells that the first group had been sent out by the French, instructed to bring back not captives but "only their scalps." Three days later came the Springfield attack and, two weeks after that, the deaths at Northfield.[30]

Still, the deaths at Northfield did not galvanize Deerfield into action; Schenectady did. On the night of February 18, 1690, a French and Indian force surprised the frontier settlement of Schenectady, New York, some eighty miles to the west, killing almost sixty people and burning most of the houses in town. The strike horrified the English. It also shocked them: A full-sized raid, in mid-winter, on a village outpost far from French lines, had succeeded brilliantly.

Deerfield quickly started to prepare. Within a week of learning of the Schenectady disaster, a special town meeting was called. The agenda had just one item: to discuss the building of "a good sufficient fortification . . . upon the Meeting hous hill." As a sense of urgency gripped the town, every man was required to build "his part or proportion of fortification." With a seven-man committee overseeing the operation, residents were given less than two weeks to finish their work.[31]

The fort surrounded the heart of the town, measuring roughly forty by sixty rods.[32] Within it stood the meetinghouse, the town common, and perhaps fifteen houses. Settlers whose houses lay outside the fort were also taken care of. If they could not find room to sleep in another's home inside the fort, the town built them "habitations" within—all at town charge.[33]

Like all New England towns, Deerfield had its own militia. The idea of universal military service for men from sixteen to sixty was both law and tradition. Every year a town's able-bodied men would muster on the town common, show the clerk their required arms and ammunition, and go through training sessions. Each town had to have its own "sufficient Watch house" as well, and selectmen were responsible for maintaining "a stock of powder and ammunition in each town."[34] Yet while militias were a constant in New England, vigilance was not. Indeed, "frantic efforts to build or repair fortifications because of a sudden threat were characteristic of the New England military system."[35]

County efforts complemented Deerfield's in the months after Schenectady. In late March of 1690, Hampshire's Colonel Pynchon established "a weekly Scout of 14 or 16 men" to search out the enemy. A month later Pynchon wrote to the General Court that the "safety of the whole County" might well depend on Deerfield, since it was "a frontier to the whole county." He urged the placing of a garrison of "thirty or forty men" in the town, whose people were at the time "under grt discouragements." Two months later the Hampshire County Court sent a scout "as far as the falls that are above Northfield to make what discovery they can of the Enemie."[36]

The reward in 1690 for all these preparations was quietude. The only force that struck the valley in 1690 was an epidemic (which disease is unknown) that swept downriver, leaving a "hundred persons sick at Deerfield, about forescore at Northampton, many at Hadley & Hatfield." "The arrows of mortality and death, are flying thick from town to town, & from family to family," grimly reported a valley resident.[37]

Both illness and the Indians spared Deerfield and the valley in 1691. Still, all was not restful. A large band of Indians struck Salmon Falls, New Hampshire, killing thirty, burning twenty-five houses, and taking fifty prisoners. Attacks had now hit the New England frontier both east and west of Deerfield.[38] Tensions rose higher with the arrival of a band of about one hundred fifty Indians at a site near Deerfield. These natives were "friendly" Indians who carried "a written Pass Subscribed by y[e] Mayor of Albany." Still, John Pynchon wrote in December, "difficultys many ways" could well arise with the Indians so close, residing "under y[e] Side of y[e] Mountain" east of Wapping, just two miles south of town. Pynchon again suggested putting a garrison of soldiers at Deerfield, sending out "scouts" each week, or perhaps forming a band of forty to sixty men out of the upper valley towns to "be in readiness." "If such a company in their Arms should only march once or twice this winter to Dearefeild," he continued, "y[e] very sight of them might awe these Indians." At the same time, Pynchon feared that valley residents were starting to let down their guard, in spite of the fact that "ye talke is y^t the French [are] coming down on us this winter." And Deerfield, Pynchon noted in closing, was in particularly bad straits. By "a sad froune of God," Lieutenant Thomas Wells, Deerfield's "very useful & . . . much wanted" military leader, had died.[39]

Fortunately for Deerfield and the valley, all remained calm. Pynchon set up specific restrictions for the Albany Indians, and relations remained peaceful. Meanwhile, the war continued, but on other fronts far from town. Thus 1692 passed quietly as well.

But even if Deerfield did not see actual combat, the war was taking its toll. Certainly the Indian threat stayed in people's minds. In late December of 1692, while drawing up the town contract for the corn mill Joseph Parsons was to build, Deerfield's committee inserted a clause that Parsons would not lose rights to his mill if the townspeople were "driven out by an Enimie."[40] Beyond this, Deerfield reaped a lean harvest that year. Worms had infested local crops, and only "some meate or few barrels of Porke wch are scarce may be in Dearefield."[41] Most telling was a petition the town sent to Massachusetts governor William Phips in early 1693. It told of the town's "present Afflicted state," explaining how Deerfield had "for a long time Been Much Exercised And at great Expenses in purchaseing and seteling our place anew" and how by "Hazzard of ye Approaching of enimies" townspeople were now spending "a great part of our Time in Watchings Wardings Scoutings and Making of fortifications." Family, church, and town were all threatened. To conclude, Deerfielders sought "help And releife" from the "Extreame Difficulties" in this "Exposed" place. Any funds from "their Majesties treasury" would help, as would a "sutable supply of Amunition we haveing no town stock." An abatement of taxes would be appreciated, too.[42]

The General Court heard Deerfield's plea and answered it. In March it established a valley committee to manage the town's defense, sent men to help repair the fort, and supplied ammunition. The Court acknowledged that Deerfield was the spearhead of the valley's defense, declaring that the place must "be mainetained, & not Deserted."[43] At roughly the same time, Governor Phips wrote the Connecticut governor and Council seeking aid for the valley. As in 1675, the region's defense was to be an intercolonial affair. Phips urged that there "be some souldiers detached & sent to secure Dearfeild." He left the details "to Coll: pincheon."[44]

By April Connecticut, too, had responded.[45] Deerfield now had more attention and aid than at any time since the attacks on Northfield and Springfield in 1688. Yet it was not enough. On the night of June 6, 1693, around midnight a band of Indians struck the town and committed a "Barbarous murther." Attacking two houses, they killed thirty-two-year-old Thomas Broughton, his pregnant wife, Hester, and three of their children, plus scalped three of widow Hepzibah Wells's daughters, two of whom died. One escapee reported that as he lay hidden in his bedchamber he heard the settlers "plead for their lives"; Broughton "pleadd if his own life might not be spared his children might," but the Indians retorted, "we don't care for ye xdren & will kill y^m all."[46]

Less than two months later violence rocked the valley again. On July 27 a band of thirty or forty "Canida Indians" attacked Brookfield, killing six settlers. One Brookfield man who escaped rushed to Springfield, where authorities put together a thirty-man force to pursue the enemy. By following tracks, the colonial force moved northwesterly—toward Deerfield.[47] The town quickly sent out scouts and prepared to face the enemy. Although trackers found that the Indians had traveled "near about ye falls above dearefeild" and not directly to the town, they were aware that "ye enemy are sett upon mischeife & in all likelihoods to doe it in small ptes [parties] scattering y^m-selves to alarm & doe small exploites wth ye killing of men at their Labors." Townspeople dared not ease up in their vigilance, either, for the Indians might lurk in the valley's woods for "two months or thereabouts." The town lay in an unseen state of siege.[48]

Fortunately for Deerfield, Captain George Colton and his soldiers freed the town. Tracking the enemy successfully, they surprised them just after sunup on July 30. Killing six and routing the rest, they seized the Indians' gunpowder plus nine guns, twenty hatchets, four cutlasses, and the plunder taken at Brookfield.

The valley was spared further attacks for the rest of the summer. That did not mean that enemies were not lurking, however. Deerfield was painfully reminded of this on the morning of October 13 when settler Martin Smith was seized and taken to Canada.

As the threat of war abated with the winter of 1693, Deerfielders sent another petition to the General Court. The "frontier town" had been "much Infested" with the enemy that year, causing "Grate Impoverishment." Conditions were so bad, the petitioners continued, that without assistance "we must of necessity forsake o^r habitations and draw off to some neighboring tounes." Assistance might come in two forms: exemption from taxes "dureing the present distress" and establishment of a garrison of "Eighteen or twenty souldrs" to reside in town.[49]

If the petitioners were bluffing with their threat to abandon Deerfield, the General Court was not prepared to call their bluff. The town had obviously suffered, and it remained the spearhead of the western Massachusetts frontier. With these points in mind, on November 28 the General Court ordered that the town be allowed a £40 "discount" in their taxes, to be used to pay for the fortifications. Later that session the Court "abated their share or part of the next Tax and until the court take further notice."[50]

The next summer passed uneventfully—until yet another sneak attack struck the town. On September 15, 1694, a French-allied Indian force crept to the edge of town through the woods to the east. Young Daniel Severance caught sight of the Indians as they were emerging from a ravine, and he paid for his discovery with his life. With the gunshot that killed Severance, however, the Indians lost their surprise. As settlers scrambled for their guns, the Indians rushed down from the northeast toward the town fort. Just ahead of them flew Hannah Beaman, the town's school dame, and her young students, sprinting for the fort's north gate. As town chronicler George Sheldon engraved it, "fear gave wings to the children," for they all got inside the fort just before the Indians could catch them. With the gate closed and the town alerted, the settlers held off their attackers with no further loss of life.[51]

Once again Deerfield had been reminded of its perilous position. John Pynchon set the tone for Massachusetts' attitude "about continueing or quitting ye Garrison at Dearefeild" in a letter to the Council on December 3, 1694. The winter gave "hope of some respit & allowance of some ease," since attack was so unlikely, and thus a garrison could be "dismissed or abated for a month or sixeweike [six weeks]"—but "not much longer." By early February the enemy could be on the move again and, Pynchon reasoned, "may as wel come to Dearefeild." The town therefore needed a garrison "provided & Setled in January."[52]

As weeks passed and no help came from Massachusetts or Connecticut, Deerfield became nervous. In late winter the town anxiously sent Pynchon a letter beseeching help. By that point, Pynchon later reported, townspeople had "been so frighted . . . that they dare not stay there if naked of men." Pynchon sent a few soldiers up to town, yet "Dearefeild being a large fortification cannot wel be secured [with] under 32 men," and Pynchon himself could not spare more.[53]

Neither could—or would—Connecticut. An exchange of increasingly acrimonious letters between Massachusetts and Connecticut yielded no more soldiers from the colony below.[54] By the summer of 1695 a short-handed John Pynchon was struggling to defend the valley. He could not quite do it. On August 10 a band of "Enymy Indians" attacked a smaller group of friendly "Albany Indians" who were "Hunting above Deerfield," just a few miles north of "where Northfield once stood." Pynchon immediately sent twenty-four soldiers into the area and tried to raise more troops as well, hoping he could put off the enemy's "atacqueing of Deerfield."[55] His efforts fell short. On August 21, in the only attack on valley settlements that summer, Indians ambushed three Deerfielders as they crossed a bridge on their way to the mill. Joseph Barnard was hit by gunfire and mortally wounded. Godrey Nims had his horse shot out from under him, yet survived by getting a ride back to the fort from Philip Mattoon.

The next thirteen months passed without incident in the valley. Then, on September 16, 1696, the enemy surprised Deerfielders John Smead and John Gillett in the woods near town, capturing Gillett, and then attacked the home of Daniel Belding outside the fort. Belding and two children were captured, his wife and three children killed, and one other wounded. For the fourth straight summer, blood had been spilled at Deerfield. Although the town held firm, these continuing strikes—and Deerfield's state of siege—continued. Looking back, Massachusetts had been right about the need for more defenses at the outpost—and yet Connecticut's reticence was understandable. Ambushes by small groups of Indians, as these were, were almost impossible to stop.

Other events of 1696 reflect the depth of Deerfield's plight. That summer the General Court had acknowledged the town's distress by granting a sum of £10 from the treasury "towards the Maintenance of the Ministry at the Garrison & Towne of Deerfield."[56] In October Connecticut renewed its recognition of the importance of this "garrison and town." This time, responding to a plea by Reverend John Williams and other valley authorities about Deerfield's "distressed condition" and "great and continuall fear," Connecticut sent forty men "with all possible speed" to the outpost.[57]

This speed reflected yet another new phase of the region's agony, for Hadley resident Richard Church had been killed—by gunshot in the head, arrow in the body, and scalping—by a small band of supposedly friendly Indians from the Albany area. Although four Indians were arrested and tried, and two executed, the region hardly needed this kind of difficulty.[58]

The responses to this apparent betrayal show the increasing strains of war. In the summer of 1695 Connecticut had abandoned its long-standing practice of trade with friendly Indians in the upper valley. Massachusetts quickly did the same, forbidding settlers to "give, trade, sell, deal, truck or barter any goods, wares, merchandizes, ammunition, or . . . stray liquors" under pain of a £100 fine.[59] In 1696 the General Court went further, declaring that "all Indians . . . found within twenty miles on the westerly side of the Connecticut River, shall be deemed enemies and treated forthwith." Within three years the region had gone from open relations with friendly Indians to restricted trade and now to the banning of the natives entirely. War had altered the very nature of the frontier. No longer could English colonists consider the edge of settlement a fluid region of interaction and exchange. The risks had proven too high, the destruction too great. A letter from March of 1697 reflects the settlers' fears and frustrations. Hatfield's militia leader Samuel Partridge decried "what a deceitful nation & people we have to deal with. . . . these Indians that pretend freindship" have brought only "agrevation of our trouble & difficultie."[60] In truth, he wrote in a different letter, these "treacherous & deceitful" Indians are "worse than open Enemys."

As a further reflection of the growing bitterness of this guerrilla war, the Massachusetts government now increased the bounties to be paid for Indian prisoners and scalps, a practice in place since the beginning of the war. By summer of 1697 officers and companies would receive £50 for an Indian man, and £25 for any Indian woman or child, slain or brought in. Scalps could be delivered to the commissioner of war.[61]

In Deerfield itself, citizens of that "hazzardous place" remained understandably "fearful" about their "pretended freinds."[62] Thus, taking advantage of forty "Train Soldiers" sent from Connecticut, they used the winter of 1696–1697 to repair the town's palisade. The following March the citizens decided to add three new "mounts" to the fort as well as construct three new town gates "strong and substantiall with Conveniencyes for fastning both open and shut." Deerfield received a scare during this period when unknown Indians killed some cattle of Joseph Brooks near town on Decmeber 11, 1696, but otherwise the war stayed at arm's length from the village.[63]

All this strengthening of defenses paid off, of a fashion, for the enemy did not strike Deerfield again in the last two years of the war. It appears the Indians now recognized the strength of the Deerfield garrison, for the last two valley attacks of the war came below Deerfield at Hatfield. Of course, this did not mean Deerfield could let down its guard. The town remained the linchpin of valley defense, as evidenced by the distribution of Massachusetts garrison soldiers in the summer of 1698: two each to Northampton, Hadley, and Westfield, three to Hatfield, and *sixteen* to Deerfield.[64] And Deerfield remained an explicit Indian target. As late as June of 1698 the Massachusetts Council received a report from a friendly Indian that a war party of "near seventy" French and Indians was on its way down from Canada, with sixteen "designed for Deerfield."[65] With "all yᵉ soldiers" of the valley at Deerfield and the town regularly sending out scouts, however, the Indians struck below at Hatfield, killing three in the last valley assault of the war.[66]

After July of 1698, with word of the Treaty of Ryswick reaching across the Atlantic, the fighting ceased. King William's War had resolved very little of France and England's rivalry for North America. Ryswick reflected this lack of resolution, restoring borders and territories in North America to *status quo ante bellum.*

At the same time, the war had a profound effect on the Indian-European balance of power in America. The 1690s had proven disastrous for the Iroquois. Although the English had promised great help, they had delivered precious little; indeed, as allies they had proven "nearly useless."[67] The Iroquois had their share of military success against the French and their allies, but while "Iroquois harassment caused great suffering in Canada, it fell far short of decisive triumph."[68] Meanwhile, the toll of war proved appallingly high. By the end of the war, Iroquois fighting strength had been cut by as much as one-half and total population had declined similarly. As early as 1693 Mohawk losses were so severe that they could not "function effectively as a fighting force." By the middle of the decade the Iroquois were "desperate men, reeling in pain from the shock of French blows and outraged by unfulfilled promises by the English."[69] They split into three blocks—Francophiles, Anglophiles, and neutrals—with the first two at times actually fighting each other.[70] On top of all this, Ryswick did not end the war for the Iroquois, for the French would not settle and Iroquois fighting with other Indians out west continued. By 1700 the Iroquois "teetered on the brink of annihilation."[71]

The result was a fundamental shift in the balance of power. Even as the French and their allies kept fighting the Iroquois, they also offered sanctuary to individuals, a policy that proved increasingly effective. By 1700 the Iroquois began to talk peace. Although defeated, they did not surrender to the French. Rather, they chose a diplomatic path that kept them independent of both the English and the French. With the English they negotiated to rebuild the Covenant Chain, both for protection and for trade. With the French, by the "Grand Settlement of 1701" the Iroquois ended their long struggle and established neutrality. And they did much more. By this treaty, they brought Iroquois factions back together; they became an important buffer for both the English and the French; they enhanced their position as traders with different markets to ply; and they got a chance to recover from the devastation of the 1690s.[72]

While outwardly stable, Deerfield and the Connecticut valley had been shaken by the war. For the second time pioneers at Northfield had failed to sustain a town in the face of Indian attacks. Thus, the line of settlement remained as it had been for a quarter century. No villages north or west of Deerfield protected the town, nor would any be established for almost two more decades. Although not as destructive as the fifteen months of King Philip's War, eleven years of conflict took their toll. Deerfield's losses were by far the highest of any town: twelve dead, five wounded, and five captured in a population of 250. Six valley towns had been attacked. Four saw the enemy only once, Hatfield bore two blows—and Deerfield took the other seven.

Deerfield's losses can be measured in other ways. This village which had rebuilt so rapidly in the 1680s had its growth stunted by the war. Indian attacks destroyed men and families and homes; they also kept prospective settlers away from the town. The town might even have been abandoned entirely were it not for a 1695 Massachusetts statute which forbade residents of frontier towns from moving elsewhere without express authority.[73]

Beyond the numbers were other losses. Feeding and maintaining a garrison and fort had turned Deerfield into a military outpost, which strained the town's resources and spirit. Sickness and famine, the result of ruined crops, plagued the village in two different years. Men on watch lost days, weeks, months of time better spent in the fields. The town fell into such dire straits that twice it put the possibility of abandonment before the General Court. The Court aided Deerfield with tax abatements, soldiers, money for fortifications, and support for the ministry. Yet all this petitioning and aid bespeak a town in desperate shape. The town lived in a virtual state of siege for fully half the decade, trying to survive amidst the continual threat of attack. For Deerfield in the 1690s, the frontier meant war, and war brought unending fears, pressures, and losses.

Coda: The Trials of Sarah Smith

If all this were not enough, just as the tensions of war were finally easing in 1698, Deerfield suffered the most dramatic and perhaps terrible personal horror in its first half century. The story of Sarah Smith brings together the dominant themes of Deerfield's life through this entire period—war, the pressures of the frontier, living a proper Puritan life, townspeople closely bound up with one another, living with sin, and living with death—and binds them together in a story of adultery and murder which ended with western Massachusetts' first known public execution.

Sarah Smith's origins are unclear. Local tradition would tie her to a family in Hadley where one Philip Smith was "murdered with a hideous witchcraft,"[74] but there is no direct evidence to support this. All that is clear is that she was living in Deerfield with her husband, Martin, in 1693 when he was captured by "Canada Indians." Of Martin more is known. One of Pocumtuck's first settlers, as a young single man he got in trouble with the law in 1674 when he tried to kiss Jedediah Strong's wife and offered her "some abuse." After Bloody Brook he had moved to Northampton, yet returned early in the resettlement efforts, securing a home lot in 1682. Two years later he married Mary Phelps of Northampton; within a year of her death in 1692, he married Sarah. Although he served as a fence viewer in 1689, he left no record of further service to the town before his capture on October 13, 1693, near Wapping.

From that point on Sarah was alone, for she had no children and her family apparently did not live in Deerfield. In the summer of 1694, she became a public figure, though hardly through any wish of her own. On the night of July 31 Deerfielder John Evans came to her house just outside the fort and talked with her for a few minutes. After a while he turned to go "look after his watch," but then, declaring it was not yet time, he turned around and, "putting his hand under my apron," as Sarah later testified, attacked the woman. As she drew away, he threw her onto the floor, got on top of her, and pulled up her petticoat. Then, Sarah continued, he "fell on my Naked body On my prwy pts [private parts] & after open his privy pts so y^t I Saw them." Though she resisted, Evans continued to try "forceing an Unclean act" upon her. Once she almost freed herself, but Evans got her under him a second time. Still she resisted, now crying out. Two watchmen, sixteen-year-olds Ebenezer Stebbins and Henry White, heard the "noyse" of "distress." Rushing to the house, the moonlight pouring in the door revealed Evans's attempted rape and Sarah's "striving and strugling." Stunned with "fear and trembling att such actions," the two lads stood transfixed as she resisted "his Evil Intent"; as Evans "was getting up," they "ran away from that door" and did not speak out until five days later.[75]

No record has been found of what, if any, punishment John Evans suffered for this attempted rape. Nor is there any way to gauge the trauma that Sarah Smith felt as she continued alone, a young wife without family living in a besieged frontier town with her husband captured by Indians and probably dead. For three more years Smith lived under these conditions. Then came a new and greater tragedy.

On the winter afternoon of January 11, 1698, in an upstairs bedroom of Daniel Weld's home in Deerfield where she was evidently living, Sarah Smith secretly gave birth to an infant bastard daughter. Sometime later that afternoon, by a combination of withholding care from the child and then smothering it, Smith killed her baby. Then she tied it up in an apron, bringing the four corners together, and placed the body under her bed.

Her crime was quickly discovered. For some time Reverend John Williams and some neighboring women had suspected Smith's pregnancy and questioned her about it. She had denied all, however, and had held off any direct action by others. Clearly she hoped to continue this charade, for she bore the child alone and the Welds knew nothing of what was taking place upstairs. But she could not conceal her pain, or the signs of delivery, from other women of the town. Hearing that Smith was ill, thirty-three-year-old Mary Allin went over to see her and found Smith in great travail, for her water had broken. Seeking out thirty-one-year-old Mehitable Nims and two of the older wives in town, Mary Catlin and Elizabeth Smead, the four returned to find Smith in such a condition that she had to have given birth already. They confronted Smith, but again she denied all, claiming only an ague, a sickness. This time Goodwife Allin lit a candle and searched the room until she found the corpse at the foot of the bed.

The next day twelve Deerfield men formed a jury of inquest and examined the child. Their discovery of blackened lips and a flat nose made them suspect strangulation or smothering. In any event, there appeared no question about the crime, only about the method.

Because the winter was so severe, Deerfield's officials kept Smith in town for a month. Then, on February 11, they moved her to Springfield. As the law required, the Massachusetts Council called for a trial of the Court of Assizes and General Gaol Delivery, to be led by three justices of the Superior Court of Judicature. Proceedings began with an inquest by a sixteen-man grand jury, followed by the trial, on August 18, 1698. The trial took just one day. Rather than addressing the issue of adultery at all, the court focused wholly on the charge of murder, that Smith had been "led by the instigation of the devil" to do "Malice [a]forethoug" in killing her child. Smith pleaded not guilty. The court heard as testimony the sworn statements of Smith and the other women of town who had found her. The issue arose of what man was involved. Smith "vehemently charged" garrison soldier Joseph Clesson with the act, claiming that she had told him she was pregnant. In response to that, she continued, he had offered her money to keep quiet. Clesson denied all, though, and there is no surviving record of action against him.

The twelve-man jury did not take long to reach its verdict. The court swiftly sentenced Smith to the "pains of death." She was ordered to "be led back again to the place whence she came, and from thence be led to the place of Execution" in Springfield, to "be hanged by the neck until she be dead." The court set the date of execution as August 25, 1698, between twelve and four in the afternoon.[76]

On Sarah Smith's day of doom, Reverend John Williams gave the "lecture" that preceded the hanging. He called it "Warnings to the Unclean." It offers much insight into Deerfield's world in 1698. Williams's sermon was a long one, running some sixty-four printed pages. Through most of it he preached against "whoredom," murder, and adultery, those "sins of darkness." In part a jeremiad, Williams's lecture railed against such sins as "a prevailing, growing evil." He hoped his sermon would prove a "matter of Awakening to all unclean Sinners, Adulterers or Fornicators."

Not until the last few pages of his sermon did Williams turn and give a "word of Warning" to Smith herself, "the occasion of our being here this day . . . under the Righteous Sentence of Death." Williams assailed her "moral evils, lying, Stealing, Adultery, and Murder." He looked into her past and saw that over the years she had "sinned more and more," leading up to her "wantonly doting on . . . Lovers," she who had "idled, slept away, yea whored away part of so many Sabbaths." Now she should die, for her life could not "be saved without injustice."

The tirade continued: "Don't think your Prayers, good promises, and others praying for you, will save you." Yet he urged that she "Hasten" to Christ, for only he might bring her "out of

the pit." "Oh that you may be saved from the unbelief, hypoc-
risie, worldliness, hardness and carnality of your heart," he
concluded.[77]

Williams's sermon contained no mercy, nor is there any evidence that anyone sought it. The vicissitudes of war had not
bent the minister from his course, and the firmness, even rigid-
ity, of his beliefs and tone match the cries that had come from
the Hampshire County justices in these same years after 1675.
The true path of righteousness was not wide: It demanded
careful following lest the sins of the world overwhelm the people. At no time did Williams suggest that God had brought
King William's War upon New England as punishment, as some
had suggested about King Philip's War in 1675. Yet neither did
he allow that the terrible strains of war might bring with them
some ease from the harsh dictates of Puritanism. Williams's
path remained clear, and his sermon suggests that he expected
nothing less of his congregants. Even after a decade of war, and
in a town struggling to survive—or perhaps especially there—
God's law remained fixed.

Of Sarah Smith many things could be said. John Williams's
fury implies a woman who had been an evil influence on the
town for years. Yet her struggle against John Evans in 1694
suggests a different picture. So, too, do certain facts surrounding her crime. If she were as sinful as Williams claimed, she
simply might have kept the child. But enough in her evidently
told her of the evil of bastardy that she tried to conceal her act,
and in so doing committed a more heinous crime. Without
knowing more about her life, she cannot be judged as so wantonly evil as Williams portrayed her. And yet her sins were
horrible.

It would add immeasurably to know what Sarah Smith's fellow townspeople knew of her and felt about her. But it cannot
be. Instead, only one more note in the town records pertains to
the case. In December of 1698, having been gone for five years,
Martin Smith was reported "newly returned out of captivity."

EIGHT

The Wheel Turns Again: Deerfield and Queen Anne's War

T HE AGREEMENT that England and France had concluded at Ryswick in 1697 was more an armistice
than a treaty. Both the actual fighting of the war and
the settlement proved inconclusive. The reason for
this was clear: Charles II of Spain, an aged, crippled, impotent,
pathetic product of generations of royal inbreeding, was about
to die without an heir. By 1697 Europe anxiously awaited his
death and the determination of the fate of the Spanish empire.
When it finally came in 1700, Charles's death interrupted negotiations between Louis XIV of France and William of Orange
over the control of Spain and the dispensation of her overseas
trade. When it was surprisingly announced that Charles had
left a will, the negotiations broke down entirely. The will shook
Europe and drove it once again into war.

In essence, Charles had ceded the Spanish throne to Louis
XIV via his grandson, duc d'Anjou, and further stipulated that
if Louis did not take the crown it would go to the son of the
Hapsburg emperor. Although Louis was not anxious to plunge
into another war, he could hardly forgo the chance to gain
control over the Spanish empire, much less let such power slip
from his hands to the rival Hapsburgs. Therefore, though he
knew that accepting the will's terms would likely bring a re-
sumption of war, he took the risk and accepted Spain for his
grandson.[1]

England quickly responded. To oppose France and Spain,
William brought together the "Grand Alliance," composed of

much the same forces as he had led in 1689: England, Holland, Rome, Brandenburg, Portugal, and Savoy. Thus began what became known in Europe as the War of the Spanish Succession.

When war broke out in Europe in 1702, prospects for renewed war in North America rose quickly. In the lull between storms—the five years of peace between New England and New France from 1697 to 1702—both sides had moved to strengthen Indian alliances. By 1701 the French had succeeded. The English never wholly did.

French success turned on their ability to establish neutrality with the Iroquois.[2] They did not need a full-blown alliance with the Iroquois to shift the balance of power in North America. Simply to be spared more fighting with those Indians, plus gaining a buffer zone between New France and the English, represented huge gains. For their part, the Iroquois had been more than willing to agree. With Iroquois power at its nadir, neutrality and the chance to rebuild economic, political, and military strength were ideal.[3]

While the French were shoring up support in the upper New York and Great Lakes region, the English moved to improve relations with the Abenaki of northern New England. In fact, the English made covenants with the Abenaki in January 1699, September 1699, and June 1701, and Massachusetts governor Joseph Dudley negotiated with these Indians at Casco Bay in Maine in the summers of 1702 and 1703. These bonds of peace were but loosely tied, however—and even if they had not been, the French quickly moved to loosen them.

The English negotiations with the Abenaki drove the Marquis de Vaudreuil, the new governor general of New France, into action. As a military man who had first come to Canada in the 1680s, Vaudreuil knew well the importance of keeping the Abenaki on the French side, for they were essential in keeping the English enclosed in New England and defensive in posture. Thus Vaudreuil rushed to shore up the French-Abenaki alliance by promising them a war. Within six weeks of Dudley's June 30, 1703, conference at Casco Bay, the Maine towns of Wells and Saco were assaulted by French-inspired and clearly

unconverted Indians. Queen Anne's War, as the conflict was to
be known in North America, had begun.[4]

The attacks on Wells and Saco in 1703 alarmed all of New
England, particularly those settlers living along the two-hundred-
mile frontier that stretched from the Maine coast in the east to
Deerfield in the west. In Deerfield, as in the other frontier
outposts, townspeople once again tightened up their defenses.
Following Massachusetts law, local officers trained the town
militia. The town was also required to have a "sufficient Watch
house" and to maintain a "watch," a vigil of sentinels for the
town.[5] As of 1702, Deerfield did not have as many fortified
houses as many other frontier towns—only three versus as many
as ten or twelve[6]—but the town did have its palisade, or fort,
enclosing the center of town. This "good and sufficient fortification" had been built in 1689, at the beginning of King William's War, and improved in 1697. In June, with the threat of
war building, the town agreed that the fort needed to "be righted
up" and petitioned the governor for help.[7]

Within two weeks the Massachusetts Council responded to
this plea. Acknowledging Deerfield as "the most westerly frontier of the Province" and that "a considerable part of the Line
of Fortification about their Plantation is decayed and fal^n down,"
the Council ordered John Pynchon to send ten men from neighboring towns to provide support.[8] The work proved fruitful.
The fort was not only repaired but expanded significantly, from
roughly 200 rods in circumference to 320 rods.[9]

Deerfield prepared in other ways as well. The house of John
Wells, just outside the fort on the south end of town, was heavily fortified. The town selectmen were impowered to build up
the "town stock of Amunition." As in the 1690s the town also
secured places inside the fort for all townspeople where they
could sleep each night. Those with houses inside were required
to shelter fellow townsmen, receiving a tax break for their pains.
The town even gave "little pieces of land" inside the fort to at
least two townsmen on which to build their own small houses.[10]

Deerfield was wise to take these precautions, for by the middle of 1703 there were ominous signs that war might soon strike

the town. As early as May of 1703, even before the attacks on Wells and Saco, New York governor Cornbury sent notice to Massachusetts governor Dudley that "a party of French and Indians, . . . near one hundred, may be expected every day at Deerfield." Dudley quickly alerted the town to "be in readiness and to scout and range for a discovery."[11] Dudley also communicated the information to Connecticut governor Fitz-John Winthrop, both as a precaution for his colony and because Massachusetts again expected Connecticut to help defend the upper valley. Winthrop felt that such an attack would be "a bold attempt at this tyme," with war still only smoldering, and especially at Deerfield, a place "soe remote & hazardous" from Quebec. Still, counseling "tis best to have an eye upon them," he urged preparedness in all frontier towns.[12]

Two months later the tension in the valley rose higher. In early August Colonel Samuel Partridge of Hadley, the region's military commander, reported to Governor Dudley that he had "intelligence of a party of French & Indians from Canada who are expected every hour to make some attaque on ye towns upon Connecticut River." This warning coincided almost to the day with the actual outbreak of war in Maine—the burning and destruction of Wells and other small posts, and the assaults on the forts at Saco, Blackpoint, and Casco.[13] Warnings also went to Connecticut governor Winthrop when Major John Pynchon relayed word that "scoutes from Deerfield saw the enimies tracks" only five miles from town "& expected to be attacked presently." Immediately Connecticut sent fifty-three soldiers up north. Stopping at Northampton, they learned that "the scouts were misstaken in the tracks they found." Still, the threat remained. The company went up to Deerfield for two days while scouts patrolling from there journeyed over thirty miles farther north. They found nothing.[14]

The rest of the summer passed quietly but uneasily. New York governor Cornbury shared his fears with the English Lords of Trade in both June and September, warning of the French and Indian threat which his spies had uncovered. Even with the summer over he feared enemy attacks, claiming that the Indians were "ready to attempt something upon our Frontiers this Winter."[15] Yet by the end of September Connecticut officials were preparing to draw off their men from Deerfield, despite a message from Albany that "some hundreds of Indians" were gathering to raid the Connecticut valley.[16]

Finally, on the evening of October 8 the first blow of Queen Anne's War struck the valley—at Deerfield. While they were watching after the town's animals in the pasture outside the fort, Indians ambushed Zebediah Williams and John Nims. After firing but missing, the Indians quickly seized Williams. Nims ran away toward a pond nearby, but then, afraid he would be shot, he gave himself up.[17] The Indians quickly marched the men off into captivity.

Deerfield redoubled its defense efforts. One week after the attack, at an unusual mid-October meeting, the town agreed upon their "nesasaty of fortifying," and set up a committee to "joyn with Colonell Partrigg to consult agree and determin" how to shore up local defenses still further.[18] After meeting with the committee, Partridge asked the General Court for financial support, either out of the "publique Rates" or by an abatement of those "Rates now to be collected" in Deerfield.[19]

No one doubted Deerfield's willingness to fight; in fact, Connecticut governor Winthrop commented that the Hampshire County people had "allwaies fallen to their post in all tymes of difficulty."[20] Yet Deerfield's poverty certainly complicated the town's ability to defend itself. At this point Deerfield was as poor as any town in Massachusetts. Two steps taken by the General Court reveal this. On November 20, 1703, the Court, "Considering the Extraordinary Impoverishing Circumstances" of Deerfield, granted the town £20 to support the ministry.[21] Even more dramatic, however, is the tax rate that the General Court levied for the province in late October of that year. To raise the money needed to run the colony, each town was taxed an average of roughly £200. Yet Deerfield's share was *zero:* It was the *only* town in all of Massachusetts not taxed at all.[22]

Deerfield's poverty made defending the town more problematical. In a dangerous situation the town could expect provincial authorities to send soldiers—as few as two or three, as many as forty or fifty—to help defend it. That town was expected to house and feed those soldiers, however. Thus Deer-field had a dilemma born of its poverty: either to bring in soldiers it could not afford to care for, or to try to defend without needed military support.[23]

In late October of 1703, the town's plight spurred its minis-ter, the Reverend John Williams, to write a poignant appeal for aid to Governor Dudley. Williams thanked the governor for his "care and concernment for our safety," both in helping rebuild the fort and in supplying soldiers the previous year. Yet, Wil-liams explained, now "we have been driven from our houses & home lots into the fort, (where there are but 10 house lots in the fort)." With some settlers moving "a mile some two miles" to live in the fort, the town had

suffered much loss . . . we have in the alarms several times been wholly taken off from any business, the whole town kept in, our chil-dren of twelve or thirteen years and under we have been afraid to improve in the field in fear of the enemy . . . we have been crowded together into houses to the preventing of indoor affairs being carryed on to any advantage . . . so that our losses are far more than would have paid our taxes.

Seeking any kind of assistance from the colony, Williams con-tinued:

Strangers tell us they would not live where we do for twenty times as much as we do . . . several say they would freely leave all they have & go away were it not that it would be disobedience to authority & . . . discouraging [to] their brethren. The frontier difficulties of a place so remote from others and so exposed as ours, are more than be known, if not felt.[24]

Solomon Stoddard, Northampton's prominent minister, also pleaded Deerfield's case to Governor Dudley. He asked that Deerfield "be freed from the Country Rates during the time of the war." Like Williams, Stoddard recited Deerfield's dire cir-cumstances: alarms in the fields, inability to improve outlying lands due to the danger, crowded houses—"sometimes with souldiers"—making home life difficult. Further, Stoddard claimed, the townspeople's "spirits are so taken up about their

Dangers, that they have little heart to undertake what is needful for advancing their estates."[25]

Massachusetts heard Deerfield's cry. Not only did the General Court exempt the town from taxes for 1703 and send money to support the ministry, but in late October it sent sixteen more soldiers as well.[26] As the snows of early winter came to the valley, however, these soldiers went home. Winter was not a time of fighting, certainly not a time of invasion by forces coming from three hundred miles away.[27] As military leader John Pynchon had written on an early December day during King William's War, "ye approaching winter gives hope of some respit & allowance of some Ease. . . . The entring upon Winter wil give som security, for in Reson noe attempt can be fro[m] Canida now at this season." Then he added one eerily prophetic line: "tho when winter is setled al Rivers strong [frozen], Passage good, days lengthen and warmer weather"—"then may be ye Enemys motion."[28]

The early winter of 1703 passed without incident. The notes from the December 27 town meeting suggest it was an ordinary year-end session: mostly establishing local apprizements, tax rates, and methods of tax payments. By February 20 news of "bloody & misschevious" attacks on Haverill and Exeter near Boston reminded Deerfielders of their danger. The next day regional commander Samuel Partridge wrote to Connecticut governor Winthrop, telling of the rising danger at Deerfield and requesting soldiers. At this same time, Massachusetts governor Dudley sent twenty soldiers to the town, and they were in place by about February 24. Partridge's letter contained both hope and anxiety: "through the goodness of God we are p^{r}served yet and hope for respitt till ye rivers break up . . . but as soon as there be passing, we look for troubles."[29]

Winter did not give Partridge, or Deerfield, their desired "respitt." Even as the twenty-man garrison was arriving at Deerfield, an army of two hundred to three hundred French and Indians was moving south toward Deerfield.[30]

The Frenchmen included both regular army men and *coureurs de bois*. The Indians came from two groups: the Caughnawagas, or French Mohawks, and a larger group of Abenaki, formerly of Maine and now living—like the Caughnawaga— under French protection near Montreal.

Leaving Canada in the depths of winter, the party made its way south on snowshoes, walking atop frozen lakes and rivers, up the Sorel River to Lake Champlain, from the eastern side of Champlain up the Winooski River, and eventually onto the upper Connecticut. As the French and Indians neared the end of their three-hundred-mile journey, they left a few of their party, plus sleds and provisions, some twenty-five miles above Deerfield. From there they moved overland toward the fron- tier village.[31]

Leading the war party was Sieur Hertel de Rouville, a regu- lar French officer of the line. De Rouville's father, François Hertel, had been a great military leader, a hero in early New France particularly for leading a successful French and Indian raid on Salmon Falls, New Hampshire, in 1690. Now his son was about to launch a similar strike.[32]

As daylight waned on Monday, February 28, 1704, the French and Indians moved into position two miles north and across the river from Deerfield. From there they observed the activities of the town and planned their attack. As night fell, the villagers of Deerfield moved as usual into the fort. Roughly three-quar- ters of the townspeople had homes outside the palisade, but all took the precaution that night of sleeping within the ten- or twelve-foot-high wall. With fortifications recently rebuilt and twenty garrison soldiers newly arrived, the town seemed well protected. Living conditions were extremely cramped and un- comfortable, though. With the addition of the twenty soldiers, Deerfield now held 291 people, all packed into ten or twelve houses inside the fort plus the one fortified house of Captain Jonathan Wells just to the south. Still, it was better to be cramped and safe inside the fort than left outside to the mercies of the enemy. As the town went to bed, a watch regularly patrolled, protecting Deerfield's people as they slept.[33]

Through the night, as the town slept, the French and Indians waited. And as they waited, what they observed gave them promise of aid. First, they saw that heavy snows of winter, some three feet deep, still blanketed the area. That snow had made their travel to Deerfield difficult. Yet here it had drifted up against the palisade, and they now saw that they could easily mount the drifts and climb over that wall. Toward morning, they saw something even more important: There was no watch.

Local legends about the failed watch vary. Some have him propped up against the door of a house in town, listening to a mother's lullaby for a crying infant. Others have him simply inside and asleep. Recalling the incident three months later, New York's Lord Cornbury harshly accorded it to "the negligence of the people, who did not keep guard soe carefully as they should have done." A military report filed within the week claimed that the watch "shot of a gun & cryed Arm," but "very few heard." John Williams, Deerfield's minister, chose the richest, if ambiguous, description: The watch was "unfaithful."[34]

Two hours before daybreak the French and Indians struck. They moved the final miles across the frozen fields toward town, stopping and starting every so often, it was said, so that if any sentinels heard the crunch of snowshoes on the snow they might mistake it for rising and falling gusts of wind. To the palisade the warriors moved, past the silent, darkened empty houses north of the fort. Over the palisade a handful went, still unseen. Opening the gates at the north end of the fort, they let in the rest of their force. Then, "with horrid shouting and yelling," they swept over the town, as John Williams recalled it, "like a flood upon us."[35]

As the settlers opened their eyes to the terrifying scene, the French and Indians seemed everywhere. Some of the attackers seized the watch and others who got outside first. Quickly they took them to different members of the war party whose job it was to secure and lead away captives. Others broke open doors and windows of the houses and, rushing in, seized or slew the still groggy occupants. Still others broke into the empty houses outside the palisade, rifling them of "provisions, money, cloathing, drinks." The "greatest part" of the attackers, though, battled with those townspeople able to fight back, while also "fireing houses, killing all they could y^t made any resistance: alsoe killing cattle, hogs, sheep."[36]

One of the first houses attacked was that of the Reverend John Williams:

They came to my house in the beginning of the onset, and by their violent endeavors to break open doors and windows, with axes and hatchets, awakened me out of sleep; on which I leapt out of bed, and running towards the door perceived the enemy making their entrance into the house; I called to awaken two soldiers in the chamber, and returned to my bedside for my arms; the enemy immediately brake into the room, I judge to the number of twenty, with painted faces and hideous exclamations. I reached up my hands to the bed-tester for my pistol, uttering a short petition to God for everlasting mercies for me and mine . . . expecting a present passage through the valley of death. . . . Taking down my pistol, I cocked it, and put it to the breast of the first Indian that came up; but my pistol missing fire, I was seized by three Indians who disarmed me, and bound me naked, as I was in my shirt, and so I stood for near the space of an hour.

While Williams stood shivering he watched the enemy ransack his house, "entering in great numbers into every room." Some Indians threatened Williams, "holding up hatchets over my head, threatening to burn all I had." More horrible, Williams stood bound while some "cruel and barbarous" Indians murdered two of his children, six-year-old John and six-week-old Jerusha, as well as one of his two black servants, the children's nursemaid Parthena.

About an hour after sunup, Williams and his surviving family members were "carried out of the house for a march, and saw many of the houses of my neighbors in flames, perceiving the whole fort, one house excepted, to be taken." Then, even as the Indians set fire to his house and barn, Williams and his family were taken from town. Carried over the Deerfield River to a spot a mile or so northwest of town, they met "a great number" of their "Christian neighbors, men, women, and children."[37]

The fighting and pillaging went on for perhaps three hours. Although Deerfield's settlers had been horribly surprised, once aroused—to use Governor Dudley's appraisal—they "defended themselves tolerably."[38] As the fighting continued and the number of dead and captured rose, one Deerfield house held fast. It was the home of Benoni Stebbins, located just north of Reverend Williams's home in the middle of the fort. Although not "fortified" in the classic sense of having heavy doors and slots for shooting, the house had walls "filled up with brick" which repulsed Indian rifle fire. Since the house was "attaqued later than some others," those inside were "well awakened": seven men, plus the women and children of their families. Standing "stoutly to their Armes, firing upon ye Enemy & ye Enemy upon them," "with more than ordinary Couridge" they kept fighting, ultimately discouraging the enemy so that they "betook themselves to the next house & ye Meeting house."[39]

At the "next house," in the northwest corner of the fort, the attackers were again frustrated. Now they were trying to break into Ensign John Sheldon's fortified house, but its small windows and overhanging second floor made this difficult. Eventually the Indians chopped a small hole in the heavily reinforced, nail-studded front door. Aiming a gun inside, one of the Indians shot and killed Mrs. Sheldon in her bedroom. Still, the Indians could not break in, nor did they succeed in setting the house on fire.[40]

Meanwhile, after the mass of French and Indian attackers had moved on from the Stebbins house, its defenders kept fighting. In fact, the small band inside battled with "no Respite" for over two hours, from "about an hour before day till ye Sun about one hour & half high." Firing as many as forty times each, the seven men made the enemy pay. One Indian captain was shot, as well as "one Frentchman, a Gentile man to appearance" (an ensign), plus many others. Finally, though, their ammunition and their energy were "almost spent."[41]

"At that very pintch, ready to yield," thirty men from Hadley and Hatfield "rushed in upon ye Enemy & made a shot upon them, at wch time they Quitted their Assaileing ye house & ye fort alsoe." At the very beginning of the attack, one lad from the fort had escaped. Leaping out a back window and then clambering over the palisade, young John Sheldon had rushed through the darkness toward the valley towns below, tearing his shirt into strips of cloth to bind up his bare feet. Even before he reached the settlements below, the light of the burning town had given notice of the attack on Deerfield. Quickly a party of thirty men had raced north toward the town.[42]

It was roughly nine o'clock in the morning when the soldiers from Hadley and Hatfield burst into town through the south gate. Seeing them, the Indians still fighting in town (many had already left with the prisoners) quickly fled. Others who had continued looting the empty houses also raced away; some panicked, leaving behind guns, hatchets, pistols, blankets, and other supplies. As soon as the Indians were outside the town's north gate, the women and children from the Stebbins house ran to Captain Wells's fortified house south of the fort. Meanwhile, roughly fifteen surviving Deerfield men and six garrison soliders joined the troop of thirty. Now the English—"whose courage was more worthy of applaus than their conduct," as one contemporary later noted—chased the fleeing Indians north across the meadows toward the river. At first they had great success, "killing and wounding many of them." But they rushed on headlong, as they later claimed, "with utmost earnestness and resolution," yet mindlessly and "imprudently" according to a different witness. Many even cast off their bulky coats and gloves during the chase. Captain Wells called for a retreat, but the men paid him no heed.

They soon paid a price for their wild chase. A mile from the fort the soldiers dashed into an ambush, sprung by the larger number of Indians who had already left the village and were by now rested and ready. Overpowered, the band of fifty retreated to the fort, but not before nine of their party were killed and several others wounded.[43]

Once the soldiers got back inside and secured the garrison, the Indians drew off. Soon they were all across the river, and by day's end they were six miles away. With them the Indians had taken 109 prisoners—almost two-fifths of the townspeople of Deerfield.[44]

Back in town, even as houses and barns continued to burn, the exhausted, numbed survivors bound up their wounded and counted their losses. They were staggering. Of the 291 people who had gone to sleep in Deerfield just hours before, only 133 remained alive in town. Beyond the 109 captured, 44 residents of Deerfield had been killed: 10 men, 9 women, and 25 children. Five of the garrison soldiers also died, as did seven Hadley and Hatfield men who fell in the meadows fight, for a total death toll of fifty-six. Seventeen out of forty-one houses in town, both within and without the fort, were burned. Personal possessions were lost not only in those houses that burned but in many more that were rifled.

The destruction and death were not spread evenly over the town. As might be expected, the houses to the north took the heavier blows, while the south end of town below the fort remained largely intact. Some men and their families escaped entirely; others were obliterated. John Hawks, Jr., his wife, and three children smothered to death in a cellar while fire raged above them. Godfrey Nims endured a day of hell: four children slain, his wife and three other children captured, his house, barn, and all within burned. John Williams, too, bore terrible losses. Although one son, Eleazer, was spared by his absence that day in Hadley, two of Williams's children were slain on the first day and his wife on the second; his two black servants were also killed; and the minister himself and his other five children were all captured.[45]

The French and Indians were not without their losses. Although Canadian governor Vaudreuil later boasted that his forces lost but eleven men, John Williams learned through French soldiers in Canada that the attackers had lost over forty French and Indians, including a prominent "Macqua" Indian and a French officer.[46]

News of the English disaster spread quickly. By midnight of the day of the attack, close to eighty men had gathered in Deerfield. With the snow so deep and without snowshoes, however, an attack on the retreating party seemed impossible. Besides, the more the colonists contemplated such an attack, the more difficult it sounded. It was

doubtfull whether we could ataque y^m before day, being in a capacitie to follow y^m but in their path, they in a Capacitie to flank us on both sides, being fitted with snow shoes, & with treble our Numb^r, if not more, & some were much concerned for the Captives, Mr Wm's famyly Especially, whome ye enemy would kill, if we come on, & it was concluded we should too much Expose our men.

By two o'clock the next afternoon Connecticut men began to come into town, and by nightfall there were 250 men in Deerfield. Again, though, plans to pursue the enemy fell through:

the afores^d Objections, & the weather verry Warme, & like to be so, (& so it was with Raine) we judge it impossible to travill, but as afores^d to uttermost disadvantage, Especially when we came up to y^m to an attaque, (Providence put a bar in our way) we Judge we should Expose o'rselves to ye Loss of men and not be able, as the case was circumstanced, to offend the Enemy or Rescue our Captives, which was ye End we aimed at in all, therefore desisted, & haveing buried the dead, saved what we Could of Catt^ll, hogg, & sheep, & other Estate, out of ye spoyles of ye Remayneing Inhabitants.[47]

There was to be no third marshaling of forces. Some Hampshire County men remained in town and "settled a Garrisson of 30 men or upwards, und^r Capt Wells." The rest "drew off to other places."[48] Deerfield was left alone, barely alive.

The French and their allied Indians had achieved an enormously successful raid. In this, fortune surely had smiled on them. They could not have expected to gain such total surprise; they could not count on an "unfaithful" watch; they could not predict that the deep snows would drift up against the palisade, making their entry into town so easy. In fact, they may even have expected to split up their forces and send small raiding parties throughout the valley, as they had done in previous wars, but found Deerfield too vulnerable to pass up.

Yet beyond good fortune lay plans and tactics which explain a great deal about why the French and Indians struck where, when, and as they did. The attack on Deerfield was far more than a random assault on some "unoffending hamlet."[49] Overall military strategy for Queen Anne's War dictated such a strike. As of 1703, when the war was still in its infancy, the French wanted to establish the "ground rules" for the conflict. By making strong thrusts along the two-hundred-mile New England frontier, they could—and did—force the colonists onto the defensive. The 1703 summer raids on Wells and Saco began the process. By then attacking Deerfield, at the extreme other end of the frontier, the French served notice that all of New England was in jeopardy. As in 1689, at the beginning of King William's War, the French had dictated the war's battleground.

French and Indian tactics were equally effective. By attacking in late winter, "out of season," they added a new level of terror to New England. The blow to Deerfield meant that the English could never let down their guard. Through the two previous wars fought in the valley, fifty-five of fifty-seven enemy attacks had taken place between March and November. As it turned out, twenty-eight of twenty-nine blows during Queen Anne's War also fell during that period. Yet the fateful twenty-ninth attack, on February 29, 1704, was the strike at Deerfield. In planning this winter raid, Governor Vaudreuil may well have recalled the great success of a similarly "aberrant" assault, the surprise attack on Schenectady in early February of 1690. That raid, near the start of King William's War, had resulted in sixty English dead and twenty-seven captured.[50]

The actual type of assault—a well-planned, pre-dawn sneak attack—was nothing new. Over three wars now, the colonists of New England had become accustomed to this style of fighting. Even when the Indians sent a large war party, attacks invariably came without warning.[51] The surprise attack on Deerfield may have been larger and bloodier than most, but it was different in degree, not in kind.

The size of the force that struck Deerfield was unusual, though not unique. During these wars the Indians usually sent out parties of fewer than fifty men. Still, the two-hundred- to three-hundred-man force that shattered Deerfield in 1704 was not without precedent.[52] Schenectady and Salmon Falls in 1690, York in 1692, Oyster Bay in 1694, Wells and Saco in 1703, Haverhill in 1708—all were raids of roughly the same scale.

The identity of the French-allied Indians in this raid was distinctive, however. In fact, the identity and goals of the Indians that attacked Deerfield make the incident emblematic of the complexity of these wars. As noted above, French strategy in this war depended on keeping New England on the defensive, and the Abenaki Indians were the key to control. Since 1701 the French had worked hard to maintain good relations with these allies and seemed to be successful. At a meeting in 1701, after the peace pipe was passed, the Abenaki representative had reassured the French that his tribe would be "always attached" to them.[53] Nevertheless, when Massachusetts governor Dudley engineered his series of meetings with the Abenaki, Vaudreuil had every reason to be alarmed. Although he successfully urged the Abenaki into raids on Wells and Saco in the summer of 1703, the Canadian governor remained apprehensive. Writing to French minister Pontchartrain about these Eastern Indians, he reminded his Minister of Marine of "the absolute necessity which we [are] under to embroil them with the English . . . not only for their safety but even for our proper advantage." If the French could convince the Abenaki to continue fighting for them, those Indians would "be a cover to the entire Southern frontier of the government of Montreal." In essence, Vaudreuil commented, "English and Abenaki must be kept irreconcilable enemies."[54]

By late 1703 Deerfield had become an explicit part of French-Abenaki relations. According to a report from Vaudreuil to Pontchartrain, after the French-inspired Abenaki raids in Maine the previous summer, "the English having killed some of these Indians, they [the Indians] . . . demanded assistance. This obliged us . . . to send thither Sieur de Rouville, . . . who attacked a fort"—Deerfield. The raid on Deerfield proved of great consequence, Vaudreuil later claimed. It "accomplished everything expected of it, for independent of the capture of a fort, it showed the Abenakis that they could truly rely on our promises; and this is what they told me at Montreal . . . when they came to thank me." Vaudreuil acknowledged that bringing in the Abenaki would "not fail to cost his Majesty something, but the advantage we derive from it will richly compensate us in the end."[55] The Abenaki, too, were pleased. When they met in council with Vaudreuil, the tribe's representative thanked the Canadian governor for "the pleasure you have made [given] me to send me this winter a party to avenge me against the English . . . I knew in this more than ever that you regarded me as your true child."[56]

The French had another motive for bringing the Abenaki to their side. It centered, predictably, on the Iroquois. Although the French and Iroquois had agreed to neutrality in 1701, the previous half century of strife kept the French nervous. The Iroquois might be weakened, but their residual strength and strategic importance remained critical. Thus, at a conference on October 24, 1703, Vaudreuil promised the Iroquois that the French would stay away from them and would "not wage war against the English except in the direction of Boston." This the Iroquois approved, for they now wanted no part of the English-French conflict; in fact, they even urged the French to seek peace with the English. At the same time, the French realized that the Iroquois might still rejoin their traditional ally. For this reason, Abenaki support was crucial, for if those Eastern Indians could provide protection for the French frontier along the St. Lawrence, that "would enable us," in Vaudreuil's words, "in case of a rupture, to resist the Iroquois." Even well after the assault on Deerfield, Vaudreuil continued to regard "the continuance of the peace with the Iroquois as *the principal affair* of this country [emphasis added]."[57]

From the Indian standpoint as well as from the French, the raid on Deerfield proved important. No mere pawns in a European game, the Indians involved in the attack had their own goals. First, French and Abenaki aims coincided in the attack on Deerfield because each side wanted to make sure it could trust the other. Apart from their relationship with the French, though, the Abenaki had their own reasons for wanting to strike at New England. Until the 1670s the Abenaki had lived throughout Maine. When King Philip's War broke out in 1675, they had not joined the fighting. The English failed to appreciate this, however. This soon proved "very disastrous to the English," for by attacking "without exception all the . . . tribes who Surround them," they only added to the ranks of their enemies.[58]

Among these new enemies were the Abenaki. Late in the

war the Abenaki took in Indians from some of the shattered tribes of southern New England, apparently including some from the Connecticut valley. At this same time, many of the Abenaki decided "to take Refuge in the country inhabited by the French." Those Abenaki "found shelter at . . . Sillery"— the place from which the French and Indians launched their raid on Deerfield some twenty-seven years later.[59] It is likely, then, that some Abenaki were anxious to strike at Deerfield because it stood on native land, land from which they had been driven a generation before.

One other force that motivated the Indians to attack Deerfield was money. By 1704 Europeans had profoundly altered the economies of many if not all of the tribes of eastern North America. It is doubtful that there were Indians by then who did not seek European guns, knives, tools, and clothing. Thus, the idea of exchanging English prisoners for money appealed to the Abenaki; it also helps explain why so many Deerfielders were captured and not killed. That this kind of exchange took place is clear. The Indians holding young Stephen Williams, the minister's son, got £40 for selling him to the French, and Stephen's father reportedly brought even more.[60] Even more crucial for understanding initial Indian motives for the attack on Deerfield, though, was Governor Vaudreuil's standing offer for English prisoners: As he recalled for the Abenaki in 1706, "since the beginning of this war I declared to you that this manner of paying for scalps seemed too inhuman, but that I would give you *ten Spanish crowns for each prisoner* [emphasis added]."[61]

Thus, general French military strategy, French concern for Indian alliances, Indian concern for French support, possibly Indian desire to avenge earlier English destruction, even the Indian economy—all played parts in bringing about the devastation at Deerfield.[62] Vastly more complex than simply some wanton act, the raid made sense—at least from the French and Indian points of view.

The success of the strike at Deerfield can also be measured by the strong reactions it brought throughout New England. Although French and Indian attacks had bloodied the region in the summer of 1703, the English had only clumsily and reluctantly risen to the challenge. But February 29, 1704, electrified New England. As word of the attack spread, it became apparent that the French and Indians had done what the English could not do alone: shock the colonies into unity and action.

Word of the disaster spread swiftly. On March 5 Samuel Sewall of Boston noted in his diary, "The dismal News of the Slaughter made at Deerfield is certainly and generally known."[63] The General Court soon reacted. On March 9, the second day of the session just begun, Governor Dudley addressed the General Court, saying, "I thought it necessary to see you at this time and to have your advice in the affayr of the warr that presses hard . . . I am sorry we have done no more against the Enemy this Winter."[64] That very day, the General Court determined that it should "keep a day of fasting and prayer, and that the neighboring ministers might be desired to be present . . . to implore the divine protection in the arduous affairs under present consideration."[65] Later that same month Governor Dudley, the Council, and the Assembly issued a "Declaration against Prophaneness and Immoralities," a warning and a plea published "under a deep sence of the Divine displeasure express'd in various calamities already Inflicted, and still awfully threatning us, Because we have not hitherto been reformed."[66] The spiritual message coming from the disaster at Deerfield was sometimes harsh. On the Sunday directly after the Deerfield attack, the Reverend Timothy Edwards of Windsor, Connecticut, devoted his sermon to its meaning. Bewailing "ye awful and dreadful dispensation of Gods hand at Deerfield," he warned, "[t]he sins of a professing people do sometimes provoke God to do such things amongst y^m as are very dreadful."[67]

Military responses came quickly. On March 6 Governor Dudley wrote to Connecticut governor Fitz-John Winthrop, urging him to reinforce the towns of the upper Connecticut valley: "I hope your men at Hartford, as well as any at Springfield, will not let the enemy pass from Deerfield without some impression to let them know we are awake, tho the poor inhabitants were asleep." Within two weeks Connecticut had posted sixty men in Hampshire County, "both for garrisoning and scouting." On March 16 the Massachusetts legislature called for "not less than six hundred . . . Voluntiers against the French and Indian enemy." Through the next two years Massachusetts maintained a force as great as 750 men to search "all the Usuall places of the Indians abode" and to patrol the frontier the two hundred miles "from Deerfield to Wells."[68]

Open anger and retaliation were also among Boston's responses. On March 18 Dudley put Benjamin Church, an aging but experienced and tough Indian fighter, in charge of an expedition aimed "against the *French* and *Indian* Enemy" in Maine, "to the *Eastward* of *Casco-Bay.*"[69] Church's purpose was clear. He set out, he wrote,

because of many cruelties . . . particularly the horrid action at Deerfield, this last winter, in killing . . . and scalping, without giving any notice at all, or opportunity to ask quarter . . . and carrying the remainder into captivity in the height of winter of which the journey killed many . . . and exposed the rest to the hardships of cold and famine worse than death itself.[70]

That summer his seven-hundred-man force stormed a number of French settlements on the Atlantic coast. While the strategic value of the raids was slight, the psychological value to the English was doubtless higher.

Some of the reactions to Deerfield might seem fanciful were they not so reflective of the tragedy. On March 14 the General Court ordered that "there be five hundred pair of good snowshoes provided at the public charge, one hundred and twenty-five pair thereof to be put into the hands of [the] . . . chief military officer . . . within the county of Hampshire."[71] The sobering reason for this came from Governor Dudley: "I am oppressed with the remembrance of my sleepy neighbours at Deerfield, and that all that came to their assistance could not make out snow shoes to follow a drunken, loaded, tyred enemy."[72] At this same time the bounty for Indian scalps shot upward. In late November of 1703, the General Court had raised the reward from £10 to £40 for "every Scalp of an Indian Enemy kill'd in fight, that is ten Years of age, or more." Now, on March 29, just after Deerfield and "for the Encouragement of Voluntiers against the French and Indian Enemy," the court raised the bounty to £100.[73]

General Court actions in April bespoke the continuing reverberations of the Deerfield attack. On April 18 the Court declared that it now seemed "Convenient, if not Necessary, that . . . all the French-men residing in this Province, be Registered"; that any found corresponding with the French and Indian enemy "be proceeded with as English-men should be under the like circumstances"—that is, as traitors; and that "all French Catholicks be forthwith made prisoners of war."[74] Englishmen were even restricted to their towns. A General Court order of April 27 declared that no one in "Natick or other places presume to go one mile beyond their homes without a special permit or in Company on pain of death"![75]

The blow at Deerfield also made New England anxious to repair the Covenant Chain with the Iroquois. Writing from Albany on April 24, Indian expert Johannes Schuyler advised Connecticut governor Winthrop that "it would not be amiss" for Massachusetts governor Dudley "to send some gentlemen . . . this summer with some presents, to renew the covenant with [the Iroquois], whereby encouragement may be given them and persuaded to lift ye hatchet against y^e . . . Eastern Indians."[76] Two months later the Massachusetts Council did just that, renewing "ye antient amity between ye Maquas & this Government" with "a sutable present" worth £200.[77]

Deerfield's fate even affected colonial politics. Within Massachusetts the crisis forced the governor and the General Court to stop bickering and work together.[78] Relations between colonies also improved markedly. As late as one week before the attack, the English Board of Trade and Plantations had acknowledged Governor Dudley's frustration that so far in Queen Anne's War he "could obtaine Nothing" when he sought aid from Connecticut and Rhode Island.[79] After Deerfield, however, correspondence between Boston, Hartford, and Albany was soon filled with gestures of cooperation. Once Deerfield was struck, Connecticut authorities realized how vulnerable their colony was. It was therefore in Connecticut's best interest to post soldiers well up the valley to ward off French and Indian

attacks, especially with Massachusetts more committed to defending in the east. Although the colonies disagreed on details,
such as whether to divide up forces among various towns or
mass them in one outpost, the tone of negotiations was concil-
iatory. In the spring of 1704 Connecticut's Winthrop wrote to
Massachusetts' Dudley, "I shall be very sorry if any little mistake should leade to any misunderstanding betwene us . . . I
am sure noe thing shall be wanting on my part to observe the
stricktest type of freindship and good correspondence with your
Excellency." Massachusetts–New York and Connecticut–New
York correspondence became similarly amicable.[80]

Even overall English strategy was affected by the assault on
Deerfield. Once the town had been attacked, the whole New
England frontier appeared vulnerable, at least as long as New
England stayed on the defensive. Just two weeks after the
Deerfield disaster Hampshire County's commander Samuel
Partridge wrote to Connecticut governor Winthrop, "I hope
our authorities will consider it . . . to make attaques & subdue
Canada"; otherwise, with the French and Indians operating
freely, "we might expect nothing but blood & spoyle as farr as
they can go." A month later Winthrop suggested to both his
own Council of War and New York's Cornbury that "several
Governments in this country . . . forme an expedition to Canada."[81] These proposals were conveyed all the way to England.
In a message to the Lords of Trade dated May 30, 1704, Colonel
Robert Quarry focused his arguments on "a place called Dearfeild," concluding,

We must expect frequent misfortunes of this nature, in one province
or another, where the Enemy please to fall on us, nor is there any
other effectuall way to prevent these mischiefs but by cutting off Canada.[82]

In all these ways, then, for months the waves from the Deerfield attack continued to lap onto distant shores.

Meanwhile, as New England responded to the attack on
Deerfield, Deerfield itself struggled to stay alive. At first the
townsmen almost left: "after the Bloody Desolation . . . we

were unanimously Determined to Desert the Town and seek shelter and safty whear we could find it." Within two days of the attack, however, Colonel Partridge "Impressed into Her Majesty's service and Posted as Garrison souldiers" the twenty-five surviving men in town; the women and children were re-moved to valley towns below. The townsmen resented Par-tridge's decision. One later wrote that "our hopes of seaving our Lives by quitting our Habitations [were] superceded" only "by fear of Incuring the Penelty of Deserting Her majstys ser-vice."[83] Partridge held firm. He based his decision on three points: his military judgment that the post needed to be main-tained, the fact that half the town was "yet standing," and his knowledge that Governor Dudley was "express in holding that post."[84]

So Deerfield held on. That there were no attacks in the next two months doubtless proved encouraging to the survivors. On April 20 the town showed signs of life when it held a "lagall town meeting." Interestingly, nowhere within the brief min-utes of that meeting was there any mention of the February 29 attack. Going by these records, it appears that the townsmen did their best to conduct "business as usual." Deerfield chose a moderator and a clerk, selectmen and fence viewers. Yet a few subtle signs betrayed the fact that something had gone awry. The writing in the town book was large and awkward: Edward Allen did not show the careful hand of his predecessor, Samuel French, a captive of the February 29 raid. The meeting also took place a month later than the usual March gathering, and no new business was conducted.

Reports from both outside Deerfield and inside make it ob-vious that the town and the upper valley were struggling. Col-onel Partridge reported, "O^r people are so tranceported with the late stroak at Deerfield that I can hardly pacifie them. . . . The enemy rush in at unawares and do spoyles; in this way we shall dye a lingering death, & do no great spoyle on ye enemy, but alwayes be upon ye loosing hand."[85] The Deerfield survivors had further discouraging words: "we are uncapable of Attend-ing our businese to Procure a maintenance for our selves and families . . . being obligated to be in actuall Duty as souldiers three fifth parts of our time."[86] Connecticut's Colonel William Whiting visited Deerfield in May and found the townspeople "laboring under some difficulties and many discouragem^{ts}." Even though Connecticut supplied as many as sixty men to reinforce the town, Deerfield remained a bleak outpost for the demoralized settlers.[87]

As spring became summer, military matters worsened. On May 10 Deerfielders John Allen and his wife were killed two miles south of town. Two days later a party of seventy French and Indians struck Pascommuck, a hamlet outside Northampton, killing nineteen and capturing three. Particularly disquieting for Deerfield was the fact that these enemies had passed within eight or ten miles of town, "made a very great track and yett were not perceived by the garrison, a matter which," Connecticut governor Winthrop remarked, "argues that a carefull scout was not kept from that post."[88]

The threat of attack continued unabated. In mid-May Colonel Partridge reported that

the enemy in greater numb^{rs} are intending speedy mischiefes on Northampton, Hatfield, or Hadley [all just below the more heavily fortified Deerfield] . . . we dayly expect mischiefs manyfold, & are so surprized that we day & night stand on our guard, & most of o^r men keep watch every other night & spend o^r whole tyme in the day to fortifie & be in posture of deffence; so that it becomes an extremitie upon us. . . . The awfull appearances of warr, blood, fire & desolations by the comon enemy moves & shakes our people with such consternation and amazement that its hard for us here to sitt quiet under our p^{r}sent circumstances.[89]

On June 12 Governor Dudley informed his Council that he had just received word "from Albany via Northampton, advising of a body of French and Indians to the number of five hundred that were upon their march towards the frontiers on Connecticut River."[90] Deerfield and the valley braced for attacks. On July 20 Thomas Russell, a Hatfield resident then serving as a soldier at Deerfield, "was sent out into ye woods with others as a scout, but he rambling from his company, was kill^d by ye Indians.[91] Then, at ten o'clock in the morning on July 22, a lone

French soldier walked up toward the Deerfield garrison, fired his gun into the air, and approached the fort. He was a deserter, who then entered the fort and began talking. Through this almost miraculous action, the region learned that a force of some one hundred forty French and three hundred forty Indians was indeed closing in on the valley. But they never attacked. Apparently discouraged by their loss of surprise, the enemy force broke up and headed back north. Even so, small, sniping attacks continued through the summer.[92]

During this tense period Massachusetts did what it could for Deerfield. Military and civilian authorities alike showed their concern for "that poore little place."[93] First, both regional and provincial authorities kept Deerfield fortified and protected, a practice shared by the government of Connecticut. The General Court also compensated Deerfielders for their losses of February 29. All specific losses of equipment—coats, guns, hats—were covered; all surviving participants in the fight received £3; and the widows of those slain each received £5. In addition, since it was not clear who had taken the one Indian scalp brought in after the fight, a £60 allotted bounty was "equally divided amongst them together with all Plunder whereof they gave account."[94] During the next year the Court further provided individual payments to Deerfield men or valley soldiers who had been injured in the February raid. For example, in 1705 Benjamin Church received £4 "for his losse of time & being wounded."[95]

The remainder of the summer passed without incident. By mid-autumn the war seemed to have moved well away from the Connecticut valley. Yet Deerfield continued to struggle. In late October the General Court received a petition from constable Thomas Wells. Wells acknowledged that Deerfield owed the province its regular payment of taxes, yet with "at Least One halfe of the inhabitants that should have paid it . . . killed & taken captive & their Estates destroyed & burnt up," Wells sought an abatement. The Council "immediately concurred."[96]

The Massachusetts government apparently felt Deerfield needed more than an elimination of taxes. On November 1 the Council decided that "there be a chaplain sent to the Town and

Garison at Deerfield," and that £20 "be allowed him out of the publick Treasury for his Service there for Six months." The man selected was Benjamin Choat, a twenty-four-year-old Harvard graduate, not yet ordained, who promptly headed to the post.[97]

From all these actions, it is clear that the Massachusetts government did not want to lose Deerfield. As the spearhead of the Connecticut valley, the frontier outpost was simply too important to give up. Even though the remaining settlers at Deerfield were deeply discouraged, Massachusetts kept the town—albeit largely as a military post—alive.

On January 22, 1705, Governor Dudley issued a proclamation naming March 1 "a day of public fasting and prayer." On that day, Dudley urged the people of the province to attend services, repent, and pray to God for protection of their queen, government, lands, and citizens. The governor also urged prayer that the "Designs of the barbarous Salvages against us [be] defeated; Our exposed Plantations preserved, And the poor Christian Captives in their hands, returned."[98] These last prayers must have struck deeply into the hearts of the Deerfield survivors. What is probably more poignant, though, is that the day of the fast was set for the first anniversary of the trauma of February 29.

When Governor Dudley urged the people of Massachusetts to remember the "poor Christian Captives," the prisoners from Deerfield were undoubtedly on his mind. One hundred nine men, women, and children had been taken from Deerfield to a fate New Englanders could only imagine. The story of the captivity and redemption of these colonists helped immortalize Deerfield in the annals of early New England. Within a few years it became a well-known tale of trial and suffering, yet also of survival and triumph.[99]

Even before the battle in Deerfield was over on the morning of February 29, 1704, the Indians had started to prepare their prisoners for their journey. The attacking party clearly had planned to take captives, for they outfitted the prisoners with moccasins and snowshoes that they had brought along. As they climbed the hills two miles north of town, John Williams and the others took a final look back at their homes and "saw the smoke of the fires in the town and beheld the awful desolations."[100] Then their odyssey began.

For the first three days of the journey, the party worked largely overland the twenty-five miles north to the spot on the Connecticut River where the French and Indians had left their sleds and other gear. The group was forced to move along quickly, for the Indians still feared English pursuit. The dazed prisoners also had to endure continued horror. In the first three days nine prisoners, ranging in age from "a suckling child" to three elder women, were killed. Of especial pain to the minister was the death of his wife, Eunice. Having borne a child just seven weeks before, she proved weak from the beginning of the trek. On the second day, some seven miles north of her home, in her weakened state she tried to cross "a smal river which water runing very swift flung her down She being wet was not able to travail any further," as her son Stephen later recalled. At that point an Indian "slew her with his hatchet at one stroke."[101]

Deaths continued to mount up as the party made its way the next sixty miles north, up the Connecticut River. In fact, by the time the journey to Canada ended, 21 of the 109 prisoners had been killed. The killings were not random or wanton. Rather, they fell upon people who could not keep up with the party as it moved, especially older women and young children. For example, on the eighth day out the Indians slew Mary Brooks on the day after she suffered a miscarriage brought about by a fall upon the ice. Even the killing of a four-year-old girl two days later was not without reason, for the snow was then so deep that her Indian master could not carry both his pack and her. Rather than leave her alone in the woods, he slew her.[102]

That the Indians could be kind as well as barbarous became one of the journey's lessons. At times the Indians carried children "upon their shoulders and in their arms." John Williams was particularly grateful for the ride the Indians gave his seven-year-old daughter, Eunice. And Williams's Indian master took particularly good care of him, giving him snowshoes, of food "the best he had to eat," and even " a piece of a Bible."[103]

On the ninth day of the captivity, the party reached the place where the White River joins the Connecticut. At this point the forces split up. While the French army marched along on its own, the Indians and their captives broke down into smaller groups—for convenience, for speed, and for safety.

As John Williams and his Indian captors headed up the White River, the trip became extremely difficult for the minister. Even with plenty to eat—the benefits of five moose killed by Williams's Indian party—Williams struggled to keep up. Carrying a heavy pack, even with snowshoes the minister suffered great pain in his feet and legs. Each night, he reported, "I wrung blood out of my stockings when I pulled them off." Even when the Indians took his pack off, "my bones seemed to be misplaced and I unable to travel with any speed." Williams's shins, too, were battered, "being cut with crusty snow in the time of . . . traveling without snowshoes." Moving off the White River onto the Winooski River on the way to Lake Champlain, Williams thought it "impossible to hold out": "my feet were so tender, swollen, bruised, and full of pain that I could scarce stand upon them without holding onto the wigwam." But he did hold out, aided that day by a favor of God in the form of mid-winter manna from heaven: "a moist snow about an inch and a half deep that made it very soft for my feet."[104]

Within three weeks, Williams and his party had moved north along the shore of Lake Champlain and followed the Sorel River north, by now traveling with the luxury of a canoe. On April 15, the forty-seventh day of the journey, they reached the town of Chambly, just twelve miles below Montreal. Except for some later movement within Canada, for Williams the journey was over.[105]

As the Deerfield minister came under French care, he learned that many of his fellow townsmen had been in Canada for as much as three weeks already, and he was doubtless cheered by the fact that there were no reports of further deaths en route. There were some captives still unaccounted for at this time, though, and prominent among them was the minister's eleven-year-old son, Stephen.

Stephen, it turned out, was alive, but he was a long way and many months from seeing his father. When the Indians had split up at the White River, unlike most of the parties Stephen and his captors had headed further up the Connecticut River. They journeyed past the lower "Cowass," or "place of pines," a well-known Indian rendezvous. Then, in an area near the north branch of the Wells River, they settled in to live for nearly five months. Stephen helped make maple sugar, traveled back and forth between different Indian forts, and hunted. Only in August did young Williams and his Indian masters move on to Chambly. By the time Stephen arrived, his father had been moved to St. Francis and Montreal. It would be another ten months before father and son would be reunited.[106]

Eighty-eight of Deerfield's 109 captives reached Canada alive. Veterans of different journeys and scattered to different locales, their stories—and fates—varied widely. The Indians sold many of the captives to the French, presumably receiving their promised ten crowns in return. Many of the younger prisoners were kept by their French and Indian captors, who tried to integrate them into their respective societies. And almost all the captives were proselytized by the Roman Catholic Church—often by the Jesuits, yet by converted Indians as well.

Through some severe religious trials, the adults held firm. In John Williams's *The Redeemed Captive*, the chronicle of Deerfield men and women resisting Catholicism is impressive. Stories of real courage—people refusing to attend mass, kneel, or kiss a crucifix—mark those pages. In fact, Williams reported proudly, "One day one of the Jesuits came to the governor and told the company there that he never saw such persons as were taken from Deerfield." The adults were so strong in their beliefs that at one point the Jesuits suggested the separation of any united parents and children, since the adults "hindered the children's complying."[107]

Williams remembered his own battles with Catholicism vividly. Soon after his arrival in Canada, he refused an order to go to mass and his life was threatened. Williams held firm. Soon thereafter, he was hauled "by the head and shoulders out of the wigwam" and forced to attend mass, though he smugly viewed it only for its flaws. A short time later Williams's Indian master put a hatchet to his head, but saying, "I would sooner choose death than to sin against God," Williams was "not moved." Next the Indian threatened to pull out all of Williams's finger-nails. Again the minister remained strong. At this point, calling Williams "as bad as the devil," the Indian finally gave up. Some time later, a Jesuit at Quebec offered Williams the safe return of his children if he would but profess Catholicism. Responded the minister, "Sir, if I thought your religion to be true, I would embrace it freely without any such offer, but so long as I believe it to be what it is, the offer of the whole world is of no more value to me than a blackberry."[108]

The trials of Christianity were not all won so handily. In fact, the most painful story of a captive's submission to Catholicism was that of Williams's own son, fifteen-year-old Samuel. Two hundred miles away from his father, Samuel proved unable to withstand the pressures of his Jesuit masters. Their threats to return him to the Indians, their promises, warnings, whip-pings, and other physical torments pushed him to kneel and accept Catholicism. John Williams's reaction bespeaks the fierceness with which he held to his religion and the unbending resolve that carried him through his captivity. Writing to Sam-uel, he termed the news "the most distressing, afflicting, sor-rowful . . . that ever I heard . . . Oh! I pity you . . . I pity your weakness." Some weeks later, he penned a long, formal, rea-soned letter to his son, carefully citing scripture in the hope of helping him see the fatal flaws in the "Romish" practices. Al-though he sent his continuing love to his son, Williams ended the letter "your afflicted and sorrowful father."[109]

While the religious trials were great, daily life was comfort-able for many of the captives. For the most part, those in the hands of the French were treated well and, as the most promi-nent captive, John Williams lived especially well. Governor Vaudreuil made sure Williams had good and ample food, fresh clothing, a comfortable bed chamber, and even medical care when needed. In addition, he gave the Deerfield minister con-siderable aid in locating his children and redeeming them from the Indians. Part of this kind treatment may have stemmed from Vaudreuil's ultimately unsuccessful efforts to secure a peace treaty with New England,[110] but even so, the good care was a blessing.

Captives also took heart in the communication and movement they were allowed amongst themselves. Although some prisoners remained isolated from their comrades, others were kept together or in close proximity. The French also allowed captives to exchange letters, both with one another and with New England. Some of the letters proved disheartening, like John Williams's painful correspondence with his son Samuel. More, however, kept hopes alive and gave relief to prisoners who might otherwise have thought that they were lost forever. As early as October 21, 1704, John Williams "received some letters from New England" with the good news that "many of our neighbors escaped out of the desolations in the fort, and that my dear wife was recarried and decently buried."[111] In 1705, through a letter from James Adams, a captive in Canada who had been taken at Wells, Maine, in 1703, John Sheldon of Deerfield learned that his daughters Hanna and Mary had survived the march to Canada, something he had doubted "noing How Lame they war."[112] In April of 1705 Sheldon himself spread news around. Writing to his captured son Remembrance, Sheldon acknowledged receipt of Remembrance's letter, "which was a comfort to me," and passed on news of others: John Williams "gives his love to al the captives there," as did fellow townsmen John Wells and Ebenezer Warner. Even locations of different captives were shared. Again from the letter of James Adams to John Sheldon: "Remembrance lives near cabect [Quebec], Hannah also Lives with the frenc, Jn in the same house i doe."[113]

As the Deerfield survivors adapted to their new life, New England and New France began formal negotiations for their release. As early as April of 1704 Massachusetts governor Dudley initiated contact with Vaudreuil. Dispatching letters via Albany, Dudley blistered the Canadian governor for his military action:

you have boasted of massacring my poor women and children, and carrying away into a miserable captivity the reste, and they are made a matter of trade between the savages and . . . you. . . . Such treatment of Christians will be esteemed barbarous by all Europe . . . and I expect you to withdraw all these Christian captives from the hands of savages, and return them to me, as I have several times returned *your* people to Port Royal, and shall continue to do, until I have your reply in this.

In August Dudley threatened reprisals if the captives were not taken from the Indians:

I cannot admit the pretext that the Indians have the right to retain these prisoners, because I would never permit a savage to tell *me* that any Christian prisoner is at his disposal.[114]

With his outcries and threats ignored (or possibly never delivered),[115] Dudley moved to a more traditional means of redeeming the captives: negotiation. In December of 1704 John Sheldon and John Wells, Deerfield men with relatives in captivity in Canada, approached the Massachusetts governor, "very urgent to have license to travail thither." Soon thereafter, Captain John Livingston of New York fortuitously appeared in Boston. A veteran of the overland journey to Quebec, he appeared to be an ideal man to lead the two Deerfielders on their mission. For £100 plus expenses, Livingston agreed to take the two newly appointed envoys to Canada. With them the three carried a proposal for a full exchange of prisoners.[116]

Leaving Boston in late December, the party traveled west through Deerfield toward Albany and then north to Canada. They arrived at their destination in late winter. The visit proved a partial success. They met the governor and laid out Dudley's proposals, and also got to see John Williams. From him Sheldon received the good news that his own children still lived; Wells received bad news, that his mother had been killed on the march. As for a prisoner exchange, Vaudreuil sent back to Dudley a series of counteroffers. With these in hand, in early May 1705 the envoys headed back to New England—accompanied by five freed captives.

Livingston, Sheldon, and Wells had done a great service for Deerfield and New England. As John Williams wrote to Liv-

ingston's wife on April 21, 1705, "I should be guilty of ingrati-
tude if I should forget to offer my thanks for your denial of
yourself the desirable company of your beloved consort for the
sake of poor captives. . . . hundreds here are obliged to you."[117]
Still, most of the Deerfield prisoners, and over a hundred others taken from other places during this war, remained in Canada.

Dudley continued his efforts. In the summer of 1705 he sent
Captain Samuel Vetch, along with his own eighteen-year-old
son, William, by ship to Quebec with new proposals. The men
arrived in August, delivered their messages, and went away
with "some few" (four or five) more captives, including John
Williams's son Stephen.[118] The following January the Massachusetts governor and Council dispatched John Sheldon on his
second mission to Canada.[119]

Sheldon arrived in Canada with both proposals and some
prisoners in early March of 1706. At this point, negotiations
intensified. John Williams perceived a change in the wind,
noting that "the adversaries did what they could to retard the
time of our return to gain time to seduce our young ones to
popery."[120] Sheldon stayed in Canada, "treating" with the governor, for a full three months. Finally, in early June the French
bark *Marie*, sailing a flag of truce, left Quebec with forty-four
freed captives from Deerfield and other locales. They arrived
in Boston on August 1, 1706. Although "many more" were "yet
left behind," as Cotton Mather acknowledged in his diary, the
logjam of prisoner exchanges in Queen Anne's War had been
broken.[121]

John Williams was among the "many more" left behind, for
he was someone special to the French. From the time of his
capture the French and Indians had realized that the Deerfield
minister was an unusually valuable prisoner. In fact, Williams
later recalled that he alone "was pinioned and bound down"
every night on the march to Canada.[122] Soon after arriving in
Canada, Williams became the key piece in the chess game of
prisoner exchanges. While Dudley called for a full exchange of
all prisoners, Vaudreuil and the French wanted one special

prisoner. His name was Jean Baptiste, and he was an expert pilot, one who could navigate the coastal waters of New England and Acadia as well as any Frenchman alive.

Baptiste had a long and, to the French, illustrious record of sailing and fighting reaching back to 1690. In 1704, though, he sat in a Boston jail, for the English had caught this "most mischievous enemy." And Vaudreuil wanted him back. Williams learned of this when he first came to Montreal, for even at that point in spring of 1704 the governor told him, "I should be sent home as soon as Captain Baptiste was returned and not before, and that I was taken [presumably by the French from the Indians] in order to his redemption."[123] Vaudreuil communicated this message to Dudley early in their negotiations. Upon his return from the first expedition to Canada, which netted but five prisoners, Captain John Livingston wrote, "I beleve there will bee no exchange of prisoners, for [Vaudreuil] demands Basett [Baptiste], and ye Govr wont relese him."[124]

The English in Boston had no desire to let this "notorious" Frenchman go. A petition from Boston's "Merchants, Traders & Sailers" was explicit: A "Dangerous Consequence . . . will unavoidably attend his release." In recent months Boston had been "Signally Preserved from any Attacks or Insults on our Sea: Coasts by the French." This was "Chiefly Attributed" to "the due retention of one Baptist . . whose former Piracies, Murders & Villanies" were well known.[125] Understandably, then, Dudley refused to include him in his proposals for prisoner exchanges. Even in the face of Vaudreuil's general peace treaty proposal of 1705, Dudley refused to budge.

Dudley's refusal may well have kept New England's captives in Canada an extra year. By the middle of 1706, though, the Massachusetts governor's position softened. For one thing, word filtered back to Boston that Reverend Williams was growing ragged, at least in appearance if not in spirit.[126] For another, Dudley may have been tiring of negotiations with the French or perhaps felt he needed a new initiative. In any event, on August 8, 1706, the English took a large step: The Council ordered Dudley to "send away the French prisoners, *without exception*, to Port Royal and Quebeck, and demand the English prisoners . . . in return of theirs . . . and that a suitable vessel be forthwith sent to Quebeck for our prisoners, in the hopes of seeing them before winter [emphasis added]."[127] Following this order, Baptiste was taken to Acadia, and Dudley sent Captain Samuel Appleton of the brigantine *Hope* to pick up the remaining captives. Vaudreuil quickly acceded.

When it became apparent that Williams and many others were about to leave Canada, "the clergy and others labored to stop many of the prisoners," offering freedom and money, and even threatening them with visions of shipwrecks or damnation in hell. It was all for naught. On October 29, 1706, Williams and fifty-six other New Englanders left Quebec, arriving safely in Boston on November 21. After almost three years of captivity it was, to use Cotton Mather's term, a joyful "Harvest."[128]

Although Williams extolled "the kindness of the Lord" in making safe the captives' return, God had frowned as well. By Williams's own estimate, a "great number" of New Englanders remained in Canada, "not much short of a hundred." Included in this total was a large group from Deerfield. Of the 109 prisoners taken from the town three years before, eighty-eight had survived the journey to Canada. Of these, fifty-nine had come home—yet twenty-nine remained behind.

The twenty-nine were an especially painful group to lose, for they were the young. Consistent with a pattern seen throughout the colonial wars, the French and Indians particularly wanted to keep children. They were the easiest to control, to convert, and to integrate into society, whether Indian or French.[129] John Williams claimed that the French worked particularly hard to "seduce our young ones." Some, he explained, "were sent away [set free] who were judged ungainable, [but] most of the younger sort still kept, some still flattered with promises of reward."[130] The results were painfully effective. All of Deerfield's twenty-nine unredeemed captives were under twenty years of age; what's more, fifteen of the eighteen girls were under twelve and nine of the eleven boys under fourteen, generally the pivotal ages in deciding whether to keep youths.[131]

Over the years, news about many of the twenty-nine filtered down to New England. John Stebbins's daughter Thankful, twelve years old in 1704, converted to Catholicism in 1706 and married a Frenchman in 1713. Mary Harris, Mercy Carter, and Joanna Kellogg, girls of nine, ten, and eleven years, all ended up at the Indian village of Caughnawaga, where they married Indian men.[132]

Probably the most poignant story was that of Reverend Williams's own daughter, Eunice. Although Governor Vaudreuil "labored much for her redemption" in 1704 and 1705, once even offering "a hundred pieces of eight" for her, her Indian master refused. Vaudreuil tried to exchange an Indian girl for Eunice, but again had no success. The French governor's wife vainly pleaded for the girl as well. By 1707 the child, only seven years old when captured, had "forgotten to speak English."[133] Although emissaries tried to redeem Eunice in 1707 and for years thereafter, by then Eunice herself seemed "unwilling to return" and her master still "not very willing to part with her." New York governor Peter Schuyler's efforts to redeem this "pritty girll" fell short, as did the repeated attempts of Massachusetts governor Dudley. Even as the war ebbed after 1711, both men kept trying. Yet Vaudreuil could supply "no satisfactory Answer" to Eunice's "unaccountable Detention": She was now beyond "her tender years" and beyond any European influence as well.[134] In 1713 she married a Caughnawaga Indian and never again set foot in Deerfield.[135]

While the people of New England did not forget the prisoners still in Canada, the return of so many captives in late 1706 was a time of celebration and thanksgiving. Close to fifty Deerfielders, and over one hundred captives total, had come home in the space of four months. The people of Boston showed the redeemed captives great kindness, great "love and charity," as John Williams noted.[136]

Most of those newly freed headed for their homes and families. John Williams, though, again received special treatment. By the time he arrived Williams was a figure well known to Bostonians. In August of that year, just after the first large boatload of captives had come home, Cotton Mather had published a book entitled *Good Fetch'd Out of Evil*. The heart of this slim, three-part volume was a "pastoral letter" that Williams had written in May of 1706, on the eve of the departure of those captives.[137]

Williams's letter is a Puritan model of hope and faith in the face of great hardship. He urged his departing flock, "Oh! let it be evident that you were brought into captivity for your good. . . . Oh! make all haste to get into a converted state." He closed his letter, "I wish you a healthy, a safe, a speedy passage to your desired port; if it be the will of God. But above all I wish you a gracious, truly penitent, Christ prizing, and soul enriching, sanctifying voyage to another port." Within a few weeks, Mather's publisher had "sold off a Thousand of the Impression."[138]

Immediately upon his return Williams was in great demand. Cotton Mather persuaded him to preach a lecture, "unto a great Auditory (the General Assembly then also sitting) and, directed him, to show how great things God had done unto him." Williams duly preached on December 5, just two weeks after his return. On December 20 he preached again, this time at the meeting of a Mr. Bromfield.[139] Meanwhile, he also was hard at work writing a narrative of his captivity, *The Redeemed Captive Returning to Zion.*

While fame and a full schedule kept Williams busy in Boston, his "flock" strived to bring their shepherd home. On November 30, less than ten days after Williams had reached Boston, the Deerfield town meeting resolved to send Thomas French and its two heroes of redemption, Captain Jonathan Wells and Ensign John Sheldon, to Boston to "treat with thair pastor the Reverant Mr Jno Wms in order to his rejoining with them a gaine in ye work of ye ministry." The town also petitioned the General Court for "a grant of moneys for ye incouragment" of the minister, for they feared they might not get him back.[140] Their worries were well founded. In fact, Williams was "importunately invited to settle where his Worldly Interest might be more promoted, than if he return'd to *Deerfield.*"[141] Fortunately for Deerfield, the General Court quickly gave the townspeople the support they sought. In December the Court offered

£40 to Williams, but only if he would return to Deerfield "within the space of three weeks next coming," and settle there for the next year.[142]

Honoring the General Court's pointed invitation, on December 28, 1706, Williams went home. Reported the *Boston News-Letter*, the people of Hampshire County were "fill'd with joy, for the Arrival of the Captives; especially, for the Return of the Reverend and Pious Mr. *John Williams.*" The minister stayed for about two weeks while the townspeople, both those settled and those resettling, made plans for "Rebuilding the Town more commodiously, and regularly fortifying" it. They also held a special town meeting on January 9, 1707, and voted to "buld a house for m^r Jno Williams in derfield as big as ens Shelldens a back room as big as may be thought convenient."[143] Williams then returned to Boston for a short while, where he finished his writing and preached again to the General Court "at the publick lectures." Eight days later, with his narrative *The Redeemed Captive* "in the press," he headed back to Deerfield.[144]

The town Williams returned to in March of 1707 was only a shell of the one he had known three years before. Since the day of the attack, Deerfield had become more garrison than town. Deerfield's impressed citizen-soldiers had all been required to serve through July of 1705, and many had continued through at least May of 1706. The General Court had continued to aid the post throughout this period. In addition to supplying and paying for soldiers, in both 1705 and 1706 the Court had sent £20 to continue supporting and maintaining Mr. Benjamin Choat, Deerfield's assigned chaplain.[145] Still, during these three years townsmen's military responsibilities had made it difficult for them to farm.

After Williams's return the General Court continued to aid the town. On May 28 valley commander Samuel Partridge petitioned the government on behalf of the town's inhabitants. The General Court's previous support, he wrote, had proven "greatly adventageous to us all for which myself in the behalf of all do Return Our thankfulness." With their minister back, the women and children of Deerfield could return. Yet now there was a new concern: "The Nessessitie of Rebuilding the Forts," a step "absolutely Nessessary both for the people & Church of Christ there & of absolute advantage to the whole Country." Partridge proposed to strengthen and enlarge the fort, the latter step especially to "take in m^r Williams his home & Several Other houses." In June the Court granted £30 toward 120 new rods of fortification built "with square timber."[146]

In the fall of 1707 the town sought and received still more aid. The petition the Deerfielders wrote vividly portrays the town's plight. Settlers found themselves "Labouring Still under many Difficulties & streights being but a small handful of us, & the most of us very low in the World, are at Considerable charges among o^rselves in Building A House, & providing other Necessarys & Conveniencys for the Resettling of o^r Rever^d Pastor." In addition, "many who Disserted ye Place quickly after ye Desolation" had been encouraged by Williams's return into "giveing hopes of Settleing again amongst us . . . with many other who Returned out of Captivity." Yet those newly returned to town, "Instead of helping" support the ministry and fortify the town, "have rather need of help to build Houses for themselves."[147] Deerfield was trying to rebuild, but this town, so terribly poor even before Queen Anne's War had begun, continued to struggle just to survive.

From 1707 through the war's end in America in late 1712, Deerfield remained both a military outpost and a frontier town. The dangers of war certainly did not abate after 1707. Through the summer of 1708 the Deerfield garrison tried to protect Hampshire County by sending scouts as far as 120 miles up the Connecticut valley. In so doing they hoped to push the line of fighting farther north, away from the settlements below. The town continued to pay the price of war, though, for on one such mission in August 1708 Martin Kellogg, Jr., was captured by Indians—for the second time. Closer to home, some two months later Hatfield native Ebenezer Field was slain near Bloody Brook.[148]

In 1709 the war crept back still closer to Deerfield. On April 11, "while driving his teem from Northampton loaded with apple trees, without any fear of indians," Deerfield resident Mehuman Hinsdale was captured just south of town—he, too, for the second time.[149] Soon after, the town faced a sterner challenge—indeed, a true test of its reconstruction and readiness. In early June a war party of forty French and one hundred forty Indians set forth from Canada "designed for *Dearfeild.*" They planned, the English later learned from an Indian deserter, to "post themselves Near the Fort and then send out a skulking party to draw out the English, thinking by that means to take the place." As the war party closed in on Deerfield, however, this time alert sentries sounded the alarm and got most townspeople into the fort safely. Although the Indians killed two, "caught two alive," and wounded two more, Deerfield held. It was the last attack on the town in this long, drawn-out, and destructive war.[150]

The costs had been terribly high. While all of Hampshire County had suffered during the nine years of war, Deerfield had taken by far the worst losses. Of a total of twenty-nine attacks on seven different valley towns, Deerfield had taken ten. The only two massed attacks in the valley by large French and Indian forces both came at Deerfield, in 1704 and 1709. In a valley population of 3,000 to 4,000, Deerfield had fewer than 300 people—yet the town suffered 56 of the valley's 103 dead, 5 of its 18 wounded, and 113 of its 130 captured.[151]

As late as 1712, as the war ebbed, Massachusetts was still carefully defending its frontiers. In November of 1711 the General Court required "a good Pair of Snow-Shoes & Moggasons" for at least half the soldiers in every frontier town in New England, including every town in Hampshire County. The following spring Governor Dudley explained to the Council of Trade and Plantations in London how he had fortified "the frontier . . . from Deerfield in the west, to Wells in the east" with soldiers, fortified houses, "stoccadoes, and flanckers." Scouts continued to be vital to "repell the enemy," Dudley noted, for "four or five times in this warr they have come in bodyes of three or four hundred French and Indians."[152] Even as hostilities were coming to a close, New England had not forgotten Deerfield and the lessons—as well as the agony—of February 29, 1704.

NINE

The Frontier Moves On: Survivors and a New Deerfield, 1704-1729

THE QUARTER CENTURY after 1704 brought profound changes to Deerfield. Although the outpost remained small and fragile in the first years after 1704, by 1729 Deerfield exhibited many signs of security and stability. By 1729 Deerfield was no longer the region's northwestern outpost: New towns and forts now flanked the town. As Deerfield became less exposed and more secure, its land values quickly rose. Population stopped turning over so rapidly as well. In part because of that, for the first time a clear second generation of townsmen moved to take the reins of political power from their fathers. War again afflicted Deerfield and New England in the 1720s, but it was a smaller war and was fought largely away from the Connecticut valley.

Deerfield paid a price for these changes. By the 1720s population growth slowed, as fewer new families settled in the town. By 1729 the political processes showed the first signs of contention. Deerfield's proprietors separated themselves from the town government, thereby severing previously shared control of town land. There were religious disputes, over meetinghouses and ministers alike. In fact, the Reverend John Williams's death in 1729, marking the end of this quarter century, soon led to serious disputes in town over his replacement. In all these ways, from 1704 to 1729 Deerfield showed the evolution of a small, communal village into a more secure, less unified, and more contentious New England town.

By late 1712, when the hostilities of Queen Anne's War finally ended, Deerfield had already engineered a remarkable recovery. In 1704 the town had been literally decimated, reduced from a village of 265 to a military outpost of just twenty-five. Yet within eight years, even in the face of continued war, the town had built its population back up to 214, almost 80 percent of its former size.[1]

The main reason Deerfield rebuilt so quickly was that so many of its old families, its settlers from 1704, continued to cast their lots with the town. Of the people living in Deerfield in 1712, over four-fifths had lived there before the war. Vital to this resurgence was the number of redeemed captives who came back to their town. Of the fifty-nine Deerfield captives rescued from Canada, thirty-three resettled in town. It is noteworthy that thirty of these thirty-three had other family members in town in 1712: Redeemed captives usually returned to Deerfield if their families had. The obverse is also true: Only one-quarter of those redeemed captives who did not return to Deerfield had family still living in town. The other factor that affected the decision about returning was age. The captives who returned averaged twenty-seven years of age, while the non-returnees averaged nineteen.[2] It seems that the older one was, the deeper the attachment to home—an attachment perhaps both emotional and material.

Even as many families returned, both from captivity and from valley towns below, they often did so in sharply reduced numbers. The Barnard family, one of the largest in town since the 1670s, had just three members in Deerfield in 1712. Of the Frarys, descendants of the first settler back in 1669, there was just one resident. Some Deerfield families split up in the aftermath of the war. Curiously, John Sheldon, the hero of repeated rescue missions to Canada, left Deerfield for Connecticut some time after 1708, although two sons stayed. And some simply gave up on Deerfield. Samuel Carter, of one of the original founding families of Pocumtuck, suffered terrible losses in 1704: his wife and three children killed plus three children captured. In 1705 he left Deerfield forever.

Newcomers made up almost one-fifth of Deerfield's 1712

population. Thomas Bardwell of Hatfield had served as a garrison soldier in Deerfield in 1711, at the age of twenty. Apparently he was attracted to the place and its people, for soon after
he took residence in Deerfield and apprenticed himself to
Deerfield resident (and former sergeant of Bardwell's garrison)
Thomas Taylor to become a saddler.[3] Judah Wright's story is
more romantic. Like Bardwell, Wright first came to Deerfield
as a garrison soldier. A survivor of the 1704 assault, Wright
remained in town and in 1707 married Mary Hoyt, another
1704 survivor. By 1712 the Wrights had three children and
Judah was actively engaged in town government.[4]

By 1712 Deerfield displayed many of the vital elements of a
healthy New England village. Town meetings annually chose
full slates of officers to handle much of the business of the town,
with over twenty offices regularly filled. The meeting schedule
itself regained the rhythm of the seasons, a pattern lost during
the war. Deerfield had restored the steady pulse of life it had
known before 1704.[5]

Yet the war still weighed heavily on the town. At least as late
as 1710 the town continued to maintain the "Great Fort" around
its center—a continual reminder of the threat from without.[6]
The war also brought irregularities in religious affairs. John
Williams was twice called away from Deerfield to serve the
cause of New England, first as a chaplain on a 1710 expedition
to Canada and then in 1712 as an emissary to the French governor. During both these absences Deerfield had to make do
with itinerant clergymen.[7] Deerfield also remembered the war
because it would not forget its captives. Even after 1712 the
town was still sending representatives to Canada to try to redeem those still "lost."

Beyond this, however, most vestiges of war quickly slipped
away with the formal end of hostilities in 1712. Deerfield soon
moved into a period of peace and growth. From 1712 until
1729, Deerfield matured—both grew and changed—in a number of vital areas: population, economy, land distribution, and
governance.

The first area of change was in the population of the town.
After forty years of having its growth stunted by wars, Deerfield

expanded steadily over the next two decades. Back in 1675, before it was destroyed, Deerfield (then Pocumtuck) had held roughly 200 people. The Deerfield that was rebuilt after 1680 had a population of 265 when attacked in 1704. By 1712 Deerfield had been restored to 214 citizens. By 1729 it held 320.

Such steady increase seems to speaks well for the attractiveness of the town. Yet growth came largely from natural increase, not from waves of new settlers. In fact, Deerfield's population was also getting older and more entrenched. In the twenty-five years after 1704, only twelve new families settled and remained in Deerfield. At first glance this seems most curious. The war was over; new and protective settlements were growing to the north; and the town still held unusually fertile land. Nevertheless, as strange as it sounds, by the 1720s it was getting difficult to obtain land in town. This does not mean that Deerfield tried to limit new settlement.[8] Rather, the town had simply "filled up": It had given away all its house lots in the town center and at Wapping. While the town could make divisions of other lands, these two prime settlement areas were full. As long as Deerfield maintained a nucleated settlement, its growth was frozen. (It is telling here that six of the twelve new men who settled in town chose Deerfield brides, thereby marrying into rights or opportunities to gain home lots and lands.)

Migration out of town also hints at a problem of land shortage. Eight men left Deerfield between 1704 and 1729 for valley towns below. Since there were many family ties throughout the valley, this fact alone is not surprising. Yet twelve other men all left town for Northfield, a new, open, and more exposed hamlet farther up the Connecticut River. Given the risks in moving to such a place, such a major shift suggests that Deerfield land was either limited or expensive.[9]

A further hint of the scarcity of land comes in the ages at which Deerfielders first married. By 1729 these ages had risen sharply for both men and women. In the 1670s and 1680s, on average, Deerfield men had married at age twenty-five and the women at nineteen, earlier that at almost all other places in New England.[10] By 1729, however, Deerfield's average for men stood at over twenty-seven years, higher than in other towns.[11] Deerfield's average for women also went up by 1729, from ninteen to twenty-one. In this case, the women shifted from being the youngest in comparison with other towns to simply being among the younger.

The shift in marriage age for men is particularly striking. The decision to "delay maturity," to hold off the step of marriage, has familial and economic implications. It suggests that men in Deerfield by 1729 were increasingly without land and thus unable to marry without that key to independence. Overall, then, between these higher marriage ages, an older generation in town, and the fact that the town parceled out few new lands, Deerfield was becoming increasingly closed, insular, inbred.

At the same time, Deerfield continued to grow steadily. Not only were Deerfield families larger, but the town also enjoyed a lower mortality rate.[12] In contrast to the twenty-four men who had died between 1680 and 1704 (including the 1704 attack), only seven died from 1705 through 1729. There was no further massive war to take away many men, or any known epidemics such as those which had struck the valley in 1683 and 1690.[13]

The settlers who lived in Deerfield through this period saw increasing prosperity as well as population. Starting from 1704, of course, the town's economy had nowhere to go but up. Signs of growth soon appeared. Between 1709 and 1714, plans moved ahead on three local projects: a grist mill in 1709–1710, a saw mill in 1714, and another corn mill in 1714. During these same five years, the town also approved the tapping of pine trees for making turpentine. Deerfield further built one new road, improved others, and also "reset" the common fence that surrounded the "great meadow" north of town.[14]

The biggest boost to Deerfield's economy, though, did not even take place within the town. Rather, it took place all around Deerfield, for "it" was the expansion of English settlement in the upper Connecticut valley. For over forty years Deerfield had stood at the extreme northwestern tip of the New England frontier. After 1714, with peace assured, permanent settlers and settlements finally came up the Connecticut River valley. Within five days in February of 1714, the Massachusetts Gen-

eral Court established two new towns near Deerfield. Swampfield had failed as a town when its proprietors had first tried to
build between 1673 and 1675. Although its few buildings had
been destroyed in King Philip's War, the site on the Connecticut River, some six miles below Deerfield, remained promising. By 1715 some forty new settlers, largely from Hatfield and
Hadley, had divided up lands, drawn house lots, and started to
build. By 1717 Swampfield (soon to be renamed Sunderland)
even had a meetinghouse and a minister.[15]

Of much greater significance to the people of Deerfield was
Northfield's reconstruction. After two failed attempts at settlement, in the early 1670s and late 1680s, the site had lain abandoned through King William's War and Queen Anne's War. In
1713, though, Northfield's original proprietors and their heirs
successfully petitioned the General Court for another opportunity to build. Like Swampfield, the new town grew quickly.[16]
The success of this venture had great importance for Deerfield,
for Northfield was situated fifteen miles *above* Deerfield, north
along the Connecticut River. After almost a half century of
being the first line of defense for the entire Connecticut valley,
Deerfield now had its own sentinel above.

These were not the only signs of expansion along the frontier
line, either. In a flurry of activity in the aftermath of Queen
Anne's War, new towns went up from the coast of Maine to the
Connecticut valley.[17] In 1715 the General Court studied plans
for new roads that would more closely bind eastern and western
Massachusetts.[18] And in 1724 Massachusetts established the
first fort on the western frontier, Fort Dummer, located some
ten miles above Northfield. This blockhouse, posted with forty
men, gave Deerfield yet another layer of protection.[19]

The effects of all these on the town were profound. In essence, Deerfield was no longer on the edge of the frontier. With
their town no longer a key military outpost, Deerfield's townsmen could devote full time to their farming and other work.
With new settlements around them, they were more secure.
With these measures of safety, people within and without
Deerfield could again appreciate the quality of the site and the
soil.

"Appreciation" came quickly—in an upsurge of land values. From 1704 to 1710, when war had still threatened the Connecticut valley, Deerfield lands understandably were worth little. In fact, in compiling estate inventories for Deerfield men killed in the 1704 attack, appraisers often did not even try to estimate the value of lands. Instead they would simply list the parcels and their acreage. Sometimes they did not even bother with that step. In concluding John Allin's inventory in 1704, the two "apprizers" wrote, "The Lands not Inventoried by Reason of Troubles not knowing What to Value Them."[20]

Over the next few years, as war continued, Deerfield lands were occasionally sold, but usually for small sums. In 1705 a six-acre house lot with a house on it, plus twenty-six acres of farmland, plus all attendant proprietary rights sold for as little as £17.[21] In 1709 former Deerfielder Daniel Weld sold off a similar package—a four-and-a-half-acre house lot, twenty-seven acres of lands, and all rights—for £44. In that same year Joseph Morton also sold out. For his three-acre home lot with a house, plus thirty-three acres of prime farmland, he received only £86.[22]

Prices, of course, depended not just on quality but also on location. Parcels of land in the "Great Meadow," just north of town, held higher value than those in the "New Fort Meadow," perched more precariously across the Deerfield River. Similarly, a home lot in Wapping, two miles from the town center, could be bought for as little as £5 as late as 1720. There were differences even along the main street. In 1708 one house lot in Deerfield brought £16, yet another, listed specifically as "within the Great Fort," brought £30 in 1710.[23]

Once the war moved away from Deerfield, values rose quickly. In 1712 an estate of a four-acre home lot, thirty-two acres of farmlands, and all proprietary rights sold for £204—a huge jump from the £44 and £86 offered for similar estates just three years earlier. Within a year of that, a similarly landed estate (though also including livestock) sold for £262. By 1717 a six-acre home lot, house, and barn without any farmlands or rights sold for £140, and four years later a three-acre home lot alone brought £70.[24] Farmland, too, soared in value. As early as 1713, a sixty-

six-acre tract of prime land in the Great Meadow sold for £500,
or almost £8 per acre. By 1720, a seven-acre tract of that same
prime farmland brought £13 per acre.[25] By 1732 a homestead at
Wapping, plus moderate acreage, brought £310.[26]

There were other, subtler signs of Deerfield's growing prosperity. Not only did the General Court stop granting Deerfield
support for its ministry after 1712, but the townspeople themselves steadily improved the minister's salary through this period. In 1707, the year of John Williams's return from captivity,
the town had paid its minister by giving him a day's labor from
each townsman. By 1708 they were again able to grant him a
salary, but one of only £40. By 1711, with the General Court
still supplying £20 annually, the town raised the salary to £60.
By 1714, now paying the full salary itself, Deerfield still granted
a salary increase up to £65 while also granting Williams eighty
acres. As of 1727, while the town still at least occasionally supplemented the minister's pay with loads of firewood, they also
provided a salary of £90.[27]

By the end of this period, Deerfield's growing financial security also permitted the town to end twenty years of almost
constant maintenance and repairs on the old meetinghouse and
construct a new one. In 1728 plans were approved, and on April
28, 1729, with "a Sutable quantyty of Drink and Cake" supplied
"on ye towns charge," Deerfield raised a new meetinghouse.[28]

Schooling, too, reflected the town's improving economic for-
tunes. In 1707, the town had sold off its old schoolhouse, idle
since 1704, for £5. By contrast, in 1720 the town meeting pledged
£20 for "ye encouragement of a school" and set up a committee
to find a schoolmaster. Three years later the town started to
build a new schoolhouse.[29]

A final sign of Deerfield's prosperity comes from the records
of townsmen who died during this period. They show that residents after 1704 were significantly wealthier than those who
had settled Deerfield in the seventeenth century. Estate values—combining real and personal estates and subtracting debts
outstanding—ranged in size from £54 to £2,655, and averaged
a substantial £803. Even excluding John Williams's large estate
of £2,655, free estates averaged £341 in value.[30] These figures

contrast extraordinarily with the Deerfield of the twenty-five years before 1704, where free estates averaged only £61 in value.[31] Deerfield's dramatic increase should be seen more as a rise from acute poverty to respectability than as one from respectability to great wealth, however.[32]

Deerfield's rising prosperity also can be seen in some of the goods townspeople now owned that a previous generation had not. By 1729 many men had large holdings of livestock; a number also now individually owned the bulls and oxen that were more often collectively or publicly owned a generation earlier. John Sheldon died in 1713 with oxen, three steers, and a bull, and a total of £46 worth of livestock. John Williams, too, owned his own "yoke of oxen" amidst livestock valued at £105. Books were common, too. Reverend Williams had an uncommon collection: over one hundred books, worth £45. Yet Sheldon, of different occupation and far more modest means, owned two Bibles and "a parcel of old books."

While Deerfield's men all had the necessities of early-eighteenth-century life—bed, linens, clothing, cookware, cups and plates, work tools—hints of finery also began to appear in the years after 1704. Both John Sheldon and Nathaniel Frary owned glass bottles, not seen before 1704. John Smead owned four waistcoats; his own brewery—"funnel . . . beer barrel, mashing tub, stillwards"; and pewter, brass, and tinware. Nathaniel Frary owned a £7 brass kettle, an unusual seven chairs, a looking glass, a cider press. John Williams died in 1729 with £74 worth of stored food in his home, as well as a silver tankard worth £19. He also owned two slaves, a "molatto boy" named Meseck and a "black Boy," Kedar, each valued at £80.[33] There is even evidence during this period of imported ceramics: a chamber pot from Rhineland.[34]

For all this, there are signs that Deerfield's interdependent, barter economy lived on. Inventories from this period also include acknowledgment of debts which averaged £31 per estate. Itemization of the debts, when it exists, suggests that the people of Deerfield still exchanged myriad goods and services with their neighbors.[35] This network of exchange does not mean that Deerfield remained poor. Rather, the exchange of items, crops, and labor, and the lack of cash as a medium of exchange, were common even in prosperous parts of Massachusetts through the mid-eighteenth century.[36]

Thus, while Deerfield maintained some vestiges of this interdependent local economy, the town was not the impoverished outpost of a generation before. With the town more secure, farmers successfully farmed their rich lands and prosperity followed. That prosperity turned largely on whoever owned and controlled the land of the town—and by 1729 that number had narrowed. Although it seems ironic to talk of a "land shortage" in a town almost surrounded by wilderness, Deerfield's town plan restricted the number of families who could live in or near town. Many Deerfield families had seen a second generation grow up in town, and now some had a third generation. With limited lands locally and abundant lands elsewhere, it makes sense that some of Deerfield's sons, or grandsons, would leave.[37] For outsiders the prospects were even dimmer. Thus, Deerfield's growing wealth of 1729 may also be a comment on the younger, poorer families who could not get enough land to stay in Deerfield, or who could not even get in.[38]

While Deerfield's population and economic life changed a great deal from 1704 to 1729, its pattern of politics and government remained strikingly consistent. In general, Deerfield remained isolated from provincial and county affairs while maintaining its extremely broad-based, egalitarian local government.

In the fifteen years before 1704, Deerfield's town government had been marked by the fact that virtually every adult male served in local office. During the twenty-five years after 1704 that pattern continued. No fewer than eighty-one men held office in Deerfield sometime between 1704 and 1729. This represents almost nine-tenths of all the men who lived in Deerfield at any time during this period. Equally telling, these eighty-one men gave an average of almost seven years of service to the town, in one or more offices.[39] This means that every townsman was typically holding office once every two or three years throughout this period.[40]

Deerfield's town meeting practices helped give rise to this

impressive degree of participation. With twenty positions open each year, the town virtually required widespread participation. Deerfield also made its government broad based by continuing its practice of deciding matters by consent of the entire meeting, not by simple majority votes. As before 1704, "the town" or "the meeting" "agreed" or "decided" matters. There is no record of any majority vote taken before 1728.[41]

Yet another sign of the broad-based and egalitarian nature of this local government was the turnover of townsmen who held each office. Admittedly, a couple offices showed great continuity as the town returned the same people to office year after year: the clerk, the treasurer, and the clerks of the market. All other posts turned over frequently, however. Even those men who might spend four or five years as fence viewers or tithingmen or selectmen rarely did so in consecutive years. Instead, positions rotated steadily and men served off and on over a period of many years.

Deerfield encouraged broad participation in government in another way as well. In Deerfield men were elected to office for the first time on average at about age twenty-nine, some five to ten years earlier than their counterparts in other New England towns. Consistent with that, Deerfield's selectmen first moved into that important office at age thirty-eight on the average, again earlier than in other New England towns.[42] In this light, Deerfield continues to have used town office, consciously or unconsciously, as a "rite of passage" for young men in town. Given that Deerfield men at this time did not on average even marry until age twenty-seven, officeholding by twenty-nine is even more telling.

Again as before 1704, Deerfield men followed a clear path in the jobs that they might hold. Their "apprenticeship" in public office began with service as a fence viewer, a hayward, or a field driver.[43] Men served as fence viewers for anywhere from one to ten years during this period, averaging about three years. Haywards served from one to six years and averaged under two years in that office.

During these years many men in Deerfield served only in these "lower-level" positions. Townsmen who moved beyond these three offices, however, were moving up. As before, two jobs of higher importance and greater responsibility loomed: tithingman and constable. Between 1704 and 1729, nineteen different men served as tithingman, with one or two chosen each year and an average length of service of just under two years. As before 1704, the sensitive job of constable continued to turn over virtually every year.[44]

While Deerfield's government was generally marked by widespread participation and extensive turnover, the town continued its practice of the 1690s of maintaining stability in a few offices. Only five men served as town clerk, with Thomas French and Edward Allen serving eighteen of the twenty-five years. Continuity also marked the treasurer's post, held from its establishment in 1721 by just two men: Thomas French for the first four and Samuel Childs for the next five. Deerfield's market, too, was under consistent control. Only five men served as clerk of market, packer, or sealer during these years.

In choosing its most critical officers, its selectmen, Deerfield again followed seventeenth-century patterns and displayed a strikingly wide degree of participation. From 1704 to 1729 twenty-nine different men served as selectmen, for an average of three years apiece.[45]

Looking carefully at the selectman group makes it appear even more egalitarian. First, the job turned over regularly: Officeholders rarely stayed in for consecutive terms. Only three men served as many as three consecutive terms, and each did it only once. More common—and remarkable—was Lieutenant Thomas Wells's record. Wells served eight terms between 1707 and 1728, yet never twice in a row. In addition, only six of Deerfield's twenty-nine selectmen served for more than four years: The job was passed around. Over the years townspeople also chose a blend of old and new selectmen to serve each year, especially as Deerfield's children of 1704 became its adults of 1729. Nine men served as selectmen for the first time in the 1720s, while three of the eight selectmen who had served Deerfield between 1704 and 1709 also served at some point in the 1720s. Eleazer Hawks first served as selectman in 1704—and last held the office in 1726.

Still another sign of equality in Deerfield government is the fact that townsmen rotated through major and minor offices. Only two of Deerfield's twenty-nine selectmen were elected to the post without first holding some lower office. In addition, selectmen could and did move "back down." In 1722, after ten terms as selectman, Deacon Eleazer Hawks became a fence viewer. One year later he was again chosen selectman. About the only clear criterion for choosing selectmen was picking people committed to Deerfield, people who would stay in town. Whether such attachments grew after men were elected is impossible to say, but the fact remains that twenty-six of the twenty-nine selectmen chosen over these twenty-five years remained in town through 1729 (or their death earlier).

As broad based as all this was, Deerfield again had a "pool of leaders." Among the twenty-nine selectmen were two men who served six terms, two who served eight, and one who served twelve. They did not accrue power through consecutive years in office, yet they held power over a long time. This sense of a pool, indeed a political elite, is borne out by study of the final town office: moderator. Twenty-one different Deerfielders served as moderator between 1704 and 1729, a large number in a town that held only ninety-two men throughout this period. At the same time, though, four men—four of the five long-term selectmen—dominated the office. John Wells served twelve times, Eleazer Hawks twenty, Thomas French thirteen, and Thomas Wells seventeen; none of the other seventeen moderators ever served more than four times. Moderators in Deerfield were generally chosen from among the current or previous year's selectmen. Thus, the extensive selection of the four men reflects their frequent roles as selectmen. It also shows that amidst generally broad-based political participation, there was a core of leaders.

Unlike Deerfield before 1704, it appears that wealth had a significant effect on membership in this elite: Four of the five long-term selectmen were among the top 15 percent of landowners.[46] This is not surprising. In Deerfield, as throughout New England, government service was a burden—a time-consuming and therefore expensive proposition. In Deerfield the burden was shared widely, at least in the great number of offices and officeholders generally. The selectmen and moderator's jobs were different, however. Selectmen had to conduct the business of the town between meetings and had much more constant work. For this reason, the task more often fell to those who could afford to do it. Wealth was also a sign of success in God's eyes, a sign of ability. Thus it is no wonder that townspeople would often choose wealthier people to lead: They had shown themselves to be able and they could afford the time to serve.

Deerfield did not strictly follow wealth as its criterion for leadership. One of the elite group, Thomas French, was a man of modest means, with barely average landholdings. And wealth did not automatically bring political power. In fact, the largest landowner in Deerfield, Mehuman Hinsdale, never served as selectman, and the second largest, Samuel Barnard, served but twice.[47] Still, in general, wealth played a significant part in Deerfield's choosing of leaders.

In summary, Deerfield maintained its impressively broad-based local government for the quarter century after 1704. Officeholding was not absolutely egalitarian, yet governance was shared widely. Consensual, interdependent, wide ranging in their choices of officers, Deerfield's townspeople sustained the communal model of local governance they had established a generation before.

Even as Deerfielders wove an intricate web of local government, from 1704 to 1729 few strands tied them to Hampshire County in any official capacity. Certain legal actions bound village and county. Deerfield men regularly served as jurors and grand jurors in the county courts, a step required by law.[48] Even here, though, Deerfield's attention occasionally flagged: In 1729 Samuel Childs was admonished by the court for failing to serve.[49] Deerfield men also appeared in court, of course, when involved in cases. By the 1720s these were overwhelmingly debt actions. One Deerfield man entered the courts in a more distinguished way. In 1723 John Wells became the town's first justice of the peace.

Deerfield also had contact with Hampshire County because

its court licensed the town's innkeepers. In fact, in 1729, for the first time, it licensed two for Deerfield, Edward Allin and Samuel Field, each to be an "Innholder Taverner & Common Victualler." Deerfield was growing, of a fashion. And yet the town must still have seemed small and poor to county officials. In 1728, when establishing the proportion of the county tax that each town would pay, the judges placed Deerfield near the bottom of the list. Of twelve county towns sharing the £150 rate, Deerfield was to pay just £7.[50]

In some respects Deerfield had more contact with the government of Massachusetts than of Hampshire County. From 1704 to 1712 Deerfield's ties with the General Court revolved around Queen Anne's War, as the government sent aid, usually money or soldiers, to the besieged town. Through these years Deerfield never sent a single representative to the General Court. Townsmen likely felt they could not afford one, and since the Court supported Deerfield steadily through this period, such a decision evidently did not hurt the town.

For most of the next decade, Deerfield became less of a General Court concern. Deerfield's only ties from 1712 to 1720 involved residue from the previous war: continued negotiations over prisoners of war or, more commonly, compensation to Deerfield people who fought or suffered losses in the war.[51] In the 1720s, though, Deerfield and the General Court began to work together more. One reason was that the town finally started to send representatives to the General Court. John Wells became Deerfield's first representative to the Assembly in eighteen years when he ventured to Boston in 1716. He was followed the next year by his nephew Thomas Wells, who served for the next five years.[52] The other reason was that, once again, war loomed in New England. Father Sebastian Rasle, a Jesuit missionary, rallied the Abenaki in the early 1720s to take up arms against their English enemies. From 1722 to 1725 Deerfield again became embroiled in conflict.

The threat of war rose as early as 1720, when the General Court offered £100 to anyone who could capture "Monsr Ralle" who had "been the incendiary that has instigated & stirr'd up those Indians."[53] Although Father Rasle's War never became a major conflagration, Deerfield and New England could not scale down their preparations. To begin with, the government of New France, not just one isolated missionary, urged the Abenaki into the war. Governor Vaudreuil felt that he could not get into open war with New England, and in fact had to make New France appear neutral, since France and England were at peace. Still, he secretly provided aid for the Abenaki and encouraged other tribes to aid or join them, too.[54] The Abenakis, enemies of the English since King Philip's War, had enough resentment built up against the English that the French support was sufficient to push them into war.

The opposing forces then fell into place. In addition to gearing up their own armies and militia, the English in Massachusetts and New York soon began to recruit the Iroquois, a force Vaudreuil knew and feared. With presents and entreaties, the English eventually brought a few Mohawks to their side.[55]

While Massachusetts prepared the entire New England frontier for war, it paid particular attention to Hampshire County and the west. Instead of focusing the bulk of its energies on Deerfield, though, now efforts were centered farther north, at Northfield. This young, small settlement had been supported with money and soldiers from Boston almost since its birth in 1714. In 1720, with war threatening, help increased. The General Court soon granted to the outpost tax abatements, garrison soldiers, and aid for fortifying houses.[56] Northfield was becoming the Deerfield of Father Rasle's War.

In July of 1722, after peace entreaties failed, Massachusetts governor Shute declared war on the Eastern Indians. For a year the west stayed quiet. Then, in August of 1723, a band of five Indians struck at Northfield, killing two. Within ten days Deerfield had its own garrison posted. A month later Colonel Samuel Partridge, still the valley's military commander, requested gunpowder, lead, and flints for all the western frontier towns.[57]

Although the valley took no more blows that summer, tensions rose as 1723 ebbed. Through the end of that year Deerfield billetted Connecticut soldiers sent up the valley to help protect it.[58] In December the General Court voted that it would be "of Great Service to all the Western Frontiers . . . to build a Block House above Northfield . . . & to post In it Forty Able Men . . . to be employed in Scouting at a good Distance . . . for the discovery of the enemy Coming towards any of the Frontier Towns."[59] Situated up the Connecticut River some ten miles above Northfield, Fort Dummer pushed New England's frontier still farther from Deerfield.

Even with this added protection, townspeople in the twice-shattered town were apprehensive. Lieutenant John Stoddard, the valley's second-in-command, noted this in March of 1724: "The people of Deerfield grow uneasy (now the spring comes on) at their having but 10 men."[60] A committee of townsmen petitioned the governor, seeking "a sufficiency of men, both to guard our forts, & men in the field. . . . we stand in great need of 30 men." Revealing is the townsmen's rationale, strongly reminiscent of 1704:

by reason of the war [we] are much afraid to go about our occupations, expecting daily a descent of the enemy on our Western frontiers . . . indeed the difficulties of the war lie so hard on us, that several families, & also several young men have drawn off from us, & several more are going in a little time, to the great discouragement of those who are left behind.[61]

Massachusetts heard Deerfield's cries. In April the Court sent fifteen additional men to Deerfield.

War still came. On June 18, a band of eight or ten Indians struck at Hatfield, killing one and capturing two others. Nine days later they ambushed and killed three men just four miles north of Deerfield. Then, on July 10, the Indians drew blood at Deerfield, as three natives ambushed Deerfielders Samuel Childs and Samuel Allen at the south end of Pine Hill, just a mile north of town.[62] The next day Colonel Partridge wrote to Governor William Dummer of the danger of the lurking enemy: "in the midst of our harvest we are forced to go 30 or 40 men in a day with their arms and a guard to accompany and work to gather." In October, even after three quiet months, he wrote of the same troubles, made vexing by the number of enemy tracks still being found in the region.[63]

For all this, Deerfield and the valley had thus far suffered relatively little. Besides, with scouts out that summer and through the following winter, Partridge's forces successfully deterred any large enemy parties from coming anywhere near the valley.[64] Massachusetts also remembered other lessons of Queen Anne's War. That winter the Assembly ordered the outposts in the Connecticut valley to provide "Snow Shoes & Moggasins" for its garrison soldiers.[65] Not again would the English fail to pursue the enemy for lack of equipment.

Hampshire County's preparations paid off; in fact, they alone may have been enough to discourage the enemy from fighting in the west. While scouts continued to push north through 1725, the valley itself lay quiet—so quiet, in fact, that in mid-summer Colonel Stoddard warned Governor Dummer about the valley people's "careless way of living . . . [I could not] persuade them to order a watch."[66] Stoddard's fears were well founded. On August 25, 1725, six Deerfield men taking a cow to pasture across the Deerfield River at "Green River Farms" were ambushed by Indians, with Deacon Samuel Field seriously wounded.[67]

Fortunately for Deerfield, that was the last blow the town took in this brief and sputtering war. With Father Rasle killed in August of 1724 and Governor Vaudreuil's death fourteen months later, the Indians lost their strongest allies. Soon peace returned to the Connecticut valley and New England.

This war proved to be more smoke than fire for Deerfield. The town lost no one killed, just three wounded, and one captured; was never assaulted or threatened by any large force; had the buffers of Northfield and Fort Dummer to protect it; and was never forced into major construction of defenses. Yet the smoke of Father Rasle's War did cloud Deerfield's life for two years. The town had to absorb and support as many as twenty-five soldiers and had twenty-six of its own townsmen serve as well.[68] It had to endure yet another period of intense pressure, of constant vigilance for the attack that could come at any time—the tension of guerrilla warfare. Compared to Queen Anne's War, Deerfield fared well. But this was still war.

Once Father Rasle's War was over, Deerfield seemed on a path toward unprecedented peace, security, and prosperity. The population had grown steadily; people were increasingly prosperous; and local government appeared smooth and successful. Deerfield also had new neighbors who offered protection, and as soon as the war ended still more new settlements began to bloom.[69] Yet Deerfield paid a price for this progress. The town suffered growing pains, and they ultimately made it less a small, communal village than a more developed—and contentious—town.

By the 1720s Deerfield's growth had slowed. Beyond the fact that few new residents settled in town, apparently because it was difficult to acquire land, two other issues relating to land became problems. They were the splitting off of Deerfield's proprietors and the "Cheapside/Green River lands" controversy.

Like most New England towns of the seventeenth century, when Deerfield was founded it did not separate the political functions of the town from the affairs concerning land, which legally were the concern of the town's proprietors. The town meeting simply handled both. This was both logical and practical. It was logical because most if not all of the original settlers of a town were also its proprietors. It was also practical because early New England towns depended on their townspeople working together, and to separate a proprietors group from the residents could have been destructive. Deerfield had followed this practice since its inception. Except for one separate proprietors meeting in 1699, for the forty years from 1674 to 1714 Deerfield had dealt with all land affairs at town meeting.

In 1714 this changed. By virtue of a 1713 General Court order, proprietors in Massachusetts towns were required to make their affairs distinct, regular, and orderly.[70] Thus, in December of 1714 Deerfield's proprietors gathered as a separate body. At that meeting, and occasional others over the next three years, they handled the routine land affairs of the town. These included granting "wanting lands" to petitioners; occasionally giving out new grants of land, such as small additions to house lots; and regulating and maintaining common fence. Interestingly, the records of these proprietors meetings still ended up in the town meeting book: The legal change had not pushed Deerfielders too far.

Such mundane activity did not affect Deerfield's economic world, as proprietors and townsmen continued to interweave their affairs. The proprietors met less than once a year through this period and the town meeting continued to handle at least some proprietary matters, such as decisions about fences. From 1718 on, though, the proprietors began to make decisions which were more profound. Symbolizing these changes was the decision in 1719 to purchase a separate proprietors' book and transcribe all proprietors' records from the town book into this separate volume. The proprietors were slowly breaking away.

Fittingly enough, it was at a town—not proprietors—meeting that the most significant step in this separation began. In March of 1718 the town decided to draw up articles to vote on "respecting the undivided lands within ye township of Deerfield." Deerfield had not divided any common lands since a wood-lot division in 1688. Now it was about to set the rules for any future divisions. The way to do that was to establish for all townspeople "their rights or interest by Commons in the Eight thousand acres formerly granted to Dedham." In other words, the town would make clear who held what rights to the original 532 "cow commons" parceled out in Dedham in the 1660s. Because by 1718 so many Deerfielders held lands without these proprietary rights, the committee also recommended that settlers should be accorded one share for every 13.5 acres of land they owned.[71]

It took five years to sort out Deerfield's shares, but in May of 1723 the town's proprietors finally got together to ratify the list and proportions of proprietary rights. It was clearly an unusual meeting. For the only time in Deerfield's records before 1730, the clerk recorded a list of all townsmen present. Then the proprietors voted to accept the list of fifty-nine Deerfield proprietors and their total of 687 commons rights.[72]

In some respects the meeting was largely symbolic. Almost everyone on the proprietors list was a resident; in other words, there were almost no absentee proprietors. This meant that while proprietors and residents were legally different groups, at this point they were still largely the same people. Yet the list had great implications for the future. No longer would newcomers in Deerfield stand on equal footing with established residents, for the proprietors list now stood as the basis for "all Divisions of Land hereafter to be made."[73] Further, the list established and confirmed, both for 1723 and after, a measure of inequality among Deerfielders. Over one-third of the fifty-nine proprietors held just two or three shares, and almost two-thirds held fewer than ten. On the other hand, Mehuman Hinsdale owned 103 shares, and seven others held more than twenty.[74]

Of more immediate impact and controversy were conflicts over the Cheapside and Green River lands, located some two to three miles north of town across the Deerfield River. When Deerfield had been growing rapidly in the 1680s, the town had laid out roughly twenty house lots and accompanying parcels of farmland for new settlers at Green River. It appeared at that time that Green River would be the northern complement to Wapping, the hamlet of about twelve home lots located two miles south of town. But Green River "did not take." While some houses may have been built there in the 1690s, the threat of war drove settlers back to the town center. As of 1704, no settlers lived as far from town as Green River, especially since those lands sat on the far side of the Deerfield River. While townsmen may have farmed the lands, there are no signs that anyone lived across the river at any time in the early eighteenth century.

By 1716 that situation had changed.[75] That March the town chose a committee to negotiate with "yᵉ ocupiers of yᵉ chepside"—Cheapside, an appropriate enough name for lands across the Deerfield River. Two years later the town tacitly encouraged such expansion when it established a committee to lay out common fence for "yᵉ proprietors and improvers of land at . . . Cheapside."[76]

Deerfield also renewed its interest in the "Green River lands" laid out in the 1680s. At that same 1718 meeting the town "resited" the twenty-five house lots up along the Green River just above where it emptied into the Deerfield. The committee also issued regulations for settlement consistent with those of 1680s Deerfield. To gain full title to his land, a grantee would have two years to build "a mansion house" on his lot and would have to live there three years after building; in case of further wars, each would have five years after the war's end "to make good their title."[77]

Although the records do not tell why, this proposal was not accepted. For the next decade, Cheapside and Green River affairs became increasingly acrimonious in Deerfield. In the winter of 1720–1721 the town voted to buy a new scow to go up on the Deerfield River near Cheapside—but specified that "ye mill men Cheapside or Green River men" must care for the boat, and if it "be lost throrow their carelessness they . . . Bear ye loss of it."[78] Eighteen months later the town appointed a committee to consider building a bridge across the Deerfield— yet nothing came of it for five years.

With the threat of Father Rasle's War dominating local affairs from 1723 to 1726, little was done for the people living or farming across the river. At last, in March of 1727 the town chose a new committee "to lay out ye green river homelots." With terms now explicitly "Encludeing . . . Conditions" for proper settlement, the town laid out twenty-five lots well up on the Green River, perhaps four miles from town. Green River was finally a settlement.[79]

That there was controversy in all this comes from more than the problems of delay and "conditions." In December of 1727 the town meeting again took up the issue of building a bridge over the Deerfield River to connect Green River and Cheapside with the town center. This time a vote to build a bridge passed. Two months later, however, at an unusual February meeting the town reversed itself. Now the vote to build a bridge "passed in ye negative." Instead, the meeting tossed crumbs at the residents across the river, offering instead "a Scow and 2 cannoes."[80] It is only the second recorded negative vote in the entire Deerfield town book to this point, and the only one since the town had decided not to send a General Court representative to Boston in 1698.

The circumstances surrounding land issues in Deerfield from 1715 to 1729 do not suggest sudden trauma or grave crisis. Instead, they offer more a sign of change. That the proprietors became independent was a common and reasonable evolutionary step. That they made clear their proprietary rights is similarly sensible. Yet these steps suggest changes from the communal Deerfield of a generation before. Likewise the efforts of the Cheapside and Green River people to get full support from the town for their settlement make sense, particularly from the perspective of those outlying settlers. With land in town so limited, moving across the Deerfield River was possibly the only way those settlers could remain Deerfield residents and have sufficient home lots and lands of their own. Yet it is only fitting to note that after one more generation of conflict, the Green River settlement would break off to become the independent town of Greenfield, established by the General Court in 1753.

Town governance, too, showed change in a gradual, not sudden or violent, way. One sign of change was the development of a political elite in town. Such a core was normal for early New England towns,[81] yet Deerfield had not had one before 1715. By 1729 Deerfield had simply become more like other New England towns.

Other political changes eased into Deerfield's world as well. Again, they were not violent, and they only made Deerfield like other New England towns. Yet they also represented important changes in this growing community, for they revolved around contention, disagreement, division.

The first glimmerings of dissent in town governance came in 1713. On March 16 the town held its usual annual meeting to elect town officials for the year. While the meeting addressed some minor land issues as well, there are no signs that the meeting was in any way unusual. Exactly one week later, however, the town met again and voted that the men selected for office the previous week "were not Legally chosen."[82] As it turned out, most of the men elected to office the previous week were reelected, though Captain Jonathan Wells was replaced as selectman by Edward Allen.

This curious action could be seen as a legal quirk or an aberration, except that within several years contention grew. At a 1721 proprietors meeting six Deerfield men took the extraordinary step of putting their disapproval of a decision on record when they "did Actually Enter y^r desent" against the granting of a home lot to Edward Allen. Heading the list of dissenters was Captain Jonathan Wells—the very man Allen had replaced as selectman eight years before.

By the mid-1720s another form of dissent touched Deerfield. In 1725, for the first time, a Deerfielder refused to serve in his elected office. When Ensign John Wells turned down the job of constable, the town had to vote in a new man. One year later the problem broadened. John Catlin refused to serve as selectman and the town was forced to make a new choice. Later in the same meeting, John Nims announced that he, too, refused to serve as selectman, and the town chose Jonathan Hoyt. But now Hoyt refused to serve. Finally, Sergeant Benjamin Mun took the post.[83]

Contention soon reared its head still higher. In 1727 and 1728 the town struggled through granting the Green River home lots; those same months also saw the Cheapside bridge controversy and the town's vote reversal. By 1729 public disagreements even spilled over into religious affairs. Controversy had been rising steadily throughout this period over seating in the meetinghouse. In the years before 1704, this public ranking of citizens by "age, estate and dignity" took place infrequently, perhaps once every ten years. With growth, however, came growing disagreements. When the town voted for a new seating in 1713, it was the first such action since 1701. Eight years then passed before the town approved a new arrangement in 1721. But in 1724 the issue arose again, with the town clerk recording the intriguing restriction that seating be established only for "all White persons above ye age of sixteen years." Less than a year later the town approved two new "seaters" to join the three-man committee already selected. Now even the committee was struggling over seating. Within two months the town tried to help the enlarged committee by establishing new rules for the meetinghouse: "ye flank seats" were made into pews made "the Equal With ye second seat in ye body."[84] Deerfield was wrestling with equality.

Quarrels continued through the end of the decade. At a special town meeting on October 28, 1728, Deerfielders voted to build a new meetinghouse some forty by fifty feet in size. Yet controversy stalked even this project. After determining where to spot the meetinghouse at the December 1728 meeting, dissent arose over the decision. At an unusual mid-spring meeting on May 19, 1729, the town proved unable to agree on a site. Thus, the town "concluded to move out [outside] and stand at the 3 places discoust [discussed]." More significantly, they agreed to disagree, to let a vote decide the matter. Far from achieving consensus, much less unanimity, Deerfield decided that "ye bigest number shall have ye place."[85] The communal decisions of a small outpost were being replaced by the votes of a growing town.

One more facet of daily life betrays these changes in Deerfield: the courts. In Deerfield's early years, townspeople rarely went to the Hampshire County Court unless they were involved in criminal proceedings. By the 1720s that, too, had changed. At both General Sessions of the Peace and the Inferior Court of Common Pleas, Deerfield men began to appear regularly, usually for debt actions. Sometimes the cases involved significant sums of money, as in 1729 when Deerfield husbandman Daniel Arms took former Deerfielder Michael Mitchell to court for recovery of one hundred gallons of "Merchantable Mollasses" and fifty-three gallons of "Good Barbadoes Rhum." Yet other times the cases were small. In 1727 Deerfield yeoman George Swan took Joseph Sheldon to court for £10. In a local land case in 1728, Samuel Dickinson took fellow townsman Mehuman Hinsdale to court on a plea of "Trespass and Ejectment" over a five-acre piece of land in the Great Meadow.[86]

These cases have significance on at least three levels. For one thing, Deerfielders appear to have become more litigious. Perhaps with more time and money they could afford to take the step of going to court to handle disputes, a marked change from before. For another, relationships between litigants had become more formal. Disagreements over £10 or a five-acre piece of meadowland now became county court cases, not local matters. Finally, and perhaps most telling, Deerfielders were taking Deerfielders to court. Local disputes between neighbors, whether over land or money, were blown into county court cases. Once again, it seems that the spirit of a small, intertwined group of villagers had given way to the more individualistic and combative mores of a developing town.

In looking back over Deerfield's changes from 1704 to 1729, there is a danger in reading too much into the record. The poor village of the late seventeenth century was still a small farm town in 1729; it was just a bit larger and more secure. The increases in population and wealth that Deerfield saw after 1704 did not make the town large or wealthy; they only made it more like other towns. The rise of a political core of leadership, too, was normal, and must be acknowledged in the context of a local government that continued to share its authority unusually widely. The rise of proprietors and the edging away of new settlers across the Deerfield River—even as they remained Deerfield citizens—were also common stages of development for eighteenth-century New England towns. Even the contention and division in Deerfield by the 1720s were not unusual. Dissent at meetings, disputes over major town decisions like building new bridges or meetinghouses, debt actions, even refusals to serve in office were evolutionary signs common in many towns.

But such contention had not existed in Deerfield before 1715. In early Deerfield a smaller number of more closely bound citizens had resolved their problems differently. Disagreements over town affairs ended in consensus, not majority votes. Local disputes over money or land were handled privately in town, not in a courthouse in Northampton or Springfield. Deerfield would not allow itself to have factions or major divisions in town. Then again, townspeople could not have expected to survive the wilderness and the wars if they were not bound closely together.

By 1729 Deerfield had changed. When the frontier moved on, so did many of the reasons for the town to live as it had. And the trade-off was not a bad one. In 1704 Deerfield had been a poor, rude, fragile frontier outpost surrounded—and almost obliterated—by constant, threatening war. By 1729 it was a growing, protected, more prosperous town. Deerfield was not a boiling sea of faction and fighting. It was simply a different town.

Conclusion: Deerfield and the New England Frontier

THE YEAR 1729 did not see any magical or instantaneous changes in Deerfield. Yet the date has meaning. That it marked a quarter century since the devastation of 1704 makes it an appropriate point of reference. That it marked the death of the Reverend John Williams makes it symbolic as well.

As Deerfield, the Connecticut valley, and Massachusetts all mourned the loss of the well-known "captivity minister," Williams's death became a sign of the end of an era. "But alas!" cried Boston minister Thomas Foxcroft, "how great is the scarcity of real Saints in our Day!"[1] Indeed, Williams's death came at a time of decline in New England's churches, a time of great soul searching among the region's clergy about their faded errand into the wilderness.[2]

Williams's death had particular meaning for Deerfield, of course. The shepherd who had led the town's flock since 1686, almost the beginning of permanent settlement, was gone. And he had been a good leader. A neighboring minister eulogized Williams as just and humble, a man who loved his work and had displayed "his Zeal against Sin." Courageous as well, Williams had fought against the Indians and wilderness back in the years when Deerfield "was *the* Frontier Plantation [emphasis added]." The implication, if unintended, was clear: By 1729 Deerfield no longer was "the frontier." Williams had been a frontier pastor, but both he and the frontier had now passed. The neighboring minister also praised Williams for being "publick Spirited." In a sentence more didactic than eulogistic, he stated, "We are not born for our selves, but are members of Communities, and ought to be concerned for the publick Welfare."[3] One can only wonder whether this was a compliment or a warning to the people of Deerfield in 1729.

For as Deerfield changed ministers, the town's ways of working continued to evolve. Townspeople struggled for three years to replace Williams. In fact, the struggle itself demonstrates Deerfield's changing nature. In 1730, in the town's first recorded explicitly majority decision, Deerfield voted "by a great majority" of 36 to 14 to bring in twenty-three-year-old Benjamin Pierpont as its new minister.[4] Ironically, then, John Williams—the man eulogized as standing for the need for a close community—was being replaced by a minister chosen by majority vote. That step did not succeed, however, for as new and damaging information about young Pierpont filtered into Deerfield, the "great majority" dwindled and the town withdrew its offer. Not until 1732—and after a second candidate had rejected Deerfield's offer—did the town hire Mr. Jonathan Ashley, again by "a great majority of votes."[5]

The year 1729 took on religious significance for another reason as well. During that year two other giants of the Connecticut valley clergy also died, Northampton's Solomon Stoddard and Westfield's Edward Taylor. The loss of these three ministers, all of whom had been at their pulpits since the late seventeenth century, stripped the valley of many of its ties to the past. With a new generation of young clergymen installed by the early 1730s, plus rising concern for the decline of Puritan zeal, Hampshire County was ripe for change. By 1735, under the leadership of one of these new leaders, Northampton minister Jonathan Edwards, the Little Awakening aroused the citizens of the Connecticut valley. Within a few years, the Great Awakening shook all of British North America.

By the 1740s the Great Awakening had splintered the unity of Deerfield's church. Although Reverend Ashley at first supported the Little Awakening, as early as 1742 he was speaking out against the "disorder and emotional excess" he saw around him. The split within Deerfield's church steadily widened.

By 1750 a minority in Deerfield, displaying "disdain and defi-
ance," left the town church to join with other "New Lights" at
Green River.[6] Three years later Green River broke off from
Deerfield entirely to form the new town of Greenfield.

Religion was not the only area of change in Deerfield after
1729. Indian-English relationships in the valley were also shifting. Natives now traded regularly with the English at a "truck
house" located above Northfield on the Connecticut River.[7] In
1735 Deerfield became the site of a peace conference between
Massachusetts governor Belcher and representatives of the six
Iroquois nations (the sixth, the Tuscaroras, had joined around
1715). The town that had been the site of so much violence now
echoed with cries of good will and alliance between colonists
and natives.[8] Some Indian forces remained enemies, to be sure.
Yet just one generation after 1704, Deerfielders forged amicable relations with at least some regional Indians. Relations were
not conducted on terms that were purely red and white.

Even so, Deerfielders still had not seen the end of Indian
violence in town. In the 1740s New England and New France
plunged into King George's War, the third of the French and
Indian Wars. In 1745 and 1746 the French sent allied Indians
on a series of raids along the New England frontier and up and
down the Connecticut valley. On August 25, 1746, a band of
ten to twenty French-allied Indians struck at "the Bars," a small
cluster of houses two miles below the center of Deerfield. When
it was over, five members of the Allen and Amsden families lay
scalped and dead, one of the Amsden boys was captured, and
one girl, Eunice Allen, was tomahawked in the head but survived.[9] By 1747 Massachusetts and Connecticut were once again
negotiating the question of which colony would send men "into
Hampshire County for the defense of Deerfield and Northfield."[10] Although that 1746 assault was the last Indian attack
that ever struck Deerfield, Indians attacked settlers on the
north side of Greenfield, less than ten miles away, as late as
1766.[11] Thus, for another generation after 1729, war still threatened the town.

Although sporadic violence shook Deerfield, the frontier
moved steadily away as Massachusetts constructed a line of

forts across its northern border. By the mid-1740s the chain of forts stretched from "Fort No. 4" a few miles east of Brattleboro, Vermont, to Fort Dummer on the Connecticut and then west toward New York, with the forts five to ten miles apart: Forts Sheldon, Morrison, Pelham, and Massachusetts. In fact, it was at Fort Massachusetts in 1746 that a Deerfield son, Sergeant John Hawks, led twenty soldiers in a valiant but fruitless defense against a huge French and Indian force that ultimately captured the outpost. By the 1740s, though, these forts protected Deerfield and the Connecticut valley, for even in defeat they provided the region with a buffer, a line of defense.[12]

While war and the frontier remained part of the lives of Connecticut valley people, Deerfield and the region grew quickly after 1730. Deerfield's population increased steadily from the 310 of 1729 to 737 by 1765.[13] As the region's population soared, the number of towns in Hampshire County exploded, rising from fourteen in 1740 to forty-three by 1776. Deerfield itself spawned a pair of new towns on the western edges of its township, first Shelburne in 1742 and then Conway in 1750.[14]

As ever, growth brought costs of change. While Deerfield's population grew through the mid-eighteenth century, it also became more stagnant. Continuing a trend visible by the 1720s, few new families settled in town. Deerfield's population became two populations: a small number of newcomers and transients, and a larger, ever more entrenched core of the town's oldest families.[15] The region's growth was not an unmixed blessing, either. The dramatic population increase caused "overcrowding and political instability"; as many settlers moved into the newly created "hill towns" away from the river, they set up new and at times challenging lines of authority; and the process of separating new towns from old often proved bitter and divisive. The splitting off of Greenfield from Deerfield in 1753 is a good example. Settlers of the two towns clashed violently over rights to hay in disputed fields as late as 1768—fully fifteen years after the towns had separated.[16]

While the region's population growth had its negative effects, economic development did not. Deerfield thrived in the years after 1729. Farmers began to practice more intensive agriculture, using such techniques as dung spreading, cutting ditches for drainage, and the "grain cradle." New crops were planted—potatoes, turnips, beans—and animal fodder was changed as well. The town saw a "dramatic increase" in the number of cattle that families owned. Finally, and most profound, Deerfielders were taking their produce to market. They shipped peas, wheat, corn, and flaxseed by cart to markets in Hatfield, Northampton, and Hartford. They also soon developed a thriving market in cattle which took them all the way to Boston. On their return from those trips they brought back various scythes and other specialized equipment. They also brought luxuries: yard goods, clothes, hardware, and ceramics from England; tea and spices from the East Indies; molasses, rum, sugar, and salt from the West Indies.[17]

This does not mean that Deerfield's farmers were all commercial entrepreneurs by 1750; far from it. Like most Massachusetts farm towns Deerfield continued to maintain elements of a local barter economy. Likely spurred by the lack of cash, Deerfielders' exchanges of crops, goods, and labor continued to be "an essential and necessary part of subsistence." Yet such local networks now coexisted with rising commercial activity.[18] By 1771 Deerfield was one of Massachusetts' most prosperous farm towns, a place where "the majority of farmers . . . were capable of producing a marketable surplus."[19] Deerfield had raced through the classic historical model of agricultural development: "communal and group values" had quickly given way to a more "individualistic and commercial form of society."[20] By the American Revolution the town's economy bore little resemblance to that of the frontier outpost of earlier times.

If Deerfield by 1750 was a thriving little farm town, what then was early Deerfield? What had this place been in the years before 1729 and why did it struggle so? And what does Deerfield tell us about the New England frontier?

Deerfield's story is, first of all, the dramatic tale of a town's enduring struggle to survive. Deerfield bore thirty attacks in its first half century, a frightening, eloquent testimony to the violence of this frontier and the fortitude of its pioneers. New

England battled through four different wars between 1670 and 1729, wars that consumed twenty-seven of those years. Yet amidst this almost constant conflict, Deerfield's men and women carved out a town in the "howling wilderness," and they made it work.

The story of this place reverberates with drama and violence. Taking advantage of the ideal site, the Pocumtuck Indians had dwelled on this spot in the upper Connecticut valley for decades, if not centuries. Their destruction in 1664 at the hands of the Mohawks foretold the violence that Deerfield would endure. Indeed, the English settlers who soon followed had been living on the site for just six years when King Philip's War erupted in 1675. Deerfield, then called Pocumtuck, suffered the ultimate loss in that war: total destruction. In the face of the Bloody Brook massacre, perhaps the most one-sided English defeat in the entire war, Pocumtuck's pioneers had to give up their settlement. Because of Bloody Brook, the town gained notoriety throughout New England.

Deerfield's next generation was burdened with still more unwanted fame. The town that began to rebuild in the 1680s was crushed by the devastating French and Indian attack of February 29, 1704. Although Deerfield was not abandoned this time, the losses were staggering: three-fifths of the townspeople killed or captured, nearly half the town burned. Fame again came quickly, and this time lasted longer. John Williams's *The Redeemed Captive* was an immediate "best-seller" when published in 1707, and Americans continued to read it, through six editions, right through the eighteenth century. Deerfield's place in the history books, in the genre of captivity narratives, and in early American literature was assured.

So Deerfield's story deserves to be told, if simply as a drama of life in early New England. Yet Deerfield is far more. It is also the story—and a model for study—of America's early frontier. Indeed, the single most important force that molded Deerfield was the frontier. Although in many respects Deerfield was a New England town like others, the frontier shaped and constantly reshaped Deerfield for over half a century. When New England's lines of settlement, both west from Boston and northward up the Connecticut River valley, had reached Deerfield in 1670, they stopped—and essentially did not move for over forty years. Deerfield sat on the edge of English settlement for an unusually long time, and while it did the frontier dominated its life.

But what was "the frontier"? Or, better yet, "which frontier"? Ever since 1893, when Frederick Jackson Turner galvanized thinking about the nature and significance of America's frontier, historians have been blessed and burdened with a jumble of powerful images. Turner claimed that the frontier brought forth democracy, selfishness, "dominant individualism," a restless spirit, and the "buoyancy and exuberance that comes with freedom."[21] In addition, "removal from the customary usages of the older communities and from the conservative influence of the body of the clergy increased the innovating tendency": The frontier opened "a gate from the bondage of the past" to a "freshness, and confidence, and scorn of older society, impatience of its restraints and ideas, and indifference to its lessons."[22] In an essay written specifically about the Massachusetts frontier, Turner added, "Individualistic and democratic tendencies were emphasized . . . by the wilderness conditions. . . . Remove[al] away from the control of . . . the older communities and from the conservative influence of . . . the clergy, increased the innovating tendency." The Massachusetts frontier, he concluded, was " 'the Wrong side of the Hedge.' "[23]

The problem with applying all these ideas to Deerfield, however appealing they might be, is that they are essentially wrong.

Throughout American history, "frontier" has had vastly different meanings to different people in different contexts; it did in 1704, and it does now. To understand early Deerfield requires recognition of these "different frontiers." Each helps one understand early Deerfield—and New England.

It is not surprising that Turner spoke of the early New England frontier as a hedge: New Englanders had been doing so since the seventeenth century. In pondering King Philip's War, contemporary William Hubbard had asked, "Why are our Hedges broken down?" Religious references were frequent. Cotton

Mather used the image, as did Thomas Shepard. In fact, there seemed to be a common "ecclesiastical Hedge." It is easy to see why. The image was clear and understandable, and it sent a strong message. A hedge, a firm and well-defined though not insurmountable barrier, divided light from dark, good from evil, civilization from savagery. If a "Hedge of grace sur-rounded New England," then settlers and outsiders alike would understand the meaning and purpose of New England's "errand into the wilderness." If it were breached, either from within or without, all of New England was at risk.[24]

Such a frontier was important, at least in spiritual terms, to early New England. Yet daily life brought other, more imme-diate "frontiers" to the people of early Deerfield. Most compel-ling was the frontier that separated colonists and natives. This was no sharp dividing line between "civilization" and "sav-ages," however. Instead, this frontier was a zone of exchange between peoples, an area of interaction between cultures.[25]

For early Deerfield this "frontier" was a normal, active, ongoing part of town life. Starting with the first Connecticut valley colonization in the 1630s, Indians and English had lived side by side. Not until King Philip's War did the natives leave their local village sites. Even then, "friendly Indians" contin-ued to move through the valley, stopping to hunt or fish for periods of time, into the 1690s. Valley Indians had also begun trading with their English neighbors from the time of first set-tlement. Although the region's fur trade started to ebb by the 1650s, other exchanges continued until King Philip's War. While such interaction declined during the early French and Indian Wars, Indian-English trade returned by the 1730s.

Law and government proved to be other fields of interaction. Especially before 1675 valley natives were frequently held accountable for their actions under English law, a practice with profound implications. Although the English controlled such a situation, Indian acquiescence to shared laws, practices, and court procedures suggests considerable coexistence. While the number of Indian cases declined after 1675, that stemmed in part from the radically diminished postwar native population. At the same time, though, Indians continued to settle land claims in county courts through the end of the seventeenth century.[26]

Deerfield's frontier also involved valley colonists with inter-Indian affairs. From first settlement the valley's English colonists distinguished between friendly and unfriendly Indians. They carefully cultivated friendships and alliances, as both cultures realized the value of such interdependence. The colonists also learned quickly about inter-Indian conflicts and rivalries, and from the 1640s on at times played active roles in them. Through the seventeenth century the English were only one force among many in this still-fluid region; the stage was not all theirs.

The major force that changed the frontier was war. When war broke out between English and Indians, especially when it closed in on the Connecticut valley, the areas of interchange would narrow; the types of interaction—economic, social, legal—would diminish or collapse. If there was a time for the English when differences between Indian and Indian would disappear, war was it. That was understandable. Deerfield and the other valley towns were fighting for their very existence in the 1670s, the 1690s, and the early 1700s. Yet even through these wars, while this frontier contracted, it only rarely became a solid line of division. In 1675 "friendly Indians" still dwelled near Springfield until the day Philip's forces attacked that English town. In the middle of King William's War, Deerfield was still allowing "friendly" Indians safe passage through their region; they even let a large band encamp within a few miles of town. In the 1690s the Hampshire County Court heard two different murder cases where Indians stood accused. Even amidst war the courts held off vigilantism, or "frontier justice."

The colonists' ability, willingness, and desire to maintain good relations with friendly Indians continued through the 1720s. During Father Rasle's War, Hatfield doctor Thomas Hastings treated a number of wounded Indians. This was no show of kindness to vanquished enemies. Rather, these were members of a native force allied with the English.[27] In 1735 representatives of the Massachusetts government rode out from Boston to

Deerfield to cement alliances with Indians from New York. That this meeting could take place in Deerfield is the ultimate testimony to the continued maintenance of the frontier as a region of exchange. Even after four wars, Deerfield's frontier was no solid line of separation, nor were the Indians a "single, oppressive entity."[28] This does not mean the forces were equal—by 1735 the Indians had given up most land, law, and economic control—but such an imbalance in a frontier zone was not unusual.[29] What is far more important is that this type of frontier persisted. Fluid, capable of expanding and contracting, it was a far cry from Turner's—and Cotton Mather's—hedge.

As there were these "different frontiers," so, too, did these frontiers define colonists' existence in many ways. Whether amidst a zone of interaction or along a sharp line of division, the fact remains that Deerfield was isolated, separated from its English neighbors, in many ways alone on the edge of the "howling wilderness." Deerfield was not one of a continuous, sweeping line of settlements linking New England's frontier. Instead, to the north, east, and west it had no neighbors: Deerfield sat alone on the very tip of a knife blade of settlement up the Connecticut River valley. The blade was thin, and Deerfield remained alone at the tip for nearly half a century. Such a position could not help but define the town.

And so it did. Deerfield's place on the frontier made its existence tenuous indeed. In times of war—and such times comprised over half of the town's first fifty years—Deerfield was simply an "easy mark." As the Connecticut valley's sentinel through these wars, the town took vastly more blows than any other town in the region. In King Philip's War, all towns risked attack from the allied, indigenous New England Indians. In this war Deerfield shared its fate with many other outlying villages. When the later French and Indian Wars ensued, however, battle lines shifted. In wars between New England and New France, Deerfield stood as the region's first line of defense. The village paid a high price for this. After all, Deerfield's position on the frontier in many ways defined 1704: It was the "closest place" for the French and Indians from Mon-

treal to attack. To put it in other terms, Deerfield offered settlers the ultimate risk: It could disappear. Indeed, it did once,
in 1675, and almost did again in 1704.

Beyond actual warfare, Deerfield's tenuousness showed in
other ways. For one thing, the town's growth was stunted. After
Bloody Brook Deerfield had to start over, and its population of
the 1680s and 1690s was largely new. While many survivors of
1704 stayed in town or returned with John Williams after 1707,
close to half of the redeemed captives never lived there again.
Not until after the wars abated and the line of settlement moved
on did Deerfield's population start to grow.

The uncertainties of life in early Deerfield also made the
town extremely poor. If county and provincial tax rates can be
relied on, to say nothing of the anguished petitions that ema-
nated from the town, early Deerfield was as poor as any village
in Massachusetts, if not New England. Its lands were surely
rich enough, but in possessions, in personal and real estate, in
its dearth of luxuries, its settlers lived close to the line.

This poverty cuts two ways. First, Deerfield's place on the
frontier made it difficult to carve out a living. The endless struggles of war—the constant vigilance, the time away from work,
the losses of people and property—took their toll. So, too, did
the isolation from other settlements, from more and easier trade,
from resources. Deerfield's precarious position also defined to
a degree the types of men and women who would settle in such
a place. Marginal people, people who were poor, landless,
without family support, exiled or eased from previous towns,
transients, drifters, debtors, lawbreakers, troublemakers—all
these could, and many did, find Deerfield a viable option. Here
Turner's ideas make sense, for Deerfield offered a fresh start,
with all the attendant risks and opportunities.

Yet while Turner may have been right about the frontier as a
place of new possibilities, he was wrong about the nature of
New England frontier society. The New England frontier defined Deerfield's world as anything *but* individualistic, democratic, impatient, and free. Although the town was in many
ways isolated from both county and provincial government, an
internal dynamic vastly different from Turner's appeared in

town. In Deerfield the frontier drove people together: It *inhibited* individualism.[30] In governance, economics, religion, and social order, Deerfield was inward directed, closed, interdependent—communal.

Town government exhibited unusually widespread sharing of officeholding and responsibilities, as Deerfield went well "beyond" democracy toward all-inclusive, consensual governance. Local economic practices, centered on subsistence farming and shared specialized skills, came together to forge a close-knit, interwoven, local barter economy. Reflecting valley practices inspired by Solomon Stoddard, Deerfield's church embraced the inclusive practice of open communion. All of these developments reflect the zeal and drive of New England's Puritans. At the same time, they are also a powerful comment on the desires and demands of the frontier.

For all this interdependence, it is important to remember that "communal" does not necessarily mean "utopian." Presumably Deerfield's Puritans were inspired by a vision of what their village could be. But they were also driven by what existed, by what had to be. Theirs was a rough, rude, violent, and unpredictable world. That their village was communal was a product of necessity as well as design.

Deerfielders often turned to traditional ways of living, to a world they knew. Far from Turner's liberating, innovative frontier, Deerfield's first settlers followed English patterns of settlement. In town planning, in farming, in daily economic life, Deerfield demonstrated the "persistence of European culture in the American wilderness."[31] In its first town layout in 1670, Deerfield resembled a medieval English village. Fifty years later it was still using a common-field system.

In many ways Deerfield's world was quite simple. These frontier settlers had their lives defined by what they could do, where they could do it, how, and with whom. Governance provides one good example of this. Deerfielders had no great aversion to county or provincial government; in times of war or need they readily appealed to both. Still, on an ongoing basis their world of governance was local. Local issues—field regulation, fence building, tax rates—were the issues that mattered, and they were handled locally. Between the town's poverty, its lack of an elite, its rough equity, and the immediate importance of local decisions, widespread sharing of governance made sense.

Lines of trade, too, extended as far as was practical. Deerfield's local barter economy did not arise out of some careful plan. People bartered with one another to survive. While most exchange was local, networks were extended to other valley people when feasible. Deerfielders did not resist trading outside town; they just did not have much surplus or opportunity.

In all these areas—governance, defense, economics, and trade—as well as in religious, social, and family patterns, Deerfielders followed no code or plan. Instead, they did what they could as they could. In this sense, they maintained not one community but a web of communities, or perhaps a series of concentric rings of association with other towns and people. The ring of governance was small and tight, rarely extending beyond Deerfield itself. The band of economic ties was slightly wider, reaching through barter and trade to towns nearby. Kinship patterns and networks stretched still farther down the valley, as did religious ideas and practices. Military measures, when called for, tied Deerfield to a still wider world, to Springfield and Boston. All this does not change Deerfield's fundamental isolation, yet neither was the town hermetically sealed off from its neighbors. Frontier Deerfield was alone, yet it was also part of a larger world.

All of this contemplation of Deerfield and the New England frontier would be richer if there were fuller records of what the settlers felt and thought. Unfortunately, that frontier *"mentalité"* remains elusive.[32] Without direct evidence of settlers' ways of thinking, it is hard to know if Deerfielders' institutions mirrored their ideas.

Some clues do emerge from the historical record, however. Certainly the town's residents portrayed their plight as painful, even pathetic. Their many petitions are full of despair—about the threats of impending war, the horror of past attacks, the sufferings that continued, their poverty, and their inability to farm and live free from fear.[33]

Left unclear is whether the settlers viewed attacks on Deerfield as firestorms or hailstorms. Did Deerfield's settlers know of and dread attacks as acts of men that could be avoided? Or were they passing storms, acts of nature that, however horrible, were an ongoing part of life? It is hard to imagine that Deerfield's people did not know the risks they were taking by living there. Their decision to stay seems an act of resignation and thus an acceptance of risk.[34] The source of risk, however—whether man or God—remains clouded.

In his stimulating study of the mythology of the American frontier, Richard Slotkin suggested that the wilderness symbolized "two opposed visions": "a starting place for the renewal and revival of purified Christianity . . . or . . . a place in which Christians would be tempted by devilish seductions to degenerate into base Indians, lecherous, materialistic, demonic."[35] While these visions certainly appeared in Puritan literature, and John Williams presented them to his flock at Deerfield,[36] it is also possible that these represent a false dichotomy for Deerfield's frontier residents. For these people, the wilderness simply "was." If war was an ongoing part of life, so were wolves; so, too, was poverty; so, too, were sowing and reaping, and life and death. The frontier offered powerful images, yet the people of Deerfield did not live by the imagery of Cotton Mather. The frontier was simply where they lived.

When the frontier line of English settlement moved on after 1715, Deerfield changed quickly. The reestablishment of Northfield above Deerfield, the line of forts to the north and west, and the settling of hill towns throughout the region had a profound effect on the town. Deerfield gained a security it had never had before. That security brought continuity. After a half century the town finally kept a generation of settlers intact. For the first time the town saw steady growth from within.

Security also brought prosperity. By 1750 the growing little town showed increasing signs of a market economy and of increased income. Protected by water and hills, rich in prime, fertile farmlands, Deerfield had always been an ideal site for settlement. The vicissitudes of the frontier had made it impossible for the town to grow and flourish. Now that arrested development was over.

The change from communal village to growing farm town, from poor frontier outpost to thriving valley town, from subsistence to growing commerce, did not come smoothly or steadily. As long as Deerfield sat on the frontier, and as long as there were wars, Deerfield could never fully develop. As those passed, however, change came quickly. The frontier had retarded growth; its passing accelerated it.[37]

Not without a cost. Ironically, it was precisely not until the frontier line of settlement had passed that Deerfield began to exhibit some of the traits that Turner ascribed to the frontier.[38] Not before the 1720s and 1730s—a half century after Deerfield's founding and a generation after the frontier moved on—did Deerfield start to become Turner's American frontier town. Only then did dissent appear in town. Only then did the town move to majority decisions. Only then could one afford to disagree, to become less conservative, to become more independent. Deerfield, New England, America were still a century away from the individualism of Alexis de Tocqueville, but by now they had also left behind the collective vision of John Winthrop.

Was the New England frontier like other frontiers of early America? The question deserves future study. Certainly there are apt areas of comparison between regions. Recent work on the seventeenth-century Chesapeake Bay region suggests economic patterns similar to those of Deerfield, but that work does not bind that region's society to its wars. Study of Indian affairs in the middle colonies illuminates comparable complexities and patterns in warfare, yet such work offers no local perspective.[39] A venerable study of the southern frontier below Virginia from 1670 to 1730 reveals striking similarities. Verner Crane's 1928 work, too, examines no frontier "line, but rather a zone"; sees the advance of English settlements along with various "frontiers . . . among the Indians"; explores the European "contests for empire" and "intrigues and wars in the Indian country"; and chronicles English border settlements destroyed and the frontier pushed back.[40]

In the south as in the north the natives often dictated how fragile the English hold on settlement was. Amidst the Yamasee

War, some forty years after initial English settlement—just as King Philip's War took place forty years after Massachusetts was founded—Indians controlled the colonists' fate. In Carolina, if the Cherokees had joined the war, "then the ruin of the colony" would have been "inescapable."[41] How close that sounds to similar claims of Iroquois might in New England in 1700: "if the Five Nations should at any time in conjunction with the Eastern Indians . . . revolt . . . they would in a short time drive us quite out of this Continent."[42] The Indian threat was huge; the problems were frightening; the future of the continent was hardly preordained.

In sum, the colonial frontier merits new work. The work of the most recent generation of scholars has both opened new areas of inquiry and rekindled old ones. The nature of war, reasons for Indian-European conflict, the dynamic of Indian life, inter-Indian complexities, the nature of frontier settlements and society—all these offer rich comparisons with Deerfield's experience.

Two final points. First, this study of a New England frontier town is largely a study of a town at war—and that is how it should be. As Fred Anderson has noted in his study of Massachusetts soldiers in the Seven Years War, "War, as much as peace, typified New England life in the eighteenth century."[43] This was equally true of the seventeenth century. That Deerfield endured so many years of war may seem distressing, but it was not exceptional. That it sat exposed on the edge of English settlement makes its plight more daunting, but this, too, was not unusual. A look at a map of New England settlements in 1675 or 1700 or even 1725 shows that a large number lay exposed, if not as completely as Deerfield, at least on one flank. Deerfield suffered terribly through these wars, but it did not suffer alone.

A study of war implies a study of warriors, and here, too, Deerfield's story serves as an important reminder of what early New England was like. Amidst the many excellent studies of New England towns and colonial life that have appeared in the last twenty years, the Indians of the region have too often gotten lost. But Indians, and wars, were a basic part of New England's development. To study the path from Puritan to Yankee or from village to town without examining the staccato of wars and conflicts is to excise a critical element of New England's story. The time has come to integrate colonial social history more fully with the study of Indians, wars, and the frontier.

Finally, Deerfield's story is also a reminder of the long and torturous path that New England settlers took from being the English of the seventeenth century to becoming Americans of the eighteenth. In 1675 the New Englanders fighting against King Philip were referred to as "the English" or "Our English." A century later, at the beginning of a very different war, "the English" no longer comprised New England's settlers. The English now were outsiders, enemies.[44]

Somewhere amidst the evolution of this New England frontier town, amidst its growth and development, and also amidst the near half century of conflict it endured, this English Puritan village became a New England—American—town. In this respect, then, Turner was right: The frontier made Europeans into Americans. By the 1730s Deerfield's citizens were hardly the "revolutionary" Americans of 1775. Then again, in their long and largely isolated struggle for security on the New England frontier, they had achieved a different kind of revolution: a deep-seated, even unconscious revolution that necessarily preceded a later, more famous, but no more important one.

ABBREVIATIONS

CSP-C	Massachusetts Council, *Calendar of State Papers— Colonial*
DTB	*Deerfield Town Book*
DTR	*Dedham Town Records*
HCCourt	Hampshire County Court Records
HCDeeds	Hampshire County Deeds
HCProbate	Hampshire County Probate Records
JR	*Jesuit Relations*, Reuben Gold Thwaites, ed. (Cleveland: The Burrows Brothers Co., 1896)
MA	*Massachusetts Archives*
Mass. A&R	*The Acts and Resolves, Public and Private, of the Province of Massachusetts Bay*
Mass. Recs.	*Records of the Governor and Company of the Massachusetts Bay in New England, 1628–1686*
MHS	Manuscripts of the Massachusetts Historical Society
NYCD	*Documents Relative to the Colonial History of New York*
PVMA MSS	Pocumtuck Valley Memorial Association Manuscript Collection
PVMA Proc.	*History and Proceedings of the Pocumtuck Valley Memorial Association*
Recherches Historiques	*Le Bulletin des Recherches Historiques* (organ du bureau des archives de la province de Quebec)
Winthrop Papers	Massachusetts Historical Society Collection, "The Winthrop Papers"
WMQ	*William and Mary Quarterly*

Notes

1. Native Peoples, Native Lands

1. Erastus Worthington, *History of Dedham (1635–1827)* (Boston: Dutton and Wentworth, 1827), 19.
2. For a vision of the remarkable abundance of early New England, see William Cronon, *Changes in the Land* (New York: Hill and Wang, 1983), ch. 2.
3. It is with trepidation that anyone today uses the word "tribe" to describe a group of seventeenth-century Indians. The concept is more Eurocentric than Indian and is too simplistic: It belies the considerable degree of individualistic or kinship-based tendencies that Indians showed. At the same time, given the connotations of alternative words like "band," one must choose some word to characterize a group of natives who shared habitats, life-styles, language, enemies, and common English identification. For this reason I use the word "tribe" particularly to describe a second state of political evolution (one beyond "band"). The word seems especially appropriate for the Pocumtucks because they were one of the larger, more stable, and more significant Indian groups in seventeenth-century New England. This concept of stages, as well as a larger, carefully constructed discussion, comes from Morton Fried, *The Evolution of Political Society* (New York: Random House, 1967), ch. 4. See also Peter A. Thomas, "In the Maelstrom of Change: The Indian Trade and Cultural Process in the Middle Connecticut Valley, 1635–1665" (Ph.D. thesis, University of Massachusetts, 1979), 399–400.
4. Connecticut General Court Record, February 1638, cited in George Sheldon, "The Pocumtuck Confederacy," in *History and Proceedings of the Pocumtuck Valley Memorial Association* (hereafter known as *PVMA Proc.*), vol. 2 (1880–1889) (Deerfield, Mass.: Pocumtuck Valley Memorial Assoc., 1898), 396.
5. For an evolving look at attitudes toward whites and Indians in colonial America, begin with Cotton Mather, *Magnalia Christiana*, move through Francis Parkman, and then contrast the modern scholarship of Alden Vaughan, *New England Frontier: Puritans and Indians, 1620–1675* (1965; rpt. New York: Norton, 1979), with Francis Jennings, *The Invasion of America: Indians, Colonialism, and The Cant of Conquest* (Chapel Hill: University of North Carolina Press, 1975). See also, however, Vaughan's thoughtful essay on the study of Indian / white relations which accompanies the Norton paperback reprint of *New England Frontier* (1979). A valuable article focused on these problems comes from James Axtell, "Ethnology in Early America: A Review Essay," *William and Mary Quarterly* (hereafter known as *WMQ*) 35 (No. 1, 1978):110–144.

6. Gordon M. Day, "The Indian Languages of the Upper Connecticut Valley," in William R. Young, ed., *An Introduction to . . . the Connecticut Valley Indian*, vol. 1; no. 1 (Springfield, Mass.: Museum of Science, 1969), 74–77. See also John R. Swanton, *Indian Tribes of North America* (Washington, D.C.: Bureau of American Ethnology, Bulletin 145, 1952), 23–24.

7. Sheldon, "The Pocumtuck Confederacy."

8. See Gordon M. Day, "Western Abenaki," and Dean R. Snow, "Eastern Abenaki," in *Handbook of North American Indians*, William Sturtevant, gen. ed., vol. 15, "Northeast," Bruce Trigger, ed. (Washington, D.C.: Smithsonian Institution, 1978), 148–159, 137–147. Day's essay is particularly important here in extending the Western Abenaki lands all the way to the Sokokis at Squakeag, less than twenty-five miles north of the Pocumtucks.

9. The issue of New England's Indian population is a vexing one, yet one which has seen careful scholarship brought to bear on it in recent years. Francis Jennings, *The Invasion of America* (New York: Norton, 1976), ch. 2, provided valuable challenges to older estimates. William Cronon's survey of recent research, including Jennings, Sherburne F. Cook, *The Indian Populations of New England in the Seventeenth Century* (Berkeley: University of California Press, 1976), and Dean R. Snow, *The Archaeology of New England* (New York: Academic Press, 1980), leads him to estimate a population of 70,000–100,000; see Cronon, *Changes*, p. 42 and fn. 14. Finally, Peter A. Thomas's fine dissertation, "In the Maelstrom of Change," suggests a population of "at least 90,000" and likely 90,000–110,000; see pp. 25–28.

10. See Charles C. Willoughby, *Antiquities of the New England Indians* (1935; rpt. Cambridge, Mass.: Peabody Museum, 1973), 278; Chandler Whipple, *First Encounter: The White Man and Indian in Massachusetts and Rhode Island* (Stockbridge, Mass.: The Berkshire Traveller Press, no date), 35; Swanton, *Indian Tribes*, 23–24; Howard S. Russell, *Indian New England Before the Mayflower* (Hanover: University Press of New England, 1980), 35. George Sheldon also guesses as high as 5,000 in *A History of Deerfield, Massachusetts*, vol. 1 (1895–1896; rpt. Deerfield: New Hampshire Publishing Company and P.V.M.A., 1972, 2 vols.), 51. See also Sheldon, "The Pocumtuck Confederacy," *PVMA Proc.* 2:396ff.

11. Thomas, "Maelstrom," 34ff.

12. Russell, *Indian New England*, 27.

13. Letter of William Pynchon, 5 July 1648, cited in Thomas, "Maelstrom," 77.

14. Neal Salisbury, "InterIndian Affairs in Seventeenth Century New England" (unpublished 1985 paper), 31.

15. Russell, *Indian New England*, 125; Thomas, "Maelstrom," 307–308.

16. Swanton, *Indian Tribes;* see also Bert Salwen, "Indians of Southern New England and Long Island: Early Period," in *Handbook of North American Indians*, vol. 15 (Washington, D.C.: Smithsonian Institution, 1978), 160–176.

17. Salwen, "Indians of Southern New England," 163.

18. William Morrell, "Poem on New England," in *Massachusetts Historical Society Collections*, 1st series, vol 1 (1792), 125–139.

19. M. K. Bennett, "The Food Economy of the New England Indians, 1605–1676," *Journal of Political Economy* 62 (No. 5, October 1955), 373.

20. Eva L. Butler, "Algonkian Culture and Use of Maize in Southern New England," *Archaelogical Society of Connecticut Bulletin* 22 (1948), 3–39. See also Cronon, *Changes*, 42; Bennett, "Food Economy," 391–393.

21. Salwen, "Indians of Southern New England," 160.

22. William Wood, *New England's Prospect* (London, 1634; rpt. Boston: John Fleet, 1764), 18.

23. Russell, *Indian New England*, 125.

24. Thomas, "Maelstrom," 106–107; Cronon, *Changes*, ch. 2, 3, *passim*.

25. "Governor Winslow's Account of the Natives of New England," in Nathaniel Morton, *New England's Memorial* (1669; rpt. 6th ed. Boston: Congregational Board of Publication, 1855), 490.

26. One local confirmed site is at Vernon, Vermont; another, unconfirmed, lies on Smead's Island, in the Connecticut River just over the East Mountain from Deerfield. More generally, see Bennett, "Food Economy," 376.

27. Butler, "Algonkian Culture"; M.K. Bennett, "Food Economy," 375.

28. Salwen, "Indians of Southern New England," 164.

29. Russell, *Indian New England*, 51.

30. Salwen, "Indians of Southern New England," 166.

31. Recent scholarship suggests that "squaw sachems" may have been a recent innovation in the seventeenth century, brought about by the ravages of epidemics. My thanks to Daniel Richter for this important corrective.

32. Deerfield Town Papers, Folder 4, Manuscript Collection, Pocumtuck Valley Memorial Association (hereafter known as PVMA MSS), V.

33. William Wood, *New England's Prospect*, 103; Robert Austin Warner, "The Southern New England Indians to 1725: A Study in Culture Contact" (Ph.D. dissertation, Yale University, 1935).

34. The fort's existence is confirmed in many ways, perhaps best in *Documents Relative to the Colonial History of New York* (hereafter known as *NYCD*), E.B. O'Callaghan, ed. (New York: Weed, Parsons, and Co., 1850–1861, 15 vols.), vol. 13, 308–309. Its exact location is a matter of some conjecture, with George Sheldon, as usual, quite firm in placing it one-half mile northeast of town; see *A History of Deerfield*, vol. 1, 69. Some recent historians claim that forts like this came only after the English arrived and started raising rivalries, questions of territoriality, and fur trade pressures, cf. Salwen, "Indians of Southern New England." However, there is no direct support of this view, and given the ethnohistorical evidence of inter-Indian conflict before and apart from European contact, such forts seem likely to have existed solely due to Indian pressures and conflicts.

35. T.J. Brasser, "Early Indian-European Contacts," in *Handbook of North American Indians*, vol. 15, 82.

36. Nathaniel Morton, *New England's Memorial*, 37.

37. Ibid., 44–45.

38. Massachusetts General Court, March 9, 1637 / 1638, cited in Sheldon, *History of Deerfield*, vol. 1, 51–52; Russell, *Indian New England*, 14.

39. Stephen C. Innes, "A Patriarchal Society: Economic Dependency and Social Order in Springfield, Massachusetts, 1636–1702" (Ph.D. dissertation, Northwestern University, 1977), 83–92 and *passim*. Innes's subse-

quent book *Labor in a New Land: Economy and Society in Seventeenth Century Springfield* (Princeton: Princeton University Press, 1983) provides a somewhat more positive and restrained view of the Pynchons' acquisition and use of wealth and power. Much evidence of the Pynchons' extraordinary power comes out of John Pynchon's Account Book, at the Connecticut Valley Historical Museum, in Springfield, Mass. See also Ruth McIntyre, *William Pynchon: Merchant and Colonizer (1590–1662)* (Springfield, Mass.: Connecticut Valley Historical Museum, 1961); Francis Armytage and Juliette Tomlinson, *The Pynchons of Springfield: Founders and Colonizers (1636–1702)* Springfield, Mass.: Connecticut Valley Historical Museum, 1969).

40. A great number of the deeds exist, in the Hampshire County Registry of Deeds, in the Court House, Springfield, Mass. See Books A,B,C, *passim*, which interestingly include many deeds duly sealed after King Philip's War of 1675–1676. The issue of Indians and land, one more complex, is dealt with below, when looking at the "buying and selling" of Deerfield. Discussions of the meaning of alienation of land to English and Indians abound. See, for example, Jennings, *Invasion*, ch. 8; Cronon, *Changes*, ch. 4.

41. Robert A. Warner, "Southern New England Indians," 69–77.

42. T. J. Brasser, "Early Contacts," 84.

43. J. Hammond Trumbull, ed. *The Public Records of the Colony of Connecticut (pre-1665)* (Hartford: Brown and Parsons, 1850), 14.

44. The Hampshire County Court Records, *passim,* provide fascinating passages amidst general eyestrain. Early records can be more comfortably read in Joseph H. Smith, ed., *Colonial Justice in Western Massachusetts: The Pynchon Court Record* (Cambridge: Harvard University Press, 1961), *passim.*

45. *Public Records of Connecticut*, 294.

46. It is a classic Eurocentric conceit to think that the English "controlled" inter-Indian strife in the mid-seventeenth-century Connecticut valley. See Salisbury, "InterIndian," *passim;* Thomas, "Maelstrom," 211–225.

47. Even Wilcomb E. Washburn, who is greatly concerned with the English role in fomenting Indian strife, concedes this point. See "Seventeenth Century Indian Wars," in *Handbook of North American Indians*, vol. 15, 90.

48. P. Richard Metcalf, "Who Should Rule at Home? Native American Politics and Indian-White Relations," *Journal of American History* 61 (December 1974): 651–665.

49. 3 September 1659, United Colonies Commissioners, at Hartford, cited in Sheldon, *History of Deerfield*, vol. 1, 62.

50. Ebenezar Hazard, ed., *Records of the United Colonies of New England,* in *Historical Collections. . .* , vol. 2 (rpt. Freeport, N.Y.: The Books for Library Press, 1969), 105–106; Thomas, "Maelstrom," 77.

51. Salisbury, "InterIndian," 28.

52. Metcalf, "Who Should Rule?" 651–665; Thomas, "Maelstrom," 224–226.

53. Trumbull, *Connecticut Records,* 12 August and 1 October 1657, 300–308.

54. 3 September 1659, United Colonies Commissioners, at Hartford, cited in Sheldon, *History of Deerfield*, vol. 1, 62.

55. Message of the Pocumtucks to the United Colonies, 12 September 1659

from Pocumtuck, via Thomas Stanton, in Sheldon, *History of Deerfield*, vol. 1, 67.

56. Warner, "Southern New England Indians," 148.

57. Thomas, "Maelstrom," 226.

58. This theme of Indian-European interdependence is well laid out in Neal Salisbury, "Social Relationships on a Moving Frontier: Natives and Settlers in Southern New England, 1638–1675" (unpublished ms., 1985). See also Thomas, "Maelstrom," 215–225.

59. See, for example, Patrick M. Malone, "Indian and English Military Systems in New England in the Seventeenth Century" (Ph.D. dissertation, Brown University, 1971), 1–34.

60. William Wood, *New England's Prospect*, 67–69.

61. Roger Williams, letter to John Winthrop, 11 September 1648, in *Massachusetts Historical Society Collections*, 3rd series, vol. 1, 178.

62. Relation of Jerome LaLemant, in *Jesuit Relations* (hereafter known as *JR*), Reuben Gold Thwaites, ed., vol. 45 (Cleveland: The Burrows Brothers Co., 1896), 203–205.

63. Daniel Gookin, "Historical Collections of the Indians in New England" (1674), published in *Massachusetts Historical Society Collections*, 1st series, vol. 1, 161–167.

64. Letter of William Pynchon, 1647, in Josiah H. Temple, *History of North Brookfield, Massachusetts* (Boston: Town of North Brookfield, 1887), 37–38.

65. An immensely helpful documentary survey of seventeenth-century Mohawk history comes from Thomas Grassmann, *The Mohawks and Their Valley* (Caughnawaga: Eric Hugo Photo. and Printing Co., 1969). Valuable detail of battles comes from *NYCD*, especially vol. 3, 13, and *passim*, much of which is well used by Allen W. Trelease in *Indian Affairs in Colonial New York: The Seventeenth Century* (Ithaca, N.Y.: Cornell University Press, 1960). Other early record of French-Mohawk strife can be found in Daniel Gookin, "Historical Collections."

66. See also Daniel Richter, "The Ordeal of the Longhouse: Change and Persistence on the Iroquois Frontier, 1607–1720" (Ph.D. thesis, Columbia University, 1984), esp. ch. 1. Richter's argument is beautifully presented in his article "War and Culture: The Iroquois Experience," *WMQ* (October 1983): 528–559.

67. George T. Hunt, *The Wars of the Iroquois: A Study in Intertribal Trade Relations* (Madison: University of Wisconsin Press, 1940), 1–22.

68. See a letter of Reverend Jonas Michaelius to Reverend Adrianus Smoutius, 1628, in *NYCD* 2:760.

69. Franklin Leonard Pope, *The Western Boundary of Massachusetts: A Study of Indian and Colonial History* (Pittsfield, Mass.: privately published by the author, 1886), 11–14.

70. Thomas, "Maelstrom," 85.

71. Sherburne F. Cook, "Interracial Warfare and Population Among the New England Indians," *Ethnohistory* 20 (no. 1, 1973):1–24.

72. Cook, "Interracial Warfare"; Russell, *Indian New England*, 14.

73. Record of this action is found in Hunt, *Wars of the Iroquois*, 32.

74. Cited in Sheldon, "The Pocumtuck Confederacy," in *PVMA Proc.* 1:402ff.

75. Salisbury, "InterIndian," 26.

76. *JR* 36:83–103; Gordon Day, "Western Abenaki," 150; Salisbury, "Inter-Indian," 25–30.
77. Thomas, "Maelstrom," 215–216; Salisbury, "Social Relationships," 8–9.
78. Richter, "Ordeal," 71.
79. Thomas, "Maelstrom," 238.
80. Salisbury, "InterIndian," 29–32; Richter, "Ordeal," ch. 1–3; Thomas, "Maelstrom," ch. 5–6; Salisbury "Social Relationships," 8–9.
81. Salisbury, "InterIndian," 30.
82. Relation of Jerome LaLemant, in *JR*.
83. Relation of Paul LeJeune, S.J., in *JR* 47:105.
84. *NYCD* 13:224–227, 239–240.
85. *NYCD* 2:462.
86. Grassman, *The Mohawks*, 226ff.
87. *NYCD* 13:303–304.
88. Thomas, "Maelstrom," 250–255, 291; Salisbury, "InterIndian," 29–30.
89. *NYCD* 13:298, 308.
90. Ibid., 308–309; see also *Calendar of Historical Documents—Dutch*, E.B. O'Callaghan, ed., (CHM-D), 1630–1664 (Albany: Office of Secretary of State, 1865), D304 at 72a, cited in Grassman, *The Mohawks*, 240.
91. Letter of David Wilton of Northampton, in John Winthrop Mss., vol. 20, 71, Massachusetts Historical Society Collections.
92. Ibid.; *JR* 49:11, 143–149; Thomas, "Maelstrom," 251–255; *NYCD* 13:378–382.
93. Letter of Jeremias van Rensselaer to his brother Jean Baptiste, 26 July 1664, *JR*, 358, cited in Grassman, *The Mohawks*, 241–242.
94. Salisbury, "InterIndian," 30–31; *NYCD* 13: 378–382; letter of Henry Clark to John Winthrop, Jr., 26 July 1664, Winthrop Papers, Massachusetts Historical Society Collections.
95. *NYCD* 13:336, 378–382, 389.
96. Trelease, *Indian Affairs*, 190.
97. *NYCD* 3:67.
98. 11 July 1666 report of Samuell Willis to Colonel Nicholls, for the Connecticut Governor and Assistants, in *NYCD* 3:120–121.
99. Hampshire County Probate Records, Northampton, Mass. (also on microfilm and available at Henry N. Flynt Library of Historic Deerfield, in Deerfield, Mass.), vol. 1, 102–103.
100. Gookin, "Historical Collections," 166–167.
101. *JR* 60 (1675–1677):231–234; Kenneth M. Morrison, "The People of the Dawn: The Abnaki and Their Relations with New England and New France, 1600–1727" (Ph.D. dissertation, University of Maine, 1975), 111–113.
102. *NYCD* 3:254–265, 273–276.
103. Trelease, *Indian Affairs*, 226–227.
104. Francis Jennings has effectively shattered the mythic vision of "virgin land" in *Invasion*, ch. 2.

2. *"Some Controversey," and New Proprietors*

1. Alden Vaughan, *New England Frontier: Puritans and Indians, 1620–1675* (1965; rpt. New York: Norton, 1979), ch. 9 and 10, p. 264. Francis Jennings, in *The Invasion of America: Indians, Colonialism, and the Cant of*

Conquest (Chapel Hill, N.C.: University of North Carolina Press, 1975), ch. 14, blasts Eliot, portrays his efforts as cunning, shady, almost diabolical, if ingenious. In his dissertation "Conquest of the 'Savage': Puritans, Puritan Missionaries, and Indians, 1620–1680" (Ph.D. dissertation, UCLA, 1975), Neal Salisbury acknowledges the zeal and depth of belief of Eliot, while bordering his analysis with a frame of Puritan misdirection, overbearing paternalism, and inevitable failure. See especially ch. 1, 2, 5, 6.

2. John Eliot, "A Late and Further Manifestation of the Progress of the Gospel Amongst the Indians of New England," Massachusetts Historical Society Collections, 3rd series, vol. 4, 269–270; also cited in Vaughan, *New England Frontier*, 264.

3. Wilbur R. Jacobs, *Dispossessing the American Indian* (New York: Charles Scribner's Sons, 1972), 13–14.

4. *Massachusetts Archives* (hereafter known as *MA*) 30:16.

5. Nathaniel E. Shurtleff, ed., *Records of the Governor and Company of the Massachusetts Bay in New England, 1628–1686* (hereafter known as *Mass. Recs.*) (Boston: William White, 1853–1854, 5 vols.), vol. 3, 246, 301, 385, and *passim;* vol. 4, *passim*. See also *MA* 30:103–104 and *passim;* the Appendix to *Dedham Town Records* (hereafter known as *DTR*), Donald Gleason Hill, ed. (Dedham, Mass.: 1886–1891, 4 vols.), vol. 4, 241–245, 268–275.

6. In his *History of Dedham* (Boston: Dutton and Wentworth, 1827), Erastus Worthington notes that Dedham began with 19 proprietors and as of 1642 had 47; thus, this coincidence of the number 47 as the number of petitioners as of 1662 probably represents a hefty percentage of the town's proprietors.

7. *MA* 30:112.

8. General Court order of 7 May 1662. *Mass. Recs.* 4 (pt. 2): 49.

9. *MA* 30:117–118; cited in *DTR* 4 (Appendix):273–274.

10. *DTR* 4:75, 88–89, 97, 102–103. A more general look at Dedham's land holdings and distribution comes in Kenneth A. Lockridge's *A New England Town: The First Hundred Years* (New York: Norton, 1970), *passim*. Lockridge discusses the concept of land scarcity at greater length in his essay "Land, Population, and the Evolution of New England Society, 1630–1790," in *Past and Present* 39 (1968):62–80. That scarcity, however, is a phenomenon which had not yet come as of the 1660s.

11. *DTR* 4 (Appendix):275. See also *Mass. Recs.* 4 (pt. 2):282; Gertrude Cochrane Smith, "First Maps of Pocumtuck," in *PVMA Proc.* 8 (1931):38–50, wherein she describes Fisher's map.

12. *DTR* 4:103.

13. Ibid.

14. *DTR* 4:117.

15. The *Dedham Town Records* shows Dedham's continuing exploration of the region, its negotiations with Pynchon, and its attitudes toward the Pocumtuck venture. See *DTR* 4:117, 133–134, 136–137, 142–143, 161–162, 167, 173–174, 178, 185. The issue of proprietorship in Pocumtuck is a complicated one, and is described in greater detail in Chapter 3. As for Indian deeds: Although Eleazer Lusher brought "severall" deeds back to Dedham in 1669, only three can be confirmed, the three which this chapter discusses at greatest length. A fourth gains mention in the text, but nothing of it remains but tempting allusions in another deed. A fifth was signed in

1672, after Dedham had started its new plantation at Pocumtuck, and was probably in response to the General Court's granting of additional lands. See C. Alice Baker, "Historical Paper," in *PVMA Proc.*, op. cit.; see also Harry Andrew Wright, *Indian Deeds of Hampden County* (Springfield, Mass.: privately printed, 1905), esp. 65, 67–68; see also PVMA MSS., V.

16. Some lingering expenses apparently brought the final total up slightly, to roughly £100. £96.10, though, was Pynchon's precise bill on September 24, 1669. See *DTR* 4:173–175.

17. Francis Jennings, *Invasion of America*, ch. 8.

18. See Neal Salisbury, "Conquest of the 'Savage,'" ch. 2, esp. 54–55; see also Jennings, *Invasion of America*, ch. 8; William Cronon, *Changes in the Land* (New York: Hill and Wang, 1983), ch. 4.

19. Winthrop Papers, vol. 2, 91 (in Massachusetts Historical Society Collections), cited in Charles M. Segal and David Stineback, *Puritans, Indians, and Manifest Destiny* (New York: G.P. Putnam's Sons, 1977), 50.

20. See Wilcomb E. Washburn, *Red Man's Land / White Man's Law* (New York: Charles Scribner's Sons, 1971), ch. 1, esp. 40.

21. John Cotton, "God's Promise to His Plantation," excerpted in Segal and Stineback, op. cit., 51–53.

22. Jennings, *Invasion of America*.

23. See Jennings, *Invasion*, Chapter 1, and also the records of the Hampshire County Courts, held at Springfield and Northampton, 1662–1675 (records available in Northampton or on microfilm at Henry N. Flynt Library, Historic Deerfield, Mass.).

24. Cronon, *Changes*, ch. 4, esp. 58–65. Cronon's emphasis on usage, or "usufruct rights" versus English ownership, is critical here. For a look at how historians' views of this complex subject have evolved, see, for example, various works of anthropologist Frank G. Speck and compare those with Alden Vaughan, *New England Frontier*, esp. 105ff.

25. Francis Jennings, *Invasion of America*, 136–137.

26. C. Alice Baker, "Historical Paper," in *PVMA Proc.* 1:97.

27. Harry A. Wright, *Indian Deeds*, 74–75. This selling of land more than once was not unique, especially given the Indian concept of usufruct rights to land. See Cronon, *Changes*, ch. 4.

28. The land the Indians called "Tomholissick" was purchased in both 1666 and 1667, and the colonists secured "Mantehelant" in both 1667 and 1672. See Wright, *Indian Deeds*, 61–75.

29. The whole set of questions about authority in Algonkian tribes—economic, political, social—is difficult to grapple with, to say nothing of authority in a tribe that has been decimated and scattered. And all this does not address the issue of whether the Pocumtucks should be considered a "tribe" versus a "band" versus a "remnant," especially after 1665.

30. Deed is located in PVMA MSS, V, Town Papers, File 1. Deed is dated 24 February 1665–6; for confirmation, see also C. Alice Baker, "Historical Paper," in *PVMA Proc.* 1(1870–1879):79–80.

31. *DTR* 3:142.

32. For a look at the place of land in the life of Dedham, see Kenneth A. Lockridge, *A New England Town*, Part I; Lockridge, "Land, Population, and the Evolution of the New England Town, 1630–1790"; *DTR* 3:141–146 and *passim* 4:228–231.

33. In establishing Dedham, Pocumtuck, or any early New England town, age, status, wealth, family size, and position were considered before granting proprietary rights. For a wonderful, lucid overview of this issue of democracy in early New England, see Edmund S. Morgan. *The Puritan Dilemma* (Boston: Little, Brown, 1958), esp. ch. 7. For a more specific look at proprietary rights, see Roy H. Akagi, *The Town Proprietors of the New England Colonies* (Philadelphia: University of Pennsylvania Press, 1924).

34. *DTR* 3:141–144. This concept has been confusing for many a student of Deerfield history who has looked on cow commonage as having to equal a set amount of land. It is not; it simply represents a percentage of divided land.

35. *DTR* 4:112–144 and *passim*.

36. *DTR* 4:171.

37. Massachusetts laws about proprietor meetings came in 1698, but they were still vague. Formal, legal procedure came in 1713. The best overall study of this topic is Roy H. Akagi, *The Town Proprietors of the New England Colonies*, ch. 3. The process of drawing lots for land existed from the time of the first Massachusetts Bay settlements in 1629–1630. See John W. Reps, *Town Planning in Frontier America* (Princeton: Princeton University Press, 1969), ch. 5. On Dedham and Pocumtuck, see *DTR* 4:187–192.

38. *DTR* 4:192. Significantly, this same meeting record also was copied in the *Deerfield Town Book* (hereafter known as *DTB*) (transcription by Richard I. Melvoin, 1981), 1b–1c.

39. Lots were sized not just to the acre but to the "rood" (fraction of an acre) and even to the rod (1/40 of ¼ acre). See *DTB*, 1c–1d; George Sheldon, *A History of Deerfield, Massachusetts*, vol. 1, 17–19, has a couple of minor errors in its copy but is essentially accurate.

40. The map of the 1671 allotment displays the fruits of the proprietors' labors. Although this surviving fragment covers only from the town's center northward, it graphically shows the different size apportionments of land that different proprietors received. For example, John Hubbard drew house lot number five. Since he held only three cow commons rights, the committee made his house lot proportionately small, less than one and one-quarter acres. By contrast, Hubbard's neighbor to the north, Dedham minister John Allin, held sixteen cow commons, and when he drew house lot number four, the committee made his lot over five and one-half acres. The map also shows that the artist remembered to locate a site for "Meetinghouse Hill." It lay in the center of town (the bottom of the map), on the highest land, on the west side of the street, an unnumbered house lot which to this day embraces the town church and village green.

The original of this map resides in the collection of the Pocumtuck Valley Memorial Assoc. J. Ritchie Garrison copied the map and its divisions of land for help in a study of farming practices in Deerfield. The author took Garrison's work and, based on the original fragment, added the lot numbers where they appeared on the original. These crucial numbers help explain the divisions of land that the proprietors first apportioned. The map is also remarkable because it is so startlingly similar to the way Deerfield looks today. The "north meadows" remain almost entirely farmland, while the houses sit on the same north-south "highway"—today called Main Street, or just "the street"—that existed in 1675.

This practice is wholly consistent with other Puritan New England towns. See Ola Elizabeth Winslow, *Meetinghouse Hill* (New York: Norton, 1972), esp. ch. 4.

41. As for how house lots were placed relative to farmlands, two patterns dominated early New England. The "compact" pattern of a center area with houses scattered along a number of intersecting streets could be seen in places like New Haven and Hartford. By contrast, a "linear" pattern of houses all close by one another on long strips of farmland existed at Wethersfield, Springfield, Sudbury. Pocumtuck was a hybrid. It had a linear pattern, with its houses along the town street at the end of small strips of land planned for house lots, yet its residential area was nuclear, with houses placed thickly on both sides of the street and with the main fields of arable strips beyond this town center. In this respect, Pocumtuck was probably the product of three forces: English heritage, Puritan vision, and frontier pressures for compactness and defensibility.

42. Recent students of New England towns have identified a whole host of parts of Pocumtuck's plan that reflect an English heritage. The manorial system from the "drowsy corners" of northern England also included open fields all around the village, divided into strips, owned individually yet farmed and managed in common. This basic "common-field" system came across the ocean largely intact and planted itself in many of the first Massachusetts settlements, such as Sudbury, Dedham, and Rowley. The result thus "combined ownership in severalty and ownership in common" so that settlers could farm for themselves—yet would also succeed only insofar as town planning and cooperative venture allowed.

There is a wealth of good, careful studies now out on this subject. In particular, see Sumner Chilton Powell's study of Sudbury, *Puritan Village* (Middletown: Wesleyan University Press, 1963). For a comparative study of both English and American patterns of rural life, see David Grayson Allen, *In English Ways: The Movement of Societies and the Transferral of English Local Law and Custom to Massachusetts Bay in the Seventeenth Century* (Chapel Hill: University of North Carolina Press, 1981). Lockridge, *A New England Town*, ch. 1, shows the place of land in the larger context of the life and dreams of the people of a New England town. See also John W. Reps, *Town Planning in Frontier America* (Princeton: Princeton University Press, 1969), 148. For details on Deerfield's experience, see John Sheldon, "The Common Field of Deerfield," *PVMA Proc.* 5 (1908 meeting):238–254.

43. Lockridge, *A New England Town*, 95.

44. Harold Roger King, "The Settlement of the Upper Connecticut Valley to 1675" (Ph.D. dissertation, Vanderbilt University, 1965). Concerning Hadley, see Sylvester Judd, *A History of Hadley* (1905; rpt. Somersworth, N.H.: New Hampshire Publishing Co., 1976), ch. 1 and 2, esp. 3–9.

45. *DTR* 4:*passim*.

46. Dedham apparently did not want townspeople playing "fast and loose" with their proprietary rights. It was expected that sales of Pocumtuck land or rights be publicly approved, and thus one finds in the Dedham town record of 11 November 1668 that Lieutenant Fisher had "liberty granted to alienate his Rights at Pawcompticke." The Registries of Deeds of Hamp-

shire and Suffolk Counties also show evidence of sales. However, few transactions ever made it into the town or county records. After 1668 the vast majority of trades or transactions evidently never got recorded—yet they are the ones which tell the most about what happened in Dedham. See *DTR* 4:157; Hampshire County Deeds, Book A, 78.

47. *DTR* 3:142–144, 4:174–175. The difference of one person is easily attributable to an estate which has been divided among heirs.

48. *DTR* 4:171, 174–175.

49. *DTB*, 1c.

50. Hampshire County Deeds (henceforth known as HCDeeds), Book A, 77–78.

51. King, "Settlement of the Upper Connecticut Valley," ch. 8 and esp. 267.

52. Viewing such taxes as based on proprietary shareholding, no one among the eighty proprietors was assessed more than £2.8.8 that year; only five people were required to pay as much as £2; and most paid about £1.

53. *DTR* 3:142–144, 4:174–175, 192–194. The six men who at some point went to live in Deerfield were Samuel Hinsdale, Robert Hinsdale, John Stebbins, Samson Frary, Samuel Daniel, and John Farrington; Farrington was the only Dedhamite. Of these, only Frary and Stebbins lived in town after 1680.

54. When the tax of September 29, 1669, was levied, the assembly of proprietors obviously acknowledged their failure to pay previously, first by the very fact that they levied another rate to pay off Captain Pynchon for his work, and second because they declared the levy of October 2, 1667, "heereby made nulle." *DTR* 4:174.

55. For example, Lieutenant Fisher was "allowed to sell" some commonage to Nathaniel Sutlief of Medfield; John Plympton was "allowed to purchase" John Bacon's land; and for some unknown reason Thomas Weld's brother Daniel was "not granted . . . libertie to purchase Lande at Paucomptucke." *DTR* 4:209, 216; Sheldon, *History of Deerfield*, vol. 1, 36.

56. *DTR* 4:219–220.

57. Sheldon, *History of Deerfield*, vol. 1, 37.

58. Ibid.

59. Nathaniel Shurtleff, ed., *Mass. Recs.* 4 (pt. 2):558–559, also copied into *DTB* 73.

3. *"Make a Toune of It"*

1. This rich and vital record does not appear in the *DTB;* it rests in Sheldon, *A History of Deerfield, Massachusetts*, vol. 1, 38–39, "recovered," Mr. Sheldon reports, "from a collection of old papers in Connecticut." Given the references to wood lots and proprietary disputes which are indeed picked up in subsequent documents, the material appears to be in order. See *DTB*, 1a; Sheldon, *History of Deerfield*, vol. 1, 40–41.

2. Hampshire County Probate Records (henceforth known as HCProbate) (Northampton, Mass.), vol. 1, 143, 152, 157, and *passim*. Although this volume is titled "Probate," its record up to 1690 includes both probate and other court activities, from reporting of civil offices in the county's towns

to criminal and civil cases. The confusion in the title stems from the multiplicity of tasks that these early court sessions, held twice annually and alternating between Springfield and Northampton, bore.

3. General Court order of 8 October 1672, in "Miscellaneous Bound, 1672–1680" in Manuscripts of the Massachusetts Historical Society (hereafter known as MHS) (Boston); see also Gertrude Cochrane Smith, "The First Maps of Pocumtuck," *PVMA Proc.* 8:38.

4. Actually, this proved consistent with many early New England settlements which placed only plowlands in severalty and kept pastures and woods common and open to all. PVMA MSS 5 ("Pocumtuck"); see also Sheldon, *History of Deerfield*, vol. 1, 39.

5. See the early inventories of Deerfield men, copied from the HCProbate, in William A. Doubleday, transcription, "Deerfield Probate Inventories prior to the Year 1740," (unpublished manuscript). See also Mary Tigue, "Colonial Standards of Living: Economic Progress in Deerfield, Massachusetts" (unpublished 1980 Historic Deerfield Summer Fellowship paper).

6. Peter Bolles Hirtle, "Agrarian Economy in Flux: Agricultural History of Deerfield, 1670–1760" (unpublished 1973 Historic Deerfield Summer Fellowship paper), 11 and 1–15, *passim;* Harold Roger King, "The Settlement of the Upper Connecticut Valley to 1675" (Ph.D. thesis, Vanderbilt University), ch. 7; Doubleday, "Inventories," 1–10; Tigue, "Colonial Standards," 31 and *passim.*

7. Negotiations like these between absent proprietors and local Pocumtuck settlers would continue into the eighteenth century, though they became increasingly rare. HCDeeds, Book A, 60, 129.

8. John Pynchon Account Book (Springfield, Mass.: Connecticut Valley Historical Museum), vol. 5, pt. 2, 470–471; Sheldon, *History of Deerfield*, vol. 1, 201; *DTB*, 1a. The minister's rate can only be estimated, and that from a fragment: John Pynchon's minister's rate for 1674 of £3.18. Because Pynchon was buying and selling cow commons all though this period, it is impossible to get an exact count, and hence a clear ratio between holdings and taxes. However, assuming he still held his 54 commons of 1671, Mather's salary would be approximately £40. Thinking Pynchon might have sold some rights, the estimate based on a holding of 40 cow commons comes to about £50.

9. Concerning the style of the ministry in this period, see Perry Miller, *The New England Mind: The Seventeenth Century* (1939; rpt. Cambridge: Harvard University Press, 1954), ch. 1, 2, and 6 and *passim.* As for the idea of the meetinghouse as town center, see Ola Winslow, *Meetinghouse Hill*, (New York: Norton, 1972), esp. ch. 4.

10. Doubleday, "Inventories."

11. Noted in John Pynchon's sale of a home lot in Deerfield to John Earle, 19 August 1673, in John Pynchon Account Book, cited in Sheldon, *History of Deerfield*, vol. 1, 201. Suffolk County Deeds, vol. 9 (published 1897), 21; HCDeeds, Book A, 84.

12. HCProbate 1:158, 162.

13. Rather than citing sources for each individual bit of information, listed below are the sources used in building the data bank for Pocumtuck's first generation. Sources for this section include:
    Hampshire County Court Records

Hampshire County Probate Records
Doubleday, "Inventories"
John Pynchon Account Book
PVMA MSS—family papers, subject files
Shurtleff, ed., *Massachusetts Records*
Judd, *History of Hadley*
Sheldon, *History of Deerfield*
MHS—miscellaneous documents
Hampshire County Deeds
Suffolk County Deeds

Charting of the data in this section, as well as the section that covers Deerfield's second and third generations, is annotated and available from the author or in the Henry N. Flynt Library of Historic Deerfield.

Credit for the general direction of many ideas in this section should go to Kevin M. Sweeney. As a summer fellow at Deerfield in 1971, he wrote an impressive study of Deerfield's first two generations entitled "The Children of the Covenant." Although I disagree with Mr. Sweeney at times, both in interpretation and some data, and have in fact refrained entirely from using any of this data, I am indebted to him for exhuming important ideas and sources about early settlement at Deerfield.

Pocumtuck's total population figure must remain approximate. The exact count of 68 adults depends on available records and thus may be incomplete. Data on children suffer from a lack of records for 4 of 29 families plus incomplete records of deaths of infants.

14. Data on Pocumtuck's women proved difficult to find; here the data represent 7 of a possible known 29 women.

15. The relative youth of Pocumtuck's adult population is comparable to Bristol, Rhode Island, a similarly new town, where women averaged 34 years of age and men were "comparably young." See John Demos, "Families in Colonial Bristol, Rhode Island: An Exercise in Historical Demography," *WMQ* 25 (no. 1, 1968):40–57.

16. Pocumtuck's average for men at first marriage was 24.9; Hingham's first-generation men's average was 26.8; Northampton's was 26.4. Although not perfectly comparable, Andover's first two generations of men married at age 26.7; Plymouth's (from 1650 to 1675) at 25.4; and Dedham's (from 1640 to 1690) at 25.5. Pocumtuck's women married earlier than women of many New England towns, at an average age of 19.2. This measures significantly below Andover's average of 22.3, Hingham's of 22.6, Plymouth's of 21.3, Northampton's of 22.3, and Dedham's of 22.5. On Andover: Philip J. Greven, *Four Generations: Population, Land, and Family in Colonial Andover, Massachusetts* (Ithaca, N.Y.: Cornell University Press, 1970), 21–27. On Plymouth: John Demos, "Notes on Life in Plymouth Colony," *WMQ* 22 (1965):275. On Dedham: Kenneth A. Lockridge, "The Population of Dedham, Massachusetts, 1636–1736," *Economic History Review*, 19 (1966):330. On Hingham: Daniel Scott Smith, "Population, Family and Society in Hingham, Massachusetts, 1635–1880" (Ph.D. thesis, University of California at Berkeley, 1973), 36ff. On Northampton: Russell W. Mank, "Family Structure in Northampton, 1654–1729," (Ph.D. thesis, University of Denver, 1975).

17. Pocumtuck also shows a greater difference in age at marriage between men

and women than other towns. Pocumtuck's gap stood at 5.7 years, versus those of Andover (4.4), Plymouth (4.1), and Dedham (3.0).

18. Demos, *Plymouth*, 67, and Appendix, 194; Mank, "Northampton," 92ff.; Greven, *Four Generations*, 29.

19. These data exist for 25 of Pocumtuck's known 29 families. Thus, these numbers stand as low estimates. For further explanation of data based on this "slice of life," see Daniel Scott Smith, "A Perspective on Demographic Methods and Effects in Social History," *WMQ* 34 (no. 3, July 1982):448. It is critical to understand here that this study uses the idea of this slice of life at one point, so that these figures reflect the town's status only in 1675, not the total number of children born to families over a generation. For example, of the 25 families for whom there is evidence in 1675, at least 9 had more children after 1675; another 9 were cut off from that path because the husbands were killed in King Philip's War.

At the same time, these figures do not take into account infant mortality, and the records show that at least 14 of Deerfield's 131 children died young. The total number also does not account for older offspring now grown up and moved out, of whom there were at least a few. Counterbalancing those two forces which would reduce estimates of the town's total population is the fact that these data account for only 25 of the 29 known families, and count not at all Pocumtuck men whose marital status is unclear. In sum, there is no way to provide an exact count for Pocumtuck's settlers, so one must "take what one gets" and hope that countervailing forces—especially on estimates of children in town—prove roughly equal.

20. While the town's average stands as slightly lower than some places like Dedham and Andover, this may be attributable to the relative youth of the adult population. In Andover, average births per marriage through the three decades between 1650 and 1680 stood at 5.8, 5.3, and 5.7, all close to Pocumtuck's rate of 5.2. Early Dedham's rate was slightly higher—a 6.1 average as of 1648—as was Northampton's first-generation average of 6.5. A more general study of twenty New England towns shows a higher range of 6 to 8 children. See Greven, *Four Generations*, 23; Lockridge, "Dedham," 146ff.; Mank, "Northampton," 92ff.; Robert Higgs and H. Louis Stettler III, "Colonial New England Demography: A Sampling Approach," *WMQ* 27 (no. 2, 1970):282–294.

21. Edward M. Cook, Jr., *The Fathers of the Towns: Leadership and Community Structure in Eighteenth Century New England* (Baltimore: Johns Hopkins University Press, 1976), 165–184. While Cook had studied the eighteenth century, his typology remains valuable for exploring seventeenth-century New England, especially in his look at small villages and "frontier towns," both of which were numerous in both centuries.

22. For example, John Plympton and his wife, Jane Dummer Plympton; Robert Hinsdale and possibly his wife, Ann Woodward Hinsdale; probably Francis Barnard. See especially Sheldon, *History of Deerfield*, vol. 2, Genealogy.

23. Not only were the Farringtons the only Dedham resident proprietors to come to Deerfield, but they returned to Dedham after 1675, where John died the next year. Thus, by 1680 the original group was entirely erased from the roll of Deerfield settlers.

24. Stockwell was not a bad fellow necessarily, only a bit of a drifter. In 1664,

for example, the Dedham town meeting had allowed him to cut timber, for apparently there was none to be "found on his own land." However, he must have had some respectability, for Pocumtuck allowed him to board the town minister, Samuel Mather, in 1674. Stockwell gained great fame after 1677 when he was captured by Indians and lived to write a narrative of his adventure. Although he received land in Deerfield at the time of the town's resettlement after 1680, there is no evidence that he ever returned, and a few years later he was found living in Connecticut.

25. Petition to General Court, 3 May 1667, from "west side" inhabitants of Hadley; cited in Judd, *History of Hadley*, 78–80.

26. James Russell Trumbull, *History of Northampton*, vol. 1 (Northampton, Mass.: 1898), ch. 12.

27. *Northampton Town Records* (Northampton, Mass.: Forbes Library), Reel 11.

28. Ibid. See also Russell Walter Mank, Jr., "Family Structure in Northampton, Massachusetts, 1654–1729" (Ph.D. thesis, University of Denver, 1975), 9–33.

29. The cases are termed "serious" because they involved more than a town's constable—they ended up in the Hampshire County Court at its semi-annual sessions in Northampton and Springfield. This material was all gleaned from the Hampshire County Court Records, with some citations as part of the County Probate Records, 1660–1690.

30. Actually, one other force that merits discussion—though it is not a significant factor here—is *inheritance*. In early New England, eldest sons often received double portions of inheritance, while youngest sons often received single portions including little or no land. While this practice suggests that Pocumtuck might have held a disproportionate number of younger sons who would settle there for the abundant land it offered—land they would never get if they stayed "home"—Pocumtuck's record does not support this. Instead, the places of Pocumtuck men in family lines show a normal distribution. For further discussion, see Richard I. Melvoin, "New England Outpost: War and Society in Colonial Frontier Deerfield, Mass." (Ph.D. thesis, University of Michigan, 1983), 126–128.

31. See Stephen Chandler Innes, "A Patriarchal Society: Economic Dependency and Social Order in Springfield, 1636–1702" (Ph.D. dissertation, Northwestern University, 1972), ch. 2 and p. 92. Pynchon's 54 cow commons holding at Pocumtuck included 3 different house lots; he also owned one of the 150-acre "farms" in the north meadows originally given the Dedham "explorers."

32. HCDeeds, Book A, 6, 133a; Judd, *Hadley*, 3; Henry W. Taft, "Address," *PVMA Proc.* 1:169–199.

33. Innes claims that most of Pynchon's trade lay in food and livestock. However, a review of his account books makes it clear that he sold far more: He seems to have been running the valley's "general store."

34. Not surprisingly, that person was John Stebbins, Jr., son of one of Northampton's wealthiest citizens and the young man who had had two scrapes with the county judges by 1675. Between 1672 and 1675, Stebbins ran up £35 worth of debts to Pynchon—especially for items like wine and rum, for which he placed 14 separate orders in 11 months! By contrast, while the names of 3 of the wealthier, more established pioneers do appear

in Pynchon's books, each case involved only small debts and almost all in the 1660s. Typical of these was William Smead, who in 1664 bought £4.16.6 worth of "severals" but who had paid in full by 1666. John Pynchon Account Book, vol. 5, pt. 1, 278–279. The other following cases are all gleaned from the Pynchon Account Books, vol. 1–6.

35. The idea of Pynchon as patron for the valley, one who helped make it go (as opposed to Pynchon the acquisitive capitalist merchant), can particularly be seen in Innes's article on Pynchon found in Stephen Innes, Peter Thomas, and Richard Melvoin, *Early Settlement in the Connecticut Valley* (Deerfield: Historic Deerfield and Institute for Massachusetts Studies, 1984).

36. Grant, *Kent*, 94–95.

37. Again, see David Grayson Allen, *In English Ways, passim*.

38. This vital idea lies at the heart of Michael Zuckerman's important essay, "The Social Context of Democracy in Massachusetts," *WMQ* 25 (no. 4, October 1968):523–544.

39. The idea of Pocumtuck as a second-generation town is best developed in Kevin Sweeney, "Children of the Covenant." For a look at New England's mission, read Edmund S. Morgan, *The Puritan Dilemma* (Boston: Little, Brown, 1959). To see that mission in decline, one may look at Morgan; Darrett Rutman, *Winthrop's Boston* (Chapel Hill: University of North Carolina Press, 1965); Perry Miller, *The New England Mind: The Seventeenth Century;* Lockridge, *A New England Town;* Powell, *Puritan Village;* and others.

40. Cook, *Fathers of the Towns,* 181–183.

41. Pocumtuck stands by itself in terms of New England Puritan town studies. Charles Grant's fascinating *Democracy in the Connecticut Frontier Town of Kent* (1961; rpt. New York: Norton, 1970) comes to mind. However, Grant has studied different forces and issues a full sixty years later, and thus did not prove relevant here.

42. Pocumtuck's frontier status also bears notice when considered among the other valley towns. While the three older, established towns of Springfield, Northampton, and Hadley held roughly 700, 500–600, and 360 people, respectively, Pocumtuck and Hatfield were the larger new settlements, with roughly 200 inhabitants; the others held perhaps half that number.

No sophisticated population estimates exist for the Connecticut valley before 1700. The estimates given here are based on the numbers of male settlers, "residents," voters, or petition signers at each of the towns between 1668 and 1685. For Springfield, see Innes, "A Patriarchal Society," 31–32; for Northampton, *Northampton Town Records;* for Hadley and Hatfield, see Judd, *History of Hadley,* 76–77. I then worked out a crude formula, estimating that roughly five-sixths of the settlers (83%) remained in these towns in the years before 1675, and that (based on Pocumtuck) 90% were married. I then multiplied the result by an estimated family size of 8, based on Pocumtuck and Andover results. (Northampton proved especially tough to estimate because its settler list included everyone who had entered the town from 1653 to 1674.) Except for clear data on Hatfield, data on the new towns are crude. Estimates are based largely on the paucity of claims, court appearances, and resettlement efforts of the others in the years after 1675.

4. The Wheel Turns:
Pocumtuck and King Philip's War

1. The major known conflicts were apparently inter-Indian. See chapters 1 and 2 of this book.

2. See Douglas E. Leach, *Flintlock and Tomahawk: New England in King Philip's War* (New York: Macmillan, 1958), 79; Francis Jennings, *The Invasion of America: Indians, Colonialism, and the Cant of Conquest* (New York: Norton, 1975), 200.

3. Joseph H. Smith, ed., *Colonial Justice in Western Massachusetts (1639–1702): The Pynchon Court Record* (Cambridge: Harvard University Press, 1961), 296–341 and esp. 268–269.

4. Neal Salisbury suggests that this was a period of mutual dependency for English and Indians in the Connecticut valley. See his article, "Social Relationships on a Moving Frontier: Natives and Settlers in Southern New England, 1638–1675" (unpublished paper, 1985), *passim.*

5. See the works of Woodrow Borah and Sherburne F. Cook, Henry F. Doyns, and—from a seventeenth-century observer—Daniel Gookin, all of which are cited in Jennings, *Invasion*, ch. 2. These selections all consider the reduction to have been drastic, quite possibly literal "decimation." Douglas Leach offers a more subdued and conservative set of estimates of losses, suggesting that population declined by a factor closer to 3 than Jennings's 6 to 10.

6. See Neal Salisbury, "Conquest of the Savage" (Ph.D. dissertation, UCLA, 1975).

7. Speech of Metacom/King Philip, 1671, in Mr. Easton, "A Relacion of the Indyan Warre," in Charles H. Lincoln, ed., *Narratives of the Indian Wars, 1675–1699* (1913; rpt. New York: Barnes and Noble, 1959), 10.

8. The best, and contrasting, accounts of this war are Douglas Leach's careful, traditional, scholarly *Flintlock and Tomahawk* and Francis Jenning's angry, also scholarly, impassioned, and occasionally polemical *The Invasion of America.* See also Douglas E. Leach, *The Northern Colonial Frontier, 1607–1763* (New York: Holt, Rinehart and Winston, 1966), 59.

9. George M. Bodge, *Soldiers in King Philip's War* (Boston: 1906), Appendix A, 479–480, shows at least 184 Indians sold into slavery in August and September of 1676 alone. The note on proportion of casualties comes from Lincoln, *Narratives*, 4.

10. "N.S." (Nathaniel Saltonstall?), "A New and Further Narrative of the State of New-England, 1676," in Lincoln, *Narratives*, 98; William Hubbard, *A Narrative of the Indian Wars. . .to 1677* (1677; rpt. Stockbridge, Mass.: Heman Willard, 1803), 111; Rev. J.H. Temple, "Address," in *PVMA Proc.* 1 (1872):120–122.

11. Bodge, *Soldiers*, 69.

12. See Bodge, *Soldiers*, Appendix A, 479–480; Charles M. Segal and David C. Stineback, ed., *Puritans, Indians and Manifest Destiny* (New York: G.P. Putnam's Sons, 1977), 203–207.

13. The most careful account of the war's beginning, with thoughtful balance of different forces and motivations, comes in Leach, *Flintlock and Tomahawk*, ch. 1–3, and esp. pp. 30–44.

14. Hubbard, *Narrative*, 27.

15. Leach, *Flintlock and Tomahawk,* ch. 4.
16. Letter of John Pynchon to Connecticut Council of War, dated Springfield, 22 August 1675, in J. Trumbull, ed., *Records of the Connecticut Colony, 1665–1678* (Hartford, 1850), 353. Pocumtuck's 10 soldiers noted in Judd, *History of Hadley,* 133; Sheldon, *History of Deerfield,* vol. 1, 89.
17. Reported in a letter of Rev. Solomon Stoddard to Rev. Increase Mather, 15 September 1675; extracted in Judd, *History of Hadley,* 133–134.
18. A peace pact with the Nipmucks was signed 13 June 1675. Sheldon, *History of Deerfield,* vol. 1, 82.
19. This conclusion is based upon research compiled about Indian tactics, personnel, and general strategy. See Richard I. Melvoin, "Strategy and Savagery" (paper for seminar under the direction of John Shy and Kenneth Lockridge, University of Michigan). Not all of southern New England's tribes joined King Philip. The "Pequots and Moheags" were called upon to attack Philip in the valley: 5 September 1675, Hartford, Connecticut War Council meeting, in Trumbull, *Records of the Connecticut Colony,* 363.
20. Stoddard letter of 15 September 1675, in Judd, *History of Hadley,* 134–135; Hubbard, *Narrative,* 106. The claim of only 2 garrisons (versus Sheldon's of 3) stems from a report about the subsequent September 12 attack on Pocumtuck, where Stoddard's 15 September letter claims that the settlers fled from one garrison to "the other." The figure of 17 houses burned comes from Increase Mather's diary, as cited in Richard E. Birks, "Samuel Mather, the Pioneer Preacher . . ." in *PVMA Proc.* 5:216.
21. Stoddard, in Judd, *History of Hadley,* 135.
22. At least Connecticut's 10 men, under Treat's command, are clear. See Treat's Commission from the Connecticut War Council, 2 September 1675, in Trumbull, *Records of the Connecticut Colony,* 360.

    Often normal houses with modifications, these "blockhouses" had thick walls, "projecting flankers at two or more corners, and perhaps a surrounding palisade. Strong doors, shuttered windows, and loop-holes in the walls were desirable, as was a second story which provided good shooting positions for the defenders." The upper story also helped fulfill another colony requirement, that of having a watch tower in each town. Patrick M. Malone, "Indian and English Military Systems in New England in the Seventeenth Century" (Ph.D. thesis, Brown University, 1971), 223–224; *Colonial Laws of Massachusetts,* 1675–1676 supplements, Military, 109, 112.
23. The claim of destruction of one garrison stems from Hubbard's contemporary account which, first, notes specifically that the 27 men went to *the other* garrison, and, second, observes that the day after Bloody Brook, Indians passed close by *"the garrison house."* See also Stoddard letter in Judd, *History of Hadley,* 135–136; Increase Mather, "A Brief History of the Warr . . ." (1676), in Richard Slotkin and James K. Folsom, ed., *So Dreadful a Judgment: Puritan Responses to King Philip's War, 1676–1677* (Middletown: Wesleyan University Press, 1978), 96–98.
24. Stoddard, in Judd, *History of Hadley,* 136; John Pynchon to Connecticut Council, dated Hadley, 30 September 1675, in Judd, 142.
25. Record of 13 October 1675, in Shurtleff, ed., *Mass. Recs.* 5:52.
26. Sheldon, *History of Deerfield,* vol. 1, 101.

27. Hubbard, *Narrative*, 113–114.

28. Ibid.

29. One nineteenth-century writer termed it "the most terrible massacre of whites furnished by the annals of New England." Josiah G. Holland, *History of Western Massachusetts* (Springfield, Mass.: Samuel Bowles and Co., 1855), 89. Even Herbert Osgood, a detached twentieth-century imperial historian, called it "one of the most serious disasters of the war." Herbert L. Osgood, *The American Colonies in the Seventeenth Century* (New York: Macmillan, 1904), vol. 1, 555.

30. Hubbard, *Narrative*, 115.

31. Hubbard, *Narrative*, 115–116.

32. Sheldon, *History of Deerfield*, vol. 1, 111.

33. Letter of Hadley reverend John Russell to John Pynchon, 6 (?) October 1675, in Gregory H. Nobles and Herbert L. Zarov, ed., *Selected Papers from the Sylvester Judd Manuscripts* (Northampton: Forbes Library, 1976), 529.

34. The probate records of Pocumtuck men killed in 1675 show that either these people had been extremely poor or simply had not had the time or opportunity to secure their possessions in a safer town. Both are probably true. Of the eight estate records of any kind, only one man left an estate (after debts) of more than £16; one had more debts than assets; and on the average the surviving estates were worth only a paltry £13.1. And this was in a world where a horse and a cow alone were worth £5, and a feather bed with pillows, blankets, and pillow case the same. Data come from William A. Doubleday, transc., "Deerfield Probate Inventories to 1740" (unpublished; Historic Deerfield, 1975), 1–9. See also HCProbate, *passim*.

35. The Hinsdales' trials continued the following spring when yet another brother, Experience, died in the war.

36. M. Halsey Thomas, ed., *Diary of Samuel Sewall* (New York: Farrar, Straus & Giroux, 1973), vol. 1, 13.

37. Mather, "A Brief History," in Slotkin and Folsom, ed., *So Dreadful a Judgement*, 3.

38. Mather, "An Earnest Exhortation," in Slotkin and Folsom, ed., *So Dreadful a Judgement*, 3.

39. Of the 20 points listed, the first 3 read: "1. Let no man presume to blaspheme the holy & blessed Trinity . . . under payne to have his tongue bored with a hott iron. 2. Unlawful oaths, & execrations, & scandalous acts, in derogation of God's honour, shall be punished. . . . 3. All those who often & wilfully absent themselves from the public worship of God & prayer shall be proceeded against. . . ." General Court session of 13 October 1675, in *Mass. Recs.* 5:49–50.

40. General Court session of 3 November 1675, in *Mass. Recs.* 5:59–63.

41. September 1675, Hampshire County Court Records (henceforth known as HCCourt); *Mass. Recs.* 5:44–45, 55–56, 66.

42. These figures do seem unduly high, however, given the scale of battles and the Indians' initiative in most battles during this war. See Captain Wheeler's narrative of the Brookfield battle; Rev. Stoddard's 15 September letter to Increase Mather; Mather's own history of the war; Judd, *Hadley*, 130–145.

43. Sheldon, *History of Deerfield*, vol. 1, 126.

44. Reverend John Russell's report puts the death total at 145. (Judd, *History of Hadley*, 149.) My own research shows the inconsistency of casualty figures given in different accounts, and therefore a range of totals: between 114 and 172 dead, 21 to 34 wounded, 5 to 13 captured.

45. A scout reported this sighting on about October 15. Sheldon, *History of Deerfield*, vol. 1, 122.

46. *Some words about methodology.* To find the main body of evidence for this discussion of Indian strategy, I tried to find out everything I could about each incident which occurred in western Massachusetts in 1675 and 1676. This included study not only of documents which discussed the various raids but also a mass of local histories, chronicles of Indian wars, histories of colonial New England, and captivity narratives. What emerged was a file of Indian attacks on record for this period. The records proved quite uneven. For some incidents I had only one fragmentary report; for others, as many as eight or ten detailed summaries. Even the details provided problems, though, for the numbers of casualties, identification of enemies, and locales would at times vary considerably. With no way to verify various details, I decided to include the range of casualties in my data. While this fuzziness is not wholly satisfactory, I am confident that it does not destroy the strength of the data or the writing. Discrepancies in dates and even years sometimes occurred. The matter of a few days, however, did not seriously affect the results here. Further, while in the writing I have tended to say "at least" followed by the low figures I arrived at, the numbers of casualties and losses remain serious and significant.

One other word about casualty figures. Clearly, some of the casualties in King Philip's War were soldiers, not settlers, a consideration which could alter the picture of how much the Connecticut valley suffered. To deal with this, I first excluded from my data any losses incurred in either colonial attacks or while on scouts. Thus, for example, the 38 soldiers—and citizens—killed at Turner's Falls in May of 1676 were not counted here. Second, it is noteworthy that many of the soldiers of Massachusetts were in fact residents of the region, so their loss was both military and local. Third, this study does not account for local men lost in fighting elsewhere during the war. Finally, the extent of property loss helps show that far more than human casualties were involved in this war.

For students of this war—and the subsequent wars that rocked Deerfield—more information is available in the author's thesis. Specifically, the thesis includes the record of all Indian attacks on the Connecticut valley through King Philip's War (1675–1676), King William's War (1688–1698), and Queen Anne's War (1703–1712). Also included are maps which graphically show the paths and patterns of Indian strategy. Richard I. Melvoin, "New England Outpost: War and Society in Colonial Frontier Deerfield, Mass." (Ph.D. thesis, University of Michigan, 1983), Appendices.

A last note: thanks to Barbara Glass Melvoin for her forays into these sources and her clear and accurate data.

47. Sheldon, *History of Deerfield*, vol. 1, 110–122; Leach, *Flintlock*, 89–91.

48. Hubbard, *Narrative*, 117.

49. "N.S.," "The Present State . . . ," in Lincoln, *Narratives*, 33.

50. Hubbard, *Narrative*, 110ff.; George Sheldon, "The Pocumtuck Confederacy," in *PVMA Proc.* 2 (1888):405.

51. Letter of John Pynchon, 1675, cited in Sheldon, *History of Deerfield*, vol. 1, 98.
52. 21 February 1675/1676, General Court, in *Mass. Recs.* 5:70–74.
53. Letter of Rev. John Russell, dated Hadley, 15 May 1676, in Judd, *Hadley*, 161–162; Trumbull, *Northampton*, 298–300; Sheldon, *History of Deerfield*,, vol. 1, 150.
54. See Bernard Bailyn, *The New England Merchants in the Seventeenth Century* (Cambridge: Harvard University Press, 1955), esp. ch. 2.
55. Trumbull, *Northampton*, 298.
56. At this point, a couple caveats need to be borne in mind. Although this scheme looks quite clear and clean, one should not be carried overboard with it. It may be that a number of the incidents reported herein, at least the small ones, were not incidents at all so much as they were accidents. If Indians and whites ran into each other in the wood, the whites may have been sure it was an ambush, but falsely so. In like fashion, it is impossible to know if the burning of an isolated house by a small party of Indians was anything more than a random attack by some isolated natives. Still, the fact that the Indians were in those locations, at those times, and took the actions they did suggests planning, and if the exact schemes did not exist, general plans did. Also, the major attacks could hardly be called "accidents"—and they form a clear pattern by themselves. On the other hand, one should be careful to keep possible Indian goals in mind. Did they hope to eradicate all whites? That probably sounded as quixotic to them as it does to readers today. Rather, the Indians had realistic goals and worked toward them by reasonable, effective means—at least in western Massachusetts.
57. General Court, 3 May 1676, in *Mass. Recs.* 5:81.
58. James Axtell, "The Scholastic Philosophy of the Wilderness," *WMQ* 25 (no. 3, 1968):335.
59. Letter of Thomas Savage, 15 May 1676, located in Sylvester Judd Manuscripts, "Massachusetts," vol. 2, 2.
60. Bodge, *Soldiers*, 243–244.
61. Report of Rev. John Russell, dated Hadley, 15 May 1676, in Bodge, *Soldiers*, 244; Judd, *Hadley*, 161–162.
62. Increase Mather, "A Brief Narrative," in Slotkin and Folsom, ed., *So Dreadful a Judgement*, 119.
63. Bodge, *Soldiers*, 246.
64. Report of John Russell, dated Hadley, 15 May 1676, in Bodge, *Soldiers*, 244.
65. Hubbard, *Narrative*, 217–218.
66. Hubbard, *Narrative*, 239.
67. Hubbard, *Narrative*, 248; Sheldon, *History of Deerfield*, vol. 1, 177.
68. From "A Short Account of the General Concerns of New-York," Governor Andros, March 1678, in *NYCD* 3:254–256.
69. A letter of 8 men of Hadley to General Court, 29 April 1676, spoke directly of "proofe" of Mohawk support "in those they slew up this River," cited in Bodge, *Soldiers*, 242; Sheldon, *History of Deerfield*, vol. 1, 143–144.
70. This crucial point is supported, if vaguely, by a letter dated 5 July 1676 from Governor Andros to the Government of Connecticut which said in part: "Our Indians, the Maquas, &c. . . have done very great execution on

your Indian enemys . . ." *(NYCD);* cited also in Hubbard, *Narrative*, 218; see also Sheldon, *History of Deerfield,,* vol. 1, 178. Trumbull, p. 344, also acknowledges three separate Mohawk strikes, though others—notably Judd and Palfrey—dispute it.

71. "N.S.," "A New and Further Narrative . . ." (London: Dorman Newman, 1676), in Samuel G. Drake, ed., *The Old Indian Chronicle* (Boston: The Antiquarian Institute, 1836), 88. Drake's excerpts appear to include certain key elements of this "narrative" that Lincoln chose to omit in his anthology of Indian narratives.

72. Hubbard, *Narrative*, 217–218.

73. Traditionally, historians of the war ignored the Mohawks. In the history of the war that became the standard for a generation after its publication in 1958, Douglas E. Leach did not focus on the Mohawk role. More recently, at least four historians have challenged this, though with varying degrees of success. Although Francis Jennings acknowledges the importance of the Mohawks in the war, he overstates New York governor Andros's role in handling them. In *1676*, Stephen Webb has similarly given undue credit to Andros, making the Mohawks unduly submissive to him. Daniel Richter has explained Mohawk fragility and independence from the English better in "The Ordeal of the Longhouse," and Neal Salisbury has followed this lead well.

74. For example, while many tribes joined Philip's forces in 1675, Uncas and the Mohegans served the English, and quite well.

75. Letter of 8 men of Hatfield to General Court, 29 April 1676, in Bodge, *Soldiers*, 242.

76. "Extracts from Edward Randolph's Report to the Council of Trade," 1676, in *NYCD* 3:242.

77. Randolph's whole role in this must be viewed with caution. As a firm ally of Andros and an enemy of Massachusetts, Randolph may have been using this opportunity to support his friend and cripple his enemies in Boston. See Bailyn, *The New England Merchants in the Seventeenth Century* (Cambridge, Mass.: Harvard University Press, 1955), ch. 6 and 7. See also Webb, *1676*, 234–236.

78. Lawrence Leder, ed., *The Livingston Indian Records, 1666–1723* (Gettysburg, Pa.: The Pennsylvania Historical Assoc., 1956), 155; Jennings, *Invasion*, p. 314; *NYCD:* 3:265.

79. Letter from New York governor Andros to Government of Connecticut, 5 July 1676, NYCD; Hubbard, *Narrative*, 178, 218.

80. This theme provides a significant thrust in Stephen Webb's view of King Philip's War in *1676* and Francis Jennings' in *The Invasion of America*. It also raises the key issue of how Andros is viewed overall. Here Webb and Jennings give him extremely high marks; Jennings called him "loyal, intelligent, and bluntly aggressive" in his ability to understand and control Iroquois affairs (Jennings, *Invasion*, 300–301).

81. See Jennings, *Invasion*, ch. 18; Richter, "Ordeal," p. 213; Salisbury, "Social Relationships," 42–44.

82. The presence of each Indian group allied with Philip can be explained, for all had reasons to be with him. The Mahicans, long enemies of the Mohawks, had been driven into Philip's camp by the English. The Scaticookes were a new group, made up largely of Algonkians who had fled from New

England—including two bands from the Connecticut valley. By 1676 they were a center of Indian resistance. Under Montreal's influence, "French Indians" had joined to strike a blow against the English; some perhaps joined to attack any Europeans; and some may have been hoping to fight against the Mohawks with whom they had split. Finally, it is important to remember that in the seventeenth century Indians did not always stay bound by tribal unity. Given the vortex of forces in 1676—English, French, Algonkian, Iroquois, and inter-Indian—it is not surprising that some Indian groups split up.

While the numbers and range of forces here may thus have seemed unlikely, they make sense. Besides, one report came from a former English prisoner, Thomas Warner, and another came via two Natick Indians who reported what they had seen while on a spy mission. Sheldon, *History of Deerfield*, vol. 1, 129–136. See also Franklin Hough, ed., *A Narrative of Causes of. . .Philip's War* (New York: 1858), 145; Jennings, *Invasion*, 314; Richter, "Ordeal," 173–183; Salisbury, "Social Relationships," 39; and Webb, *1676*, 367.

83. See Webb, *1676;* Jennings, *The Ambiguous Iroquois Empire* (New York: Norton, 1983).

84. There is a story that says that at this point Philip tried a dangerous ploy that backfired disastrously. As local records tell it, rebuffed in his efforts to get more Mohawks, Philip and his force then ambushed a Mohawk party away from camp and sent a group to tell the Mohawks that the English had committed the act. However, one of the Mohawks survived the attack, returned to camp, and told all. From that point on, the Mohawks sought revenge.

This remarkable story is not accepted by all historians of the region. At the same time, it is no convenient nineteenth-century fable, having been first reported within a year of the war's end by a contemporary, Increase Mather (see Samuel G. Drake, ed., *The History of King Philip's War* [Boston: by the editor, 1862], 168). Further, its credence has not been shaken by any firm evidence to the contrary and in the described pattern it makes sense.

85. Cook, "Interracial warfare," 3.

86. Reported in, though not pursued by, most historians of King Philip's War, including Douglas Leach, *Flintlock*, 202.

87. Webb, *1676*, 239.

88. Thomas Reed reported this to Captain Turner on May 15, and colonists confirmed this when they came up to Pocumtuck on August 22, 1676, and cut it down. Letter of Rev. John Russell, 15 May 1676, in Bodge, *Soldiers*, 244; Sheldon, *History of Deerfield*, vol. 1, 177.

89. Hubbard, *Narrative*, 248; Sheldon, *History of Deerfield*,, vol. 1, 161–175.

90. Cook, "Interracial Warfare," 19.

91. Hubbard, *Narrative*, 281.

92. Letter from five commissioners in Hartford to Governor Andros, 6 September 1678, in *NYCD* 3:273.

93. *NYCD* 3:273ff.; Sheldon, *History of Deerfield*, vol. 1, 191–192.

94. See Webb, *1676;* Jennings, *Ambiguous Iroquois;* Salisbury, "Social Relationships," 45–47.

95. Cook, "Interracial Warfare," 21.

96. Wilcomb F. Washburn, *The Indian in America* (New York: Harper and Row, 1975), 132. For a study of the nature of Indian-white legal relations, see Yasu Kawashima, "Jurisdiction of the Colonial Courts over the Indians in Massachusetts, 1689–1763," *WMQ* 26 (no. 4, 1969):532–550.

97. See Bodge, *Soldiers*, 251.

98. Doubleday, "Deerfield Probate Inventories," 9.

99. Sutlieff, Mun, and Hinsdale did so as part of the mixture of local militia and regular soldiers that fought with Turner at the falls fight. John Stebbins and John Plimpton served as volunteers in Captain Mosely's militia in the latter months of 1675. See the list of Samuel Mosely's militia, taken at Dedham, 9 December 1675, in Bodge, *Soldiers*, 476–477.

100. *Colonial Laws of Massachusetts*, 1675–1676 supplement, 238, 248.

Pocumtuck Epilogue:
"A Dwelling for Owls . . ."

1. See John Demos, *A Little Commonwealth* (New York: Oxford University Press, 1970), ch. 4.

2. Sherburne F. Cook, "Interracial Warfare and Population Decline Among the New England Indians," *Ethnohistory* 20 (no. 1, 1973):21.

3. 22 October 1677 Court Record in Shurtleff, ed., *Mass. Recs.* 5:162; Silas G. Hubbard, "Historical Address," *PVMA Proc.* 2 (1889):451–473.

4. Hubbard, *PVMA Proc.* 2:459.

5. Letter of Edmund Andros, dated New York, 28 September 1677, in J. Hammond Trumbull, ed., *The Public Records of the Connecticut Colony, 1665–1678* (Hartford: Brown and Parsons, 1850), 507.

6. "Narrative of Benoni Stebbins," taken 6 October 1677 at Northampton, Mass., in *NYCD*, 25; "Account of Attack on Hatfield and Deerfield. . .1677," Bradford Series, no. 1, 57, at Mass. Historical Society. Stebbins escaped soon after his capture on September 19. "Norwooluck" could mean Norwalk (Connecticut) Indians—or more likely means Norwottuck, some of the local "River Indians" and possibly including Pocumtucks.

7. "Stebbins Narrative," 57.

8. While this shift in attackers is genuine, a couple caveats should be considered. First, 1677 was not the first time the French had tried to influence Connecticut valley Indians. As early as 1651, the Jesuit Father Druillette had tried to get Pocumtucks, Sokokis, Pennacooks, and Mahicans to attack the Iroquois. "French Indians" appeared in the valley before 1675 as well, notably in 1663. See *JR* 26:101–105; Peter Thomas, "Maelstrom," 211–212, 251. Second, New England Indians who fled after King Philip's War to take French protection did not become mere pawns of the Europeans. Rather, their goals—including attacks on the English—may well have co-incided with French goals.

9. Quinton Stockwell letter, 22 May 1678, in Hubbard, *PVMA Proc.* 2:459; Sheldon, *History of Deerfield*, vol. 1, 185.

10. Found in HCProbate 1 (26 March 1678):195 concerning a case of "ffornication." "This day of our Calamity" is another comment of the time, seen in a broadside issued by the Massachusetts Council, Boston, 9 April 1677, looking specifically at the problem of horse racing.

11. HCProbate, 1676, vol. 1.
12. See Mary P. Wells Smith, "A Puritan Foremother . . . ," *PVMA Proc.* 4 (1900):85–98.
13. General Court letter of 22 October 1677 to Captain Salisbury of New York, in Shurtleff, ed., *Mass. Recs.* 5:166–168.
14. General Court session of 22 October 1677, in *Mass. Recs.* 5:170–171.
15. Petition of inhabitants of Pocumtuck/Deerfield to General Court, 30 April 1678, in Sheldon, *History of Deerfield*, vol. 1, 189–190; Nobles and Zanov, ed., *Judd Manuscripts*, 536–538.
16. General Court session of October 1678, in *Mass. Recs.* 5:209.
17. Some residents never gave up on the town. John Plympton's probate record showed him to be, to the last, a resident "of Deerfield," and in 1677 Philip Mattoon of Springfield signed an 11-year lease with John Pynchon on a tract of Pocumtuck land. Even the October 1678 General Court response was addressed to "the remayning inhabitants" of the town. Hampshire County Probate, 1678, 1:197. John Pynchon Account Book 5 (pt. 2):536–537, Connecticut Valley Historical Museum, Springfield, Mass.
18. Massachusetts General Court, Proclamation of 2 October 1678 (Cambridge: Samuel Green, 1678), found at Clements Library, University of Michigan.

5. *"Plant that Place Again":*
Deerfield, 1680–1688

1. *DTB*, p. 1a; Hampshire County Probate Records (HCProbate), vol. 1, session of March 1676, 171; Hampshire County Deeds (HCDeeds), Book A, 130.
2. Measurement of town population has to begin with adult white males, for only they received grants of land, appeared on town fence, tax, and land lists, or became officers of the town. Obviously, the women of Deerfield meant a great deal to the very existence of the town, as did the children, and they are accounted for and discussed as fully as possible later on in the chapter. However, one cannot but begin with the men.

   As in Chapter 3, material for the study of the town's settlers has come from a variety of sources: the town book, probate records, court records, deed and land records, family papers, Massachusetts colonial records, and the Massachusetts Archives. Helpful secondary sources include Sheldon's *History of Deerfield*, genealogies, and a number of other local town studies. This material has been assembled in a series of charts, in possession of the author, with copies to be placed in the Henry Flynt Library of Historic Deerfield, and may be seen upon request.
3. The total number of adults in town was likely higher still, for the town's records reveal the names of 8 more men beyond the 54 who by dint of their landholding in town may well have been settlers. However, since the 8 appear only in grant records, and not in the town meeting, probate, or genealogical records, they remain on the periphery of this study and are not included in future calculations. The 8 "on the periphery" were Ephraim Beers, John Earle, Samuel Field, Jonathan Hunt, Jr., Francis Keet, Thomas Seldon, Quinton Stockwell, and Ebenezer Wells. Earle and Stockwell held land from before 1675, but apparently sold off and moved out. The other 6

all received grants, but made no signs—via the records—to show they followed up on their grants and actually settled before 1689.

The 6 deceased Pocumtuck men who still held listed proprietary shares but gave no signs of family persistence in town as of 1688 were Peter Plympton, Zechariah Field, Nathaniel Sutlieff, and Ephraim, Samuel, and John Hinsdale.

Beyond those 8 peripheral figures, a 1688 wood-lot division, with proportions based as usual on cow commons, reveals that as many as 6 original Pocumtuck families still held proprietary rights in town. All the rights were in the names of now-dead Pocumtuck men, all but one of whom were killed during the struggles with the Indians. Perhaps the widows, or possibly the children, lived in town on the old home sites. Because it is impossible to know, however, they, too, cannot be counted among Deerfield's new settlers.

4. The approximate number of living children was derived thusly. Town and genealogical records yield a total of 174 children born, with 9 reported to have died young. This would lave a total of 165 living children. However, mortality rates for youths under age 21 suggest a much higher incidence of death; Deerfield, like other towns, likely had deaths—especially of youths—underrecorded. If we take John Demos's estimate of a maximum of 25% death rate for youths, one arrives at a living child population of 130. (See Demos, *A Little Commonwealth* [New York: Oxford University Press, 1970], ch. 4.)

On the other hand, Daniel Scott Smith writes of evidence suggesting infant mortality as low as 100 per 1000 (albeit challenged by David Hackett Fischer as "inherently implausible"). This would yield a child population of about 150. (See Daniel Scott Smith, "A Perspective on Demographic Methods and Effects in Social History," *WMQ* 39 [no. 3, July 1982]:452; David Hackett Fischer, *Growing Old in America* [New York: Oxford University Press, 1978], 225.) Maris Vinovskis's survey of the literature indicates that infant mortality ranged somewhere between 10% and 30% of all children. This leads me, for purposes here, in the absence of further evidence, to compromise at 140. (Maris A. Vinovskis, "Angels' Heads and Weeping Willows: Death in Early America," *American Antiquarian Society Proceedings* 86 [pt. 2, 1976]:279–286.) Some of the older children had doubtless moved away from Deerfield or had never even come with their parents. In general, though, the number should be accurate, for it is based on individual family reconstitution and considers such matters as previous residences, infant mortality rates, and the overall youth of the town.

5. Daniel Scott Smith, "Perspective on Demographic Methods," 448. John Demos, "Families in Colonial Bristol, Rhode Island: An Exercise in Historical Demography," *WMQ* 25 (no. 1, Jan. 1968):40–58. The youthfulness of Deerfield's 1688 adults compares closely overall with that of the population of Bristol, Rhode Island, in 1689. Like Deerfield, Bristol was a young town in 1689, also laid out for farming (though showing signs of growing commerce). In studying Bristol John Demos also took the same kind of "slice of life at a point in time," what demographer and historian Daniel Scott Smith has called "period analysis." While Bristol's women were a bit older than Deerfield's, averaging 33.6 years of age versus Deerfield's 29, the men were "comparably young."

6. And this excludes two Deerfield men, reported to have married before the age of 16, as highly questionable—though it includes three men who married before age 21.

7. Their marriage age is consistent with those of men of other New England towns. Deerfield's measure of 24.7 years compares closely with studies of Bristol, Rhode Island (23.9 years); Plymouth (26.1 for those born 1625–1650, 25.4 for those born 1650–1675); Dedham (1640–1690, 25.5 years); Northampton (first-generation average of 25.4); Hingham (1641–1700 average of 26.8); and Andover (first-generation average of 27.1). The numbers for women are: Bristol (20.5), Plymouth (20.2 and 21.3), Dedham (22.5), Northampton (22.3), Hingham (22.6), and Andover (22.8). See Demos, "Bristol," 49–58; Demos, *A Little Commonwealth*, Appendix, Table 4, 193; Lockridge, "Dedham, 1636–1736: The Anatomy of a Puritan Utopia" (Ph.D. thesis, Princeton University, 1965), 146; Russell W. Mank, "Family Structure in Northampton, Mass." (Ph.D. thesis, University of Denver, 1975), 95; Daniel Scott Smith, "Population, Family and Society in Hingham, Mass., 1635–1880," (Ph.D. thesis, University of California, Berkeley, 1973), ch. 2 and p. 236; Philip Greven, Jr., "Family Structure in Seventeenth Century Andover, Mass.," *WMQ* 23 (no. 2, April 1966):241–242.

8. There were 54 known adult men and 41 known adult women (all of whom were married), yielding a sex ratio of about 4:3.

9. Mank, "Northampton," 89–92; Demos, *A Little Commonwealth*, 66–67 and Appendix, Table 5, 194.

10. In Deerfield, fewer than 60% of the men married just once. Although Plymouth's rate is similar, Andover's first-generation rate of 68% and Northampton's of 78% suggest that in other towns fewer men faced the prospect of remarriage. For Deerfield's women, the picture is bleaker still: While almost 70% of Plymouth's women married only once, only 52% of Deerfield's women could make that claim. Mank, "Northampton," 89–92; Demos, *A Little Commonwealth*, 66–67, 194; Philip Greven, Jr., *Four Generations: Population, Land and Family in Colonial Andover, Massachusetts* (Ithaca: Cornell University Press, 1970), 29.

11. (See Footnote 4 for a discussion of infant mortality rates.) This sample is necessarily based on genealogical records of the men of Deerfield and their families, not on the records of the women. Some men had children from more than one wife; some widows had doubtless borne children before "marrying into" Deerfield. Scanty records limit study of these spin-offs, and force data to be based on the men.

12. Since this measure is based on a period analysis, the data must be studied with care. Given the comparable data for Bristol, Rhode Island, which indicate there an average of 3.3 children per family, Deerfield seems quite prolific. The same holds for a comparison with 1648 Dedham, where total family size stood at 6.1, an implication of 4 children per family. (A study of the Deerfield of 1704 reflects significant growth in the number of children per family; see Chapter 6 of this book.) Demos, "Bristol," 45; Lockridge, "Dedham," 138ff.

13. On 17 June 1703, John Baker gave power of attorney to his son Samuel of Northampton, for action of recovery to "recover lands" at Deerfield, or at least debts due thereon. PVMA MSS: Deerfield Town Records, Box 1, #3c; HCDeeds, Book B, 192.

14. These data exclude the 8 settlers and 3 sons of settlers who returned to Deerfield and are based on evidence of most recent residence for the 40 new men and 30 new women of Deerfield.

15. Ronald K. Snell, "The County Magistracy in Eighteenth Century Massachusetts, 1692–1750" (Ph.D. thesis, Princeton University, 1971), 224–227.

16. The three ministers were Solomon Stoddard of Northampton, John Russell of Hadley, and William Williams of Hatfield. John Pynchon Account Book, 5 (pt. 2):467, 536–537, 6:144–145.

17. General Court session of 4 June 1685, in Shurtleff, *Mass. Recs.* 5:482.

18. See discussion in Chapter 3 of this book and, more generally, Stephen Chandler Innes, "A Patriarchal Society: Economic Dependency and Social Order in Springfield, Massachusetts, 1636–1702" (Ph.D. thesis, Northwestern University, 1977), 2, 56ff.

19. John Pynchon Account Books, 4:200; 5 (pt. 2):374, "index volume 5," 22–23; 5 (pt. 1):18–19.

20. Innes, "A Patriarchal Society," 236–237.

21. 31 July 1677, John Pynchon Account Book, 5 (pt. 2):536–537.

22. John Pynchon Account Book, 6:144–145.

23. That the focus was the valley's youth seems inescapable when one considers that the oldest of the 8 future Deerfielders named was 25 years old. Also, the Deerfielder at Hadley was Joseph Seldon. 29 March 1676, HCProbate 1:177–178.

24. 26 September 1671, HCProbate 1:127.

25. 26 March 1678, HCProbate 1:195.

26. HCProbate 1:91–92, 177–178; Hampshire County Court Records (HCCourt) 2:8, 33, 58, 84.

27. 28 September 1686, HCCourt, 109; 27 September 1681, HCCourt, 49; 28 March 1682, HCCourt, 56.

28. HCCourt 2:8, 30; Smith, ed., *The Puritan Court Record*, 289, 292–293.

29. HCProbate 1:158, 160–161; HCCourt 2:71.

30. It is also noteworthy that the majority of Deerfield's citizens with court records came from a classic "dangerous class": low in wealth and status, young, unmarried, and usually male.

31. Charles Grant, *Democracy in the Connecticut Frontier Town of Kent* (1961; rpt. New York: Norton, 1972), 66–82.

32. Innes, "A Patriarchal Society," 56, 132–141, and *passim*.

33. It is important to note here that Deerfield was not exceptional in allowing former criminals to live in town. Rather, seventeenth-century Massachusetts was marked by the fact that "convicted offenders were rather easily reabsorbed into the community." See Douglas Greenberg, "Crime, Law Enforcement, and Social Control in Colonial America," *American Journal of Legal History* 26 (no. 4, October 1982):298.

34. Greven, "Family Structure," 256; Greven, *Four Generations*, p. 98 and ch. 2 and 4.

35. Laurel T. Ullrich, *Good Wives* (New York: Oxford University Press, 1983), Introduction and *passim*. Illuminating the lives of seventeenth-century Deerfield women takes determination. Ullrich's fine book explores the wide range of roles that women played generally—yet short of helpful poems by Anne Bradstreet or rare pieces of prose, it is difficult to find out

what individual women thought of their work and lives. Further, Ullrich wisely chose to generalize about women of a region, allowing a wide range of sources. The study of a single town is obviously more limited. Thus, most of the study of women here comes from analyses of genealogical material, with some information coming via county court, deed, and probate records; town and proprietors' records sometimes help.

36. HCCourt, vol. 2, session of 30 March 1680 at Northampton, p. 34; *DTB*, 39–40. Snell, "County Magistracy," 227–234, 339–344, 369. "Disinterested committees" like this had been used to establish other valley towns, including Brookfield, Enfield, and Suffield, between 1667 and 1679. That the committee members had prestige in the county is clear: All served as local justices of the peace. At the same time, it was assumed that none had any stake in Deerfield's resettlement.

37. 12 December 1680, in *DTB*, 1.

38. *Mass. Recs.*, vol. 5, General Court session of 27 May 1681, 321; *Colonial Laws of Massachusetts*, 1675–1676 supplement, 267–268.

39. 30 March 1682, in *DTB*, 1–2.

40. This concept was not new to the valley: Northampton had required four years' residence for newcomers to gain title to land. 6 March 1681/1682, in *DTB*, 1; Mank, "Northampton," ch. 1.

41. *Mass. Recs.*, vol. 5, General Court session of 27 May 1682, 360–361.

42. Timothy Mather bequest of land to his son Samuel, 10 September 1677, in "Miscellaneous Collections," Massachusetts Historical Society; Reverend Richard E. Birks, "Samuel Mather, the Pioneer Preacher of Deerfield, and his English Antecedents," *PVMA Proc.* 5 (1907):214–226; 1678 petition to General Court, in Sheldon, *History of Deerfield*, vol. 1, 189–190.

43. William Smead and Richard Weller returned; William Bartholomew headed for Branford, Connecticut, in 1679; and Moses Crafts was living in Wethersfield, Connecticut, by 1682.

44. Such as Philip Mattoon. John Pynchon Account Book 5 (pt. 2):536–537.

45. HCDeeds, Book C, p. 568; HCDeeds, Book A, 116; HCDeeds, Book C, 494. Another pattern shows Deerfielders trading land amongst themselves. See HCDeeds, Book A, 130; PVMA MSS—Family Papers; HCDeeds, Book A, 128.

46. HCDeeds, Book C, 413, Book A, 140, Book A, 136; PVMA MSS 5-VIII, Folder 1, Lot #16.

47. This figure of 16% includes the lands John Pynchon leased to Philip Mattoon.

48. HCProbate 1:245; HCDeeds, Book A, 95; HCCourt 2:92.

49. The town also gave out some proprietary rights early on, but although 5 men received either 6 or 7 cow commons during the first couple years of resettlement, that practice quickly ended. For the vast majority of new settlers who received land, their proprietary status remained unclear until 1688. Then, in granting wood lots to established settlers, Deerfield showed that it already granted *de facto* proprietary rights to them as well.

All of these data on land come from the *DTB* between 13 December 1680 and 20 April 1688. See *DTB*, 1–20, 32–33, 40. As for the distinction between a town's "inhabitants" and "proprietors," Deerfield did not make its proprietors group distinct until 1699; see Chapter 3 of this book for how Dedham worked through this intriguing distinction. At the same time, though, the wood-lot division of 1688 clearly shows that no fewer than 48 men now held proprietary rights at Deerfield, including a great number of new settlers. Unfortunately, the town record gives no indication of when or how it granted such rights.

50. Green River's distance from town and isolation across the Deerfield River caused problems, though. Three of the 13 men who received home lots and acreage forfeited them by failing to settle on the lands for the required 3 years. Ultimately its isolation proved so severe that in 1753 Green River broke from Deerfield to form the town of Greenfield.

51. Meeting date is unclear; probably late 1684 or early 1685. *DTB*, 2, 41.

52. Jonathan Church received his 64 acres "in ye boggie meadow," to make up for his missing 16 in the meadows that he claimed he had bought from Samson Frary (presumably first-division lands) on 5 February 1687. *DTB*, 12.

53. 5 February 1687, *DTB*, 11.

54. Wanting land granted by the town amounted to a known 446.5 acres, plus 7 cases where no exact acreage was noted in the town book. Using the determined average grant of 17.8 acres for those 7 cases, one can project that an additional 124.6 acres of land were granted, making the total 571.1 acres.

At the same time, "New and additional grants" made during the period totaled 545 acres (using the rough average of 3 acres per cow common to account for commonage granted). In addition there were 6 cases of unspecified acreage. Using the determined average of 11.8 acres per grant then adds 70.8 acres more. Thus, "new and additional" lands total 615.8 and, combined with the amount of wanting land, one finds that the total amount of land granted by the town comes to 1186.9 acres.

55. List of wood lots drawn 20 April 1688, in *DTB*, 19a; Sheldon, *History of Deerfield*, vol. 1, 208–209. It is the second wood-lot division which shows most new Deerfield settlers as now in possession of cow commonage—proprietary rights.

56. 5 January 1686, *DTB*, 3.

57. Sheldon argues that he was preaching by June of 1686; Sheldon, *History of Deerfield*, vol. 2, 377. More definite proof comes only with the 13 October 1686 citation about John Williams "of Deerfield" found in Samuel Sewall's *Diary*, 123; see also Reverend Allen Hazen, "Some Account of John Williams, First Pastor of Deerfield," in *PVMA Proc.* 2:109.

58. *DTB*, 3, 5, 6.

59. Sewall, *Diary*, 123; Hazen, "Some Account," *PVMA Proc.* 2:107–116.

60. See Chapter 5 of this book; Snell, "County Magistracy," 339–344.

61. 5 January 1686. "The Committee's" consent was apparently required in giving Thomas Broughton even a 4-acre home lot. *DTB*, 3.

62. The dating of the town book is so haphazard in the years before 1700 that it is impossible to tell exactly which data are correct. Further, the book's pages are not in chronological order. See *DTB*, 6–7.

63. *DTB*, p. 6, tells of the town's "prudential" affairs; *DTB*, p. 17, demonstrates "the Comitte's" largesse in December of 1687.

64. *DTB*, 17–20.

6. A Communal Frontier Town

1. There were 67 men, 50 women, and 140 or so children. Virtually all the women were married; their families had an average of just under 5 children each. Family size ranged from 0 to 14 children. Of the 67 men, 28 were old settlers and 39 new. The veterans of Pocumtuck averaged 47 years of age; only one was less than 36. The new men averaged 33, with only three over 35. The new men married at an average age of 24; the women at 20.

   How much the war that encircled Deerfield from 1688 to 1698 affected the town's population is difficult to say. This chapter presents Deerfield's population and way of life in the 1690s; the next chapter explores the impact of King William's War on the town and the valley.

   As before, data here come from town birth and death records, *DTB*, HCProbate, HCCourt, and HCDeeds, the genealogy in Sheldon's *History of Deerfield*, and Pocumtuck Valley Memorial Assoc. manuscripts.

2. "Independent adulthood" is defined by marriage, ownership of land, participation in town government, and possibly participation in the local militia or battles. Few Deerfielders fell into all these categories, but any one could qualify them for this adult status.

3. 20 December 1687: 20 acres each to Jeremiah Hull and Samuel Smead on condition they stay on the land for 3 years after turning 21. *DTB*, 15.

4. The newcomers followed previous patterns, coming largely from the valley below. It should be noted that during the 1690s the town lost settlers not only from the 1688 generation but also from among these new residents. One new man, James Corse, died and as many as 5 others quit the town by 1704.

5. Smith, ed., *Colonial Justice in Western Massachusetts: The Pynchon Court Record*, 341; HCDeeds, Book A, 111; Fitz-John Winthrop's Table of 1704 Losses, in *Massachusetts Historical Society Proceedings*, 1st series (1792); also in Sheldon *History of Deerfield*, vol. 1, 304–305, vol. 2 (Genealogy), 265.

6. Smith, ed., *Colonial Justice,* 9 January 1702, 375; HCCourt, 29 March 1692, 154; Sheldon, *History of Deerfield,* vol. 1, 298, 308–309, vol. 2, 293. The slaves were valuable, too. Sheldon's 2 adults and 5 children were worth a total of £420 in 1733.

7. 26 September 1693, in HCCourt, p. 164; 26 December 1693, in HCCourt, 166.

8. PVMA MSS—Family Papers; Sheldon, *History of Deerfield,* vol. 2, 80; *DTB, passim.*

9. HCProbate, vol. 1, and HCCourt, *passim.* See also George Lee Haskins, *Law and Authority in Early Massachusetts* (New York: Macmillan, 1960), 214–215.

10. HCDeeds, Book A, pp. 98, 104–105, 130–131, 152.

11. *DTB,* 20, 26–27, 34, 58–59.

12. *DTB,* 42–43.

13. In young towns, meetings might well take place in someone's house, or even outside under a tree in good weather. There is nothing in Deerfield's records to suggest that it had a meetinghouse before 1695.

14. Deerfield's use of the Hatfield meetinghouse as a model is intriguing. On

the one hand, it may reflect nothing more than the fact that Hatfield was Deerfield's closest neighbor and of similar size. (Hatfield had a bit over 300 people, Deerfield just under 250.) On the other hand, Hatfield's meetinghouse was small and simple, and Deerfield may have seen it as a good, familiar, inexpensive model. That it took Deerfield 15 years to build a meetinghouse suggests the town's poverty. Even details about the meetinghouse construction support this. For one thing, construction took years. For another, the town deviated from Hatfield's model when it decided to use simple pineboards for the pews "and not wainscut." *DTB*, 57–58; Daniel White Wells and Reuben Field Wells, *A History of Hatfield, Massachusetts* (Springfield, Mass.: F.C.H. Gibbons, 1910), 60, 106, 116ff., 137.

15. *DTB*, 58–62, 64.
16. Ola Elizabeth Winslow, *Meetinghouse Hill* (1952; rpt. New York: Norton, 1972), ch. 9 and esp. 142–143. Unfortunately, none of Deerfield's early seating plans survived; the town book only indicates that they were drawn up and by what criteria.
17. *DTB*, 64a.
18. Probate records discussed in Chapters 3 and 7 of this book suggest that many Deerfielders owned books. The number of inventories that exist is too few to allow dependable quantification, but they suggest that over half of Deerfield's men owned books. See Kenneth A. Lockridge, *Literacy in Colonial New England* (New York: Norton, 1974).
19. See Bernard Bailyn, *Education in the Forming of American Society* (1960; rpt. New York: Norton, 1972).
20. Sheldon, *History of Deerfield*, vol. 1, 273; *DTB*, 31. The limiting of expected schooling to 4 years may be yet another comment on Deerfield's poverty: Perhaps this was as much as any family could or should afford.
21. *DTB*, 31, 48, 52, 68–69, 69a.
22. *DTB*, 40, 57, 63, 69–70.
23. *DTB*, *passim*. See Chapter 5 of this book.
24. In fairness, it should be noted that in 1688 and 1689, and also in 1701, the town chose officers back in December, not in March. Otherwise, however, the pattern holds.
25. *DTB*, 30–31, 38, 54a.
26. *DTB*, 29, 31, 34, 46.
27. *DTB*, 61.
28. *DTB*, 35 and *passim*.
29. See, for example, an order of the Massachusetts Council, Boston, April 4, 1676, found in *Colonial Laws of Massachusetts*, 1675–1676 supplement, 337. The order required towns to take "particular account of all Persons and families so coming to them." There is no evidence that Deerfield ever followed this.

Such autonomy evidently was not rare in seventeenth-century Massachusetts. As early as the 1640s, Sudbury showed a remarkable degree of separation from Boston. And Sudbury was a well-established town near Boston; Deerfield was a young and isolated western outpost. See Sumner Chilton Powell, *Puritan Village* (Middletown, Ct.: Wesleyan University Press, 1963), ch. 7.

30. Act of 30 November 1692, in *Massachusetts Acts and Resolves,* vol. 7 (vol. 2 of Appendix), 20. Under the new laws of the royal colony, freemanship no longer existed, and freeholding went to men who were 21 years of age and landholders.

31. Some New England frontier towns apparently did not mind being "under-represented" in provincial government, for they felt protected by the colony's "benevolent paternalism"; whether this was true for Deerfield is unclear. It seems that Deerfield sent representatives to meetings of the General Court only when vital issues were discussed: Thomas Weld after the overthrow of the Dominion of New England in 1689, Lieutenant Jonathan Wells and Joseph Barnard to the first General Court session of Governor Phips after the colony's reorganization in 1692, and Jonathan Wells again in the aftermath of King William's War in 1698. Otherwise, Deerfield was close enough to the 40-man freeholder level to ordinarily opt not to send a representative.

    The estimate of £10 per year comes from Lockridge, "Dedham," 343ff. The idea of different priorities comes from Michael Zuckerman, *Peaceable Kingdoms: New England Towns in the Eighteenth Century* (New York: Vintage, 1972), 27–28. See also Grant, *Kent*, 115–122.

32. Edward M. Cook, *The Fathers of the Towns: Leadership and Community Structure in Eighteenth Century Massachusetts* (Baltimore: Johns Hopkins University Press, 1976), ch. 6.

33. Ronald Snell, "The County Magistracy," ch. 7 and 8, and esp. 294.

34. This set of bylaws apparently ended Deerfield's dependence on the courts, for this is the last record of such review by the court. HCCourt, "General or Quarter Sessions," 14 March 1693, 161; 10 April 1693, 163; 6 March 1694, 170.

35. 28 September 1694, HCCourt, 2:109.

36. On criminality in the 1670s and 1680s, see Chapters 3 and 5 of this book. One critical caveat here is that the Hampshire County Court Records from 1696 to 1704 are lost. Searches through available records in Springfield, Northampton, and Worcester unfortunately failed to produce those missing years. Thus, while the ideas in the text are based on the records from 1688 to 1696, they do not cover the last 8 years before 1704. (In fact, the records do not resume until 1707, and from there to 1720 they are sketchy.) Deerfield's one major, dramatic case of the 1690s, the infanticide/adultery case of Sarah Smith in 1698–1699, required a special court. It is discussed in Chapter 7 of this book.

37. 31 March 1691, HCCourt, 139.

38. John Pynchon Account Book 2:34, 214–215, 3:162–163, 4:26–27, 176–177, 5 (pt. 2):467, 536–537, 6:144–145, 198–199; PVMA MSS—Family Papers. John Allin was still settling his debt in 1709.

39. Pynchon's reduced influence in Deerfield is consistent with a more general picture of his decline throughout Hampshire County. Although Pynchon's power remained great until his death in 1702, it had reached its zenith in the 1680s and fell after that. See Innes, "A Patriarchal Society," ch. 6.

40. The following data and analysis all come from the town meeting records found in the *DTB*, 6–71.

41. Of the 54 men on the townsmen list of 1688, 39 served in offices during the

1690s. Of the remaining 15: five were dead by 1693 and one, John Williams, as minister, was not allowed to serve. Of the last 9, not one remained in town by 1704.

42. The eastern Massachusetts town of Sudbury had 40 offices in its early years, and frontier Kent, Connecticut, had 31 offices in 1779—and only 45 able-bodied men. In Springfield, "virtually all the men held some kind of office." In seventeenth-century Dedham, 60–80% of men on tax lists served in government at one time or another. Powell, *Puritan Village*, 44; Grant, *Kent*, 146–150; Innes, "A Patriarchal Society," 123; Lockridge, "Dedham," 278. Edward Cook estimates Dedham's participation as still higher: "nearly all of the permanent residents"—in Cook, *Fathers*, 32, 35–44, 181–183.

43. See Cook, *Fathers*, ch. 2; Lockridge, "Dedham," ch. 8 and esp. 286ff.

44. Cook, *Fathers*, 23–33; Lockridge, "Dedham," 286.

45. HCProbate 1 (1678):195a.

46. Cook, *Fathers*, 1–2.

47. Ibid., 22.

48. 39% of Deerfield's men served as selectmen at some point in the years from 1689 to 1704. While 32% of Springfield's men served in similar fashion, a more general look at 27 small New England towns reveals that the "leader pool" averaged only about one-quarter of a town's men. Deerfield's average of just two and a half years of service as selectman is quite low. By contrast, while about 30% of men who served as selectman in New England towns did so for only one term, a substantial number of elected selectmen—probably 35–40%—served 5 or more years. Here again Deerfield appears more egalitarian: Only one-quarter of its selectmen served as many as 4 years. Finally, while Deerfield men's movement between major and minor offices matches the pattern established in early Dedham and was common in small New England towns—considered "necessary and even desirable" and "entirely consistent with [townsmen's] sense of personal worth"—it diverges at least from the experience of frontier Kent, where major and minor offices were "mutually exclusive." See Innes, "A Patriarchal Society," 123; Cook, *Fathers*, 36–37, 53–60, 62. One must be cautious with Cook's data on pp. 36–37. Apparently he includes moderator, clerk, treasurer, and constable in his "leader pool," and he also takes his percentage of leaders versus the pool of *all* town officials—not, as in Deerfield, out of the total male population. Since virtually all Deerfield residents served in office, this latter problem almost disappears; both, however, only serve to make Deerfield's percentage of leadership even more striking. See also Lockridge, "Dedham," 280–283; Cook, *Fathers*, 44; Grant, *Kent*, 146.

49. Northampton statute is quoted in Cook, *Fathers*, 86. The ties between wealth and political leadership are readily seen in Cook, *Fathers*, ch. 3; Lockridge, "Dedham," 280–286; Grant, *Kent*, ch. 10.

50. *DTB*, 60.

51. While legally town meetings could do anything they wanted, early Dedham and Watertown town meetings "existed largely as a passive veto power" and were "in some ways definitely subordinate" to the selectmen. Similarly, in frontier Kent, selectmen held most "major administrative powers," a point borne out by a more generalized study of Connecticut towns which indicates that selectmen had more power while town meetings only

ratified decisions. Kenneth A. Lockridge and Alan Kreider, "The Evolution of Massachusetts Town Government, 1640 to 1740," *WMQ* 23 (no. 4, October 1966):552; Grant, *Kent*, 134; Bruce C. Daniels, *The Connecticut Town: Growth and Development, 1635–1740* (Middletown: Wesleyan University Press, 1979), 66–69.

52. See Michael Zuckerman, "The Social Context of Democracy in Massachusetts," *WMQ* 25 (1968): 523–544; Zuckerman, *Peaceable Kingdoms* (New York: Knopf, 1970), esp. ch. 3–5.

53. Kenneth A. Lockridge, *A New England Town: The First Hundred Years* (New York: Norton, 1970).

54. 20 April 1688 wood-lot division, in *DTB*, 19a; Sheldon, *History of Deerfield*, vol. 1, 209. 28 of 48 men held from 10 to 20 shares.

55. *DTB*, 2–28, *passim*.

56. HCDeeds, Book A, 23 (back), 136, Book AB, 285, Book B, 42–43, 192, Book D, 112.

57. 4 April 1692, *DTB*, 54a.

58. The following work comes primarily from study of the Hampshire County Deeds; Hampshire County Probate Records, especially probate inventories; and the town record book's listings of home lots, lands, and fences.

59. One has to be cautious in ascribing all these trades and skills to Deerfield men. First, while some of these are clear from family papers and probate inventories, a few emanate from the work of George Sheldon which, though careful, is not footnoted or annotated. Also a difficulty here is trying to figure out when these people learned and practiced their trades, and especially how many did so before 1704. With these caveats in mind, I have treaded lightly upon the material.

60. This material comes from inventories of 24 Deerfield men who died between 1686 and 1704. Though not every inventory contains all relevant information, such as debts and land values, enough include enough data to yield a clear overall picture. Inventories can be found in HCProbate, vol. 1 and 3, with good transcriptions for almost all Deerfielders done by William Doubleday, in his "Deerfield Probate Inventories Prior to the Year 1740" (unpublished), 11–60.

61. Mary Tigue, "Colonial Standards of Living: Economic Progress in Deerfield, Mass." (unpublished Historic Deerfield Summer Fellowship Paper, 1981), 18.

62. This lack of furniture has also been seen in the first generations of Hampton, New Hampshire, and early Dedham, as well as early Pocumtuck. See Lockridge, "Dedham," 220–222; Tigue, "Colonial Standards," 20–33.

63. This is based on a study of 24 inventories of Deerfield men (and one woman) who died between 1686 and 1704. The generalizations made are generally corroborated by Tigue, "Colonial Standards," whose study goes up to 1704.

64. HCProbate 1:184.

65. Analysis of probate inventories of all Deerfield men who died between 1688 and 1704 yields an average holding of 66 acres at the time of their deaths. This low figure is corroborated by proprietors' records which show an average cow commons holding of just under 12 commons. With an estimated holding at that time of 3 to 5 acres per common, this yields an average holding of roughly 36 to 60 acres. For a careful discussion of some of the pitfalls involved in using probate records, see Gloria L. Main, "Pro-

bate Records as a Source for Early American History," *WMQ* 32 (no. 1, January 1975):89–99. Mary Tigue's work studies Deerfield inventories up to 1740, and still finds an average holding of fewer than 100 acres. See Tigue, 19–20.

66. Lockridge, "Dedham," 220; Greven, *Four Generations*, 59; Grant, *Kent*, 14; Innes, "A Patriarchal Society," 30–31.

67. Probate records exist for 13 estates between 1689 and 1704. As for age versus estate values, the wealthiest, Joseph Barnard, died at age 44 with a £230 estate. By comparison, Robert Alexander died at age 24 with a £24 estate; John Weller at 41 left a £28 estate; and both Richard Weller at age 70 and David Hoyt at 53 left estates of £79.

68. Lockridge, "Dedham," 220–223.

69. Actually, the correct average for *all* Springfield residents of this period is £326. However, this figure is skewed by the inclusion of the estate of John Pynchon, who left an estate at his death in 1702 of a staggering £8446. Even removing his estate from the study, though, Springfield's other 69 residents had estates worth an average of £209. In fairness, it should be noted that Springfield had a major maldistribution of wealth: 30 townsmen, 43% of the total, died with estates worth less than £100, and 15 of these had estates worth less than £50. Even so, while Springfield shows unequal distribution of wealth, Deerfield shows an equal but almost unremitting poverty. Innes, "A Patriarchal Society," 54–55.

70. Mank, "Northampton," averages derived from tables on pp. 131–132.

71. Inventories from early Dedham offer much the same types of items as seen in Deerfield; however, in that town both the quality and quantity of luxury items were evidently much higher. Lockridge, "Dedham," 220–222.

72. *MA* 11 (Ecclesiastical):106u, 188. This sense of Deerfield living a rather crude, hard life is corroborated in a fuller study of the town's probate inventories by Tigue, "Colonial Standards." Though looking mostly at personal and not real estate, Tigue sees Deerfield's lot as a difficult one in the years before 1704.

73. Of 24 Deerfield men who died between 1688 and 1704, and whose estate records survived at least in part, no fewer than 15 left records of strings of debts. See HCProbate, *passim;* Doubleday, "Deerfield Inventories," 34; PVMA MSS—Family Papers: Broughton, Corse, Barnard, Barrett.

74. Innes, "A Patriarchal Society"; Grant, *Kent*, pt. 2, *passim*.

75. In the 24 estate inventories of this time, and amidst hundreds of entries in the debt listings, money was specifically mentioned only three times.

76. See Haskins, *Law and Authority*, 85–93; Kevin M. Sweeney, "Unruly Saints: Religion and Society in the River Towns of Massachusetts, 1700–1750" (Williams College honors thesis, 1972), 10–11.

77. Robert G. Pope, *The Halfway Covenant: Church Membership in Puritan New England* (Princeton: Princeton University Press, 1969), 147–149. The author is indebted to Patricia Tracy for her careful counsel in this complex area.

78. Patricia J. Tracy, *Jonathan Edwards, Pastor: Religion and Society in Eighteenth Century Northampton* (New York: Hill and Wang), ch. 1. Here I diverge from Tracy's interpretation, noting that the shift in policy came more as an opportunity than a reaction to a problem.

79. There is no direct evidence which confirms that Deerfield followed

Northampton's lead. It seems likely, however. Not only do all historians of the subject acknowledge the sweep of Stoddard's ideas, but many also acknowledge "the usefulness of open communion in the 'isolated' Connecticut valley settlements." Pope, *Halfway Covenant*, 255; Tracy, *Edwards.*

80. Larzer Ziff, *Puritanism in America: New Culture in a New World* (New York: Viking, 1974), 256.

81. *DTB*, 55.

82. By 1704 Deerfield's land values were roughly like those of other New England towns. Through the 1680s and 1690s a cow commons (at that time the equivalent of 3 to 5 acres) would sell for £3 to £4. As the 1690s progressed, however, values went up, if only moderately. The 1702 "apprizement" of Deerfielder Benjamin Barrett's estate valued his house lot at 45 shillings per acre, his prime farmland at 52 shillings per acre, and other lands at 16 shillings per acre. In 1690, by contrast, Jonathan Church's house lot had been valued at only 10 shillings per acre, and "out lands" variously at just 3 or 4 shillings per acre. By 1704 house lots were worth as much as £4 per acre and prime meadows ranged from £2 to £3.

These values are roughly consistent with those of other New England towns. Land that was "unimproved," like Church's, was of marginal value anyplace. However, land that was cleared was valuable. Thus, in seventeenth-century Dedham plowed meadowland was worth £2 to £3 per acre, as in Deerfield, while unbroken land was worth far less. These conclusions came from a study of 19 Hampshire County deeds of Deerfield land and cow commons transactions between 1676 and 1703. HCProbate 1 (1676 valuation):190, 1:264, 3:165, 3:88. On Dedham, see Lockridge, "Dedham," 224–225.

83. For example, these 7, 29% of all selectmen chosen during these 15 years, served only 54% of all selectman terms.

84. Hoyt and Wells each held free estates of about £53 plus lands; Catlin had a free estate comprised solely of lands worth £120.

85. Cook, *Fathers*, ch. 2, 3, 7.

86. *DTB*, 39, 68.

7. *Living with Death: Deerfield,*
the New England Frontier, and War,
1680–1703

1. This phrase has been popularized by Michael Zuckerman's penetrating study *Peaceable Kingdoms: New England Towns in the Eighteenth Century* (New York: Vintage, 1972).

2. This does not mean, however, that Deerfield took care of people who normally would have been warned out, since failure to warn people out obligated the town to care for them if needed. There is no record of Deerfield helping any poor, orphaned, or indigent residents, either—a practice common even in frontier Kent. It appears that Deerfield took whoever came and neither helped nor hindered them. Or rather, the help people received came privately or through the communal nature of town affairs. See Zuckerman, *Peaceable Kingdoms;* Grant, *Kent*, ch. 6.

3. Daniel Boorstin, *The Americans: The Colonial Experience* (New York: Vintage, 1958), 5.

4. *DTB*, 38; *MA* 1:47.

5. HCProbate 1:161.

6. 29 March 1676, HCProbate 1:177–178.

7. 26 March 1678, HCProbate 1:195.

8. 26 September 1682, HCCourt, 61.

9. See Paul Boyer and Stephen Nissenbaum, *Salem Possessed* (Cambridge: Harvard University Press, 1974); John Demos, *Entertaining Satan* (New York: Oxford University Press, 1982).

10. Opening of the will of Thomas Wells, Sr., of Hadley, in HCProbate 1:188a.

11. Deerfield lost at least 14 people specifically to war between 1688 and 1700. The adult townsmen's average age was 46.6. Data compiled essentially from PVMA MSS—Family Papers; Sheldon, *History of Deerfield*, vol. 2, Genealogy, *passim*.

12. Hull had been put down to sleep in his bed chamber "with another child" when "after some time Henry s^d Godfrey Nimss son a boy of about 10 years of age went into the chamber with a light and by accident fired some flax or towe, which fired ye house, s^d Henry brought down the other child, and going up again to fetch s^d Jeremiah, the chamber was all in flame, and before other help came s^d Jeremiah was past recovery." HCCourt, Quarter Sessions, Inquest of 6 March 1694, 170–171.

13. 25 March 1684, HCCourt, 75.

14. Smith, ed., *Colonial Justice*, Case 158, 24 December 1674, 287.

15. Pierre Goubert, *Louis XIV and Twenty Million Frenchmen* (New York: Pantheon Books, 1970), 199–200.

16. Goubert, *Louis XIV*, 313–314; Francis H. Hammang, *The Marquis de Vaudreuil: New France at the Beginning of the Eighteenth Century* (Louvain: Biblioteque de L'Universite, 1938), 20–84, esp. 32; I.K. Steele, *Politics of Colonial Policy: The Board of Trade in Colonial Administration, 1696–1720* (Oxford: Clarendon Press, 1968), 36–37, 93.

17. For a good overview of Frontenac's plans, see Douglas E. Leach, *The Northern Colonial Frontier, 1607–1763* (Histories of the American Frontier Series, Ray A. Billington, ed.) (New York: Holt, Rinehart and Winston, 1966), 110.

18. Francis Jennings, *The Ambiguous Iroquois Empire* (New York: W.W. Norton and Co., 1984), 195.

19. W.J. Eccles says there was not, in his volume *France in America* (New York: Harper and Row, 1972), 96—but one must note that he holds strong views about Frontenac, the Canadian governor at that time.

20. Eccles, *France in America*, 97.

21. W.J. Eccles, *Frontenac: The Courtier Governor* (Toronto: McClelland and Stewart, Ltd., 1959), 244.

22. Leach, *Frontier*, 118.

23. The Covenant Chain represents a fascinating and critical step in Iroquois-English relations. While its existence is clear, its strength and significance are less so. For three recent, important, powerful interpretations of the Covenant Chain, see Daniel Richter, "The Ordeal of the Longhouse"; Stephen S. Webb, *1676: The End of American Independence;* and Francis Jennings, *Ambiguous Iroquois*.

24. See Jennings, *Ambiguous Iroquois,* ch. 8; Richter, "Ordeal," ch. 6.
25. Richter, "Ordeal," p. 208 and ch. 6, *passim.* Concerning "mourning wars," see Richter, "War and Culture: The Iroquois Experience," *WMQ* 40 (no. 4, October 1983), 528–559.
26. Richter, "Ordeal," 173; more generally, see ch. 5 and esp. 173–183.
27. Jennings, *Ambiguous Iroquois,* 191.
28. The only kind of action resembling an offensive came in sending out scouts to patrol the region and the valley above. At least one of these scouts had impact, for in 1698 a scout killed some enemy Indians and redeemed a handful of English captives at Vernon, in what is now southern Vermont.
29. Shurtleff, ed., *Mass. Recs.* 5:482.
30. Deposition of Lieutenant Thomas Wells before Edmund Randolph, 15 October 1688, in Sheldon, *History of Deerfield,* vol. 1, 214–215.
31. Sheldon, *History of Deerfield,* vol. 1, 215.
32. *DTB,* 24–25. A rod in seventeenth-century terms could be either 12 or 16 feet.
33. *MA* 70 (Military): "An account of the fortification . . ." made May 1693.
34. *DTB,* 24–25.
35. John Shy, "A New Look at Colonial Militia," *WMQ* 20 (3rd series, April 1963):175–185; *Massachusetts Acts and Resolves,* vol. 1, 107–116, and *Massachusetts Province Laws,* 1693–1694, ch. 3, 128–132, all in *Backgrounds of Selective Service,* 100–146. Patrick M. Malone, "Indian and English Military Systems in New England in the Seventeenth Century" (Ph.D. dissertation, Brown University 1971), 223.
36. HCProbate, 29 March 1690, 1:269a; HCCourt, 23 April 1690, 125, and 25 June 1690, 127.
37. Letter of Peter Tilton to Governor Bradstreet, cited in Sheldon, *History of Deerfield,* vol. 1, 222.
38. John F. Moors, "Mrs. Eunice Williams," *PVMA Proc.* 2 (1884 meeting):163–188.
39. Letter of John Pynchon to Governor Bradstreet, 2 December 1691, in Sheldon, *History of Deerfield,* vol. 1, 222–223.
40. *DTB,* 43.
41. John Pynchon letter to Governor Phips, 8 March 1693, in *Mass. Acts and Resolves/Province Laws,* 379.
42. MHS—"Miscellaneous Bound, 1690–1694"; *The Acts and Resolves, Public and Private, of the Province of Massachusetts Bay,* (hereafter known as *Mass. A & R,*) vol. 7 (App. II) (Boston: Wright and Potter, 1869–1922, 21 vols.) 389; *MA* 112:436.
43. *MA* 112:436.
44. *Mass. A&R* 378; *MA* 2:212.
45. In mid-March, in response to Pynchon's pleas, Phips and his Council issued a proclamation establishing a 50-man garrison in Hampshire County, a willingness to send 150 more "upon any Exigency," and providing £400 in "provision pay." A day later Connecticut confirmed its participation in the valley's defense. *Mass. A&R,* 7:379–380; *MA* 2:213.
46. *Mass. A&R,* 7:380; additional testimony in a document, undated, in Sheldon, *History of Deerfield,* vol. 1, 231. This attack on Deerfield set off a large diplomatic *contretemps* between Massachusetts and New York, for the two Indians who were arrested for these murders were Mohawks.

Given how critical these eastern Iroquois were to the entire English war effort, New York strove desperately not to offend their native allies. Ultimately the Indians were declared not guilty—but the case was extremely difficult. For a detailed study of the case, see Richard I. Melvoin, "New England Outpost" (Ph.D. thesis, University of Michigan, 1983), 397–405.

47. *MA* 30:336–337, 70:216.
48. Letter of Samuel Partridge, 1 August 1693, in *Mass. A&R* (1693–1694) 7:396.
49. *Mass. A&R* (1693–1694), 7:390.
50. General Court order of 3 March 1694. While Deerfield's situation was special, it was not unique: York, Kittery, and Wells, all outposts in Maine, received the same abatement. *Mass. A&R* (II of Appendix) (1692–1702), 7:33, 38.
51. Sheldon, *History of Deerfield*, vol. 1, 243–244; Richard E. Birks, "Hannah Beaman," in *PVMA Proc.* 6:496–513.
52. Letter of John Pynchon to Secretary Addington in Boston, 3 December 1694, in "Pynchon Family Papers," PVMA MSS.
53. Letter of John Pynchon to Governor Phips, 13 March 1695, in Greenough Collection, "Photostats, 1695–1697," MHS.
54. *Mass. A&R*, 7 (II of Appendix) (1692–1702):68, 462; *MA* 2:230, 231.
55. *MA* 30:368b.
56. *Mass. A&R*, 7:113.
57. *Colonial Records of Connecticut*, 1689–1706, 179.
58. *Mass. A&R*, 7:530–531; *MA* 30:406–408.
59. *Mass. A&R*, 7:460–464; *MA* 2:233–236, 30:368a.
60. *Mass. A&R*, 7:530–531.
61. Payment for killing or taking Indians had existed since the beginning of King William's War, but now the bounties increased. *Mass. A&R*, 7:116.
62. *MA* 30:381.
63. *DTB*, 28, 61, 61a.
64. *Mass. A&R*, 7:185–186.
65. *Mass. A&R*, 7:592.
66. Letter of John Pynchon to Massachusetts Council, 18 July 1698, in *Mass. A&R*, 7:605.
67. Richter, "Ordeal," 308.
68. Jennings, *Ambiguous Iroquois*, 195.
69. Jennings, *Ambiguous Iroquois*, 205–206, Richter, "Ordeal," 337–338. Jennings estimates a reduction in fighting men from a total of roughly 2570 in 1689 to some 1230 by 1700. Richter estimates a drop from an original 1600–2000 down to 1200.
70. See Richter, "Ordeal," ch. 7.
71. Richter, "Ordeal," 303.
72. This summary comes particularly from Richter, "Ordeal," pt. 4 and esp. 402–426, and from Jennings, *Ambiguous Iroquois*, 207–210.
73. Inez Fannie Kelso, "The Frontier Policy of the Massachusetts Bay Colony" (master's thesis, University of Chicago, 1913), 19; Leach, *Frontier*, 113.
74. Sylvester Judd, *History of Hadley* (1905; rpt. Sommersworth, New Hampshire: New Hampshire Publishing Company, 1976), 230–231.
75. PVMA MSS—Smith Family Papers. Testimonies of Sarah Smith, Ebenezer Stebbins, and Henry White, taken in Hatfield, 4 August 1694.

76. PVMA MSS—Smith Family Papers; Samuel Sewall, *Diary*, August 1698, p. 484; Hampshire County Court House Mss. 3718, 3807, 4310.
77. John Williams, *"Warnings to the Unclean"* (Boston: Samuel Green, 1699) (preached at Springfield, 25 August 1698), *passim*.

8. The Wheel Turns Again: Deerfield and Queen Anne's War

1. Although not critical to this work, the issue of why Louis acted as he did has led to considerable historical debate. See, for example, G.M. Trevelyan, *England Under Queen Anne: Blenheim* (London and New York: Longman, Green and Co., 1930); Mark A. Thomson, "Louis XIV and the Origins of the War of the Spanish Succession," in Ragnild Hatton and J.S. Bromley, ed., *William III and Louis XIV: Essays 1680–1720 by and for Mark A. Thomson* (Toronto: University of Toronto Press, 1968).
2. See Chapter 7 of this book and also Allen W. Trelease, *Indian Affairs in Colonial New York: The Seventeenth Century* (Ithaca, N.Y.: Cornell University Press, 1960), esp. 240ff.; George T. Hunt, *The Wars of the Iroquois: A Study of Intertribal Trade Relations* (Madison: University of Wisconsin Press, 1940); W.J. Eccles, "The Fur Trade and Eighteenth Century Imperialism," *WMQ* 40 (no. 3, July 1983):341–362.
3. See Richard Aquila, *The Iroquois Restoration: Iroquois Diplomacy on the Canadian Frontier, 1701–1754* (Detroit: Wayne State University Press, 1983), 16 and *passim*.
4. See Francis H. Hammang, *The Marquis de Vaudreuil: New France at the Beginning of the Eighteenth Century* (Louvain: Bibliotheque de L'Universite, 1938).
5. *Mass. A&R* 7 (vol. 1 of Appendix) (1692–1714), ch. 3; *Backgrounds of Selective Service*, 104; John Shy, "A New Look at Colonial Militia," *WMQ* 20 (no. 2, April 1963):175–185; Jack S. Radabaugh, "The Military System of Colonial Massachusetts, 1690–1740" (Ph.D. thesis, University of Southern California, 1965), ch. 10.
6. Radabaugh, "Military System," ch. 3—although his figures seem high.
7. The measure of the Deerfield fort comes from *MA* 70:649; *DTB*, 24–25, 28, 67.
8. Massachusetts Council, 2 July 1702, in *Calendar of State Papers—Colonial* (hereafter known as *CSP-C*), J.W. Fortesque, ed., vol. 20 (London, 1912), 440.
9. 27 October 1703 petition of Samuel Partridge to General Court, found in *MA* 70:649.
10. *DTB*, 24, 25, 68a.
11. Letter of Joseph Dudley to Fitz-John Winthrop, Boston, 27 May 1703, in "The Winthrop Papers," Massachusetts Historical Society Collections, 6th series, vol. 3 (hereafter known as "Winthrop Papers"), 129–130.
12. Fitz-John Winthrop to Joseph Dudley, New London, 9 June 1703, "Winthrop Papers," 131.
13. Dudley to Winthrop, Boston, 16 August 1703, "Winthrop Papers," 139.
14. Fitz-John Winthrop to John Chester, 12 August 1703; Joseph Dudley to Winthrop, 16 August 1703; John Chester to Winthrop, 16 August 1703—all in "Winthrop Papers," 138–147.

15. *NYCD* 4:1060–1062, 1069–1072.
16. William Whiting to Fitz-John Winthrop, 25 September 1703, "Winthrop Papers," 156.
17. This account was given in Stephen Williams, *What Befell Stephen Williams in his Captivity*, George Sheldon, ed. (Greenfield, Mass.: Pocumtuck Valley Memorial Assoc., 1889), Appendix.
18. *DTB*, 71.
19. Samuel Partridge to Governor Dudley and the General Court, 27 October 1703, in Sheldon, *History of Deerfield*, vol. 1, 288.
20. Winthrop to Dudley, 4 November 1703, "Winthrop Papers," 160.
21. *MA* 11:188.
22. *Mass. A&R* 1 (1692–1714):549.
23. Radabaugh, "Military Systems," ch. 13; Shy, "A New Look," 178.
24. Winthrop to Dudley, 21 October 1703, in Sheldon, *History of Deerfield*, vol. 1, 288–289.
25. Solomon Stoddard to Dudley, 22 October 1703, in John Demos, ed., *Remarkable Providences* (New York: George Braziller, 1972), 312–313.
26. *Mass. A&R* 8 (III of Appendix):1703–1707, and Notes, 350.
27. This is clear from the patterns of attacks that this author has studied and charted through three wars in the Connecticut valley: King Philip's War of 1675–1676, King William's of 1688–1698, and Queen Anne's of 1702–1713. Between 1675 and 1698, 57 of 59 attacks took place between March and November; in Queen Anne's War, 28 of 29.
28. John Pynchon to Secretary Addington in Boston, Springfield, 3 December 1694, in PVMA MSS—Pynchon Family Papers.
29. Partridge to Winthrop, 21 February 1704, "Winthrop Papers," 170–171; Massachusetts' 20 soldiers sent to Deerfield were noted by Isaac Addington to Winthrop, 6 March 1704, "Winthrop Papers," 180.
30. The issue of the exact number of French and Indians on the raid at Deerfield is difficult to pin down. The clearest French account, coming in a 17 November 1704 report from Canadian governor Vaudreuil to French minister Pontchartrain, puts the group at "nearly two hundred men." (*NYCD* 9 [Paris]:762.) Charlevoix's history of New France speaks similarly of a force sent out of 250 men. (See Sheldon, *History of Deerfield*, vol. 1, 294.) Yet is that a total or merely the number of French? Deerfield's venerable nineteenth-century historian George Sheldon opts for the latter and, taking other accounts of the event, adds 140 Indians to get a total war party of 340, with the French outnumbering the Indians. And this is not impossible. A report made just one week after the attack by Connecticut's William Whiting to his governor, Fitz-John Winthrop, estimated the enemy at "between 3 or 4 hundred, the one halfe or more being French." (4 March 1704, "Winthrop Papers," 176.) That so many—and such a large percentage—of French would take part in such a raid is highly unusual, but it is not impossible: The winter 1690 raid on Schenectady was made by 114 French and 96 Indians. (*NYCD* 3:708.) Still, more common, and more likely here, is that the party that struck Deerfield numbered "20 or 30 French," as New York Colonel Robert Quarry reported to the Lords of Trade on 30 May 1704. (*NYCD* 4:1083.) What makes this especially plausible here is the extremely limited role the French are given in the handful of firsthand accounts of the raid.

31. This likely route is based on the path that the French and Indians took back up to New France. (Whether they started from Montreal, Quebec, or some other site is not clear. Most likely since the Abenaki and Caughnawaga Indians were so vital to the mission, they left from the town of Caughnawaga or the St. Francis mission. Their "drop site" above Deerfield was roughly 2 miles from where the West River joins the Connecticut, in present-day Brattleboro, Vermont.

32. De Rouville's leadership is confirmed in a letter of Vaudreuil to Pontchartrain, 17 November 1703, in *NYCD* 9:762. The family's background comes from "Hertel de Rouville," in C. Alice Baker, *True Stories of New England Captivities* (Greenfield, Mass.: E.A. Hall, 1897), 313ff.

33. The "best guess" of 291 citizens comes from George Sheldon's painstaking reconstruction of the town's population; my own work confirms the number within about 10 people. The fact of merely 10 houses inside the fort—an important detail to recall—comes from the 22 October 1703 letter of John Williams to Governor Dudley, in which he lists the fort as being 206 rods around and containing "but 10 house lots in the fort." See Sheldon, *History of Deerfield*, vol. 1, 288–289.

34. Williams's wonderfully cryptic term comes from his famous captivity narrative, *The Redeemed Captive,* first published in 1706 after his return from Canada, and reprinted numerous times thereafter. The most recent printing came in a critical text edition, William Clark, ed. (Amherst: University of Massachusetts Press, 1976), see 144. Cornbury's harsh words come from *NYCD* 4:1099. The military report comes out of the "Winthrop Papers," and is also cited in Sheldon, *History of Deerfield*, vol. 1, 302.

35. Whiting to Winthrop, 4 March 1704, "Winthrop Papers," 176; Williams, *Redeemed Captive*, 44.

36. This firsthand "Account of Y^e Destruction at Derefd, Feb^r 29, 1703/4," found in the "Winthrop Papers" in the Massachusetts Historical Society, can also be found in Sheldon, *History of Deerfield*, vol. 1, 302–303.

37. Williams, *Redeemed Captive*, 44–45.

38. Governor Dudley to Council of Trade and Plantations, 20 April 1704, *CSP-C* 22:99–102.

39. "An Account of ye Destruction," MHS; Sheldon, *History of Deerfield*, vol. 1, 302–303. Williams also speaks of the bravery at Stebbins's house in *The Redeemed Captive*, 45.

40. Sheldon's house, known thereafter as "the old Indian house," survived until the 1840s and was the last building that survived the massacre to fall. When it was finally torn down, the great door, the hole from the hatchet marks still untouched, became a local treasure and is to this day on display in Deerfield, at the Memorial Hall Museum of the Pocumtuck Valley Memorial Assoc.

41. "An Account of ye Destruction"; Williams, *Redeemed Captive*.

42. C. Alice Baker, "Ensign John Sheldon," *PVMA Proc.* 1:414–415; "An Account of ye Destruction"; a 1736 petition of the veterans of the "meadow fight" of 29 February 1704, found in *MA* 2:311–312.

43. The comment about courage comes from Whiting to Winthrop, 4 March 1704, "Winthrop Papers," 176. Accounts of the meadow fight can be found in "An Account of ye Destruction"; Williams, *Redeemed Captive*, 45; Stephen Williams, *What Befell Stephen Williams*, 5; 1736 petition of meadow

fight veterans, in *MA* 2:311–312; 31 May 1704 petition of "the Company who encountered the ffrench & Indians at Deerfield febr:29, 1703," in *Mass. A&R*, 351; *MA* 71:46.

44. The group included 51 adults—26 men and 25 women—and 58 children under the age of 18. Exact counts of dead, wounded, and captured are difficult. The best records come from Sheldon, *History of Deerfield*, vol. 1, 304–305, and Stephen Williams's "Account." The most careful recent work with these data, and that on which this author is most relying, is from Ann McCleary, "The Child Against the Devil" (unpublished Historic Deerfield Summer Fellowship paper, 1975), App. II.

45. This itemized, family-by-family "inventory" comes from Fitz-John Winthrop's "Table of Losses."

46. This higher number is supported by three firsthand accounts of the battle. Two Deerfield soldiers, Jonathan Wells and Ebenezer Wright, reported seeing "many dead bodies and. . .manifest prints in the snow"; an account sent by valley soldiers to Connecticut Governor Winthrop estimated "about 50 men, & 12 or 15 wounded" who, it was thought, "will not see Canada againe"; and John Williams himself commented that, on the first day of his captivity, he "observed after this fight no great insulting mirth, as. . .expected; and saw many wounded persons." Wells and Wright, petition to the General Court, 31 May 1704, in *MA* 71:46; Williams, *Redeemed Captive*, 46–47; "An Account of yᵉ Destruction"; Sheldon, *History of Deerfield*, vol. 1, 303.

47. "An Account," in Sheldon, *History of Deerfield*, vol. 1, 303.

48. Ibid.

49. The phrase is Francis Parkman's, and comes at the beginning of his famous retelling of "The Sack of Deerfield," in his volume *Half Century of Conflict*. (Also found excerpted in *The Parkman Reader*, S.E. Morison, ed. [Boston: Little, Brown, 1955], 371.)

50. That surprise attack, by roughly the same size French and Indian force marching from Canada, resulted in 60 English dead and 27 captured. (*NYCD* 3:708.)

51. In fact, every one of the 29 recorded depredations in the Connecticut valley between 1703 and 1712 involved the element of surprise. See Chapters 4 and 7 of this book. In Richard I. Melvoin, "Strategy and Savagery: A Study of the Nature of War in the Connecticut Valley of Massachusetts, 1675–1715" (unpublished University of Michigan seminar paper), I reported that almost all attacks were "sneak attacks, surprise raids"—even when the Indians fought in large, massed forces.

52. One loose piece in the Deerfield puzzle is the actual number of French that participated in the raid and the role they played. Estimates of the number have ranged from 20 or 30 out of 200 soldiers total to 200 out of 340. The latter number, claimed by George Sheldon, is unlikely: Only in the Schenectady raid have I found record of an actual majority of French in an attack. (*NYCD* 3:708.) More likely is a number like 40 out of 200. For one thing, most accounts of French fighting alongside Indians accord them only "support" status. The French provided the supplies, arms, ammunition. They might have helped with general plans, but there is no sense that they were the commanders and the Indians their foot soldiers. Rather, the Indians often carried out the raid with the French simply supporting or

observing. (See, for example, Colonel James Smith, *A Treatise on the Mode and Manner of Indian War* . . . [Paris, Kentucky: Joel R. Lyle, 1812] 1–6.) Second, in Deerfield's case any large number of French seems unlikely because the firsthand accounts of the attack speak so little of them. That Rouville was in charge seems clear. Yet except for reference to a French officer killed by gunfire near the Stebbins house, the French do not enter into the story at all. John Williams's house was attacked by 20 Indians; in the meadows fight, the settlers chase Indians; even narratives of the journey to Canada are almost entirely about Indians. The only way I can see Sheldon's numbers so high is that he took the French account of "two hundred men" and assumed them to be Frenchmen, then took other accounts which suggested roughly 140 Indians or a total force of 300 to 400, and made his totals from there.

53. "Avec Les Sauvages en 1701," *Le Bulletin des Recherches Historiques* (organ du bureau des archives de la province de Quebec, Pierre-Georges Roy, directeur) (hereafter known as *Recherches Historiques*) 38 (1932):40–45.
54. Letter of Vaudreuil to Pontchartrain, 14 November 1703, in *NYCD* 9:744.
55. *NYCD* 9:762, 758.
56. "Conseil Entre les Sauvages Abenakis de Roessek et M. Le Marquis de Vaudreuil," A Quebec, Le 13 Juin 1704, in *Recherches Historiques* 39 (1933):310–311.
57. See *NYCD* 9:746; "Paroles des Sauvages au Gouverneur de Vaudreuil avec ses Reponses," 14 November 1703, *Recherches Historiques* 39 (1933):163–176; *NYCD* 9:744; 19 October 1705, Quebec, *NYCD* 9:766.
58. Extract of a letter of Jacques Vaultier, 1 January 1677, in *JR* 143:231ff.
59. Reports from the Connecticut valley indicated that some of its Indians fled there; whether any Pocumtucks or River Indians did is uncertain. *JR* 143:233.
60. The prices paid for Stephen and John Williams are discussed in Stephen's *What Befell* . . . and John's *The Redeemed Captive*.
61. "Le Gouverneur de Vaudreuil et Les Abenaquis," Quebec, 14 September 1706, *Recherches Historiques* 39 (1933):572.
62. There are two more possible reasons for the attack on Deerfield which have become local legend over the years. Neither one is true, I believe. However, they are worth mentioning. The first concerns the "St. Regis Bell." The story goes that a bell had been sent to the French Indians near Montreal, but that the English intercepted it and took it to Boston. Then the people of Deerfield acquired the bell and brought it home with them, thereby setting up revenge and regaining the bell as the impetus behind the attack. A good tale, it is utterly without substantiation.

   The second story is more enticing. In an essay called "New Tracks in an Old Trail," *PVMA Proc.* 4:11–28, George Sheldon examined the story of the captured French pilot Jean Baptiste and his "trade" for Reverend John Williams in 1706 (discussed in this chapter). Looking at various pieces of information. Sheldon theorized that Baptiste was so important to the French that they engineered the whole attack specifically so that they could capture someone prominent enough to force the English to give Baptiste up. That man was John Williams. Sheldon is on target about the actual Baptiste-Williams exchange. However, the idea of *planning* the raid for Williams's capture is unsupported.

63. Samuel Sewall, *Diary*, M. Halsey Thomas, ed. (New York: Farrar, Straus & Giroux, 1973), vol. 2, 498.

64. *MA* 108:15; *Mass. A&R*, Province Laws, 1703–1704, Notes, 328.

65. *Mass. A&R* 8 (1703–1707):40; *MA* 122:202.

66. *Mass. A&R* 8 (1703–1707):50–52.

67. Timothy Edwards, in "The Black Book" (Miscellaneous Documents), PVMA MSS.

68. Dudley to Winthrop, 6 March 1704, "Winthrop Papers," 178–179; *Mass. A&R*, Province Laws, 1703–1704, Notes, 329; House Resolution of 10 March 1703/1704, in *MA* 71:7; Joseph Dudley, 21 April 1704, in Parkman Papers, vol. 36 ("Public Record Office"), 13, in MHS; Governor Dudley to Council of Trade and Plantations, 10 March 1705, *CSP-C* 22 (1704–1705):444–445; 2 October 1706, *CSP-C* 23:232–233. In fact, the same phrase "from Deerfield to Wells" is used in both letters.

69. *Mass. A&R*, Province Laws (1703–1707), Notes, 328.

70. 20 June 1704, cited in C. Alice Baker, "The Adventures of Baptiste, Part II," in *PVMA Proc.* 4:459.

71. *Mass. A&R* 8:42.

72. Dudley to Winthrop, 30 March 1704, "Winthrop Papers," 188.

73. *Mass. A&R* 8:31–32, 38–39, 44. While it is not clear that anyone ever received a full £100 for a scalp, there is evidence that men received the £40. See, for example, *Mass A&R* 8 (Notes):462.

74. *Mass. A&R* 8:54; Addington to Winthrop, "Winthrop Papers," 191–192.

75. "Town Records/Miscellaneous," PVMA MSS; *Mass. A&R* 8:116.

76. Johannes Schuyler to Winthrop, 24 April 1704, "Winthrop Papers," 194.

77. 14 June 1704, *Mass. A&R* 8:67–68.

78. William Andrew Pencak, "Massachusetts Politics in War and Peace, 1676–1776" (Ph.D. dissertation, Columbia University, 1978), ch. 1, 2, 3. Pencak claims that with Queen Anne's War came cooperation; without it, or other colonial wars, Massachusetts government was riddled by faction and contention.

79. 23 February 1704, *Acts of the Privy Council of England, Colonial Series*, W.L. Grant, James Munro, Almeric W. Fitzroy, eds. (Hereford, 1910), vol. 2 (1680–1720), 458.

80. "Winthrop Papers," 180–181, 195–197, 222–223, and *passim*.

81. Partridge to Winthrop, 13 March 1704, "Winthrop Papers," 183–184; Winthrop to Cornbury, 22 April 1704, "Winthrop Papers," 192; Winthrop to Connecticut Council of War, 23 April 1704, "Winthrop Papers," 193.

82. Col. Robert Quarry to Council of Trade and Plantations, 30 May 1704, *CSP-C* 2:134–140; *NYCD* 4:1083.

83. Petition of Jonathan Wells for the townsmen of Deerfield (no date) (read in the House of Representatives, 6 September 1705), in *Mass. A&R* 8 (Notes):536; *MA* 71:166.

84. Partridge to Winthrop, 13 March 1704, in "Winthrop Papers," 182; Addington to Winthrop, 6 March 1704, "Winthrop Papers," 180.

85. "Winthrop Papers," 183.

86. *Mass. A&R* 8 (Notes):536.

87. William Whiting to Fitz-John Winthrop, 17 May 1704, "Winthrop Papers," 204.

88. Winthrop to Dudley, 18 May 1704, "Winthrop Papers," 205; Sheldon, *History of Deerfield*, vol. 1, 318–319.
89. Partridge to Winthrop, 15 May 1704, "Winthrop Papers," 200.
90. *Mass. A&R* 8:67.
91. Stephen Williams, *What Befell Stephen Williams*, Appendix, 17.
92. Whiting to Winthrop, 28 July 1704, "Winthrop Papers," 244–246; see also 248–249, 262–263.
93. Connecticut Council of War to Winthrop, 11 July 1704, "Winthrop Papers," 240.
94. *MA* 71:46–52; *Mass. A&R* 8:66–67, and Notes, 351–352; PVMA MSS Box 5-58, "Town Records—Miscellaneous," 55.
95. *Mass. A&R* 8:120, 128, e.g.
96. *MA* 113:258, 362; *Mass. A&R* 8:91, and Notes, 428.
97. Approved 1 November 1704, *Mass. A&R* 8:84, and Notes, 404–405.
98. *Mass. A&R* 8:104.
99. For the last century, local Deerfield historians and descendants of the captives of the 1704 raid have poured through endless sources, learning more about the fate of the captives. While I honor their work collectively here, I think it inappropriate to devote too much space to these stories within the context of this work. For this reason, while examining much of the material, I have tried to synthesize and summarize the dramatic stories of these 109 people.
100. The wonderful depth and detail here, and hereafter, come from two participants' accounts: Stephen Williams, *What Befell Stephen Williams*, and John Williams's *The Redeemed Captive*. This initial detail comes from *The Redeemed Captive*, 47.
101. Stephen Williams, *What Befell . . .* , 5–7; John Williams, *Redeemed Captive*, 49.
102. John Williams, *Redeemed Captive*, 52–53.
103. John Williams, *Redeemed Captive*, 47, 53–55.
104. John Williams, *Redeemed Captive*, 55–57.
105. A fine overall summary of the treks of both John and Stephen Williams comes from Samuel Carter, "The Route of the French and Indian Army that Sacked Deerfield . . . on Their Return March . . . ," *PVMA Proc.* 2:126–151.
106. The firsthand account of this adventure is wonderfully told in Stephen Williams, *What Befell. . . .* It is rich in giving the reader a vivid sense of the food, work, pain, fear, Indians, and French that young Williams lived with. The trek is also nicely summarized in Carter, "The Route," 126–151.
107. John Williams, *Redeemed Captive*, 69.
108. John Williams, *Redeemed Captive*, esp. 62–63, 74. Williams had a vested interest in telling the story one way, since this book was at least in part a religious tract. Still, the stories remain impressive.
109. John Williams, *Redeemed Captive*, 86–106. Given Williams's fierce, unbending response to this horrible "failure" of converting to Catholicism, especially when the "criminal" was his own son, it is tempting to speculate on whether Samuel Williams ever recovered. He reportedly saw the error of his ways and returned to the fold, yet after his redemption did not settle down. Rather, he moved about, working on exchanges of French prisoners

(since he had learned the "French tongue,"), and died in 1713 of unknown causes, at the age of just 23. Whether he and his father were ever reconciled is unknown. See Sheldon, *History of Deerfield*, vol. 1, 377.

110. Proposals went back and forth between Montreal and Boston for many months in 1705, a period during which the war almost ceased in North America. For a copy of the treaty, see *Mass. A&R* 8 (Notes):541–543.

111. John Williams, *Redeemed Captive*, 76.

112. PVMA MSS, Sheldon Family Papers, 1705; Sheldon, *History of Deerfield*, vol. 1, 327–328.

113. John Sheldon to Remembrance Sheldon, 1 April 1705, in Sheldon, *History of Deerfield*, vol. 1, 328; PVMA MSS, Sheldon Family Papers.

114. *PVMA Proc.* 1:417. Much of the information pertaining to the redemption of the captives is found in or confirmed by C. Alice Baker's wonderfully researched piece, "Ensign John Sheldon," 417–431.

115. Dudley himself acknowledged that "it was doubtful if those letters found safe conveyance." Dudley to Massachusetts Council, 13 December 1704, in *PVMA Proc.* 1:417.

116. *PVMA Proc.* 1:417–419.

117. 21 April 1705, in "Winthrop Papers," 296.

118. Williams, *Redeemed Captive*, 79–80.

119. Some Boston officials did not think Sheldon suitable for the task, labeling him "a Country farmer who was not Master of the [French] language nor of Address suitable" to being an envoy. However, Sheldon again quickly succeeded in his mission. *Mass. A&R* 8:613.

120. Williams, *Redeemed Captive*, 108.

121. *Mass. A&R* 8 (Notes):613; entry of 11 August 1706, in Cotton Mather, *Diary*, 567. These freed captives included, of course, both Deerfield and non-Deerfield people.

122. Williams, *Redeemed Captive*, 48.

123. Williams, *Redeemed Captive*, 68.

124. Livingston to Winthrop, 20 June 1705, "Winthrop Papers," 297.

125. Petition of 27 June 1705 to Governor Dudley, in *MA* 71:152–155. C. Alice Baker wrote extensively of this colorful French figure and the role he played in Deerfield's story in "The Adventures of Baptiste," pt. 1 and 2, *PVMA Proc.* 4:342–357, 450–477.

126. Sewall, *Diary* 2:549.

127. 8 August 1706, *Mass. A&R* 8:185.

128. Williams, *Redeemed Captive*, 112–113; Cotton Mather, *Diary*, 575. Williams claims the date of departure as 25 October; the *Boston News-Letter* reported that it was the 29th.

129. See James Axtell, "The White Indians of Colonial America," *WMQ* 32 (no. 1, January 1975):55–88; J. Norman Heard, *White into Red: A Study of the Assimilation of White Persons Captured by Indians* (Metchen, N.Y.: Scarecrow Press, 1973).

130. Williams, *Redeemed Captive*, 108.

131. Statistics are from McCleary, "Child against the Devil." Heard, *White over Red*, makes the claim of 12 and 14 as the key ages, at least for the Indians. That the ages roughly match passage into puberty is probably not accidental.

132. *PVMA Proc.* 3:66ff., 6:330ff.

133. Williams, *Redeemed Captive*, 66–67.
134. *MA* 2:433, 466, 633–634. The 1707 incident is also cited in Nobles and Zanov, ed., *Excerpts from the Judd Manuscript*, 544.
135. Eunice's story, tragic and romantic, is justifiably well studied. See C. Alice Baker, "Eunice Williams," *PVMA Proc.* 1:18–37; Alexander P. Medlicott, "Return to this Land of Light: A Plea to an Unredeemed Captive," *New England Quarterly* 38, No. 2 (June 1965):202–216.
136. At the same time, the costs of redeeming the captives had been high: Sheldon's 1706 mission alone cost Massachusetts over £522. The General Court also gave 20 shillings to each captive to help them as they readjusted. (*Mass. A&R* 8:630, 203; Williams, *Redeemed Captive*, 112.)
137. Cotton Mather, *Diary*, 567–568. The 40-page volume also included some poems of the captives and a compendium of some of their "remarkable and memorable deliverances."
138. Cotton Mather, *Good Fetch'd Out of Evil* (Boston: B. Green, 1706), 8ff.; Mather, *Diary*, 568.
139. Mather, *Diary*, 575; Sewall, *Diary* 2:555, 557.
140. 30 November 1706, *DTB*, 74.
141. Isaac Chauncey, *A Blessed Manumission of Christ: A Sermon Delivered at the Funeral of John Williams* . . . (Boston, 1734), 28.
142. *Mass. A&R* 8:209.
143. 9 January 1706/1707, *Boston News-Letter*, no. 144; excerpted in *Mass. A&R* 8:664; *DTB*, 74.
144. Sewall, *Diary* 2:562–563; *Mass. A&R* 8:215. The sermon Williams preached for the General Court on March 6, 1707, was entitled *God in the Camp;* it, too, was soon published.
145. In the middle of 1706, when Choat petitioned for more help, the Assembly complied, doubling their support to £40, while also ordering Deerfield's inhabitants to cover Choat's expenses for the previous year. (*Mass. A&R* 8:180–181, 191, 404–405, 610–611, 625; *MA* 11:211, 213; *MA* 122:275.)
146. *MA* 113:412; *Mass. A&R* 8:235, 718–719.
147. *MA* 11:231; *Mass. A&R* 8:242, 756.
148. Stephen Williams, *What Befell* . . . , Appendix, 17–18.
149. Stephen Williams, *What Befell* . . . , 18–19. Hinsdale finally did come back in 1712, after a redemption which took him from New France to Europe before it was over.
150. *NYCD* 5:85–86, 9:831.
151. These data were compiled from numerous local sources, and represent minimum numbers of casualties (since different sources gave such a wide range of casualty figures).
152. *Mass. A&R* 9:215; *CSP-C* 26 (1711–1712), item No. 375.

9. The Frontier Moves On:
Survivors and a New Deerfield, 1704–1729

1. This calculation and many of those following are based on genealogical tables and charts constructed for Deerfield from a number of sources. These include the Deerfield town book; Hampshire County probate, court, and deed records; PVMA manuscripts, especially Family Papers; Sheldon, *History of Deerfield*, vol. 2, Genealogy; and Deerfield Vital Records to

1850. I consider this population estimate of 214 to be on the low side, since it excludes itinerants and those whom the records relegate to the periphery of town affairs.

2. Ideas and data about age of returnees are from McCleary, "The Child"; David Buchanan, "The Population Shift in Deerfield . . . after 1704" (unpublished paper, Deerfield, 1982), 5.

3. PVMA MSS—Bardwell Family Papers; Sheldon, *History of Deerfield*, vol. 2, 58.

4. *DTB*, 78–87; Sheldon, *History of Deerfield*, vol. 2, 329–333.

5. *DTB*, 78–87. For a fuller explanation of this pattern of town meetings, see Chapter 6 of this book.

6. Noted in the home-lot description of Joseph Severance, bought from Martin Kellogg, 3 April 1710, in HCDeeds, Book C, 565–566.

7. 6 June 1712, in *Mass. A&R* 9:238; 3 November 1710, in *MA* 9:148; *MA* 11:367.

8. Only two new house lots were granted between 1704 and 1729. See *DTB*, *passim.*; Sweeney, "Children of the Covenant," 23–25. The only exception here is settlement of the Green River lands, discussed below.

9. Migration was exclusively a Connecticut valley affair during this period. Of the 20 men known to have left Deerfield between 1704 and 1729 (out of 95 who appear at any time in the town records), *every one* moved within the Connecticut valley—5 as far as Connecticut (the farthest away to Wallingford), the rest staying within Massachusetts. Similarly, of Deerfield's new residents whose origins are known, 7 men and 3 women came from neighboring Hatfield, 1 man and 1 woman from Northampton, and just 1 woman from as far as Springfield and 1 man from Connecticut. When it came to migration, Boston and the bay were not part of Deerfield's orbit.

10. See extended discussion in Chapter 5 of this book.

11. This contrasts most sharply with one study which follows a town over time, Plymouth, where the average actually declined over four quarter-century periods, from 27.0 to 24.6. The one place with which it compares closely in a rise is Andover, where prospective scarcity was apparently a factor. Significantly, the average age at marriage of sons who purchased lands from their fathers in early 1700s Andover was 28.4. See Demos, *A Little Commonwealth*, Appendix, Table IV, 193; Greven, *Four Generations*, 134–135.

12. Deerfield's 1729 average was 5.5 children per family, well above previous Deerfield averages of 5.2 in 1675, 4.5 in 1688, and 4.7 in 1704. It also stands well beyond the averages of two young New England towns also measured at a point in time: 1648 Dedham's average of 4.1 and 1687 Bristol's average of 3.3. See Lockridge, "Dedham," 138ff.; Demos, "Bristol," 45.

13. Robert Breck, "A Century Sermon," Appendix in John Williams, *The Redeemed Captive*, John Taylor, ed. (Greenfield: Thomas Dickinson, 1802), 244. Concerning the 1690 epidemic, see Chapter 7 of this book.

14. *DTB*, 81–82, 90–91, 95–96, 99–101, 118; *DTB*, 80–95; *DTB*, 78–80, 103.

15. The minister was Joseph Willard. W.H. Taft, "Address," *PVMA Proc.* 1:169–189; *Mass. A&R* 9:332.

16. J.H. Temple, "Address," *PVMA Proc.* 1:114–140; *Mass. A&R* 9:336.

17. *Mass. A&R* 9:338—Westfield and Rutland; 9:363–364—Brookfield; 9:391—Mendon/Sherburn; 9:422—Swampfield.

18. One proposal from Hampshire County suggested a road "for carts or Waggons. . .from Marlborough to Springfield & from Brookfield to Hadley." (4 June 1715, *Mass. A&R* 9:392.)

19. "Report" (Field Meeting), *PVMA Proc.* 2:364–381.

20. HCProbate 3:199; Doubleday, transcr., "Deerfield Inventories," 36–60.

21. HCDeeds, Book B, 114.

22. HCDeeds, Book B, 408–409, Book C, 565–566, 570, 600–601, Book D, 442.

23. On house-lot values, see HCDeeds, Book C, 130–131, 565–566, 570, 600–601. On farmland values, see HCDeeds, Book C, 434–435, Book D, 200, 202; PVMA MSS—Wright Family Papers.

24. HCDeeds, Book C, 389–390, 436, Book D, 155–156, Book E, 385.

25. HCDeeds, Book C, 553–554. The sale of 66 acres of Great Meadows also included a 4-acre home lot plus all rights, which I have estimated as worth £50 out of the total purchase price of £550. The 7-acre tract sold in 1720 was located in "the Neck": HCDeeds, Book C, 655.

26. PVMA MSS—Hoyt Family Papers.

27. *DTB*, 73–126.

28. The record of repairs goes back to 1708, and can be traced in the *DTB*, 79–126. The new meetinghouse planning and execution comes in *DTB*, 128–129.

29. *DTB*, 76, 109–110, 114–115.

30. While there is a risk that the six surviving inventories which come from this period may not be representative, the size and values of the estates compare well and closely with those of the period 1730–1740. In both personal and real estate, Deerfield's men died far better off than their forebears. Personal estates averaged £294 in this sample, ranging in size from £60 to £770. Real estate was also of significant value, averaging £399 (£177 without Williams).

   This wealth appears to have been only partly a function of age. While 28-year-old Matthew Clesson, Jr., died with a free estate of just £54 in 1709, 32-year-old John Sheldon, Jr., left a free estate of £283 when he died in 1713. John Williams, whose estate was four times larger than anyone else's, died at age 65, yet 77-year-old John Stebbins (whose probate included land only) left the second smallest real estate holding, at £109.

   These data are derived from HCProbate records, most of which are found in Doubleday, transcr., "Deerfield Inventories," 63–104.

31. Deerfield's late-seventeenth-century poverty stood in stark contrast to average estate values in Dedham of £294, Springfield of £326 (£209 without John Pynchon's £8400 estate), and Northampton of £395. For Dedham, see Lockridge, "Dedham," 220–223. For Springfield, see Innes, "A Patriarchal Society," 54–55. For Northampton, see Mank, "Family Structure," 131–132.

32. Deerfield's rise in wealth needs to be tempered by awareness of changes in the monetary system of Massachusetts. During Queen Anne's War the colony had felt it necessary to issue paper money, for the first time, to finance the war effort. While the new notes had the desired effect, over time they also became inflationary. The runaway inflation that ultimately

caused a crisis in Massachusetts did not come until the late 1730s and 1740s. Even by 1729, however, Massachusetts currency had fallen to half its 1712 value versus the British pound sterling. In other words, Deerfielders of 1729, while still clearly wealthier than their parents, were not quite so wealthy as the pure numbers suggest. See John J. McCusker, *Money and Exchange in Europe and America, 1600–1775* (Chapel Hill: Institute of Early American History and Culture/University of North Carolina Press, 1978), 133–141.

33. Doubleday, "Deerfield Inventories," 63–104, *passim*.

34. Elizabeth Pratt Fox, "Ceramics and Glass," in William N. Hosley, Jr., ed., *The Great River: Art and Society of the Connecticut Valley, 1630–1820* (Hartford: Wadsworth Athaneum, 1985), 415.

35. The Northampton estate of 1719 reveals debts of £71 to 32 different people, 11 of whom were in Deerfield. (16 September 1719, estate of Jonathan Patterson of Northfield, administrator is father-in-law, Deacon Eleazer Hawks of Deerfield, HCProbate 4:22.)

36. See Bettye Hobbs Pruitt, "Self-Sufficiency and the Agricultural Economy of Eighteenth Century Massachusetts," *WMQ* 41 (no. 3, July 1984):333–364.

37. Studies of generations in at least two "young" New England towns—Andover and Kent—have demonstrated that it is especially in the third generation that land pressures built significantly. See Greven, *Four Generations*, ch. 6; Grant, *Kent*, ch. 6 and esp. 98–103. The notion that Deerfield reached its first "critical land pressure" after 1715 is supported by Sweeney, "Children of the Covenant," 26.

38. See Kenneth A. Lockridge, "Land, Population and the Evolution of New England Society, 1630–1790," *Past and Present* 39 (1968):62–80.

39. The data here are compiled almost exclusively from the *DTB*.

40. Although a pure average of 7 years of service per man over 25 years yields an average of 1 year of service every 3.6 years, in fact many townsmen did not come to Deerfield until well after 1704; left before 1729; or were sons who reached adulthood after 1704. As many as 10 sons, for instance, first served the town as adults only in the 1720s.

41. The first came, in fact, in 1730 amidst a split over a new minister. (Located in the original *DTB*, no page number; see also Sweeney, "Children of the Covenant," 39.)

42. See Cook, *Fathers*, ch. 2; Lockridge, "Dedham," ch. 8.

43. Of Deerfield's 81 officeholders, 66 served as fence viewers between 1704 and 1729; 41 served as haywards. Only 6 of the 81 never served in one of these two jobs. Similar to those two tasks was the surveyor's—28 Deerfield men held this job, for an average of 2.1 years each; no one held it for more than 4 years.

44. Between 1704 and 1709, a time of small population and great stress for Deerfield, Benoni Moore served two terms and Simon Beamon three. From 1710 to 1729, though, a new constable served every year. In total, 22 Deerfield men served as constable in the 25 years after 1704.

45. Cook, *Fathers*, 36–37. Cook's definition of a "leadership pool" is not entirely clear.

46. As of 1723—as are all these figures. See proprietors list, in *DTB*, Appendix, 16–18.

47. Interestingly, both these men acquired their large holdings in proprietary rights from their parents, who had been among Deerfield's prominent founders.

48. Order of 1728 court session, in HCCourt, 1677–1728, 363. Unfortunately, records from about 1694 to 1727 appear to be lost, so it is impossible to know how long this requirement was in effect.

49. HCCourt, 1677–1728, March 1728 session (no page number).

50. HCCourt, 1677–1728, 364.

51. The General Court had three main provincial concerns during this postwar period: currency, governor-Assembly relations, and the frontier. Deerfield had no direct role in the first two issues, and as long as the frontier remained quiet, so did Massachusetts' role in Deerfield's life. (Pencak, "Massachusetts Politics," ch. 9 and esp. 143.)

52. Curiously, Deerfield then drew back. For 3 years no representative went, and while Thomas Wells served again from 1725 to 1727, Deerfield sent no representative from 1728 through at least 1734. (*Mass. A&R* 8, 9, 10, 11, *passim.*)

53. 21 July 1720, *Mass. A&R* 10:14.

54. 14 October 1723, "Lettre de Mm. de Vaudreuil et Begon au Ministre au sujet des Affaires des Abenakis," *Recherches Historiques* 41 (1935):624–629.

55. Vaudreuil to Abenaki, 1723, *Recherches Historiques* 41:624–625; Sheldon, *History of Deerfield*, vol. 1, 392–393, 403.

56. *Mass. A&R* 10:47, 54, 170, 198.

57. *Mass. A&R* 10:391–392, 459; Sheldon, *History of Deerfield*, vol. 1, 393.

58. 10 December 1723, *Mass. A&R* 10:391–392.

59. 27 December 1723, *Mass. A&R* 10:423.

60. 27 March 1724, Stoddard to Dummer, in Sheldon, *History of Deerfield*, vol. 1, 408.

61. 6 April 1724, Deerfield petition to Governor Dummer, in Sheldon, *History of Deerfield*, vol. 1, 409.

62. Stephen Williams, What Befell Stephen Williams, Appendix, 26.

63. Letters of 11 July 1724 and 1 October 1724, in *MA* 2:118, 217.

64. Sheldon, *History of Deerfield*, vol. 1, 431, 436.

65. *Mass. A&R* 10 (Province Laws, ch. 338):549–550.

66. Stoddard to Dummer, in Sheldon, *History of Deerfield*, vol. 1, 448.

67. Stephen Williams, *What Befell . . .* , 27.

68. List from Sheldon, *History of Deerfield*, vol. 1, 453, plus Samuel Dickinson, who was captured in the war. *Mass. A&R* 11:735.

69. In a flurry of activity between 1728 and 1733, Deerfield saw both Hadley and Sunderland to the south expand; a new Hampshire County township of Brimfield approved by the General Court; a "truck house" for Indian trade established above Northfield; new settlements proposed as "Ashuelot and Paquoiag," the latter just southeast of Northfield; and three new townships laid out east of the Connecticut River along the Miller's River, northeast of Deerfield. (*Mass. A&R* 11:243, 330–336, 423, 548, 758, 775–776.)

70. Akagi, *Town Proprietors*, 45–56; Sweeney, "Children of the Covenant," 26.

71. *DTB*, 90–103, *passim; DTB*, 105.

72. *DTB*, Appendix, 15–16.

73. *DTB*, Appendix, 18.

74. Landless Deerfield sons or newcomers received either two or three shares, apparently to give all residents some stake in the town and its lands. Looking at these figures by deciles, the top 10% of the population held 44% of the shares, and the bottom 10% just 2%. (*DTB*, Appendix, 16–18.)

75. By that time Green River had become the place where Deerfielders built their mills. (Sewall, *Diary* 2:829–830.)

76. *DTB*, 97, 104.

77. *DTB*, 104.

78. *DTB*, 110.

79. *DTB*, 125.

80. *DTB*, 135–136.

81. See Cook, *Fathers*, Ch. 2.

82. *DTB*, 88–89.

83. *DTB*, Appendix, 10; *DTB*, 120–122.

84. *DTB*, 89–120, *passim*.

85. *DTB*, 128–129.

86. HCCourt, 1677–1728, sessions of 29 August 1727, 20 May 1729, 26 August 1729, 236ff.

Conclusion: Deerfield and the
New England Frontier

1. Thomas Foxcroft, *Eli the Priest Dying Suddenly* (Boston: S. Gerrish, 1734), 7.

2. See Perry Miller, *The New England Mind: From Colony to Province* (Boston: Beacon, 1953), esp. ch. 28 and Epilogue, "Vale Atque Ave."

3. Isaac Chauncey, *A Blessed Manumission of Christ: A Sermon Presented at the Funeral of John Williams* . . . (Boston: D. Henchman and T. Hancock, 1734), 22.

4. *DTB*, 5 January 1730 (on microfilm—no page number).

5. *DTB*, 10 April 1732 (on microfilm—no page number).

6. Gregory H. Nobles, *Divisions Throughout the Whole: Politics and Society in Hampshire County, Massachusetts, 1740–1775* (New York: Cambridge University Press, 1983), ch. 2 and esp. 50–52.

7. *Mass. A&R*, Province Laws, 1728–1729, 330–331.

8. See Sheldon, *History of Deerfield*, vol. 1, 519–522.

9. *NYCD* 10:33, 77, 158; John Williams, *The Redeemed Captive* (1853 edition), Appendix, 162; Sheldon, *History of Deerfield*, vol. 1, 545–547.

10. *MA* 4:26.

11. PVMA MSS—Brooks Family Papers; Epaphrus Hoyt, *Antiquarian Researches* (Greenfield, 1820), 277.

12. John Adams Aiken, "The Mohawk Trail," in *PVMA Proc.* 5 (1909):333–350; *Mass. A&R*, 1733–1734, 744; Sheldon, *History of Deerfield*, vol. 1, 504–511.

13. Jerry J. Suich, "A Statistical Analysis of Deerfield, Massachusetts, 1705–1725 and 1745–1765" (Heritage Foundation paper, 1966), 19.

14. On the region's rise, see Gregory H. Nobles, "Population and Politics in Hampshire County, Massachusetts, 1740–1775" (paper presented at His-

toric Deerfield Colloquium, March 1978), 8. For example, Bernardston, located 10 miles above Deerfield and just west of Northfield, began in the 1730s as "Falls Town," a township of lands granted to participants in the "Falls Fight" of May 1676.

15. David R. Whitesell, "Population Movement and Geographical Mobility in Deerfield, Massachusetts, 1720–1820" (Historic Deerfield Summer Fellowship paper, 1974), esp. 5–13.

16. Nobles, *Divisions*, 10 and *passim*; Nobles, "Population and Politics," 14.

17. Peter B. Hirtle, "Agrarian Economy in Flux: The Agricultural History of Deerfield, 1670–1760" (Historic Deerfield Summer Fellowship paper, 1973), pt. 2; Kevin Sweeney, "From Wilderness to Arcadian Vale: Material Life in the Connecticut River Valley, 1635–1760," in Gerald W.R. Ford and William N. Hosley, ed., *The Great River: Art and Society of the Connecticut Valley, 1635–1820* (Hartford: Hartford Athaneum, 1985), 20–23.

18. Bettye Hobbs Pruitt, "Self-Sufficiency and the Agricultural Economy of Eighteenth Century Massachusetts," *WMQ* 41 (no. 3, July 1984):333–364.

19. Mary Lynn Stevens, "No Complaints: Agriculture in Deerfield, 1760–1810" (Historic Deerfield Summer Fellowship paper, 1976), 1 and *passim*.

20. John Ritchie Garrison, "Surviving Strategies: The Commercialization of Life in Rural Massachusetts, 1790–1860" (Ph.D. dissertation, University of Pennsylvania, 1985), Introduction and esp. 1.

21. Frederick Jackson Turner, "The Significance of the Frontier in American History," in *The Frontier in American History*, Ray A. Billington, ed. (1920; rpt. New York: Holt, Rinehart, 1962), 37.

22. Frederick Jackson Turner, *The Frontier in American History*, 1–66; Nobles, *Divisions*, 13–16.

23. Frederick Jackson Turner, "The First Official Frontier of the Massachusetts Bay," in *The Frontier in American History*, 65.

24. See Peter N. Carroll, *Puritanism and the Wilderness: The Intellectual Significance of the New England Frontier, 1629–1700* (New York: Columbia University Press, 1969), 109–117, 211, and *passim*; Richard Slotkin, *Regeneration through Violence: The Mythology of the American Frontier, 1600–1860* (Middletown, Ct.: Wesleyan University Press, 1973), 99.

25. See Howard Lamar and Leonard Thompson, "Comparative Frontier History," in Lamar and Thompson, ed., *The Frontier in History: North America and Southern Africa Compared* (New Haven: Yale University Press, 1981), 7; Verner Crane, *The Southern Frontier, 1673–1732* (1928; rpt. New York: W.W. Norton, 1979), xix. Lamar and Thompson have three criteria for this frontier: territory, two different cultures or societies, and a process of interaction. Deerfield has all three.

26. See HCCourt and HCDeeds, Northampton and Springfield, Mass.; see also Smith, *Colonial Justice in Western Massachusetts: The Pynchon Court Record*, *passim*.

27. This allied force was led by Deerfield's own Sergeant Williams. *MA* 224 (doc. 254):163.

28. Robert F. Berkhofer, Jr., "The North American Frontier as Process and Context," in Lamar and Thompson, *The Frontier in History*, 49.

29. Lamar and Thompson, "Comparative Frontier History," in Lamar and Thompson, *The Frontier in History*, 7ff.

30. A number of historians of early New England share this view. See James A. Henretta, "Families and Farms: *Mentalité* in Pre-Industrial America," *WMQ* 35 (no. 1, January 1978):3–32; Douglas E. Leach, *The Northern Colonial Frontier* (New York: Holt, Rinehart, 1966), esp. 208–210; Nobles, *Divisions*, ch. 1.

31. Leach, *Frontier*, 208. The common-field fence is noted in the *DTB*, Proprietors Records, 16.

32. See Henretta, "Families and Farms: *Mentalité*," in *WMQ* 35 (no. 1, January 1978):3–32.

33. At the same time, all these petitions ended in requests for aid: for the ministry, for money, for soldiers, for defense. In other words, the pleas were purposeful and thus may have been overstated.

34. Douglas Leach agrees: "Most frontiersmen accepted the French and Indian wars as a bitter condition of life in America and simply tried to carry on as best they could under difficult conditions." (*Frontier*, 122.)

35. Slotkin, *Regeneration through Violence*, 117. For further contemplation of the idea of wilderness in early New England, see Peter Carroll, *Puritanism and the Wilderness;* see also Roderick Nash, *Wilderness and the American Mind* (New Haven: Yale University Press, 1967).

36. See, for example, Williams's 1698 sermon, *Warnings to the Unclean* (Boston: Thomas Green, 1699).

37. This vision of change first retarded and then accelerated challenges the view of a steady drive toward commercialization and markets seen in William Cronon, *Changes in the Land*, ch. 4 and pp. 76–77, 167. In Deerfield, at least, the sweep was not so constant and steady.

38. Leach, *Frontier*, 210. Even here, notes Leach, changes were often "gradual, almost imperceptible." See also Henretta, "Families and Farms."

39. For example, see work by Gloria Main on poverty in the Chesapeake region. Francis Jennings's *The Ambiguous Iroquois Empire* does an excellent job of explaining inter-Indian complexities from New York through Pennsylvania and below. Main's work does not discuss the frontier, however, nor does Jennings deal in depth with the colonial frontier; his focus, properly, is on the Indians and Indian-English diplomacy. These sources notwithstanding, the indices for comparison raised in this study would need far more work than can be begun in the context of this work.

40. Crane, *The Southern Frontier*, xvii–xix, 169, and *passim*. Although Indian trade and not Puritan expansion proved the chief motive for growth in the south, there, too, the Indians often dominated colonists' lives.

41. Crane, *Southern Frontier*, 179.

42. Letter of the Earl of Bellomont to the Lords of Trade, Boston, 20 April 1700, in *NYCD* 9 (London Documents):638.

43. Fred Anderson, *A People's Army: Massachusetts Soldiers and Society in the Seven Years War* (New York: W.W. Norton, 1985), vii.

44. For example, see John Pynchon's letter to the Connecticut Council, 30 September 1675, in Judd, *Hadley*, 142–143; *Journal of the Connecticut Council*, 1 September 1675, 359. The concluding reference to different revolutions hearkens back to Gordon Wood, "Rhetoric and Reality in the American Revolution," in *WMQ*.

Selected Bibliography

Published Primary Sources

"Account of Attack on Hatfield and Deerfield . . . 1677." Bradford Series, No. 1 (privately printed). (Located at Massachusetts Historical Society, Boston, Mass.).

The Acts and Resolves, Public and Private, of the Province of Massachusetts Bay, 21 vols. Boston: Wright and Potter, 1869–1922.

Bodge, George M. *Soldiers in King Philip's War.* Boston: 1906.

Chauncey, Isaac. *A Blessed Manumission of Christ: A Sermon Presented at the Funeral of John Williams* . . . Boston: D. Henchman and T. Hancock, 1734.

Drake, Samuel G., ed. *The History of King Philip's War.* Boston: by the editor, 1862.

Drake, Samuel G., ed. *The Old Indian Chronicle.* Boston: The Antiquarian Institute, 1836.

Mr. Easton. "A Relacion of the Indyan Warre." In *Narratives of the Indian Wars, 1675–1699,* Charles H. Lincoln, ed., 1913. Reprint: New York: Barnes and Noble, 1959.

Eliot, John. "A Late and Further Manifestation of the Progress of the Gospel Amongst the Indians of New England." In *Massachusetts Historical Society Collections,* 3rd series, vol. 4.

Fortesque, J. W., ed. *Calendar of State Papers—Colonial,* vol. 20. London: 1912.

Foxcroft, Thomas. *Eli the Priest Dying Suddenly.* Boston: S. Gerrish, 1734.

Gookin, Daniel. "Historical Collections of the Indians in New England" (1674). In *Massachusetts Historical Society Collections,* 1st series, vol. 1 (1792; reprint Boston: Munroe & Francis, 1806):141–227.

Grant, W. L., Munro, James, and Fitzroy, Almeric W., eds. *Acts of the Privy Council of England, Colonial Series,* vol. 2. Hereford, England: 1910.

Hill, Donald Gleason. *Dedham Town Records,* 4 vols. Dedham, Mass.: 1886–1891.

Hoyt, Epaphrus. *Antiquarian Researches.* Greenfield, Mass.: 1820.

Hubbard, William. *A Narrative of the Indian Wars . . . to 1677,* 1677. Reprint: Stockbridge: Heman Willard, 1803.

Lincoln, Charles H., ed. *Narratives of the Indian Wars, 1675–1699,* 1913. Reprint: New York: Barnes and Noble, 1959.

Massachusetts General Court. *Proclamation of October 2, 1678.* Cambridge: Samuel Green, 1678.

Mather, Cotton. *Diary.* New York: F. Ungar, 1957.

Mather, Cotton. *Good Fetch'd Out of Evil.* Boston: B. Green, 1706.

Mather, Cotton. *Magnalia Christi Americana,* 1702. Reprint: Hartford: Silas Andrus, 1820.

Morrell, William. "Poem on New England." In *Massachusetts Historical Society Collections,* 1st series, vol. 1 (1792; reprint: Boston, Munroe & Francis, 1806):125–138.

Morton, Nathaniel. *New England's Memorial,* 1669. Reprint: Boston: Congregational Board of Publication, 1855, 6th ed.

Nobles, Gregory, and Zarov, Herbert L., eds. *Selected Papers from the Sylvester Judd Manuscripts.* Northampton, Mass.: Forbes Library, 1976.

O'Callaghan, E.B., ed. *Calendar of Historical Documents—Dutch, 1630–1664.* Albany: Weed, Parsons, and Co., 1865.

O'Callaghan, E.B., ed. *Documents Relative to the Colonial History of New York,* 15 vols. New York: Weed, Parsons, and Co., 1850–1861.

Roy, Pierre-Georges, directeur. *Le Bulletin des Recherches Historiques.* Organ du bureau des archives de la province de Quebec.

This publication includes the following sources:

"Avec Les Sauvages en 1701," vol. 38 (1932).

"Conseil Entre les Sauvages Abenakis de Roessek et M. Le Marquis de Vaudreuil," A Quebec, Le 13 Juin, 1704, vol. 39 (1933).

"Le Gouverneur de Vaudreuil et Les Abenaquis," Quebec, 14 September 1706, vol. 39 (1933).

"Lettre de Mm. de Vaudreuil et Begon au Minstre au sujet des Affaires des Abenakis," 14 October 1723, vol. 41 (1935).

"Paroles des Sauvages au Gouverneur de Vaudreuil avec ses Responses," 14 November 1703, vol. 39 (1933).

"N.S." (Nathaniel Saltonstall?). "A New and Further Narrative on the State of New-England, 1676." In *The Old Indian Chronicle,* Samuel Drake, ed. Boston: The Antiquarian Institute, 1836.

Segal, Charles N., and Stineback, David, ed. *Puritans, Indians and Manifest Destiny.* New York: G.P. Putnam's Sons, 1977.

Sewall, Samuel. *Diary,* 2 vols. M. Halsey Thomas, ed. Boston: Farrar, Straus & Giroux, 1973.

Shurtleff, Nathaniel E., ed. *Records of the Governor and Company of the Massachusetts Bay in New England, 1628–1686,* 5 vols. Boston: William White, 1853–1854.

Slotkin, Richard, and Folsom, James K., eds. *So Dreadful A Judgement: Puritan Responses to King Philip's War, 1676–1677.* Middletown, Conn.: Wesleyan University Press, 1978.

Smith, Colonel James. *A Treatise on the Mode and Manner of Indian War . . .* Paris, Kentucky: Joel R. Lyle, 1812.

Smith, Joseph H., ed. *Colonial Justice in Western Massachusetts: The Pynchon Court Record.* Cambridge: Harvard University Press, 1961.

Suffolk County Deeds, 20 vols. Boston: 1897.

Thwaites, Reuben Gold, ed. *Jesuit Relations,* 45 vols. Cleveland: The Burrows Brothers Co., 1896.

Trumbull, J. Hammond, ed. *The Public Records of the Colony of Connecticut,* 2 vols (pre-1665 and 1665–1678). Hartford: Brown and Parsons, 1850.

Williams, John. *God in the Camp.* Boston: 1707.

Williams, John. *The Redeemed Captive.* Boston: 1707. (Most recent printing is a critical text edition, William Clark, ed. Amherst: University of Massachusetts Press, 1976.)

Williams, John. *Warnings to the Unclean*. Boston: 1699.

Williams, Stephen. *What Befell Stephen Williams in His Captivity*. George Sheldon, ed. Greenfield, Mass.: Pocumtuck Valley Memorial Association, 1889.

"The Winthrop Papers." *Massachusetts Historical Society Collections*, 6th series, vol. 3. Boston: M.H.S., 1889.

Wood, William. *New England's Prospect*. London: 1634. Reprint: Boston: John Fleet, 1764.

Wright, Harry Andrew. *Indian Deeds of Hampden County*. Springfield, Mass.: privately printed, 1905.

Unpublished Primary Sources

The Boston News-Letter.

Deerfield, Massachusetts. *The Deerfield Town Book*. Town Hall, South Deerfield, Mass. (Also available on microfilm, Historic Deerfield Library, Deerfield, Mass.) (Unpublished transcription, 1670–1729, by Richard I. Melvoin.)

Doubleday, William. "Deerfield Probate Inventories Prior to the Year 1740." Historic Deerfield Library, Deerfield, Mass.

Hampshire County (Mass.) Court Records. Court Offices, Northampton and Springfield, Mass. (Also available on microfilm, Historic Deerfield Library, Deerfield, Mass.)

Hampshire County Deeds. Registry of Deeds, Springfield, Mass.

Hampshire County Probate Records. Courthouse, Springfield, Mass. (Also available on microfilm, Historic Deerfield Library, Deerfield, Mass.)

Judd, Sylvester. Manuscripts. Forbes Library, Northampton, Mass.

Massachusetts Archives. State House, Boston, Mass.

Massachusetts Council Broadside, April 9, 1677. Clements Library, University of Michigan, Ann Arbor, Mich.

Massachusetts Historical Society. Davis Papers. Boston, Mass.

Massachusetts Historical Society. Greenough Collection. Boston, Mass.

Massachusetts Historical Society. "Miscellaneous Bound, 1672–1680." Boston, Mass.

Massachusetts Historical Society. "Miscellaneous Bound, 1690–1694." Boston, Mass.

Massachusetts Historical Society. "Miscellaneous Collections." Boston, Mass.

Massachusetts Historical Society. "Papers Concerning the Attack on Hatfield and Deerfield . . . 1677." Boston, Mass.

Massachusetts Historical Society. Parkman Papers ("Public Record Office").Boston, Mass.

Northampton, Massachusetts. Northampton Town Records. Forbes Library, Northampton, Mass. (on microfilm).

Pocumtuck Valley Memorial Association. Deerfield Town Papers.

Pocumtuck Valley Memorial Association. Family Papers.

Pocumtuck Valley Memorial Association. Miscellaneous Documents.

Pynchon, John. Account Books (6 vols.). Connecticut Valley Historical Museum, Springfield, Mass.

Published Secondary Sources • Books

Akagi, Roy Hidemichi. *The Town Proprietors of the New England Colonies.*
Philadelphia: University of Pennsylvania Press, 1924.

Allen, David Grayson. *In English Ways: The Movement of Societies and the*
Transferral of English Local Law and Custom to Massachusetts Bay in
the Seventeenth Century. Chapel Hill: University of North Carolina
Press/Institute of Early American History and Culture, 1981.

Anderson, Fred. *A People's Army: Massachusetts Soldiers and Society in the*
Seven Years' War. New York: W.W. Norton and Co., 1985.

Armytage, Francis, and Tomlinson, Juliette. *The Pynchons of Springfield:*
Founders and Colonizers (1636–1702). Springfield, Mass.: Connecticut Valley Historical Museum, 1969.

Bailyn, Bernard. *Education in the Forming of American Society*, 1960. Reprint:
New York: W.W. Norton and Co., 1972.

Bailyn, Bernard. *The New England Merchants in the Seventeenth Century.*
Cambridge: Harvard University Press, 1955.

Baker, C. Alice. *True Stories of New England Captivities.* Cambridge: E.A.
Hall, 1897.

Boorstin, Daniel. *The Americans: The Colonial Experience.* New York: Vintage, 1958.

Boyer, Paul, and Nissenbaum, Stephen. *Salem Possessed.* Cambridge: Harvard University Press, 1974.

Carroll, Peter N. *Puritanism and the Wilderness: The Intellectual Significance*
of the New England Frontier, 1629–1700. New York: Columbia University Press, 1969.

Cook, Edward M., Jr. *The Fathers of the Towns: Leadership and Community*
Structure in Eighteenth Century New England. Baltimore: Johns Hopkins University Press, 1976.

Cook, Sherburne F. *The Indian Populations of New England in the Seven-*
teenth Century. Berkeley, Cal.: University of California Press, 1976.

Crane, Verner. *The Southern Frontier, 1673–1732*, 1928. Reprint: New York:
W.W. Norton and Co., 1979.

Craven, Wesley Frank. *The Colonies in Transition, 1660–1773.* New York:
Hill and Wang, 1983.

Cronon, William. *Changes in the Land.* New York: Hill and Wang, 1983.

Daniels, Bruce C. *The Connecticut Town: Growth and Development, 1635–*
1740. Middletown, Ct.: Wesleyan University Press, 1979.

Demos, John. *Entertaining Satin.* New York: Oxford University Press, 1982.

Demos, John. *A Little Commonwealth.* New York: Oxford University Press,
1970.

Eccles, W.J. *France in America.* New York: Harper and Row, 1972.

Eccles, W.J. *Frontenac: The Courtier Governor.* Toronto: McClelland and
Stewart, Ltd., 1959.

Fischer, David Hackett. *Growing Old in America.* New York: Oxford University Press, 1978.

Ford, Gerald W.R., and Hosley, William N., ed. *The Great River: Art and*
Society of the Connecticut River Valley, 1635–1820. Hartford, Ct.:
Hartford Athaneum, 1985.

Fried, Morton. *The Evolution of Political Society*. New York: Random House,
    1967.
Goubert, Pierre. *Louis XIV and Twenty Million Frenchmen*. New York: Pan-
    theon Books, 1970.
Grant, Charles. *Democracy in the Connecticut Frontier Town of Kent*. New
    York: Columbia University Press, 1961.
Grassman, Thomas. *The Mohawks and Their Valley*. Caughnawaga: Eric Hugo
    Photo. and Printing Co., 1969.
Greven, Philip J. *Four Generations: Population, Land, and Family in Colonial
    Andover, Massachusetts*. Ithaca, N.Y.: Cornell University Press, 1970.
Hammang, Francis H. *The Marquis de Vaudreuil: New France at the Begin-
    ning of the Eighteenth Century*. Louvain: Bilbioteque de L'Universite,
    1938.
Haskins, George Lee. *Law and Authority in Early Massachusetts*. New York:
    Macmillan, 1960.
Hatton, Ragnild, and Bromley, J.S. *William III and Louis XIV: Essays 1680–
    1720 by and for Mark A. Thomson*. Toronto: University of Toronto
    Press, 1968.
Heard, J. Norman. *White into Red: A Study of the Assimilation of White
    Persons Captured by Indians*. Metchen, N.Y.: Scarecrow Press, 1973.
Holland, Josiah G. *History of Western Massachusetts*. Springfield, Mass.: Samuel
    Bowles and Co., 1855.
Hunt, George T. *The Wars of the Iroquois: A Study of Intertribal Trade
    Relations*. Madison: University of Wisconsin Press, 1940.
Innes, Stephen C. *Labor in a New Land: Economy and Society in Seventeenth
    Century Springfield*. Princeton: Princeton University Press, 1983.
Jacobs, Wilbur R. *Dispossessing the American Indian*. New York: Charles
    Scribner's Sons, 1972.
Jennings, Francis. *The Invasion of America: Indians, Colonialism, and The
    Cant of Conquest*. Chapel Hill: University of North Carolina Press,
    1975.
Jennings, Francis. *The Ambiguous Iroquois Empire*. New York: W.W. Norton
    and Co., 1984.
Judd, Sylvester. *A History of Hadley*, 1905. Reprint: Somersworth, N.H.: New
    Hampshire Publishing Company, 1976.
Lamar, Howard, and Thompson, Leonard, ed. *The Frontier in History: North
    America and Southern Africa Compared*. New Haven: Yale University
    Press, 1981.
Leach, Douglas E. *Flintlock and Tomahawk: New England in King Philip's
    War*. New York: Macmillan, 1958.
Leach, Douglas E. *The Northern Colonial Frontier, 1607–1763*. New York:
    Holt, Rinehart and Winston, 1966.
Lockridge, Kenneth A. *Literacy in Colonial New England*. New York: W.W.
    Norton and Co., 1974.
Lockridge, Kenneth A. *A New England Town: The First Hundred Years*. New
    York: W.W. Norton and Co., 1970.
McCusker, John J. *Money and Exchange in Europe and America, 1600–1775*.
    Chapel Hill: University of North Carolina Press/Institute of Early
    American History and Culture, 1978.

McIntyre, Ruth. *William Pynchon: Merchant and Colonizer (1590–1662)*. Springfield, Mass.: Connecticut Valley Historical Museum, 1961.

Miller, Perry. *The New England Mind: From Colony to Province*. Boston: Beacon Press, 1953.

Miller, Perry. *The New England Mind: The Seventeenth Century*, 1939. Reprint: Cambridge: Harvard University Press, 1954.

Morgan, Edmund S. *The Puritan Dilemma: The Story of John Winthrop*. Boston: Little, Brown, 1958.

Nobles, Gregory H. *Divisions Against the Whole: Politics and Society in Hampshire County, Massachusetts, 1740–1775*. New York: Cambridge University Press, 1983.

Osgood, Herbert L. *The American Colonies in the Seventeenth Century*. New York: Macmillan, 1904.

Parkman, Francis. *England and France in North America*, vol. 6: *A Half Century of Conflict*. Boston: Little, Brown, 1902.

Pope, Franklin Leonard. *The Western Boundary of Massachusetts: A Study of Indian and Colonial History*. Pittsfield, Mass.: privately printed, 1886.

Pope, Robert G. *The Halfway Covenant: Church Membership in Puritan New England*. Princeton: Princeton University Press, 1969.

Powell, Sumner Chilton. *Puritan Village*. Middletown, Ct.: Wesleyan University Press, 1963.

Reps, John W. *Town Planning in Frontier America*. Princeton: Princeton University Press, 1969.

Russell, Howard S. *Indian New England Before the Mayflower*. Hanover: University Press of New England, 1980.

Rutman, Darrett. *Winthrop's Boston*. Chapel Hill: University of North Carolina Press, 1965.

Sheldon, George. *A History of Deerfield, Massachusetts*, 2 vols, 1895–1896. Reprint: Somersworth, N.H.: New Hampshire Publishing Co. and Pocumtuck Valley Memorial Association, 1972.

Slotkin, Richard. *Regeneration through Violence: The Mythology of the American Frontier, 1600–1800*. Middleton, Ct.: Wesleyan University Press, 1973.

Snow, Dean R. *The Archaelogy of New England*. New York: Academic Press, 1980.

Steele, I. K. *Politics of Colonial Policy: The Board of Trade in Colonial Administration, 1696–1720*. Oxford: Clarendon Press, 1968.

Swanton, John R. *Indian Tribes of North America*. Washington, D.C.: Bureau of American Ethnology, Bulletin 145, 1952.

Thomas, Peter, Innes, Stephen, and Melvoin, Richard I. *Early Settlement in the Connecticut Valley*. Deerfield, Mass.: Historic Deerfield and the Institute for Massachusetts Studies, 1984.

Tracy, Patricia J. *Jonathan Edwards, Pastor: Religion and Society in Eighteenth-Century Northampton*. New York: Hill and Wang, 1979.

Trelease, Allen W. *Indian Affairs in Colonial New York: The Seventeenth Century*. Ithaca, N.Y.: Cornell University Press, 1960.

Trevelyan, G. M. *England under Queen Anne: Blenheim*. London and New York: Longman, Green and Co., 1930.

Trumbull, James Russell. *History of Northampton*, 2 vols. Northampton, Mass.: Gazette Printing Co., 1898.

Turner, Frederick Jackson. *The Frontier in American History, 1920.* Ray A. Billington, ed. Reprint: New York: Holt, Rinehart, 1962.

Vaughan, Alden. *New England Frontier: Puritans and Indians, 1620–1675,* 1965. New York: W.W. Norton and Co., 1979, 2nd ed.

Washburn, Wilcomb. *The Indian in America.* New York: Harper and Row, 1975.

Webb, Stephen S. *1676: The End of American Independence.* New York: Alfred A. Knopf, 1984.

Whipple, Chandler. *First Encounter: The White Man and Indian in Massachusetts and Rhode Island.* Stockbridge, Mass.: The Berkshire Traveller Press, n.d.

White, Daniel, and Wells, Reuben Field. *A History of Hatfield, Massachusetts.* Springfield, Mass.: F.C.H. Gibbons, 1910.

Willoughby, Charles C. *Antiquities of the New England Indians,* 1935. Reprint: Cambridge, Mass.: Peabody Museum, 1973.

Winslow, Ola Elizabeth. *Meetinghouse Hill.* New York: W.W. Norton and Co., 1972.

Worthington, Erastus. *History of Dedham (1635–1827).* Boston: Dutton and Westworth, 1827.

Young, William R. *An Introduction to . . . the Connecticut Valley Indian,* vol. 1, no. 1. Springfield, Mass.: Museum of Science, 1969.

Ziff, Larzer. *Puritanism in America: New Culture in a New World.* New York: Viking, 1974.

Zuckerman, Michael. *Peaceable Kingdoms: New England Towns in the Eighteenth Century.* New York: Vintage, 1972.

Published Secondary Sources · Articles

Axtell, James. "Ethnology in Early America: A Review Essay." *William and Mary Quarterly* 35 (no. 1, January 1978):110–144.

Axtell, James. "The Scholastic Philosophy of the Wilderness." *William and Mary Quarterly* 29 (no. 3, July 1972):335–366.

Axtell, James. "The Unkindest Cut, or Who Invented Scalping?" *William and Mary Quarterly* 37 (no. 3 July 1980):451–472.

Axtell, James. "The White Indians of Colonial America." *William and Mary Quarterly* 32 (no. 1, January 1975):55–88.

Bennett, M.K. "The Food Economy of the New England Indians, 1605–1675." *Journal of Political Economy* 62 (no. 5, October 1955):369–397.

Brasser, T.J. "Early Indian-European Contacts." In *Handbook of North American Indians,* Vol. 15. William C. Sturtevant, gen. ed., Bruce C. Trigger, vol. ed. Washington, D.C.: Smithsonian Institution, 1978.

Butler, Eva L. "Algonkian Culture and Use of Maize in Southern New England." *Archaelogical Society of Connecticut Bulletin* 22 (1948):3–39.

Cook, Sherburne F. "Interracial Warfare and Population Decline Among the New England Indians." *Ethnohistory* 20 (no. 1, 1973):1–24.

Day, Gordon M. "The Indian Languages of the Upper Connecticut Valley." In *An Introduction to . . . the Connecticut Valley Indian.* William R. Young, ed. Springfield, Mass.: Museum of Science, 1969.

Day, Gordon. "Western Abenaki." In *Handbook of North American Indians,*

Vol. 15. William C. Sturtevant, gen. ed., Bruce C. Trigger, vol. ed. Washington, D.C.: Smithsonian Institution, 1978.

Demos, John. "Families in Colonial Bristol, Rhode Island: An Exercise in Historical Demography." *William and Mary Quarterly* 25 (no. 1, January 1968):40–57.

Demos, John. "Notes on Life in Plymouth Colony." *William and Mary Quarterly* 22 (no. 1, April 1965):264–286.

Eccles, W.J. "The Fur Trade and Eighteenth Century Imperialism." *William and Mary Quarterly* 40 (no. 3, July 1983):341–362.

Greven, Philip, Jr. "Family Structure in Seventeenth Century Andover, Massachusetts." *William and Mary Quarterly* 23 (no. 2, April 1966):234–256.

Henretta, James A. "Families and Farms: *Mentalite* in Pre-Industrial America." *William and Mary Quarterly* 35 (no. 1, January 1978):3–32.

Higgs, Robert, and Stettler, H. Louis, III. "Colonial New England Demography: A Sampling Approach." *William and Mary Quarterly* 27 (no. 2, April 1970):282–294.

Kawashima, Yasu. "Jurisdiction of the Colonial Courts over the Indians in Massachusetts, 1689–1763." *William and Mary Quarterly* 26 (no. 4, October 1969):532–550.

Leach, Douglas E. "The Question of French Involvement in King Philip's War." In *Colonial Society of Massachusetts Publications*, vol. 38, *Transactions, 1947–1951*. Boston: The Society, 1954.

Lockridge, Kenneth A. "Land, Population and the Evolution of New England Society, 1630–1790." *Past and Present* 39 (1968):62–80.

Lockridge, Kenneth A. "The Population of Dedham, Massachusetts, 1636–1736." *Economic History Review* 19 (1966):318–344.

Lockridge, Kenneth A., and Kreider, Alan. "The Evolution of Massachusetts Town Government, 1640 to 1740." *William and Mary Quarterly* 23 (no. 4, October 1966):549–574.

Main, Gloria L. "Probate Records as a Source for Early American History." *William and Mary Quarterly* 32 (no. 1, January 1975):89–99.

Medlicott, Alexander G., Jr. "Return to This Land of Light: A Plea to an Unredeemed Captive." *New England Quarterly* 38 (no. 2, June 1965):202–216.

Metcalf, P. Richard. "Who Should Rule at Home? Native American Politics and Indian-White Relations." *Journal of American History* 61 (December 1974):651–665.

Norton, Susan L. "Population Growth in Colonial America: A Study of Ipswich, Massachusetts." *Population Studies* 25 (no. 3, 1971):433–452.

Pruitt, Bettye Hobbs. "Self-Sufficiency and the Agricultural Economy of Eighteenth Century Massachusetts." *William and Mary Quarterly* 41 (no. 3, July 1984):333–364.

Richter, Daniel. "War and Culture: The Iroquois Experience." *William and Mary Quarterly* 40 (no. 4, October 1983):528–559.

Salwen, Bert. "Indians of Southern New England and Long Island, Early Period." In *Handbook of American Indians*, vol. 15. William C. Sturtevant, gen. ed., Bruce C. Trigger, vol. ed. Washington, D.C.: Smithsonian Institution, 1978.

Shy, John. "A New Look at Colonial Militia." *William and Mary Quarterly* 20 (no. 2, April 1963):175–185.

Smith, Daniel Scott. "A Perspective on Demographic Methods and Effects in Social History." *William and Mary Quarterly* 34 (no. 3, July 1982):442–468.

Vinovskis, Maris. "Angels' Heads and Weeping Willows: Death in Early America." *American Antiquarian Society Proceedings* 86 (pt. 2, 1976):279–286.

Washburn, Wilcomb E. "Seventeenth Century Indian Wars." In *Handbook of American Indians*, vol. 15. William C. Sturtevant, gen. ed., Bruce C. Trigger, vol. ed. Washington, D.C.: Smithsonian Institution, 1978.

Zuckerman, Michael. "The Social Context of Democracy in Massachusetts." *William and Mary Quarterly* 25 (no. 4, October 1968):523–544.

The following articles all come from the *Proceedings of the Pocumtuck Valley Memorial Association*, printed by the Association in 9 volumes between 1870 and 1945.

Aiken, John Adams. "The Mohawk Trail." 5 (1909):333–350.

Baker, C. Alice. "The Adventures of Baptiste, Parts I and II." 4:342–357, 450–477.

Baker, C. Alice. "Ensign John Sheldon." 1 (1870–1879):410–429.

Baker, C. Alice. "Eunice Williams." 1 (1870–1879):18–37.

Baker, C. Alice. "Historical Paper." 1 (1870–1879):79ff.

Birks, Richard E. "Hannah Beaman." 6 (1912–1920):496–513.

Birks, Richard E. "Samuel Mather, the Pioneer Preacher . . ." 5 (1905–1911):215ff.

Carter, Samuel. "The Route of the French and Indian Army that Sacked Deerfield . . . on Their Return March. . . ." 2 (1880–1889):126–151.

Hazen, Reverend Allen. "Some Account of John Williams, First Pastor of Deerfield." 2 (1880–1889):109ff.

Hubbard, Silas. "Historical Address." 2 (1880–1889):451–473.

Moors, John F. "Mrs. Eunice Williams." 2 (1880–1889):163–188.

Sheldon, George. "New Tracks in an Old Trail." 4:11–28.

Sheldon, George. "The Pocumtuck Confederacy." 2:396ff.

Sheldon, John. "The Common Field System of Deerfield." 5 (1905–1911):238–254.

Smith, Gertrude Cochran. "First Maps of Pocumtuck." 8 (1931):38–50.

Smith, Mary P. Wells. "A Puritan Foremother . . ." 4 (1900):85–98.

Taft, Henry W. "Address." 1 (1870–1879):169–199.

Temple, J.H. "Address." 1 (1870–1879):114–140.

Unpublished Secondary Sources

Foster, Mary Catherine. "Hampshire County, Massachusetts, 1729–1754: A Covenant Society in Transition." Unpublished Ph.D. dissertation, University of Michigan, 1967.

Garrison, John Ritchie. "Surviving Strategies: The Commercialization of Life in Rural Massachusetts, 1790–1860." Unpublished Ph.D. dissertation, University of Pennsylvania, 1985.

Hirtle, Peter Bolles. "Agrarian Economy in Flux: Agricultural History of Deerfield, 1670–1760." Unpublished Historic Deerfield Summer Fellowship paper, 1973.

Innes, Stephen Chandler. "A Patriarchal Society: Economic Dependency and Social Order in Springfield, Massachusetts, 1636–1702." Unpublished Ph.D. dissertation, Northwestern University, 1977.

Kelso, Inez Fanny. "The Frontier Policy of the Massachusetts Bay Colony." Unpublished masters thesis, University of Chicago, 1913.

King, Harold Roger. "The Settlement of the Upper Connecticut Valley to 1675." Unpublished Ph.D. dissertation, Vanderbilt University, 1965.

Lockridge, Kenneth A. "Dedham, 1636–1736: The Anatomy of a Puritan Utopia." Unpublished Ph.D. dissertation, Princeton University, 1965.

Malone, Patrick M. "Indian and English Military Systems in New England in the Seventeenth Century." Unpublished Ph.D. dissertation, Brown University, 1971.

Mank, Russell W. "Family Structure in Northampton (Mass.), 1654–1729." Unpublished Ph.D. dissertation, University of Denver, 1975.

McCleary, Ann. "The Child Against the Devil." Unpublished Historic Deerfield Summer Fellowship paper, 1975.

Melvoin, Richard I. "Strategy and Savagery: A Study of War in the Connecticut Valley of Massachusetts, 1675–1713." Unpublished seminar paper, University of Michigan, 1979.

Morrison, Kenneth M. "The People of the Dawn: The Abenaki and Their Relations with New England and New France, 1600–1727." Unpublished Ph.D. dissertation, University of Maine, 1976.

Nobles, Gregory Hight. "Politics and Society in Hampshire County, Massachusetts, 1740–1775: The Rural West on the Eve of the Revolution." Unpublished Ph.D. dissertation, University of Michigan, 1979.

Pencak, William Andrew. "Massachusetts Politics in War and Peace, 1676–1776." Unpublished Ph.D. dissertation, Columbia University, 1978.

Radabaugh, Jack S. "The Military System of Colonial Massachusetts, 1690–1740." Unpublished Ph.D. dissertation, University of Southern California, 1965.

Richter, Daniel. "The Ordeal of the Longhouse: Change and Persistence on the Iroquois Frontier, 1607–1720." Unpublished Ph.D. dissertation, Columbia University, 1984.

Salisbury, Neal. "Conquest of the 'Savage': Puritans, Puritan Missionaries, and Indians, 1620–1680." Unpublished Ph.D. dissertation, UCLA, 1975.

Salisbury, Neal. "InterIndian Affairs in Seventeenth Century New England." Working paper, 1985.

Salisbury, Neal. "Social Relationships on a Moving Frontier: Natives and Settlers in Southern New England, 1638–1675." Working paper, 1985.

Smith, Daniel Scott. "Population, Family and Society in Hingham, Massachusetts, 1635–1880." Unpublished Ph.D. dissertation, University of California at Berkeley, 1973.

Snell, Ronald K. "The County Magistracy in Eighteenth Century Massachusetts, 1692–1750." Unpublished Ph.D. dissertation, Princeton University, 1971.

Suich, Jerry. "A Statistical Analysis of Deerfield, Massachusetts, 1705–1725 and 1745–1765." Unpublished Heritage Foundation paper, 1966.

Sweeney, Kevin N. "The Children of the Covenant." Unpublished Historic Deerfield Summer Fellowship paper, 1971.

Sweeney, Kevin N. "Unruly Saints: Religion and Society in the River Towns of Massachusetts, 1700–1750." Unpublished Williams College honors thesis, 1972.

Thomas, Peter A. "In the Maelstrom of Change: The Indian Trade and Cultural Process in the Middle Connecticut Valley, 1635–1665." Unpublished Ph.D. dissertation, University of Massachusetts, 1979.

Tigue, Mary. "Colonial Standards of Living: Economic Progress in Deerfield, Massachusetts." Unpublished Historic Deerfield Summer Fellowship paper, 1980.

Tracy, Patricia J. "Jonathan Edwards, Pastor: Minister and Congregation in the Eighteen Century Connecticut Valley." Unpublished Ph.D. dissertation, University of Massachusetts, 1977.

Warner, Robert A. "The Southern New England Indians to 1725: A Study in Culture Contact." Unpublished Ph.D. dissertation, Yale University, 1935.

Index